All About Us!

1946 to 2006

The Royal Mencap Society
Celebrates its

60th Anniversary

and invites you to read

All About Us!

The Story of People with a Learning
Disability and Mencap

Written, Compiled and Edited by
Brian Rix
(with a great deal of help from many others)

MENCAP
Understanding learning disability

First published in 2006
by MENCAP

Although the MENCAP logo normally appears in capitals, it appears as
Mencap throughout this text for ease of reading.

Cataloguing in Publication Data is available from the British Library

ISBN 0 85537 096 3 hardback
ISBN 0 85537 097 1 trade paperback

Typeset in Aldine401BT by Avon DataSet Ltd,
Bidford-on-Avon, Warwickshire

Designed by Viv Mullett

Printed and bound in Great Britain by
Mackays of Chatham plc, Chatham, Kent

MENCAP
123 Golden Lane
London EC1Y 0RT
Registered charity No. 222377

www.mencap.org.uk

For our daughter, Shelley
1951–2005
Her life inspired this book

CONTENTS

BAGSHOT PARK

Foreword

Her Royal Highness The Countess of Wessex
Patron of the Royal Mencap Society

When I was growing up I very rarely came across anyone with a learning disability. Of course I was familiar with the then commonplace terms such as 'spastic' and 'backward', but they bore no relevance to my cosseted life.

In more recent years I have been fortunate enough to meet many hundreds of children and adults with a learning disability. On every occasion they have left a strong impression on me, reinforcing my belief that they have a rightful and contributory role to play in our society. I always have fun when I meet people with a learning disability, they give me a new perspective on life and I have learnt never to underestimate their understanding of their actions – especially when it comes to the cheeky kiss!

During my visits a large part of what I see is focused on the organisations and carers who look after, educate and help individuals. I have enormous admiration for each and every person who works with people with a learning disability. The pay is often not good, the hours can be long, the work and behaviours they face can be challenging, but the rewards are limitless. And behind each organisation is an army of fantastic volunteers, without whom many activities on a support and funding basis would not exist.

The more I learn about people with a learning disability, not just through Mencap, but a variety of my other patronages, the more issues I come across. So I hope you will allow me to mention the ones that seem to me the major areas of concern:

> **education** – where it is crucial that parents are given a real choice of either a mainstream school or a special school; **healthcare** – where improved access is needed to ensure that people with a learning disability no longer die unnecessarily; **housing** – where people with a learning disability need to be given more opportunity to live in a house of their own; **employment** – an end to the dreadful situation where so few people with a learning disability have the opportunity to work; **day services** – more opportunity for meaningful activities rather than people being left languishing at home with nothing to do; **inclusion** – above all a greater priority for people with a learning disability to enable them to have the same opportunities as everybody else.

Mentioning some of the above issues would have been unthinkable just a few decades ago. To suggest that children with a learning disability could even merit an education would have been impossible, let alone adults being considered for employment and making their own decisions.

The achievements of the last sixty years by Mencap have been remarkable and this book is a comprehensive record and a wonderful celebration of this incredible work.

Its author, Mencap's President, Lord Rix – whose involvement with learning disabilities stretches back over fifty years – has detailed meticulously the birth and sustained growth of the UK's leading learning disability charity. He has also brought together stories from a wonderfully diverse mix of people, who all have in common wholehearted support for Mencap and people with a learning disability. Brian deserves our congratulations – not only for the leading part he has played in Mencap's history, but in documenting it so well in this book.

It is this passionate commitment that formed the principal reason why I agreed to become the charity's Patron in 2004 (following in the footsteps of HM Queen Elizabeth, the Queen Mother, who had a long and much respected association with Mencap and was its Royal Patron for some forty years).

Even though so much has been achieved, Chief Executive Jo Williams has still got some tough challenges ahead, but will, I am sure, attain the goals laid out. Mencap has many good and impressive advocates, it has a will that won't tire and it has a history of making things happen. My hope is that in another sixty years' time, Mencap will have won its fight for changes at every level of society and every vestige of prejudice against, and exclusion of, people with a learning disability will have been swept away.

HRH The Countess of Wessex
Patron

The Book's Beginnings

Brian Rix (The Lord Rix Kt CBE DL)
President of the Royal Mencap Society

The House of Lords and the Royal Society of Medicine seem, at first glance, to provide an unlikely background for a book concerning the changing world of learning disability. A second glance, though, and all will be revealed.

The Royal Society of Medicine (RSM) has myriad sections dealing with most of the medical, physical, sensory and mental problems which beset mankind. One of these sections deals with the single greatest cause of disability at birth – learning or intellectual disability – and I (and others contributing to this book) serve on its Council. I also happen to be a cross-bencher in the House of Lords where I am a member of the All Party Parliamentary Disability Group and am co-Chairman, along with Tom Clarke CBE MP, of the All Party Parliamentary Group on Learning Disability. Members of both groups have struggled for many years to ensure that all legislation affecting the world of disability will be proactive, reactive and fully inclusive.

In 2003 our RSM Forum was asked to make a contribution to the

RSM's Bicentenary Appeal. I suggested we hold a seminar entitled 'Then and now: Making history with people with learning disabilities' in a committee room at the House of Lords – with lunch, a tour of the House and seats in the gallery thrown in – any surplus arising from the seminar fees to be donated to the RSM appeal. It was agreed that the lecture in the morning, which I would give, would be 'A thousand years of law on people with a learning disability', while Professor Conor Ward would present the afternoon session with a paper on 'Doctors who cared: Victorian beginnings'. Shortened versions of our lectures begin this book and give, I trust, a brief description of the tortuous journey undertaken by people with a learning disability – and their families – through the centuries.

Perhaps the most significant aspect of the day, though, was that the seminar was chaired by Simon Cramp. In his introductory remarks, Simon reminded us that a few years ago, as someone with a learning disability (albeit relatively mild), he would not have been allowed such a role, although the occasion was dedicated to the history of people whose label he shares. Simon, at that time both a Mencap trustee and a member of Mencap's National Assembly, illustrates how much the world has changed. That things have changed so much is a tribute to people such as Simon (who is now a consultant on matters concerned with learning disability) as well as family carers, parliamentarians, professionals, policy makers and Mencap itself. In the late 1990s Roger Galletley (then Chairman of Gateway, Mencap's leisure arm), Fred Heddell (then Mencap's CEO) and I (then Mencap's Chairman) went on a country-wide tour trying to 'sell' the new, fully inclusive, Mencap constitution to a somewhat doubtful membership. Simon was at one of the meetings and confounded all present by cogently arguing for this dramatic change and then informing them that he had a learning disability. Furthermore, when the time came to vote on the new constitution at an EGM, Simon made the concluding and I think, in many ways, the conclusive speech. The new constitution was approved by over 88 per cent of the total vote.

My seminar lecture was made possible by the comprehensive list of dates and events (which appear in the Appendix of this book) headed Learning Disability Time Line, compiled by another member of the RSM Intellectual Disability Forum, Brian McGinnis OBE. The libraries of the House of Lords, the Royal College of Psychiatrists and the Royal Society of Medicine were very helpful in pointing him to historical documents tucked away in box files in attics and cardboard cartons in cellars, which were invaluable sources of long-forgotten information.

A number of our audience at the RSM seminar asked if our papers would be published – which is no easy matter – but then Brian Baldock CBE, the Chairman of the Royal Mencap Society (to give it its full title), who was present at the seminar, suggested the lectures might form the basis for a book to celebrate Mencap's sixtieth anniversary in 2006. Other friends of mine (and one son, Jonty, as I would call him) offered further suggestions – and so this quick glance at the past, a longer look at the present and a hopeful vision of the future came into being and will be published in the latter part of 2006, for Mencap really began in the month of November 1946.

Originally I assembled an ad hoc editorial board to help me work out the contents of the book. They were: Professor James Hogg, Director, White Top Research Unit, University of Dundee; Dr David Towell, late of the King's Fund and Director of the Centre for Inclusive Futures; Fred Heddell, late Chief Executive, Mencap, and now Consultant to the Rix Centre, University of East London; Lesley Campbell, National Children's Officer, Mencap; Naomi Creeger, Senior Public Relations Officer, Mencap; Jonathan Rix, Lecturer in Inclusion Curriculum and Learning at the Open University (OU); and the aforementioned Brian McGinnis. Further representatives from the OU – Kate Stephens, Anne Stevens, Lesley-Anne Cull and Professor Dorothy Atkinson – then joined the assembly line, as did Andy Minnion from the Rix Centre at the University of East London. I must thank them all for giving freely of their time, support and advice.

There was one slight hiccup. One of our 'team' – Professor Dorothy Atkinson – asked me to speak at the launch of a new publication involving BILD (British Institute of Learning Disabilities) and the OU. It is entitled *Witnesses to Change* and involves parents and families – many of them members of Mencap – covering their experiences from the 1920s to the present day. It is a remarkable work but, of course, its publication made it impossible for me to produce anything similar – as did the six histories of Mencap local societies, written by Sheena Rolph, and produced by the OU earlier in 2005. I then decided – unilaterally, I fear – to write and compile a rather different book from that originally discussed: Genesis 2 is the history of learning disability and Part I Chapter 1 Mencap's sixty-year diary. Part II Chapters 2 to 6 contain the stories of the honorary officers and senior staff, while the voices of people with a learning disability are loud and clear in Part III Chapters 7 to 11. Then come the activities of Mencap, the majority stemming from work originating in our head office in Golden Lane, including profound and multiple learning disability, Healthcare and Mencap in Wales and Northern Ireland. The book ends with personal stories told by parents and siblings, penned by the family member concerned, and I trust that the overall work will give pleasure – and information – to those who now read it, as well as providing an historical record for the future when the struggles and privations suffered by people with a learning disability and their families are but a distant memory.

To all contributors – whether writers or interviewees – I owe a great debt of gratitude and the most sincere thanks. They are named individually as the book progresses so I hope they will forgive me for not listing them here. I must also explain that the early part of the book – especially Genesis and Part I – contains a good deal of material written by me, but in the history of Mencap I have referred to myself in the third person at all times and my CV, as President, is culled from the Mencap information sheet. My personal story in Part II Chapter 4 is written in a question and answer format – which is a method employed elsewhere in the book – but I must confess the questions (as well as the answers) were penned by me, while Professor James Hogg 'anonymously' interviewed his wife Loretto Lambe in Part IV Chapter 14. It saved me a journey to Dundee!

The staff, too, of Mencap – led by Chief Executive Jo Williams CBE – have been unfailingly helpful, particularly Tim Segaller who did sterling work researching all the current and future activities of Mencap, as well as scripting the interviews he conducted with Mencap's learning disabled employees. An 'outsider', Justine Williams, who interviewed all the older parents and retired members of staff while waiting to study for her PhD at Warwick University, also provided remarkable material – but that is not altogether surprising for her grandfather is Alan Phillips OBE who was my deputy when I was Secretary-General of Mencap in the 1980s and Assistant Secretary-General to my predecessor, George Lee OBE, for many years before that. You can see why I put 'outsider' in quotes.

Finally, my especial thanks to Tim Hely Hutchinson and Martin Neild of Hodder Headline for enabling Mencap to publish this book with the minimum of fuss and the maximum savings in cash. They also introduced me to Celia Kent, who did all the final editing, putting this weighty tome to bed. I am most grateful for her expertise and support. Without her, this book would never have met its November 2006 deadline.

So, a massive joint effort. We have come a long way in sixty years, especially when you look at the chequered history of learning disability which follows. Other organisations, including Enable, Down's Syndrome Association, BILD, United Response, Leonard Cheshire, Barnardo's, Home Farm Trust, National Autistic Society, Contact a Family, Turning Point, Voice UK, People First, etc. have all been participants in this long journey (and some have added their contribution to this enterprise), but the Royal Mencap Society has, I believe, been the tour leader.

A Brief History of Learning Disability from Ancient Greece to the Twenty-first Century

This abridged version of my House of Lords lecture is mainly concerned, perforce, with legislation enacted in the UK, although current differences in other countries do appear from time to time. Nevertheless, as this is a history, it would be strange if some reference was not made to earlier civilisations, including Greek and Roman, but because learning or intellectual disability has never been at the top of any agenda – except for those directly concerned – one has to hunt for information which is often based on flimsy evidence, with a degree of conjecture thrown in for good measure.

Reference can certainly be found in terminology – *idios* in Greek and *idiota* in Latin – while attitudes are also pretty clear, ranging, at worst, from putting to death to, at best, amused tolerance and even, in some rare cases, respect. We certainly know that in Sparta and the Rome of Cicero 'idiot' children were left to die on the mountainside – a view endorsed by Luther and Calvin nearly 2,000 years later, when they recommended that such children should be drowned, being agents of the devil.

The Bible does not appear to refer specifically to learning disability, although certain quotations have, from time to time, been shoehorned to fit – only to be abandoned again some time later. However, both Jewish and Christian history indicate there have been extreme views – rather as in Greek or Roman times – ranging from 'holy innocents' to the 'devil's progeny'.

The Koran, dating from c.610 AD, appears to be more practical and refers to the 'feeble-minded', advising carers to offer advice as well as support and clothing, using money raised, if possible, from the sale of the beneficiary's property. In Anglo-Saxon Britain there was a similar solution, embracing the sale of other assets as well as land. Between 935 AD and 939 AD, Athelstan ordered his reeves to support the destitute – which could include the feeble-minded – if they lived on the royal estates. As these estates covered quite a chunk of the countryside, they covered, inevitably, quite a chunk of the population, too.

Athelstan's example seems to have been followed to a great extent by the edicts of Edward I and Edward II, before the days of a real parliament, bringing *idiota* and *fatua* within the ambit of the law through property management. Later, during the reigns of Richard III, Henry VII, George II and George III, Parliament adopted similar fiscal practices. A more detailed list of these enactments can be found in the Appendix, entitled Learning Disability Time Line.

It seems, therefore, that since the days of the Koran in c.610 AD and c.935 AD in Anglo-Saxon Britain, care, supervision and control have been a prime concern of those responsible for people with a learning disability. Many laws regulating begging and providing relief for the 'impotent', including the 'mentally impotent', have been enacted over the centuries, including Elizabethan Poor Law Consolidation in the early seventeenth century and short-lived legislation in the eighteenth and nineteenth centuries, more or less ending in the twentieth century with the 1929 Local Government Act.

And what about 'the vital commoners and inland petty spirits' as they were called by Falstaff in *Henry IV Part II*? Before the Industrial Revolution much of everyday life took place in rural communities and the label 'village idiot' came into being describing, however, only a minority of people we would characterise today as having a learning disability. There are several reasons for this. Children with profound and multiple learning or physical disabilities were unlikely to survive beyond infancy and those with mild learning disabilities could often go unnoticed in a small, closely knit community, where people generally spent all their lives in the same village and where the level of literacy was extremely low, but the demand for labour was high. As now, their families would provide such support as they could, with the outside world – especially Parliament – doing little to help.

The Industrial Revolution changed all that – for the worse. Vast numbers of country-folk migrated to the cities and the majority swapped village hovels for city slums. Anyone who was aged or infirm found it almost impossible to obtain work and thus, in the reign of William IV, the 1832 Act on Care and Treatment of Insane Persons, as well as the 1832 Act to Amend Representation of the People Act and the 1834 Poor Law Amendment Act ensured that workhouses became the final refuge for the destitute and 'asylums' for those described as 'mad' or 'imbeciles'.

Actually, the idea behind the asylums had some merit. They were often developed by far-sighted people and were a genuine attempt to provide reasonable living conditions in idyllic surroundings for their intended residents. Unhappily this early promise was not sustained. The asylums became overcrowded, squalid and authoritarian. As conditions worsened the 'inmates' came to be regarded as dangerous and a drain on both the exchequer and society in general, a view which continued until well into the twentieth century.

Since those days, our long-lived parliamentary tradition has brought forth only three Acts (and some amending legislation) especially concerning people with a learning disability. These are, in the forthright language of their day, the 1886 Idiots Act, the 1899 Elementary Education (Defective and Epileptic Children) Act and the 1913 Mental Deficiency Act. Every other piece of legislation in England, Wales, Scotland and Northern Ireland (all of whom have broadly comparable laws) deals with people with a learning disability alongside others, for it is assumed that the needs of those disabled by age, physical or sensory impairment and mental illness are not dissimilar.

No subsequent legislation unscrambled this confusion. The 1913 Mental Deficiency Act repealed the Idiots Act but not the relevant parts of the Lunacy Acts. The 1930 Mental Treatment Act amended the Lunacy and Mental Deficiency Acts and changed the terminology; but 'unsound mind' is not at all dissimilar to the medieval terminology describing both groups.

The Commissioners in Lunacy, their successors the Board of Control and then the Mental Health Act Commission (England) and the Mental Welfare Commission (Scotland) all covered learning disability as well as mental illness as, of course, did the Poor Law authorities down the centuries before the counties and boroughs replaced them. In 1926 a survey showed only 10 per cent of 'mental defectives' in specialist placements, whereas 25 per cent were in hospitals for the mentally ill and another 29 per cent were in Poor Law institutions.

From this, it appears that if Parliament can protect fundamental freedoms, intervene effectively to ensure equality and accord benefits to those unable to acquire for themselves the basis of a reasonable standard of living, then Parliament believes it is serving the needs of all vulnerable people in society and thus there is no need for separate legislation affecting people with a learning disability alone. However, there is an ongoing debate about the inclusion of learning disability legislation with mental health legislation – one which has not yet been properly resolved. Even the 1979 Review of the Mental Health Act, which led to the 1983 Mental Health Act, did not unscramble the puzzle. As the then Secretary-General of Mencap, I was involved in discussions which would have excluded 'mental handicap' from mental health legislation altogether, but the powers-that-be decided that parallel legislation would be silly. They did, however, agree that 'mental handicap' on its own did not justify detention.

More recently – from September 2004 to March 2005, to be precise – as a member of the House of Lords, I sat on the Joint Committee scrutinising the Draft Mental Health Bill when the matter was thoroughly debated. I firmly believed our recommendations to amend the Bill and exclude learning disability would be accepted. Alas, the Government's response was negative, but after much discussion and lobbying there was a change for the better, as far as learning disability was concerned, anyway. On 23 March 2006, the Minister wrote to all members who had served on the Joint Committee in these terms: 'We have continued to consider further many of the issues raised by the Joint Committee's report and by the evidence given to the Committee. We have reviewed the length and complexity of the Bill and, as a result, have now decided to take a somewhat different approach to reforming the Mental Health Act 1983. We intend to introduce a shorter, streamlined Bill that, instead of replacing the 1983 Act, will amend it'. A bullet point which followed informed us that the new Amending Bill would 'preserve the effect of the 1983 Act as it relates to people with learning disabilities.' This means that only learning disabled people whose condition is 'associated with abnormally aggressive or seriously irresponsible conduct' will be subject to mental health legislation, while the vast majority will not. I experienced a sense of déjà vu on reading this, for I had negotiated that very wording with Lord Elton, when he was the Minister concerned, in our discussions before the 1983 Act. All in all, it was a singular victory for fairness and common sense.

At the risk of labouring the point, it does seem quite extraordinary that as late as March 2005 a Joint Committee and the Government were still arguing the toss about learning disabled people, when you recall that a century ago the First Principle established by the Royal Commission on the Care and Control of the Feeble-minded, which met from 1904 to 1908, was that 'persons who cannot take part in the struggle of life owing to mental defect . . . should be afforded by the State such *special protection as may be suited to their needs*'. This seems to echo edicts in the Koran, as well as those in Anglo-Saxon, Plantagenet, Tudor and Georgian times.

Nowadays, of course, people with a learning disability are becoming acutely aware of the benefits of self- and supported advocacy. Therefore, reconciling self-determination and protection is becoming more and more difficult, prompting a closer look at how law has dealt with degrees of learning disability and their implications for social participation, as well as the more complicated issue – the borderline between learning disability and mental illness.

The 1913 Mental Deficiency Act was amended in 1927. In the first place, the Mental Deficiency (Amendment) Act removed the 1913 Act's insistence on recognising only mental defects existing from birth or from an early age. Now it could be argued that persisting mental illness or some kinds of trauma could cause intellectual damage of a rather similar kind. Furthermore, the 1927 Act came forth with a list of definitions of learning disability which illustrates only too well the concerns of the early twentieth century, as well as the whole history of learning disability legislation and the attitude of the majority of parliamentarians and their constituents, before and since.

Here are those 1927 definitions: '**Idiots** are persons whose mental defect is of such severity they are unable to guard themselves against common physical dangers; **Imbeciles** are more able than idiots but are incapable of managing themselves or their affairs, while children cannot be taught to do so; **Feeble-minded persons** are more able than imbeciles but require care, supervision and control for their own protection or the protection of others, while children cannot obtain benefit from instruction in ordinary schools; **Moral defectives** (moral imbeciles in the 1913 Act) are persons whose mental defectiveness is coupled with strongly vicious or criminal propensities and who require care, supervision and control for the protection of others.' Perversely, this label was often applied to innocent young girls who had been sexually abused in their early teens by men who should certainly have been stigmatised as moral defectives.

However, it seems that in the 1913 and 1927 Acts, moral defectiveness and mental defectiveness were seen as being closely aligned (this alignment did not disappear until the 1959 Mental Health Act), although, in 1927, mental defectiveness itself is defined in terms more easily recognisable and acceptable by today's standards, for it accords more closely with modern terminology: 'A condition of arrested or incomplete development of mind arising before the age of eighteen years, whether arising from inherent causes or induced by disease or injury.'

In the light of such pejorative and insensitive terminology, can you wonder that legislators over the centuries have regarded learning disability as a subject not worth bothering about. If they did show a modicum of interest it was generally of a negative nature. Bigoted zealots such as Luther and Calvin went even further in their horrifying indifference and the Nazis actually exterminated these 'sub-humans' while others thought of extinction by more devious routes.

First came the Eugenics Movement, founded in 1885 by the biologist

Sir Francis Galton, which advocated that certain phenotypes, including those with a learning disability, should be 'encouraged to refrain from contributing to future generations even though they may be capable of doing so'. In 1908 the Radnor Commission arrived at a similar conclusion: 'Prevention of mentally defective persons from becoming parents would tend to diminish the number of such persons in the population', while in 1931 a Sterilisation Bill was presented to Parliament – as a revival of the Feeble-minded Control Bill introduced twenty years earlier – but was heavily defeated. That was not the end of a fierce parliamentary debate on sterilisation but it was effectively the end of any real likelihood that we in the UK would stop people with learning disabilities having children because of our fears about their morals, their fertility and their potential for increasing the population of people with an actual learning disability.

I say that 1931 saw the end of serious parliamentary initiatives to impose a sterilisation programme on the grounds of genetics, but in 1987, as Secretary-General of Mencap, and again as Chairman, in 1989, I was caught up in a debate in the courts, Parliament and the media as fierce as any engaged in since 1900. In 1987 the Court of Appeal ordered the sterilisation of a seventeen-year-old girl with a learning disability who was, to quote, 'showing signs of sexual awareness and sexual drive'. In the 1989 case, however, Lord Justice Butler-Sloss in the Court of Appeal said: 'It is not suggested in this case, nor could it be, that sterilisation should be performed on those unable to consent for eugenic or purely social reasons. Such reasons would be, as I already said, totally abhorrent and unacceptable.' This case, like its predecessor, eventually reached the House of Lords. Both sterilisations were allowed.

Other countries were not so lucky in escaping 'democratic' acceptance of compulsory sterilisation. Socially enlightened Sweden did not repeal its laws authorising social sterilisation of people with a learning disability until 1975. The American state of Indiana passed the first US law allowing the sterilisation of 'defectives' in 1907 and by 1925 thirty-six states had such laws. By 1975 over 75,000 people had been sterilised in what we have tended to consider as the libertarian state of California, in the 'Land of the Free'. As least on this side of the Atlantic we can claim some credit for our rejection of such legislation. As long ago as 1904 the Royal Commission on the Care and Control of the Feeble-minded stated its business was 'the protection and happiness of the defective rather than the purification of the race'.

On the other hand, the Commission did refer to people who 'are at the mercy of their animal instincts' – a phrase used, unbelievably, only a year or two ago by a learned judge in deciding that a woman with a learning disability had consented to what otherwise would have been treated as rape. I wonder what the Royal Commission would have said about allowing abortion to prevent the birth of children with mental or physical disabilities? No doubt they would have found it as difficult to find their way out of that moral maze as we do today.

I have attempted in the foregoing potted history to show how some of the laws, customs and practices came into being when referring to people with a learning disability. In more recent years legislation has addressed the same issues of mental capacity, care, control and protection which legislators down the centuries have tried to tackle, with varying degrees of success and failure. On the other hand, successive governments have introduced a plethora of services and benefits to which people have contingent rights, as well as broader disability and human rights.

For example, the ground-breaking 1946 National Health Service Act had some effect, naturally, on the lives of people with a learning disability. 'Asylums', 'institutions' and 'colonies' were all absorbed into the NHS and turned into 'hospitals' and the term 'mentally handi-capped' came into being. Ostensibly society now viewed their learning disabled brethren with greater sympathy and understanding – but still they remained segregated and isolated – even those who continued to live in the community with their families. Gradually, though, over the years (and thanks to pressure from parents and reformers) it came to be recognised that so-called hospitals were still, in fact, institutions and until they were closed down little would change. Eventually, in 1985, the Government responded to the Social Services Committee *Report on Community Care* in the following way:

Community care is a matter of marshalling resources, sharing responsibilities and combining skills to achieve good-quality modem services to meet the actual needs of real people, in ways those people find acceptable and in places which encourage rather than prevent normal living. [The Government] is firmly opposed to revamped institutions and to artificial ghettos, which have nothing to commend them except someone else's convenience and which have nothing to do with community care.

In 1990 came the NHS and Community Care Act, which brought forth new procedures for community care and recognised the right of disabled people to be an equal part of society, while having the support they need. However, it was eleven more years – in 2001 – before a White Paper, *Valuing People*, based on recommendations which Mencap had been espousing for over a quarter of a century, was published. Again in 2001, the Special Educational Needs and Disability Act, which gave parents choice and extended disability rights in the education system, reached the Statute Book, as did the Health and Social Care Act, which requires an annual report to Parliament on 'development of health and social services for persons with learning disability'.

Other disability Acts have either preceded or followed those I have mentioned and you could be forgiven for thinking that all's well that ends well. Alas, that is not the complete picture. It is true that nearly all long-stay hospitals are no more but people with a learning disability are still denied many of the things which most of us take for granted – a decent income, somewhere appropriate to live, the chance to work, leisure opportunities and a choice in education.

May I again refer you to the Learning Disability Time Line and other parliamentary references in the book, which will help fill in many of my omissions, as well as bringing you as up to date as possible with all that is going on up to the present day. Future legislation is also anticipated – but until an Act is on the Statute Book it is difficult to be certain about anything! You can be certain of one thing, though – pressure for change will continue as of yore. Largely undertaken by parents since World War II, pressure groups have now been joined by people with a learning disability themselves – warmly welcomed by Mencap. After Professor Conor Ward's 'lecture' I will try and recount some of their – and Mencap's – achievements over the last sixty years. It is a heart-warming story.

Doctors Who Cared:
The Victorian Beginnings

Professor O. Conor Ward PhD MD FRCP
Emeritus Professor of Paediatrics

Introduction

It is only in the recent past that medical interest has focused on learning disability. In 1961, living in the Republic of Ireland, and with clinical responsibility for the paediatric service for the whole area from the Liffey northwards to the border and from the east coast westwards to the Shannon, I still had a lot to learn. A Government Commission of Enquiry had been set up and in association with John McKenna, Professor of Psychology, I shared responsibility for a national survey on what was then described as mental handicap. This was a revelation. We found that training places were available for less than half the children who needed them.

Getting involved

Never having had special personal experience of the medical aspects of learning disability, the operation of the large residential centres and day centres was an eye-opener for me. My enduring impression was of stalwart dedication on the part of families and professionals, including psychologists, special teachers, social workers, therapists and doctors. Twenty years later it became possible for me to undertake some personal responsibility and, following a visit to Dublin by Dr Sig Pueschel, and with his guidance, I became Medical Adviser to the Down's Syndrome Association of Ireland and visiting paediatrician to the Children's Sunshine Home, a residential centre in Dublin. Later still my wife and I moved on to do voluntary respite care and the experience of the day-to-day problems involved in home care provided a further educational experience and increased my respect for the families whom we came to know. An interest developed and I had to satisfy my curiosity concerning the early workers in the field.

Dr Andrew Reed

Pre-eminent among the doctors who strove to develop services for learning disabilities was Andrew Reed, not a doctor of medicine but of divinity. He was a philanthropic Nonconformist minister, a founder of orphanages, schools for the poor and other charities. In 1837 his preaching mission had taken him to Cornwall and Wales and he had seen, in the language of his day, 'the wretched idiot, chained like a felon or maniac in the common lock-up house of the village green or chased hither and thither, the scoff and the outcast of the whole hamlet'.

The matter continued to exercise his mind and in 1840 he again wrote in his diary: 'The pleasure of hope! Hope to do something for a fellow creature who although human is separate, alone, knows nothing, can do nothing and wishes nothing. Some are better, some are worse; this is the maximum of incapacity: but the divine image is stamped on all.' This brings to mind the old Gaelic description of someone with a learning disability as *duine le dia*, 'one of God's people'.

Inspiration was to come later. A member of his congregation, a Mrs Plumbe, asked him what she could possibly do about her son. He needed special training and education but could not get it. She had considered sending him to Paris under the care of the famous Dr Seguin, but the cost was prohibitive. Dr Reed was a practical man. He said to her, 'Go out into the neighbourhood and come back and tell me how many destitute idiots you see.' She came back with a list of twenty-eight boys.

Dr Reed was impressed. He set out to visit Dr Seguin in Paris and he was convinced that 'the idiot could be rescued from the doom of a life of utter vacuity'.

In 1849 he devoted a month to detailed planning before announcing a meeting of well-disposed philanthropists. Two members of his provisional committee were Drs John Connolly and William Little who would be his long-term supporters. Little is still remembered for being the first to identify the connection between birth injury and spastic paralysis, a sequence now known as Little's Disease. Although himself a physician and not a surgeon, having had successful surgery for his own club foot, he learned the necessary operative techniques and applied them in practice with great success. He founded the Orthopaedic Infirmary which then became the Royal Orthopaedic Hospital. By coincidence he was clinical teacher to John Langdon Down at the London Hospital. Langdon Down was destined to become at least as famous as he was.

Dr John Connolly

John Connolly is best remembered for his reforming policy as Medical Superintendent of the Hanwell Asylum. He introduced a policy of non-restraint, saying: 'Strike off their chains.' When he died John Langdon Down wrote of him:

> Entering on my work as an untried man and finding myself allied to an institution which had become unpopular with the Lunacy Board, I was mainly decided on holding a position which had so much to overwhelm me, by the influence of Dr Connolly. That influence was magical. The humility of his character was only equalled by the real love he manifested for the mentally afflicted.

When it became possible to open an institution in Earlswood, Connolly took the chair at the meetings of the house committee and he attended once a month as official visitor. Speaking of the plight of the learning disabled in poor families he had written:

> You will find it in winter placed by the fire, and in summer by the door, seated in a little chair, or lying in a little bed. The matter of

admiration is that this imperfect little creature, which only entails privations upon them, is still to them an object of even peculiarly tender solicitude. They seem to love their affected brother or sister more than they love each other. They watch it, they protect it from danger, they try to amuse it, they draw it about, and they give it some of their own little portions of food. One by one they go from home . . . and the poor imbecile . . . becomes an even heavier burden on its father and mother when years are gathering over them.

John Connolly, an Edinburgh graduate, had been Professor of Medicine at the University of London, having previously practised in Chichester and in Stratford-upon-Avon, where he had been Lord Mayor. He resigned his university appointment to become a physician to Hanwell County Asylum. The University of Oxford conferred an honorary doctorate on him and the Royal College of Physicians nominated him as Croonian Lecturer. John Connolly was an enthusiast for clinical photography. His encouragement and support were important later, when Langdon Down undertook the research on the distribution of ethnic characteristics in the Earlswood population, leading to the recognition of what he termed the Mongolian type.

The subscribers

Action was urgent. With great drive and enthusiasm Dr Reed rallied influential community support. He gathered around him a high-level committee which included two dukes, two marquises, seven earls and seven lords. On the ecclesiastical side he had the support of the Archbishop of Canterbury and seven bishops. He recruited bankers and brokers and men of property. The objective was to found a large institution for education and training in the field of learning disability.

By coincidence the first planning meeting was chaired by Lord Wodehouse. Wodehouse, from his previous experience as an ambassador in Russia, was an advocate of large freestanding hospitals for children, and when he was Lord Lieutenant of Ireland in 1864–6 he publicly disagreed with the formidable William Stokes, who favoured having children's units in adult institutions. The founding committee met on 27 October 1847. As a first step twin institutions were opened, the first at Park House, a rented mansion in Highgate, London, in 1848 and the second at Essex Hall in Colchester, Essex, in January 1849. Only the deserving poor were eligible and only those thought capable of improvement were accepted. Paupers were excluded.

Park House

There were 133 candidates for the first ten places in Park House. Park House was set in extensive grounds. There were swings and slides for the residents, and a major effort was made to develop muscular co-ordination as a preliminary to speech training. A contemporary etching confirms that the physical training programme already in use there was the same programme that was subsequently to be further developed and refined by Martin Duncan and William Millard at the Eastern Counties Asylum. There was a school, and, for entertainment, a substantial aviary. Park House was large enough to accommodate seventy-five residents.

Essex Hall

Essex Hall had been built as a railway hotel. It could accommodate 150 residents. There were twenty-seven admissions within a week, and there was a mixture of election cases and payment cases. In 1853 everyone was moved from Park House and Essex Hall to Earlswood. It was at Essex Hall that the talents of William Pullen, the Victorian 'idiot savant', were first recognised by Sarah Pearce, the schoolmistress. He was later to become famous for his work and to become known as the 'Genius of Earlswood'.

Earlswood

Earlswood was intended to be a national centre and was built on an ambitious scale. It ultimately came to house over 500 residents. Set in grounds of over 100 acres, sited on a hillside near Redhill, in Surrey, it was built with schoolrooms, workshops, outdoor activities in the farm and gardens. The authorities had however gone too far, too fast. When it opened in 1853 the paths through the grounds were muddy tracks, and not all the windows were glazed. Staff had been hurriedly recruited. The institution got a bad press. The final blow was the case of Elizabeth Jenner, a bedridden patient, who had the misfortune to develop unrecognised gangrene of both feet. The medical superintendent was allowed to resign but the new appointee would have to re-establish the reputation of the establishment.

John Langdon Down

John Connolly and William Little recommended John Langdon Down as the new Superintendent. Although he had won four gold medals at the London Hospital, he was straight from medical school, with no higher degree, and with no relevant clinical or administrative experience. He had however been a highly commended clinical clerk on Little's farm. He was later to tell how as a young student summer rain had disrupted a seaside picnic and on taking shelter the family had been served tea by a girl with disability. He forthwith 'formed a firm resolve to give my life to such as she'.

The farm steward did not attend Board meetings and his reports were presented by Langdon Down. This experience was no doubt of use to him later in life when the grounds of Normansfield, his own private institution, extended to forty-three acres. He totally reformed Earlswood, solved the problem of wet beds, upgraded the staff, forbade punishments, developed social facilities, produced entertainments and musicals and, with his wife Mary, consolidated the training programme, following the example set by Seguin. In his hospital brass band the big drum was played by none other than George Henry Pullen. In due course the centre developed a worldwide reputation, and Seguin himself asked for permission to visit, prior to writing a new edition of his book. Langdon Down dealt with major epidemics, personally conducted over 100 autopsies and, apart from recognising the characteristics of what came to be called Down's syndrome, described the syndrome subsequently ascribed in error to Prader and Willi; he was also the first to suggest the use of the descriptive term 'idiot savant'.

An Irish initiative

The Irish philanthropist Cheyne Brady visited Earlswood in 1864 with Jonathan Pim. They were intent on setting up a centre for learning disability in Dublin. Their efforts led to the opening of the Stewart Hospital in Dublin in 1873, and in the planning stages Dr George Kidd arranged for the superintendent to visit and to profit from the Earlswood experience. Cheyne Brady found Earlswood to be a model establishment. He noted that there was extensive accommodation for private patients, paying 50–150 guineas a year according to what special facilities were provided for them. At the top end residents had a two-room suite and a personal attendant. There was a waiting list for admissions, both private and charitable. Private patients' payments helped with the costs of the charity patients. This was taken into account in the new Stewart Hospital in Dublin.

Mary Langdon Down

There were many patients-in-waiting. The talented Mary Langdon Down, drawing on her experience helping her husband, set up her own training programme. The individuals concerned lodged with asylum employees. She herself was not an employee. When they found out the Board objected. John Langdon Down replied that she had as much right to earn her living in this way as another woman might by taking in sewing or washing. He was a man of liberal views and a supporter of universal suffrage and of the admission of women to medicine, the law and the Church. He stood his ground and he resigned on principle.

Normansfield

The couple borrowed what they could, bought a house in Hampton Wick, near London, called it Normansfield and opened a private institution which went from strength to strength, starting with eighteen patients and gradually building up to 150. The Commissioners in Lunacy recommended it highly.

Death rates among residents were notably lower than in Earlswood. Two of his Down's syndrome patients lived to the ages of fifty-eight and sixty-one. Mary Langdon Down was an efficient and caring administrator, known affectionately to the residents as 'Little Mother'. The site was gradually expanded. An historic Assembly Hall, erected in 1874, survives as a listed building, the Langdon Down Centre, and is now the headquarters of the Down's Syndrome Association. High standards were expected of staff, and all were required to have the skill needed to join the orchestra, the band or the cricket team. A resident chaplain held

Sunday service and the day started and ended with prayers. The Langdon Down family themselves lived in Normansfield, as did a grandson of the founder, John, who, ironically, had the condition subsequently named after his grandfather, Down's syndrome. He lived to a comparatively ripe old age of sixty-five. Eventually, Normansfield and the work of Dr John Langdon Down developed an international reputation fostered, in the years to come, by his sons Reginald and Percival, who, in turn, were doctors running Normansfield. Finally, another grandson, Dr Norman Langdon Down, ran the place until the 1970s – a remarkably dedicated family.

Rebirth of Essex Hall

Essex Hall remained close to the heart of Andrew Reed. It lay fallow when the exodus to Earlswood took place in 1853 but it reopened in 1856 as the Eastern Counties Asylum. William Millard returned from Earlswood as superintendent. Now associated with it was Dr Martin Duncan, an unsung hero of medical history. He is listed in the Medical Directory as physician to the Essex and Colchester Hospital from 1852 to 1871. More importantly he served as physician to Essex Hall. The Medical Directory identifies him as the only member of staff without a higher qualification. Paradoxically, however, it also lists him as a Fellow of the Royal Society. This gives a clue to his other extraordinary accomplishments.

Dr Martin Duncan

The records of the Geological Society record Martin Duncan's admission as a Fellow on 16 May 1849. He was elected a Fellow of the Royal Society in 1868 in recognition of his work on fossil corals. In the year 1870 he was appointed Professor of Geology. He found time to co-author with William Millard *A Manual for the Classification, Training and Education of the Feebleminded, Imbecile and Idiotic*. This provided a comprehensive training programme covering everything from physical exercise to the details of speech therapy. A review in the *BMJ* recommended bringing 'this unpretending but valuable work to the notice of the profession, and of all who are interested in the subject which its authors have so well treated'. This might be regarded as the most important Victorian contribution in the English language in respect of training and education for the management of learning disability. William Millard had previously published an account of the development of the institutions concerned. Between them the Duncan and Millard team, from their modest base, made a disproportionate contribution to training and education in the field of learning disability.

Conclusion

The pioneering work of the Revd Dr Andrew Reed focused the attention of a number of gifted medical men on the problem of learning disability. These included John Connolly, William Little, John Langdon Down and Martin Duncan, as well as the energetic lay superintendent William Millard. Speaking personally, I came to live in England on a permanent basis some fifteen years ago, which presented an opportunity for me to become engaged in voluntary work once more – but in a new setting – which prompted a search for historical information on how services had come into being in the UK. The evolution from institutional care to care in the community has been accepted. For the early pioneers however it was only in institutions that services could be developed. The manner in which they achieved so much has not, until now, been fully acknowledged nor have they received the credit which is their due. I hope my modest contribution to this most interesting and worthwhile book will help to correct this neglect.

Prologue

Life may change, but it may fly not;
Hope may vanish, but can die not;
Truth be veiled, but still it burneth;
Love repulsed – but it returneth!
Percy Bysshe Shelley

During World War II, in the dread summer of 1940 when Hitler was preparing to invade our shores, the renowned playwright and author J.B. Priestley could be heard encouraging his listeners on the BBC to even greater wartime efforts with visions of the future, if we repelled the expected Nazi hordes and went on to the sunlit uplands of a just peace. In one of his postscripts he voiced this opinion:

> There are two ways of looking at this war. First, as a terrible interruption – as soon as we decently can, let's go back to where we started the day before war was declared. ALL WRONG, it isn't true. There's nothing that really worked that we can go back to . . . dole queues, hunger marches and appeasement. My view, for what it's worth, is that we must stop thinking in terms of property and power and begin thinking in terms of community and creation.

Later in the same year Prime Minister Churchill – no lover of Priestley – echoed those words: 'When the war is won, it must be one of our aims to establish a state of society where the advantages and privileges hitherto enjoyed only by the few shall be far more widely shared by the many.'

As though transmogrified by these words, in 1942 Sir William Beveridge (later Lord Beveridge), a one-time Permanent Secretary at the Board of Trade, together with a number of other civil servants, produced *Social Insurance and Allied Services* – known to one and all as the Beveridge Report. Sir William then went on to produce, in 1944, a further report, *Full Employment in a Free Society*. The basis of both these ground-breaking publications was a vision of the future for the Great British Public – 'a plan for social security to abolish physical want by ensuring for all citizens at all times a subsistence income and the means of meeting exceptional expenditure at birth, marriage and death'.

The only snag with both these reports was that there was utter silence when it came to the question of learning disability. Not altogether surprising, I suppose, for who wanted to tackle the problem faced by hundreds of thousands of people still classed as idiots, imbeciles, mongols, defectives, retards – not forgetting 'subnormal' – which appeared to indicate they were sub-human as well. Even 'Rab' Butler's 1944 Education Act took the same view, for those who had an IQ over 50 would be classified as 'educationally subnormal' and could attend special schools. Those below an IQ of 50 (the majority, it seemed) were described as 'ineducable' and offered places – *if* they could be found – in so-called 'occupation centres' or 'junior training centres'. In reality, the vast majority of parents had to find and pay for private education – which was largely inexpert – or keep their son or daughter at home all day, every day. It is no surprise, therefore, that desperation led to the beginnings of the Association of Parents of Backward Children.

A certain Judy Fryd of Harpenden in Hertfordshire, was concerned at the lack of educational provision for her learning disabled daughter, Felicity. She had attempted to place her in a fee-paying residential school in Surrey and it was arranged that Felicity would be admitted for a month on trial. 'We took her down there,' wrote Judy, 'with the long list of clothing requirements, and returned home happy that that she was at last to have a chance. The next morning we received in our mail a telegram, sent off at 9.00 pm the previous evening: 'FELICITY NOT SUITABLE MUST BE REMOVED AT ONCE'.

'Our feelings can be imagined. [In November 1946] I wrote a letter to *Nursery World* suggesting that parents of backward children should band together to press for the facilities we needed . . . for, being excluded from school, our children were deprived of many things – no ration of free milk, no family allowances . . .' In other words, Beveridge and Butler had inadvertently condemned children and adults with a learning disability, and their families, to a life of poverty and deprivation quite unacceptable to parents who had struggled through a fearsome war and had high hopes of a fairer world following those two reports and one Education Act.

To complement the banding together of parents, Mrs Fryd began a newsletter which was mentioned in the *Sunday People*, thus bringing a cascade of correspondence to the newspaper itself, followed by articles in various journals and yet further letters and messages. All this encouraged Judy to put parents who lived near each other in touch – so local groups began to form and in January 1949 this loosely knit conglomeration held their first meeting and a branch for the South-East was formed – along with the first friends' groups for the local 'subnormality hospitals'. These 'hospitals' were huge Victorian buildings with large wards, so overcrowded that often beds had to be crammed in round the sides and even down the centre aisle. The nurses were struggling to look after so many that it was just a question of trying to keep the 'patients' dry, fed and clean, while quite a number were kept in bed all day. The majority of the nurses were dedicated people doing an almost impossible job in an horrendous atmosphere of unhappiness and degradation with the foetid stench of urine, old cabbages and body odour permeating every nook and cranny in those ghastly institutions.

The story of Mabel Cooper illustrates this only too well. Mabel was a long-time 'patient' at one of these so-called 'hospitals' but after several decades took her place in the community. She was then given the opportunity to recount her experiences through a series of taped interviews. The resulting autobiography forms an extraordinary chapter in *Forgotten Lives* – a remarkable history of people with a learning disability – published by BILD (British Institute of Learning

Disabilities). Her story reflects the changing policies and practices since the early post-war years and tells of her early experiences in a children's home and a long-stay hospital, where conditions were exactly as already described. Here are some of her thought-provoking insights:

> There were bars on the windows when I first went to St Lawrence's. It was just like prison.

> The worst thing was I couldn't wear my own clothes, you had to wear other people's. You never got your own because the beds were too close together, so you didn't have a locker or anything, you just went to a big cupboard and helped yourself.

> The ward was blocked off [although] there were doors. You weren't allowed to sit on your beds. The beds were that close to one another, so you couldn't have anything private. I didn't have anything of my own, because they would get pinched, the other patients would pinch them.

> They had a ward, No. 3, and they used to put people in there. They used to get locked up.

> We ate on the ward together, but not with the staff. The food was vile, I didn't like it. They used to bring the dinner up at 11 o'clock and they used to sit and talk till 12 or half past. The dinners were horrible. There was no choice.

Mabel had no one to care for her outside St Lawrence's but even if she had, it would have mattered little, for parents and families were treated with the same indifference as those unfortunate enough to be incarcerated. Can you wonder that the first shoots of change were beginning to struggle towards the surface and in 1950, a further parents' meeting was held at which a constitution was adopted, a National Council elected and the Association of Parents of Backward Children came into formal being. An interesting point is that the five changes to the Royal Mencap Society's title over the intervening years give some indication as to the changes within the Society itself (as well as society in the wider world); it became the National Society for Mentally Handicapped Children, then the National Society for Mentally Handicapped Children and Adults, after that the Royal Society for Mentally Handicapped Children and Adults and, finally, the Royal Mencap Society. The logos on the letterheads also changed: the first was a profile of a child with a shadow over half the face; then, in 1957, came award-winning 'Little Stephen', a rather beguiling – but pathetic – boy named, phonetically, after the artist, Harry Stevens. There was a similar drawing of a little girl. In the 1990s, the letterheads adopted a more positive image, using wonderful photographs, taken by Caroline Cook, of people with a learning disability which raised the spirits, rather than casting them down. Nowadays, all photos and illustrations have gone and the title MENCAP is at the top of the letterhead with a strap-line underneath, 'Understanding learning disability'. Further references and illustrations can be found in the picture sections.

The label 'mental handicap' has now been rejected as offensive, confusing and inappropriate by people with a learning disability themselves but the acronym MENCAP – officially adopted in 1980 – was clearly made up from the first three and the last three letters of Mental Handicap, then in the Mencap title and in common usage worldwide. However, Mencap's National Assembly (with over 60 per cent of its members having a learning disability) voted to keep the acronym when the title of the new Royal Mencap Society was adopted, realising that a change could well cost the Society dear in both recognition and fundraising.

As I was closely involved on the joint committee which examined the draft Mental Capacity Bill and eventually with its passage through the House of Lords, I personally believe that if anyone queries the acronym Mencap, it might now be seen to derive from the 2005 Mental Capacity Act, the first principle of which states that 'every adult has the right to make his or her own decisions and must be assumed to have capacity to do so unless it is proved otherwise'. As this encompasses Mencap's current position and its fully inclusive constitution, membership and National Assembly, Mental Capacity – in my opinion – is particularly apposite.

This presumption of capacity leads to Mencap's *vision* of a world where everyone with a learning disability has an equal right to choice, opportunity and respect, with the support they need. Mencap's *mission* is to improve the lives and opportunities of children and adults with a learning disability together with their families and carers. We must never forget that:

- 1.5 million people in the UK have a learning disability.
- Learning disability affects someone's intellectual and social development all their life.
- It is not a mental illness, nor is it dyslexia.
- Mencap exists to ensure change and also to support thousands of people to live their lives the way *they* want. We've come a long way in the last sixty years. Let us complete the journey in the next sixty. That would be a Diamond Jubilee indeed . . .

PART I

The Mencap Diary

CHAPTER 1

The History of Mencap Recounted in the Society's Records 1946–2006

1946: Mrs Judy Fryd wrote that fateful letter to *Nursery World* – referred to in the Prologue – leading to an article in the *Sunday People* which brought forth many responses from parents of 'backward' children, prompting the first thoughts of an association.

1948: Miss Aphra Hargrove of the National Association of Mental Health helped Judy Fryd develop her ideas and allowed her desk space at 39 Queen Anne Street in London. One of the first to join Judy was Mrs Betty Johnson-Allen, who later ran the Home Counties North Region.

1949: A group of parents in the South-East set up an ad hoc branch, as yet without a name or a constitution. The first 'friends' group was formed to support 'patients' in long-stay hospitals.

1950: The parents met again at the Fountain Hospital, Tooting, south-west London; a constitution was approved, a Chairman (Jim White),

Hon. Secretary (Horace Hutchings) and National Executive Committee appointed and a title adopted – the National Association of Parents of Backward Children. Judy Fryd offered to edit a new magazine, *Parents' Voice*, and this was welcomed by all present. Eventually Judy was employed by the Association to produce *Parents' Voice* on a regular basis and had to give up her position on the National Executive. Nevertheless, *Parents' Voice* was so influential that Judy continued to attend all meetings in an advisory role, where the strength of her opinions held sway for many a year. In 1970 she retired as the editor and was immediately elected back on to the National Executive Committee, ending up as a Vice-President and then the Founder Member of the Society. She also received an MBE, finally elevated to CBE. How she failed to become a Dame is a mystery to all who knew her, for she battled for the rights of people with a learning disability to the end of her very long life.

1951: The first fundraising activity took place at the Scala Theatre, London – famous, at that time, for the annual Christmas production of *Peter Pan*, the 'little boy who never grew up'. This phrase could, in those days, be applied to the Society, for it reflected their title, the National Association of Parents of Backward *Children*. It was nearly thirty years before 'and Adults' was added.

1952: The money raised at the Scala went towards the opening of the Society's first short-stay home, Orchard Dene at Rainhill. The National Association also found new accommodation with two rooms in Chancery Lane and a part-time secretary, Mrs MacLaren White, employed on the princely sum of £4 per week. A founder member, Mrs Doris Drown, began to sell 'home-made' charity Christmas cards through members in the Middlesex branch. It was the beginning of an enterprise which profited both the National Society and local societies in the years ahead.

1954: The first regional group was formed in the Midlands but by 1954 there were twelve regions, one being in Northern Ireland. They met somewhat infrequently and one Hon. Secretary per region had to do all the work. Nevertheless, the regions flourished until the early 1980s, when they were replaced by five larger Divisions, plus Mencap in Wales and Northern Ireland.

1955: After rather stormy discussions, lasting throughout most of 1954 and well into 1955, new Memorandum and Articles of Association were finally agreed, drawn up and approved. The name of the Society was changed to the National Society for Mentally Handicapped Children. You will note that adults were still not included in the title – possibly because many local groups provided nurseries and classes for children labelled 'ineducable'. At that time it was known that at least 25,000 children with learning disabilities were denied schooling of any kind, so it is no surprise that desperate parents tried their very best to bridge the gap. Dudley Drown was appointed the first Chairman of the newly named National Society, while his wife, Doris – enthused by her local success – organised the widespread sale of charity Christmas cards by negotiating a generous agreement with Frank Kerry of Burton-on-Trent who, in due course, founded Fine Arts plc and Webb Ivory Ltd, eventually serving the Christmas card and merchandise needs of the majority of UK charities.

1956: A professional appeals organiser was appointed and the gift of a covenant of £500 per annum for seven years – made by an anonymous benefactor – enabled the Society to move its office to two rooms in the Strand. The building was bomb-damaged, so the rent was minimal, and the furniture would not have disgraced a jumble sale. Nevertheless it provided a rather grand address. At the end of this year the Society numbered 12,000 members in 200 local societies and declared an income of £6,817.

1957: The first General Secretary (the title was later changed to Secretary-General and, later still, to Chief Executive), George Lee, was appointed. He succeeded in implementing the new constitution and ensuring the Society grew into the great national charity it is today. This constitution remained in place until succeeded by the 1998 inclusive constitution. George Lee retired as Secretary-General in 1980 and his story appears in Chapter 3. Also in 1957 the first of a number of peers associated with the Society was appointed Chairman. He was Lord Pakenham, later The Earl of Longford. Others who played their part over the years were (or are) several barons – The Lords Stonham, Grenfell, Segal, Renton, Allen of Abbeydale and Rix. Having a voice in the House of Lords is of great importance, for all legislation affecting the lives of people with a learning disability can be closely scrutinised on its way through Parliament. This year also saw the first publication of the *Journal of Mental Deficiency Research*, organised by the Society and still published today on behalf of Mencap by Blackwell as *The Journal of Intellectual Disability Research*. It is a highly respected and widely read publication, with a list of distinguished editors and contributors.

1958: The Brooklands Experiment, funded by the Society and led by Professor Jack Tizard, was launched. This compared the progress of children with a learning disability who lived in hospital with a group of children who were cared for in a small family environment, using educational activities modelled on those in 'ordinary' nurseries. After two years, the children in the home-like setting showed marked improvements in social, emotional and verbal skills. The project's success was known worldwide. The Society was also invited to give evidence to the Royal Commission on the law relating to Mental Illness and Mental Deficiency and consequently head office asked local societies for information about the myriad problems which beset their members and their 'backward' children and this, plus the Society's manifesto, was sent to the Royal Commission. Furthermore, a delegation met with the Ministry of Education, the Ministry of Health and a group of MPs, who reported on their findings and all this activity had some bearing on the Government's proposed Mental Health Bill.

1959: Following the publication of the Royal Commission's report, the Government ensured the Mental Health Bill became an Act of Parliament in this year. A number of suggestions put forward by the Society were adopted in the Act, including the dropping of such terms as 'idiot', 'imbecile', 'mental defective' and 'feeble-minded' when describing people with a learning disability, as well as references to 'backward' children as 'ineducable'. However, this did not mean that education became readily available for the majority of such children. All that happened was that junior training centres were retitled special schools but local authorities were not required to provide services. Only 35,000 special school places were available for the 84,000 children thought to be in need of this so-called education but pejorative labels still applied: the 'mildly subnormal' were classed as ESN (Educationally Subnormal) and the 'severely subnormal' enjoyed the eponymous initials, SSN. However, the 'supervisors' of the training centres were given the opportunity to train as teachers and the curriculum of the teacher training colleges began to include courses for special school teachers. This training was fairly haphazard until it followed the example of the Society's pilot scheme at Westhill College, Birmingham, in 1970, just before the crucial Education (Handicapped Children) Act came into effect. However, in 1959 there were still eleven long years to go before education for 'handicapped children' would be formalised – but at least it was a start. Also in 1959 a most important discovery was made. Up to now, 'mongol' people had 'enjoyed' the label bestowed on them by Dr John Langdon Down in the nineteenth century, but no one had discovered the cause of the condition. Two medical men – one in France, Professor Lejeune, and one in Britain, Professor Lionel Penrose – came forward with important discoveries. Professor Lejeune declared that the condition was caused by an extra chromosome on the twenty-first chromosome, known as Trisomy 21, which was not inherited. Professor Penrose added to this, for he found there was a significant correlation between increased maternal age and the birth of infants with Down's syndrome. He went on to unearth more facts about rare conditions – chromosomal translocations and mosaicism – which can lead to inherited Down's, while he also noted the complex connection between Down's and Alzheimer's disease. These discoveries meant, at long last, that parents would no longer be asked ridiculous questions about their sex lives or whether they once had venereal disease or were drunk at the time of conception, for no one knew, until now, the cause of Down's syndrome.

1960: George Lee presided at a conference in March to explore the possibility of forming a European league of parental organisations concerned with 'the mentally handicapped'. Together with Dr van Dijk of the Netherlands and Mr Tom Mutters (also a Dutchman) of Germany, these three men defined the purpose of such a body 'to create a common bond of understanding between parents and others by the problem of mental handicap throughout the world . . .'

1961: Actor-manager Brian Rix, famous for his Whitehall farces, was asked by George Lee to become the first Chairman of a newly formed Special Functions Committee, which raised considerable sums of money, organising the first spring ball with *Beyond the Fringe* (Jonathan Miller, Peter Cook, Dudley Moore and Alan Bennett) as the cabaret. This enabled the purchase, in 1963, of a holiday home, 'Pirates Spring,' at Dymchurch in Kent. Other holiday schemes were started by local societies but floundered because they were used only in the summer. One such property, taken over by the Society, was Pengwern Hall in North Wales which became a training unit and is now part of the Mencap college, along with two other large properties, Lufton Manor in Somerset and Dilston Hall in Northumberland. The Mencap college does magnificent further education work, so those uncertain investments of long ago have more than proved their worth.

1962: HM Queen Elizabeth the Queen Mother became the Royal Patron of the National Society, having been approached by the Treasurer, Lord Grenfell, who was the father of a learning disabled daughter. The Queen Mother, who also had family interests in learning disability, remained the Society's Patron until the day she died – even approving our current title, the Royal Mencap Society, a few weeks before her demise. In the early sixties, with so many learning disabled people still incarcerated in long-stay hospitals, there was much anxiety felt by parents that, on their deaths, there would be no one to ensure the well-being of their son or daughter. The same applied, too, to those who remained at home, especially if there were no siblings prepared or able to ensure continuity of care. The National Society considered the problem and formed the Trustee Visitors' Service, guaranteeing that those whose parents had entered the scheme would be befriended and visited at least once a month by a volunteer visitor. A report would be sent by the visitor to a department in the

Society, alerting them to any problems which had arisen, or any evident unhappiness. Parents initially paid £500 for the service but as the years went by and costs rose – and more and more people left long-stay hospitals – it was decided that change was necessary and, although the scheme still exists, it is run on entirely different lines today by both professional members of staff and volunteers.

Again the headquarters of the Society moved, this time to Bulstrode Street, into premises entirely given over to its work. Whereas an earlier HQ was a couple of rooms in a bomb-damaged building in the Strand, now the Society enjoyed offices in quite a pleasant house – but with floors so rickety that the number of people who could attend meetings in one room had to be limited, lest the floor disappear to the ground below.

1963: The Queen Mother opened the National Society's new hostel and training workshop in Slough, Buckinghamshire, the first of its kind for learning disabled adults. The idea was to prove to both local authorities and communities that people with a learning disability could, in fact, work. That work consisted of set tasks – making pottery, toys, rugs, embroidery and light industrial goods, all for sale. These made a small profit and both sexes could happily live together as a family. Today we take all this for granted, but in the sixties it was a revolutionary idea. The director of this project was James Cummings, whom the Society of Friends had earlier sponsored to go to Israel and open the first training centres in that country for people with a learning disability. He was about to go to America on a similar mission when George Lee persuaded him to take on the much less rewarding job, in pecuniary terms, at Slough. George was a member of the Society of Friends, as was his deputy, Ken Solly so they knew about James's work in Israel. Later, another Quaker, Alan Phillips, joined as George's Assistant Secretary-General. In June 1963, Lord Longford retired as Chairman and Lord Stonham succeeded him. The following month Valerie Hobson (herself the mother of a boy with Down's syndrome) opened the Society's 'new' holiday home at Dymchurch, acquired from the RNIB.

1964: The National Society expanded to take in Northern Ireland, Evelyn Greer was appointed the Regional Officer and offices were opened at Ormeau Road, Belfast. In the same year – and after some hesitation – the American societies concerned with learning disability agreed to join an International League of Societies for the Mentally Handicapped. The original trio of officers who had come together in 1960, George Lee, Dr van Dijk and Tom Mutters, started work and the International League came into being. Nowadays it exists under the more politically correct title, Inclusion International, and has over 130 countries affiliated to it.

Originally the International League held conferences every four years and two chartered planeloads of members from the National Society attended the first one in Brussels. It interested everyone to see what was going on in other countries – especially in Europe, where so many people with a learning disability had been eliminated by the Nazis. It was perhaps ironic that the three societies starting the whole operation were three wartime antagonists – Britain, Holland and Germany – but in a Europe coming closer together, it was both a hopeful and imaginative step in the right direction and much was learned to everyone's advantage.

1965: Lord Segal was elected Chairman of the Society. The first International Exhibition of Art by artists with a learning disability was held in London. Entries were invited from all member countries in the newly formed International League. This was a great success and was an annual event until the nineties. It still continues, from time to time, but has largely been superseded by an exhibition of photographic works entitled *Snap!* which takes place at the Victoria and Albert Museum, sponsored by the Sorrell Foundation. Some of these photos appear in the picture sections.

1966: Alan Phillips joined the National Society as a Regional Officer before being promoted to George Lee's office as Assistant Secretary-General. (He became Deputy Secretary-General to Brian Rix in 1981.) His first major achievement for the Society, though, was in conjunction with Ken Solly, the Deputy Secretary-General. Together they formed the National Federation of Gateway Clubs to provide leisure opportunities for people with a learning disability. More can be learned about this splendid organisation in Chapter 17.

1967: Again the National Society's offices moved, this time to Newman Street, near the Post Office Tower, while another holiday home at Winterton, 'Hales House', opened. The first Gateway AGM took place, indicating there were already 1,300 members but with new clubs being formed nationwide. The Institute for Research into Mental Retardation was established in Newman Street to provide a central reference point for all professional workers in the field of 'mental handicap' and the College of Special Education, set up a few months earlier by the Guild of Teachers of Backward Children, was somehow squeezed into the same building.

1968: The Society's Founder, Judy Fryd, was awarded the MBE. The Fourth Congress of the International League was held in Jerusalem and adopted a 'Declaration of General and Special Rights of the Mentally Retarded'. Members drafting the document included the founding trio, George Lee, Dr van Dijk and Tom Mutters. In 1972 the principles enshrined were adopted by the World Assembly of the United Nations. Article 1 states: 'the mentally retarded person has the same basic rights as other citizens of the same country and age'.

1969: The Lufton Manor Training Unit opened in Somerset. Originally it was intended to be a ten-year experiment and its aim was to train people with a learning disability over the age of sixteen for jobs in agriculture and horticulture. A recent national survey of disabled people had largely excluded people with a learning disability when it came to their capability to work effectively. Lufton's task, like its forerunner, Slough, was to prove otherwise. Eventually, it did just that and was incorporated into the Mencap College, preparing young adults with a learning disability for the world outside by providing them with imaginative and practical further education. In Belfast, a nursery unit was opened at 51 Knock Road.

1970: Anticipating the Education (Handicapped Children) Act, the National Society, through its educational panel chaired by Sir David Renton MP, collaborated with Westhill College of Education in Birmingham to bring about a Special Needs Training Course which became a blueprint for all such courses in the UK. In this year, also, Alf Morris (now Lord Morris of Manchester), the MP for Manchester Wythenshawe, saw his Private Member's Bill safely on to the Statute Book as the Chronically Sick and Disabled Persons Act. Some time later, George Lee, in his capacity as the Secretary-General of the NSMHC (the National Society was generally known, then, by its initials) welcomed the Act with these words: 'Given the extent of the financial commitment involved, it called for resolve and bravery on the part of the Government to pass this Act. More than this, they showed imagination and concern in bringing into being, in 1974, a Minister of Disabled People, and wisdom in choosing Alf Morris to fill the role.'

The Act was, indeed, radical for it insisted that disabled people had a right to take part in every area of life. It was some years yet before people with a learning disability were considered capable of doing just that but, largely thanks to the Society and, nowadays, people with a learning disability themselves, inclusion is at the forefront in all relevant legislation.

The first Mental Handicap Week (now Learning Disability Week) was mounted in June. Previously the Society had participated in Mental Health Week, but increasingly the confusion between mental illness, which might well be treatable, and the lifelong condition of 'mental handicap' was causing ever greater difficulty. The week generally began with a service in St Martin-in-the-Fields, followed by a rally in Trafalgar Square, with the Secretary-General delivering a 'political' address, which usually received good coverage in the media. Events took place around the country and, at one time, national flag days were organised.

1971: The Government's White Paper *Better Services for the Mentally Handicapped* heralded a continuing shift from institutional to community care, while the new Education (Handicapped Children) Act ensured that children with severe learning disabilities were no longer excluded from school. Altogether it was a very significant year for all concerned with learning disability, with George Lee being awarded the OBE and the Gateway Federation holding its first National Festival at the Royal Festival Hall, with members entertaining a crowded house with three hours of music and laughter. These National Festivals continued until well into the nineties with matinée and evening performances.

1972: The National Society's Holiday Service was established, eventually involving thousands of volunteers who escorted children and adults to ever-expanding holiday locations. In Belfast the new HQ in Annadale Avenue was opened by (and named after) Lord Segal.

1973: In London, the Society was on the move yet again – to four houses in Pembridge Square, in the Bayswater area, which seemed vast. However, the idea was that residential courses could be held there, but after a review it was found to be impractical, as catering and housekeeping staff would have to be employed, even when there were no courses running. Houses are not always the best places from which to run an organisation and in 1979 a disused warehouse was found at 123 Golden Lane, where the Royal Mencap Society (as it is now called) exists to this day. Also, the Assistant Secretary-General, Alan Phillips, was wise enough to negotiate a favourable tenancy with the owners of the warehouse next door (115 Golden Lane) and, eventually, in the early eighties, Mencap came to own that, too.

1974: Pengwern Hall, set in twenty-three acres of land in North Wales, was established as a further holiday home to add to Pirates Spring and Hales House. Now part of the Mencap College, in 1974 the National Society's North-West Region set up the project, buying the property from the Manchester and Salford Hospital Saturday Fund for £40,000, with half the finance to pay for it coming from the region and the other half from the National Society. Within three years the region found that holidays – with the limited holiday season – were too great a drain on their resources and Pengwern was paid for and taken over as a training college by the National Society and has remained a training college ever since. Also, in this year, the Society published *Tongue Tied* by Joey Deacon, an autobiography of fifty years spent in a 'subnormality hospital'. Written by a man totally without speech, and afflicted with cerebral palsy (spastic quadriplegia) affecting all four limbs, the book was written by using the cumulative skills of three other learning disabled men. It was an instant success and the BBC documentary *Joey*, based on the book, won international acclaim and a number of awards. Doris Drown received the MBE.

1975: For years, first with the Slough project, and then with the training colleges, the National Society had been trying to establish an employment facility for people with a learning disability, with regions encouraged to develop practical ideas. The South Wales Region had been experimenting with a centre to train people for outside employment, but their scheme proved too expensive and complicated. Eventually the far simpler idea of the Pathway Employment Service came about. The Pathway Officer – generally funded by the local authority – would take on about twenty adults with a learning disability and introduce them individually to outside employers for jobs which the person concerned was willing and able to do and which the employer wished to fill. The future employee would then train for that job, *in situ*, with a 'foster' worker helping him or her at all times. Eventually, if everyone was happy, the trainee employee would be taken on and become part of the workforce. Pathway achieved its purpose surprisingly well, each local unit having about six or seven people training, a similar number actually at work and a further seven or eight who had passed through the process, but needed a little further support. The Pathway Service quickly expanded, with local authorities all over the country adopting the idea, for the service was far more effective than the local employment officers at getting people with a learning disability into full-time work. Also in 1975 the Government established the National Development Group and the National Development Team to advise on 'mental handicap policy' and inspect 'mental handicap facilities' in the UK, thus encouraging good practice. Unfortunately, all concerned had to sign the Official Secrets Act, which rather blunted the edge of their reports and recommendations. (See Chapter 4 for the full story.)

1977: The National Health Service Act provided a statutory basis for local authority health services, which included a new legislative basis for day centres. The BBC began to record the first-ever series for people with a learning disability, *Let's Go!* This was transmitted three times a week and involved two future Secretaries-General of Mencap: Brian Rix, who presented the series, and Fred Heddell, who wrote all the accompanying notes. These notes and tapes were distributed by Mencap and the Scottish society Enable (both societies adopted these acronyms later). The series continued until 1982, with forty-two episodes being transmitted.

1978: Lord Segal retired and Sir David Renton KBE TD QC MP (soon to be Lord Renton on his retirement from the Commons in 1979), who had been the Hon. Treasurer since 1976 and, earlier, Chairman of the Educational Panel, was elected as the new Chairman of the Society.

1979: The Lufton Manor Rural Training Unit had proved such a success that Lufton Manor College was the logical outcome. This offered much broader training in independent living skills and vocational opportunities, while also meeting the needs of people with more severe learning disabilities. The head office moved to 123 Golden Lane, near the Barbican and the City of London, where it has remained ever since, with suitable alterations.

1980: George Lee OBE retired and Gerald Sanctuary was appointed his successor on a pro tem basis. After six months he became Senior HQ Officer for Regional and Local Affairs. In October, Brian Rix CBE was appointed Secretary-General, with tenure of office until retirement.

The Society was renamed the National Society for Mentally Handicapped Children and Adults, with the acronym MENCAP adopted and a National Council replacing the National Executive Committee. Four Vice-Chairmen were appointed – Pauline Fairbrother, Ron Miller, Dennis Mills and Neville Thompson – each a Chairman of one of the four main committees, with Neville Thompson, the Chairman of Finance, becoming the Hon. Treasurer as well. Judy Fryd MBE continued to serve the Society on the National Council.

1981: This International Year of Disabled People (IYDP) was an important one for Mencap and people with a learning disability, for they were included in all the deliberations which went on throughout the year, along with the other organisations representing those with physical and sensory disabilities. Such cooperation had been rare indeed in the past and much of this change was due to the influence of the President of IYDP in the UK, the Earl of Snowdon. In addition, Mencap ceased to be the 'National' Society for HM The Queen graciously commanded that henceforth we became the 'Royal' Society. It was a splendid accolade in IYDP.

Also, early in 1981, the new Secretary-General, Brian Rix, formed the first-ever Parliamentary Department at Mencap with Rolf Hermelin as the Parliamentary Officer. He was soon at work, arranging for Lord Renton and the Secretary-General to meet with the Secretary of State for Education, Mark Carlisle (now Lord Carlisle) to press on him a number of important changes in the forthcoming Education Bill which, when enacted, gave children with special needs additional rights to support. The Mencap Annual Mental Handicap Week Conference, entitled 'Right from the Start '81', addressed, yet again, the perennial problem facing parents of newly born, or newly diagnosed, 'mentally handicapped' children and in the same year ATV (later Central Television) produced a documentary by Nigel Evans, *Silent Minority*. It purported to show life in a large 'subnormality hospital', St Lawrence's at Caterham, and caused a great deal of disquiet, particularly among Mencap parents whose sons and daughters lived in such places. However, the programme increased the pressure for such 'hospitals' to be closed as soon as possible. At the year's end, HM The Queen Mother opened Mencap's refurbished headquarters in Golden Lane and Lord Renton, the Secretary-General and Rolf Hermelin met with Lord Elton, the Under-Secretary of State at the DHSS, to put forward further proposals for what was to become the 1983 Mental Health Act, and many of these suggested amendments were incorporated.

1982: Lord Renton retired as Mencap's Chairman and became the Society's first-ever President. Lord Allen of Abbeydale GCB succeeded him as Chairman. Mencap's Homes Foundation was established, with Ron Miller and Herbert Bradfield as Chairman and Vice-Chairman, and Harry Neal as Director, providing some of the first accommodation of its kind in the UK. Housing was to become one of Mencap's major activities, with thousands of learning disabled people living in accommodation suited to their needs.

The Department of Health established the Opportunities for Volunteering (OFV) Scheme to support volunteering in England by providing opportunities for unemployed people to undertake voluntary work. An annual grant of £6.9 million is made to sixteen national charities – of which Mencap is one – to manage and distribute. Since 1982, to date, Mencap has allocated over £5 million in OFV grants. Brian Rix and Alan Leighton, Mencap's Director of Press and Publicity, negotiated with the producer of *Crossroads*, Jack Barton, to include a little girl with Down's syndrome in the series. Nina Weill was enchanting in this ground-breaking venture into popular TV. As a follow-up to IYDP, the Independent Development Council for People with a Mental Handicap (IDC) was initiated (see Chapter 21), with the Secretary-General in the chair, as was the Mencap Unit Trust, the first-ever for a charity. This was launched by the Chancellor of the Exchequer, Sir Geoffrey Howe, on the day the Falklands War broke out. Nevertheless, it survived and thrived, eventually becoming the United Charities Unit Trust and, finally, the Family Charities Ethical Trust. The Lord Mayor of London, Sir Anthony Jolliffe, adopted Mencap as his mayoral year charity and the Mencap Medical Advisory Panel was reinstated. The International League held their four-yearly conference in Nairobi, Kenya, and Gateway clubs raised money as a contribution to the UN Water for Life campaign and twelve members with a learning disability, plus eight volunteers, went on safari from Mombassa to Nairobi, taking water pumps and equipment to various villages along the way. Also, in 1982, Mencap in Northern Ireland became a separate division, with nearly forty affiliated local societies, and Evelyn Greer – now a JP and an MBE (advanced later to OBE) – as its first Director. Mencap in Wales, too, was formed as a separate division, embracing both North and South Wales. Up to then, North Wales had been affiliated to the North-West Region in England but, after lengthy negotiations, the North agreed to join the South in a combined body which enjoyed the rather lengthy title of Mencap yng Nghymru – later shortened to Mencap Cymru.

1983: Another year of initiatives. The Mental Health Act reached the Statute Book. The Secretary of State for Wales launched the All Wales Strategy for the Development of Services for Mentally Handicapped People. Using some of the money raised in the City by the Lord Mayor's Appeal, the Mencap City Foundation came into being. Now renamed, after the Founder Governors, the Rix-Thompson-Rothenberg (RTR) Foundation, its function remains the same: to grant-aid UK projects directly connected with learning disabled people. David Hencke of the *Guardian* and the Secretary-General organised a successful campaign to ensure that, in the future, members of the National Development Team, investigating services for people with a learning disability, would no longer have to sign the Official Secrets Act (see Chapter 4). 'Chef and Brewer' backed the first Mencap Pro-Am Golf Tournament – the Bruce Forsyth Classic – and there were two important conferences involving Mencap, with titles which are self-explanatory. The first was the annual Mencap Week Conference entitled 'Mental Handicap: Need it happen – and when it does?'; the second was organised by the Independent Council for People with a Mental Handicap (IDC), chaired by the Secretary-General, with the equally long title 'Elements of a Comprehensive Local Service for People with a Mental Handicap'. Both conferences published booklets containing their deliberations which were widely circulated and read. In the following three years the IDC published other booklets: *Next Steps, Living Like Other People* and *Pursuing Quality*. These publications were an extremely useful addition to the *Stamina* documents, which Mencap had been producing for years. These were checklists of great value and were the brainchild of the Founder, Judy Fryd, who also thought up the acronym for minimum standards: *Stamina*.

1984: Original ways of raising large sums for Mencap were particularly evident in this year: a TV series, *An Invitation to Remember*, interviewing the great and the good in the theatre and film world; a year of fund-raising by the Keep Fit Association, culminating in their annual event at the Royal Albert Hall; the Readathon in which children obtained sponsors to support their improved reading skills; parachute jumps by intrepid fundraisers and, again, the Bruce Forsyth Golf Classic. These events, plus the normal fundraising activities, kept the Appeals Department very busy. The Community Care Campaigners came into being with the Director of the Spastics Society, Sir John Cox, the Director of MIND, Chris Heginbotham, the Director of Barnardos, Roger Singleton, and the Secretary-General of Mencap, Brian Rix, campaigning – for the next three years – at party conferences, attempting to influence community care policies. The Police and Criminal Evidence (PACE) Act was placed on the Statute Book, which defined 'mental handicap' and the right to an 'appropriate adult' when being interviewed by the police. Mencap also produced, in collaboration with the Kent County Constabulary, a video for showing to all police forces on the problems which they might face as a result of the Act. Mencap members, including the Secretary-General, attended the International League conference in Rio de Janeiro.

1985: Loretto Lambe, PA to the Secretary-General, moved to Manchester to start Mencap's PRMH (Profound Retardation and Multiple Disability) project, in conjunction with the Hester Adrian Research Centre at Manchester University and based at Piper Hill School. It was one of the first to study the needs of – and provide services for – people with such diverse problems. The service continues to this day, headed by Beverley Dawkins, under the more acceptable initials PMLD – Profound and Multiple Learning Disability. Loretto Lambe and her husband, Professor James Hogg, continue their work at the White Top Research Unit, University of Dundee, with Loretto running a separate charity in Scotland – PAMIS (Promoting A More Inclusive Society).

The Mencap Medical Advisory Panel (Dr Betty Norman, Dr David Morris, Professor Gwyn Roberts, Professor 'Bill' Fraser, Frank Denny, chaired by the Secretary-General) visited Washington at the invitation of the Joseph P. Kennedy Jnr Foundation, to discuss medical ethics in regard to learning disabled people with their opposite numbers at the Kennedy Institute of Ethics, a department of Georgetown University. They also met with Eunice Kennedy Shriver regarding another Foundation-aided enterprise, Special Olympics, well-known for providing four-yearly Olympic-style Games for people with a learning disability. They visited Congress to meet Senator Chaffee and learn about his proposed Disability Bill, as well as attending a meeting with members of the Department of Health and Human Services. They were invited to the White House and hosted a reception at the British Embassy for people concerned with learning disability in the United States, arranged and co-hosted by the British Ambassador, Sir Oliver Wright. The week's visit was deemed to be very successful. Also, the Medical Advisory Panel, as well as the Mencap National Council and the Editorial Board of the *Journal of Mental Deficiency Research* (as it was still entitled), entered into the heated debate on the *Warnock Report on Human Fertilisation and Embryology* by supporting it.

1986: This was Mencap's fortieth anniversary year and was celebrated in July with a reception at St James's Palace in the presence of HM Queen Elizabeth the Queen Mother. Seven hundred guests from all the local Mencap Societies attended. After a four-year gestation period, which included raising £350,000, Mencap and the Open University launched the first course in the world for all those involved with learning disabled children and adults. It was entitled *Patterns for Living*.

This was followed by *Patterns for Living: Working Together* which was for people with a learning disability themselves. Eventually a further course for undergraduates came about, *Learning Disability: Changing Perspectives* and, more recently, *Equal People*, which is for everyone, whether learning disabled or not. Professor Dorothy Atkinson writes about these courses in Chapter 17. The Rt Hon. Tom Clarke CBE MP (who tells his story in Chapter 16) drew first place in the Private Members' Ballot in November 1985 and, initially advised by Mencap, launched his Disabled Persons (Services, Consultation and Representation) Bill which, happily, became an Act in, this, Mencap's anniversary year. The Mencap Week Conference saw the launch of *Today and Tomorrow: Mencap's vision of daytime services for people with a mental handicap into the 21st century*. It was a massive work and provided the background for a 'mobile' conference which toured the country for some time to well-attended and receptive 'audiences'. The Secretary-General led a campaign – beginning with an article in *The Times* (on the day the paper went to Wapping) – to 'give charity basic relief'. This was successful, insofar as the Chancellor of the Exchequer, Nigel Lawson (now Lord Lawson), in his March budget gave tax relief to employees making payroll donations to charities up to £240 per annum, while companies could donate up to 3 per cent of their dividends to charities, also with full tax relief. Since those early days the sums have greatly increased, but it was a good start to Mencap's anniversary year. In Northern Ireland the first group home in Bangor was opened and named Evelyn Greer House and in the Birthday Honours the Secretary-General, Brian Rix CBE, was awarded a knighthood.

1987: On 16 March the Appeal Court ordered that a seventeen-year-old girl 'with a mental age of five should be sterilised for her own good'. This was the case referred to in 'A Brief History . . .' and Mencap became closely involved in this controversy, as well as the one which arose when the media discovered that Mencap's Royal Patron had three nieces living in the Royal Earlswood Hospital. A further problem arose when, against Mencap's advice, some parents in the North-West decided to oppose the closure of long-stay hospitals, wishing to turn them into 'village communities', and formed a society, 'Rescare'. Sir Brian Rix CBE DL retired as Secretary-General, to be succeeded by Vice-Admiral Sir Geoffrey Dalton KCB.

1988: Lord Allen of Abbeydale retired as Chairman of Mencap and was succeeded by Sir Brian Rix, who had also been appointed Vice Lord-Lieutenant of Greater London earlier in the year. Lord Renton retired as President of Mencap and was succeeded by Lord Allen of Abbeydale. The *Griffiths Report on Community Care* was published, adopting a new approach to this subject. John Birt (now Lord Birt), Director-General of the BBC, apologised to Mencap's Chairman for taking out of context and misrepresenting his views on the sterilisation of yet another woman with a learning disability whose case was in the High Court. John Birt wrote: 'We owe you an apology . . . There is no doubt that on this occasion we failed in our intention to give viewers a clear account of Mencap's views on this issue. I am very sorry that you were the victim of what I consider – in my experience – to be a rare occurrence.'

1989: In February the sterilisation case went to the Court of Appeal and then to the House of Lords where, like its predecessor, the Law Lords allowed the sterilisation of the woman in question to take place. However, during the appeals process, no fewer than eight judges indicated that Mencap's long-held views on the issue needed earnest consideration.

As a result of their judgements, Mencap and the Royal Society of Medicine held a conference, 'The Legal, Medical and Ethical Issues of Mental Handicap', and a report was sent to the Lord Chancellor, Lord Mackay of Clashfern, entitled *Competency and Consent to Medical Treatment*. The Government's White Paper, *Caring for People*, responded to the *Griffiths Report* and set out their policy. Two Acts affecting the lives of people with a learning disability were placed on the Statute Book: the Children Act put the child first and emphasised support for the child through the family; the Local Government Act brought forth the Disabled Facilities Grant. Mencap became the first charity, along with two others, to benefit from an 'affinity' Visa credit card, issued by the Leeds Permanent Building Society. It still exists to this day – but as the Halifax Visa Card – having financially benefited all three charities to a considerable extent, for every time a card is used a donation is made to the cardholder's chosen charity.

1990: Evelyn Greer MBE JP retires as the first Director of Mencap in Northern Ireland and is succeeded by Maureen Piggot. HRH The Duchess of Gloucester visits Segal House. The NHS and Community Care Act comes into force, giving local authorities the lead role in assessing the needs of disabled people and coordinating services, particularly in regard to community care.

1991: Sir Geoffrey Dalton resigns as Secretary-General and is succeeded by Fred Heddell, then the current Mencap Director of Education and Employment. Roger Smythe joins Mencap for a short stay as a management accountant and finds – along with Barrie Davis, Mencap's Treasurer – that there are a number of financial problems, among which is insurance, costing the Society a disproportionate amount. As a result, Mencap City Insurance Service, assisted by the Mencap City Foundation, is formed. By 1995 the Insurance Service has grown to include many other charities and is hived off as a separate company, MCIS Ltd, with Roger Smythe as the Managing Director. Its expansion continues to this day, with the company making an annual contribution to the, what is now, RTR Foundation. Disability Living Allowance and Disability Working Allowance come into being, people with a learning disability being significant beneficiaries. In November, the Prime Minister, the Rt Hon. John Major MP, and Mrs Norma Major host a fundraising dinner and opera performance by Pavilion Opera at Chequers. Subsequently, three more events of a similar nature (with Opera Interludes giving the last two performances) are arranged at Chequers in the years before 1997. Furthermore, a cricket match at the Oval and dinner at No. 10 Downing Street is organised by Sir Philip Harris (later Lord Harris of Peckham) and Lady Harris, raising a phenomenal £800,000. It was then decided that much of the money raised at these events – over £2.5 million – would go into the newly formed Mencap Challenge Fund, with Norma Major as the President and Lady Harris as the Chairman, thus enabling local groups to apply for grants to top up or create their own fundraising projects to enhance the lives of people with a learning disability. The capital was used to provide the finance and the last tranche of money was donated to the Rix Centre for Innovation Studies in Learning Disability at the University of East London. For this work, and other charitable activities, Norma Major (later Lady Norma Major) was subsequently awarded the DBE, as was Lady Harris, and both became Vice-Presidents of Mencap.

1992: The perception of Mencap is changed. It is resolved that henceforth the Society must project a positive image of people with a learning disability. From now on the rather pathetic picture of 'Little Stephen' as the Society's logo is replaced and photographs of real people engaged in common everyday activities, together with the strap-line, 'Mencap making the most of life', appear on the Society's letterhead. This reflects the changing times and the official move from the term 'mental handicap' to 'learning disability'. The Chairman of Mencap, Sir Brian Rix, is elevated to the peerage and takes his place on the cross-benches in the House of Lords as Lord Rix of Whitehall in the City of Westminster and Hornsea in Yorkshire.

In the second reading of the Education (Amendment) Bill (a Private Member's Bill, introduced by Lord Campbell of Alloway), Lord Rix said:

> The delay before a family knows whether a child will receive a statement can be as long as a year. There can be no justification for that. Parents who have a child with special educational needs are all too aware of the problems in delaying the educational process . . . I trust that amendments are made to the timing and efficacy of statements . . .

Eventually a statement had to be available within twenty-six weeks, but to this day most parents find that deadlines are missed and appeal tribunals are not empowered to consider or adjudicate on these delays. Shortly after Lord Campbell of Alloway had introduced his Bill the Government had the first reading of their Education Bill, causing Lord Campbell to withdraw his Education (Amendment) Bill.

1993: Mencap Homes Foundation becomes Britain's largest single provider of residential services for people with a learning disability, managing over 400 homes and providing accommodation for more than 2,000 people. Note the increase, however, by the year 2005. The Education Act (and Code of Practice) receives Royal Assent and strengthens the law on education for people with special needs but by the year-end a further Education Bill dealing with teacher training 'and other related matters' is before Parliament and the Chairman of Mencap was saying: 'We know what children with special needs can achieve given proper support. We know what teachers can achieve given proper training. If we do not provide specialist training for the teachers of children with special needs, we betray the teachers and we betray the children.' In the same year he tabled the debate 'Services for people with a learning disability' and concluded his opening speech thus: 'This debate is about the future of people of all ages who, through no fault of their own, find themselves disabled. They should have no need to come to us cap in hand, as one young man succinctly pointed out. We should be there to help them with their choices when and if they ask for it.' All sides of the House supported the motion.

1994: The teacher training Education Bill becomes an Act in this year. The initial combined Mencap and Gateway Conference takes place, attracting over 700 delegates. It was the first time that a large gathering of people with a learning disability attended in their own right, as delegates, and spoke for themselves.

1995: The Disability Discrimination Act comes about after extensive campaigning, in which Mencap played a leading role. There was much debate in both Houses of Parliament, with Mencap's Chairman, and others, stressing that without a regulatory body it would be extremely difficult to enforce this legislation. Eventually, in 1999, the Labour Government created such a body with the Disability Rights Commission Act. Also, in 1995 the Carers Recognition and Services Act improved the rights of carers to assessment and services in their own right but respite care is still not obligatory.

1996: Mencap celebrates its fiftieth anniversary with many events, but specifically with the Blue Sky Appeal to raise funds to provide for the establishment of the Family Advisory Service (FAS). The Chairman of the Blue Sky Appeal was Sir George Bull (later a Vice-President of Mencap), while the Deputy-Chairman was Brian Baldock CBE who, at the end of 1998, became the Chairman of Mencap. The appeal was launched with an incredible three-day festival in Cardiff, organised by the Vice-Chairman, Alan Hill, and Nikki Gavin, who had been PA to the Chief Executive. It involved 1,000 delegates from Mencap and Gateway in a combined conference, followed by workshops, plenary sessions, celebratory dinners and an evening's fair in the grounds of Cardiff Castle, with the BBC's *Songs of Praise* being televised from the same venue. This well-publicised event ensured that within twelve months the Blue Sky Appeal had reached its target of more than £10,000,000, securing the immediate future of the Family Advisory Service. In turn, the FAS supported the development of the Mencap National Information Service (MNIS), a database which provides information about learning disability issues at national and local levels. Mencap's newly titled journal – *Viewpoint* – is launched. The Community Care (Direct Payments) Act was placed on the Statute Book, enabling a limited number of people with a learning disability to spend their own money on making their own choices in regard to the services supporting them. At Mencap's instigation the Chairman, Lord Rix, introduced a Private Member's Bill – Disabled Persons and Carers (Short Term Breaks) Bill – to ensure that local authorities would include respite care in their assessment of carers' and disabled persons' needs. The Bill was widely supported by many voluntary organisations and went through all its stages in the Lords but was talked out by the Government on reaching the Commons. The Bill was reintroduced in 1997 after the Labour Party assumed Government, but again never reached the Statute Book. Both Governments feared it would add to the financial burden placed on local authorities, even though there would be savings in the long term.

1997: Mencap became more involved with European partners on various projects, funded by European Union grants. The Chairman of Mencap (Lord Rix), the Chairman of Gateway (Roger Galletley) and the Chief Executive (Fred Heddell) toured the regions and spoke to members of local societies in an effort to persuade them to support the new inclusive constitution which would be put to an EGM the following year.

1998: Mencap's officers continued their tour of the regions and eventually, at an EGM in October, the new constitution – creating a democratic organisation with individual membership – was approved by a large majority. Over 88 per cent voted in favour of the National Council being superseded by a National Assembly of about fifty members, elected from all the regions, of whom at least one-third had to be people with a learning disability, with appropriate support. Now, over 50 per cent of the members have a learning disability. As the Chairman, Lord Rix, had seen the constitutional change through to a successful conclusion and as he was approaching his seventy-fifth birthday (then the obligatory retiring age for honorary officers), he stood down as Chairman and was elected to the role of President, taking over from Lord Allen of Abbeydale, who joined Lord Renton as the second Past-President. Brian Baldock CBE, who had been Deputy-Chairman of the Blue Sky Appeal in 1996, was elected Chairman and had the task – along with his Chief Executive, Fred Heddell – of ensuring the new constitution was successfully implemented.

Golden Lane Housing was established to add to those houses managed under Mencap Homes Foundation. Mortgages became available for potential residents and homes range from flats, where people live by themselves, to fully adapted houses where there is twenty-four-hour support.

By the end of 2005 there were 5,594 people with a learning disability living in Mencap supported accommodation, involving more than 700 properties. The Human Rights Act reached the Statute Book, giving 'further effect' to the rights contained in the European Convention on Human Rights, and the Disability Rights Commission Bill began its journey through Parliament. At the second reading of the Bill in the Lords, Mencap's newly elected President, Lord Rix, first paid tribute to two doughty fighters for disability rights, Lord Ashley of Stoke (Jack Ashley) and Lord Morris of Manchester (Alf Morris) who had been pressing for such a commission for years. He then continued:

> There is a common misconception that the provision of physical access through portable ramps and wider doors will resolve most of the barriers facing disabled people. However, access for people with learning disabilities depends more on people than on ramps, and the barriers are more often people rather than stairs. Opening minds has the edge on widening doors, necessary as that sometimes is.

1999: 'Opening minds' certainly occurred in Parliament, for in this year the Disability Rights Commission Bill was duly enacted, as was the Tax Credits Bill, although it did not help people with a learning disability as much as Mencap wished. However, when it came to the Protection of Children Bill, a Private Member's Bill by the MP for Stourbridge, Debra Shipley, the Society had no doubts and the President of Mencap 'warmly welcomed the protection this Bill will afford children with learning disabilities,' a sentiment echoed in welcoming the Care Standards Bill, which became an Act in the year 2000. In the New Year's Honours the Chief Executive of Mencap, Fred Heddell, was appointed a CBE and the initial elections took place for the new National Assembly, with its first Chairman being a long-standing member and Honorary Officer of the

Society – Joe Steen, the father of two sons, both with a learning disability. In 2004 he retired and was succeeded by Joint Chairmen, Mary Oliver and Stephen Austin, the latter having a learning disability and whose story appears in Part II Chapter 2. When the new constitution came into effect, the National Assembly had the powers to nominate seven of the eleven trustees and one of the first to be elected was Simon Cramp, referred to in 'Genesis' and who also appears appears in Chapter 2. He was succeeded in 2005 by another trustee with a learning disability, Andrew Hoof. It was a massive change – from a parent-based Society to one in which their sons and daughters – people with a learning disability – became closely involved with the policy and direction of Mencap. Nearly £2 million was granted by the Millennium Commission to fund the Mencap Millennium Award Scheme which gave learning disabled people the opportunity to take part in activities which would support them and their communities.

2000: The Learning and Skills Act, the Care Standards Act, the Welfare Reform Act, the Representation of the People Act and the Carers and Disabled Children Act (which extended direct payments) all reached the Statute Book in this millennium year, with differing effects on the lives of people with a learning disability, mostly for the good.

2001: A White Paper, *Valuing People*, based on recommendations which Mencap had been espousing for over a quarter of a century was published. Six years later, in Mencap's Diamond Jubilee year, it is still not clear if all the Society's preferred options will be accepted and turned into reality, but there are reasonable grounds for optimism. The Special Educational Needs and Disabilities Bill gave parents choice and extended disability rights in the education system. It became an Act in 2001, as did the Health and Social Care Bill, which required an annual report to Parliament on 'development of health and social services for persons with learning disability'.

The Princess Diana Memorial Fund supported the Mencap Trans-active Project which began in Birmingham. The aim of the project is to involve young people with a learning disability and their peer supporters in their transition to adulthood. The relationships which are formed help break down the barriers of disability, promoting social inclusion. Video, digital photography and drama are employed to communicate their favourite friends, family, clothes, what they are good at and what they like doing in their spare time. The CD-ROM 'passport' produced is then used at the crucial Transition Planning meeting for each student, allowing them to communicate their wishes with confidence to adults and professionals who are helping them plan their future. By 2005, eighty sites had taken up the Trans-active project, with 664 young people with a learning disability having their own online 'passports', and the project is being taken up by many other interested bodies, including the social services.

2002: The words 'mentally handicapped' were dropped from the title of the Royal Society for Mentally Handicapped Children and Adults and a new, shorter, title – approved by HM The Queen Mother shortly before she died – was adopted, The Royal Mencap Society. The Tax Credits Act came into force this year, and Mencap welcomed that parents of disabled children would be given tax credits for childcare which has to be undertaken in the home. However, Mencap was disappointed that people with a learning disability, working fewer than sixteen hours a week, would be unable to access the new tax credit. The President of Mencap sought to put forward a Private Member's Bill – the Sexual Offences (Amendment) Bill – whose aim was 'to amend the law relating to sexual relations with persons lacking capacity to consent to sexual relations, and with vulnerable adults to whom a duty of care is owed, and for connected purposes'. However, Lord Rix was persuaded to withdraw the Bill in view of the forthcoming Government 'Sex Offences Bill' which would incorporate many of the features of the Private Bill.

2003: Fred Heddell CBE, Mencap's Chief Executive, retired at Easter and Jo Williams CBE was appointed in his place. Jo Williams came to Mencap with a wealth of experience garnered as Director of Social Services in Wigan and Cheshire for, during the 1980s in Cheshire, she established a number of community-based schemes which enabled people with disability to leave institutional care. From 1999 to 2000 Jo Williams was also the President of the Association of Directors of Social

Services. Mencap began to recruit 'Ambassadors' in 2003, celebrities who would further the cause of people with a learning disability. They are, to date, Will Young, Jo Whiley, Lisa Scott-Lee, Donal MacIntyre, Christopher Eccleston, Paula Sage and Donna Air. Their biographies appear in Chapter 15. The BBC programme *Blue Peter* adopted Mencap for its Christmas Appeal and raised just under £1 million. The Sexual Offences Act received Royal Assent, strengthening the penalties for sexual offences against vulnerable people with a learning disability. The President of Mencap was closely involved with this Bill as it went through its various stages in the Lords, as he was with the Mental Capacity Bill, for he sat on the Joint Committee scrutinising the Bill before it was laid before Parliament. This Joint Committee was chaired by another disability rights campaigner, Lord Carter.

2004: In May, Her Royal Highness The Countess of Wessex graciously agreed to become Mecap's Patron in succession to Her Majesty Queen Elizabeth The Queen Mother. Lord Rix was again a member of a Joint Committee – also chaired by Lord Carter – scrutinising the Disability Rights Bill before it was laid before Parliament, and both were on the Joint Committee, chaired by Lord Carlile QC, examining the Draft Mental Health Bill. One of their recommendations, backed by all those who gave evidence to the Committee, was that the exclusions for people with a learning disability in the 1983 Mental Health Act should be retained. After much pressure from Mencap and other organisations the Government has now decided not to proceed with the draft Bill but to amend the 1983 Act, including all the safeguards for people with a learning disability. The Bill has yet to come before Parliament. In the ePolitix Charity Champions Awards 2004 Lord Rix received the Lifetime Achievement Award, presented to him by the previous year's recipient, Lord Ashley of Stoke. Mencap's Chief Executive, Jo Williams, addresses the future of Mencap with 'A Vision for Change', explaining how Mencap will continue to work to improve the lives and opportunities of children and adults with a learning disability, together with their families and carers.

2005: Just before the dissolution of Parliament in April, both the Mental Capacity Bill and the Disability Discrimination Bill received Royal

Assent. In July there was a debate in the Lords on special schools and another disability campaigner, Lord Addington, summed up the dilemma facing parents and pupils in these words:

> Each of the disability groups has a general approach towards the idea of disability and special educational needs. Some people feel they have been put aside and ignored and their special schools were dumping grounds to keep them out of the way where they were not expected to achieve. Those people will be against special schools. Others, who feel that special schools allowed them to blossom and work harder, will be in favour of them. There will also be people in the middle.

In October there was a debate on children, initiated by the cross-bencher the Earl of Listowel. In this debate, Lord Rix said:

> Mencap's *Breaking Point* report highlighted the fact that families with a severely disabled child were receiving on average less than two hours' support per week. When we neglect these families and fail to provide them with the right level of support, it all too often results in family break-up and even abuse and neglect. These unfortunate children are then further disadvantaged and made still more vulnerable. It is a simply dreadful situation.

In his reply, the Under-Secretary of State at the Department of Education and Skills, Lord Adonis, said:

> The noble Lord, Lord Rix, raised the needs of disabled children and their particular vulnerability. The National Working Group on Child Protection and Disability, membership of which is drawn from child protection and disability organisations, as well as experts from the field, published its report, *It doesn't happen to disabled children!* which highlighted many of the issues raised by the noble Lord . . . Following publication of the report, the Government have funded the Council for Disabled Children to take forward a project looking at the specific safeguarding needs of disabled children to ensure they are given equal and effective protection . . . and to produce guidance for local safeguarding children boards when they start next April.

2006: HRH The Countess of Wessex, Patron of the Royal Mencap Society, launches its Diamond Jubilee with a reception at St James's Palace, held on 24 January. It is a happy event, celebrating sixty years of steady – and, sometimes, spectacular – progress in the field of learning disability.

The Equality Act receives Royal Assent, having been reintroduced after running out of Parliamentary time before the 2005 General Election. The Act creates a new Commission for Equality and Human Rights (CEHR), which should be operational by late 2007. The CEHR amalgamates and replaces the existing Disability Rights Commission, the Equal Opportunities Commission and the Commission for Racial Equality, and also takes on new powers to tackle discrimination and promote equality in three new areas: sexual orientation, religion and belief, and age. It will have at least one Commissioner who is, or has been, a disabled person, along with a Disability Committee, at least half of whose members will be disabled people or people who have had a disability. Mencap supported the creation of the CEHR but was disappointed that there was no specific mention of learning disability. Lord Rix asked that at least one place on the Disability Committee be reserved for a person with a learning disability, but the Government refused.

However, people with a learning disability were better served by two Acts which reached the Statute Book before the summer recess in July. The first was the Electoral Administration Act 2006 which changes various aspects of common law and removes the offensive terms 'idiots' and 'lunatics' from legislation and makes it clear that disabled people have the same right to vote as everyone else. Lord Rix moved this particular amendment, with a great deal of support from the Minister, Baroness Ashton of Upholland, and the Department of Constitutional Affairs.

The Childcare Act 2006 places a duty on local authorities to improve outcomes and reduce inequalities for all children under five, and to secure sufficient childcare to meet the needs of working parents and parents preparing to work. After lobbying from Mencap, the childcare duty was extended to cover disabled children up to the age of eighteen, not just sixteen, as had been proposed by the Government.

Other Bills were wending their way through both Houses of Parliament before the recess and are likely to become law before the Queen's Speech in November. The first is the somewhat controversial Education and Inspections Bill. Mencap and the Special Educational Consortium are lobbying on a number of issues which will improve the Bill for those with special educational needs. The next is the Safeguarding Vulnerable Groups Bill which will introduce a new vetting and barring scheme for people whose jobs bring them into contact with children and vulnerable adults. Then there is the Welfare Reform Bill which will redefine the benefits system for people with disabilities and long-term health conditions and, finally, the Disabled Persons (Independent Living) Bill which is a Private Member's Bill brought forward by Lord Ashley of Stoke CH. The Bill itself is unlikely to become law but the Government have responded to it by announcing a cross-government independent living review to develop proposals on health, social care, transport, employment and housing, with the expectation that the review will publish detailed proposals in the summer of 2007.

Mencap's events team has been very busy during this Diamond Jublilee year, too. Starting with the hugely popular reception at St James's Palace, they next moved to the Tower of London, where a dinner was held in May, at the suggestion of Mencap Vice-President Dame Norma Major, and was supported by (among others) Nokia, who have helped Mencap most generously, financially and technically, for more than a decade. The evening raised £462,000.

Other fundraising events – bike rides, marathons and treks – took place in Vietnam, Mexico, Morocco, Belfast, Brazil, Canada, Kenya and America. All tested the fitness and endurance of those who took part. All these events, though, raised considerable sums of money for Mencap, thanks to the efforts of all the participants. Nearer home, there was the London Marathon, the Great North Run, the Max Mara Fashion Show in Belfast, the Chelsea Flower Show and the wonderful *Snap!* reception at the Victoria and Albert Museum.

Still to come in 2006 are many other events, including three Carols by Candlelight in the historic church, St Bartholomew-the-Great, in Smithfield, on 5, 6 and 8 December. On 19 July, Mencap, in association with PAMIS, Nottingham City Council, Dumfries and Galloway Council, the *Valuing People* Support Team and the Scottish Executive launched the *Changing Places* campaign at the Tate Modern in the City of London. This initiative is to promote the installation of fully equipped toilets for profoundly and multiply disabled people around the UK. At present, disability toilets provide neither space nor equipment to make them usable by such severely disabled people with their helpers or carers.

As Mencap's Jubilee year extends from Learning Disability Week in June 2006 to Learning Disability Week in June 2007, there will be many more events to chronicle, but as this book goes to press in September 2006 for publication in November these will have to wait until another diary is penned some time in the future. In another sixty years there will be much to report . . .

PART II

Executive and Non-Executive Officers

CHAPTER 2

Honorary Officers, Past and Present

Patron
Her Royal Highness The Countess of Wessex

Past Presidents
The Rt Hon. Lord Renton KBE DL TD PC QC David Renton, born in 1908 and educated at Oundle and University College, Oxford, was called to the Bar in 1933 at Lincoln's Inn and became the MP for Huntingdon, Cambridgeshire, in 1945, after war service in Egypt and Libya, ending with the rank of major. He served on many committees in the House of Commons as chairman or deputy chairman, and was a Parliamentary Secretary at the Ministry of Fuel and Power from 1955 to 1958 and then Minister at the Home Office from 1958 to 1962. In 1963 he was appointed Recorder of Rochester, a judicial office he held until 1968. He retired as an MP in 1979 and was elevated to the House of Lords where he served as a Deputy Speaker from 1982 to 1988. He married the late Claire Duncan (known as Paddy) in 1947 and they had

three daughters, the youngest of whom – Davina – has a profound and multiple learning disability and lives at Ravenswood, Lord Renton being a Patron of the Ravenswood Foundation. This personal experience of learning disability brought the NSMHC to the attention of Lord Renton who, as Sir David Renton KBE MP, first became the Chairman of the Educational Panel and then served as the Hon. Treasurer of the Society from 1976 to 1978, becoming the Chairman from 1978 to 1982. He then was elected as the first-ever President of Mencap, serving from 1982 to 1988. For his dedication and work on behalf of Mencap and people with a learning disability, the Renton Foundation to establish a source of funding for Gateway and the leisure and sporting pursuits of learning disabled people was named after him.

The Rt Hon. Lord Allen of Abbeydale GCB   Philip Allen, born in 1912 and educated at King Edward VII School, Sheffield and Queens' College, Cambridge, entered the Home Office in 1934 and served successively in the Offices of the War Cabinet, the Ministry of Housing and Local Government, the Home Office and HM Treasury from 1943 until he became Permanent Under-Secretary of State at the Home Office from 1966 to 1972. In 1938 he married Marjorie Coe, who died in 2002. He was awarded a CB in 1954, a KCB in 1964 and a GCB in 1970, before being elevated to the peerage in 1976. He was made an Hon. Fellow of Queens' College, Cambridge, Royal Holloway and Bedford New College and served on a number of Royal Commissions; he was Chief Counting Officer in the EEC referendum in 1975 and Chairman of the Gaming Board from 1977 to 1985. Lord Renton suggested that Lord Allen succeed him as Chairman of Mencap, which he did from 1982 until succeeded by Sir Brian Rix in 1988. He then became the second President of Mencap, succeeding Lord Renton, who became the Immediate Past President. Lord Allen of Abbeydale eventually became the Immediate Past President when he retired in favour of Lord Rix at the end of 1998, but both he and Lord Renton continue their work, sometimes on behalf of Mencap, in the Upper House.

President

The Rt Hon. Lord Rix Kt CBE DL Brian Rix was born in 1924, educated at Bootham School, York, before becoming an actor in 1942 while awaiting call-up for aircrew training in the RAF, joining Donald Wolfit's company on tour and at the, now-demolished, St James's Theatre. He then went to the White Rose Players at the Opera House, Harrogate, whence he joined the RAF. When the war with Germany was over aircrew trainees were offered alternative occupations and Brian Rix volunteered to serve down the mines at Askern Main Colliery, Doncaster. On being demobilised in 1947, he immediately became an actor-manager, with a letterhead but no company and no theatre! However, by March 1948 he had assembled a company and hired a theatre in Ilkley, opening there on Easter Monday. He transferred to the Spa Theatre, Bridlington, later in the year and in 1949 launched another company in Margate. He met Elspet Gray while holding auditions for his new company and they married later in the same year, on 14 August. They toured together in 1950, bringing *Reluctant Heroes* to the Whitehall Theatre in September of that year. The 'Whitehall Farces' had begun their protracted run (in the theatre, on film and television). Brian Rix remained in the West End for the next twenty-seven years. Brian and Elspet's first daughter, Shelley, was born in 1951 with Down's syndrome, which began their lifelong involvement in the world of learning disability. Shelley died in 2005.

Brian Rix was Chairman of the first Mencap Special Events Committee in the early 1960s, the Secretary-General from 1980 to 1987, the Chairman from 1988 to 1998 and continues as the President of the Royal Mencap Society since he succeeded Lord Allen of Abbeydale in 1998. He was a founder member and is Chairman of the Rix-Thompson-Rothenberg Foundation (formerly the Mencap City Foundation), Libertas (audio tours for disabled people), President of the Friends of Normansfield, Patron of the Langdon Down Centre, Past President of the Lord's Taverners, and was also a founder member and Chairman of the one-time Independent Development Council for People with a Mental Handicap and the Mencap Unit Trust. Brian Rix has been awarded eight Honorary Degrees, five Honorary Fellowships (including the Royal Society of Medicine and the Royal College of

Psychiatrists) and several Lifelong Achievement Awards. He was made a CBE in 1977, a Knight Bachelor in 1986 and elevated to the House of Lords in 1992. He was Chairman of Drama at the Arts Council from 1986 to 1993 as well as Chairing the Arts and Disabled People Monitoring Committee. He was also Vice Lord-Lieutenant of Greater London from 1988 to 1998 and is the Chancellor of the University of East London.

Vice-Presidents

Sir George Bull   Was already a very busy man as Chairman of Grand Metropolitan when he agreed to be the Chairman of Mencap's fiftieth anniversary Blue Sky Appeal in 1996, for at that time he was further occupied as one of the principal architects of the then largest merger in UK corporate history – Grand Met with Guinness – becoming the Joint Chairman of the merged company, Diageo, in 1997. In spite of all this work he still managed to assemble a wonderful team of the 'great and the good' suppliants around him for the appeal, with Mencap's current Chairman, Brian Baldock, as his deputy. The team aimed to raise £11,000,000 in the anniversary year to provide funds to strengthen Mencap's existing services and create new family support teams across the country. Under Sir George's enthusiastic leadership they succeeded and Mencap was honoured that he agreed to become a Vice-President in recognition of his sterling efforts on the Society's behalf. Sir George was Chairman of J. Sainsbury from 1998 until 2004.

Barrie Davis   First came across Mencap in 1970 when his daughter Caroline – now deceased – was born, for Caroline had Down's syndrome. He is still the Chairman of his local society, Avon North, and was Chairman of the South-West Region, later the Western Division, for many years. He then stood down as Chairman, becoming the Treasurer for the Western Division and also taking his place on Mencap's National Council. He was soon appointed Chairman of the Regional and Local Affairs Committee and then became the Hon. Treasurer of the Society in 1986, during which time he steered Mencap through a difficult financial period at the beginning of the nineties. Having served the Society faithfully and well for fourteen years, he retired as Treasurer in the year

2000, and was immediately nominated and elected as a Vice-President of the Society and continues to serve as a Governor of the Rix-Thompson-Rothenberg Foundation.

Pauline Fairbrother OBE   Her learning disabled daughter, Di, was born in 1950 and Pauline joined the then National Society for Mentally Handicapped Children in 1952. She was always an extremely active member, first becoming the Vice-Chairman of her local Wimbledon and District Society and then Chairman of the Surrey Group of Societies, which included affiliated Hospital Friends. She was on the National Executive and then on the National Council when that came into being in 1980, becoming a Vice-Chairman at the same time. She acted as Chairman of the sub-committee liaising with the International League and began another sub-committee – SIBS – for brothers and sisters of those with a learning disability. She was inspired to do this by another of her daughters, Ruth, and between them mother and daughter were a great help to many a worried sibling. Pauline Fairbrother was made an OBE in 1989. Now that her husband Harry has died she lives with Di in North Wales, near Di's sister, Ruth.

Dame Pauline Harris   Dame Pauline is The Lady Harris DBE for she is the wife of The Lord Harris of Peckham. However, it seems more propitious to use her own title, for she received the DBE for her charitable work, much of it for Mencap. Together, Dame Pauline and Dame Norma Major raised nearly £3,000,000 for their creation, the Mencap Challenge Fund, which matched pound-for-pound projects started by local Mencap societies. Dame Pauline has many other charitable interests as well, but Mencap was delighted when she accepted the office of Vice-President, awarded for her great efforts on behalf of the Society.

Alan Hill   The father of a daughter with a learning disability – Jackie – who was born in 1972 and died in 1988, Alan sought an active society dealing with the problems of learning disability and joined the NSMHC in 1977. By 1981 he had become the Chairman of the Croydon Local Society and remained in that role until 1988, while also serving on Mencap's National Council, to which he had been elected in 1984. He then became a Vice-Chairman of Mencap itself, chairing one of the four main committees. In 1990 this practice was changed and only one Vice-Chairman was appointed and the four main committees elected their own Chairman annually. The first solo Vice-Chairman was Leslie Wooster, to be followed by Alan, who served in this role from 1993 until 2000 when, under the new constitution, the office of Vice-Chairman was abolished and Alan became a Vice-President. Prior to this, in 1996, Alan also became a council member of Inclusion International and the honorary editor of their magazine, *Inclusion News*, as well as being responsible, along with Nikki Gavin, for Mencap's 1996 anniversary conference in Cardiff to which members of Inclusion Europe were invited. They were hugely impressed, for they saw large-scale integration actually being practised, both on inclusive social occasions and in all aspects of the conference itself. Alan and Nikki well deserved the praise bestowed on them.

Michael Mackey MVO BEM   Mike Mackey is one of those rare but precious exceptions to the rule that volunteers generally run out of steam and fade away. He joined his first Gateway club in 1972, driving Gateway members all round London without actually going into the clubhouses! He then put his nose round the door, realised why everyone came out smiling and decided to become involved in a big way. He became a Vice-Chairman of the National Federation of Gateway Clubs and for twenty years was also the Chairman of the Festival Committee organising the remarkable Gateway Festivals, when people with a learning disability put on a spectacular annual show – generally at the Royal Festival Hall in London. Even though he officially retired in 2000, becoming a Vice-President of Mencap, he still vets all the applications made to the Renton Foundation, which grant-aids Gateway club projects – a tireless volunteer, indeed.

Dame Norma Major   Dame Norma is also The Lady Major DBE, for she is the wife of the now-retired Prime Minister, Sir John Major KG CH. Originally a teacher with a strong interest in arts and music, she served on the Board of the Welsh National Opera for several years and subsequently wrote two books. The first was the official biography of the opera singer Dame Joan Sutherland, and the second was entitled *Chequers: The Prime Minister's Country House and its History*, published when her husband was the Prime Minister. Her first contact with Mencap was with the Huntingdon Local Society, for she was the sitting Member of Parliament's wife in that constituency and, as John Major's predecessor, Lord Renton, was then the Chairman of Mencap itself, it's no wonder that Dame Norma became such a wonderful supporter. She helped raise large sums of money for the Huntingdon Society and then turned her attention to Mencap, by then a Royal Society. Dame Norma and Dame Pauline worked tirelessly at fundraising events, sometimes at Chequers, sometimes at No. 10 Downing Street and, once, at the Kennington Oval. The money raised went to the Mencap Challenge Fund, with Dame Norma as the President and Dame Pauline as the Chairman. She tells her story in Chapter 15. Mencap was delighted and honoured when she agreed to become a Vice-President.

The Lady Rix   Perhaps better known to Mencap members as the wife of Brian Rix and to television and theatre audiences as the actress Elspet Gray, Lady Rix is the most recent addition to the list of Vice-Presidents. Elspet was asked to accept this honour for all the hard work and dedication she has shown in her efforts for people with a learning disability over the last fifty-odd years. She was Chairman of the Mencap Homes Foundation Area Committee when it began to operate in the Surrey area of Richmond and Kingston; she served on the Friends of Normansfield Committee for over forty years, and is now the Vice-President. She is Patron of MentAid in India and a Trustee of the Langdon Down Centre in Teddington, with its headquarters in the magnificent Victorian theatre at Normansfield. In addition, she has supported her husband at all times in whatever capacity he has been working for the Society, which has often meant long journeys, late evenings and listening to her husband's speeches! For Mencap, she accompanied Brian on demanding visits to Australia, New Zealand, India, Hong Kong, Kenya, Northern Ireland and the USA, as well as attending numerous balls and dinners. Like her husband, her motives are explained by the birth of their first child, Shelley – with Down's syndrome – in 1951. Shelley died in 2005 and her ashes are under a newly planted rowan tree in her old Homes Foundation home at Whitton, near Twickenham.

Leslie Wooster His learning disabled daughter, Hilary, was born in 1948, but it wasn't until 1962 that Leslie joined the local Wirral Society, becoming the Chairman some sixteen years later. His wife died in 1981, so Leslie took early retirement to look after Hilary at home. In 1988 she moved into a Mencap Homes Foundation house in West Kirby, and then, in 2004, she made a further move to New Brighton. In the meantime, in 1978, Leslie had been elected to the NSMHC North-West Regional Committee and then to the Mencap National Council in 1983. He served on various committees, including the Working Party on Regional Structure and Development which led to Mencap's twelve regions in England being reduced to five larger divisions, with Mencap in Northern Ireland and Mencap in Wales enjoying devolution long before both Province and Principality adopted the same system. Leslie also chaired the Welfare and Rights Committee and then the one for residential services – becoming closely involved with the Homes Foundation. In 1990 he was elected the first solo Vice-Chairman of Mencap, standing in as Chairman for Lord Rix when he had his open-heart surgery in 1992, as well as taking over the chair of the Mencap Pension Scheme for a further ten years, ensuring fairness to the staff on the one hand and protecting the pension funds on the other. Leslie retired in 1993, when he was seventy, and his successor was Alan Hill. As noted already, both became Vice-Presidents of the Royal Mencap Society in the millennium year 2000.

Neville Thompson The late Neville Thompson and the late Helmut Rothenberg are mentioned here for they were both Vice-Presidents of Mencap and their names live on in the re-titled Mencap City Foundation. It is now the Rix-Thompson-Rothenberg (RTR) Foundation to commemorate the contribution all three founder members made to the Foundation's beginning and its continued success in grant-aiding projects supporting people with a learning disability throughout the UK. Neville and Liz Thompson's interest began when their son, James, was born in 1958 with Down's syndrome. A year later, Neville became the

Hon. Secretary of the local Woolwich Society but soon was elected to the National Executive of the NSMHC. He served as the Hon. Treasurer from 1978 to 1986, but continued to chair London Mencap for over twenty years as well as acting as the Treasurer for the local Greenwich Mencap charity shop. He was the longest-serving Chairman ever of a Health Authority – Greenwich – and during his term of office he started a learning disability assessment unit and respite care facility in Bob Hope's birthplace – Eltham. He was the Hon. Treasurer of the Mencap City Foundation from its inception in 1984 to his death in 2003. His widow, Liz, continues to live in south-east London, while James shares a flat with two old friends in Greenwich.

Helmut Rothenberg OBE   Helmut and Neville were friends, both serving on the Mencap City Foundation and, by a quirk of fate, both men died in the same week, in February 2003, and their names were listed one above the other in the deaths columns of both *The Times* and the *Telegraph*. They would have enjoyed that juxtaposition. Helmut Rothenberg was born in Germany in 1915 and arrived in London just before World War II. After setting up an internationally successful accountancy firm, he endowed two Rothenberg Trusts to support people with a learning disability and those working with them, both in the UK and in developing countries. He also made generous donations to the Mencap City Foundation, and both he and Neville supported the creation of the Mencap City Insurance Service, now a separate company, MCIS Ltd, which makes annual contributions to the Foundation's work. Both men received Honorary Degrees from the University of East London for challenging discrimination in an era when people with a learning disability were shunned and ridiculed. They are greatly missed.

All the foregoing Honorary Officers are, of course, no longer engaged in the day-to-day activities of the Royal Mencap Society, but each one is recognised as being responsible – in many and differing ways – for enabling the Society to flourish and become the leading charity for learning disability in the UK. Whenever necessary, though, they still 'come to the aid of the party'.

Now it is the turn of the Honorary Officers who are engaged on a daily basis with the Society – beginning, naturally enough, with the names of the trustees serving in 2006, followed by the thoughts of their Chairman, Brian Baldock.

The Trustees of the Royal Mencap Society, 2006

Brian Baldock CBE (Chairman)	Dominic Mearing
Ann Crook	Clair Roberts
Roger Galletley	Colin Rogers
Andy Hoof	Patrick Slater MBE
Stuart Kelly	Janardan Sofat
John McKee	Fred Worth

Chairman

Brian Baldock CBE   Born in 1934, married with three sons, Brian was educated at Xaverian College, London, and, following army National Service, he began his career in international business. This included six years with Procter and Gamble, nine with Smith and Nephew, where he became a main Board director, and three in Paris with Revlon International. Returning to the UK in 1978 he eventually became Managing Director, Leisure and Retailing, the Imperial Group.

In 1986 he joined the main Board of Guinness plc and a year later was appointed Chairman and Managing Director of Guinness Brewing. By 1990 he was the Group Managing Director and in 1992 became the Deputy Chairman, retiring at the mandatory age in 1996. He was awarded the CBE in the 1997 Birthday Honours.

Brian, however, continued in the business world. From 1996 to 2004 he was a Non-Executive Director of Marks and Spencer plc and was Chairman from June 1999 to February 2000. This involved Brian in much juggling with his diary and much hard work, for he had become the Chairman of Mencap at the end of 1998 and was having to implement the new, inclusive constitution while seeking a 'permanent' Chairman and Chief Executive for M&S. He managed this incredible double act with all his usual affability and expertise. In addition, he also served at various times as a Non-Executive Director of Cornhill Insurance, Wellington Investment Co. and Dalgety and later, SYGEN, of which he has been the Chairman for the past seven years, retiring at the end of 2006. They say you should always ask a busy person to do yet another job if you want that job done well. That's certainly true of Brian!

Because of all its ever-growing support for housing and services, the Royal Mencap Society has become, in effect, a big business, with an annual turnover of over £150 million but with under 8 per cent being spent on management, administration and support services – a remarkable example of good husbandry on the part of the trustees and the management. So, when Brian Rix retired as Chairman in 1998, he realised that a sympathetic businessman or woman was a necessary replacement and knowing something of Brian Baldock's business career, and remembering how effective Brian had been as Deputy Chairman of the Blue Sky Appeal and, further back, as Chairman of the Lord's Taverners, one Brian asked another Brian to take his place. Much to the first Brian's delight, the second Brian accepted and has continued as a splendid Chairman ever since, abiding by his own guidelines, which now follow.

On being a chairman

The role of the chairman is important in any corporate activity and Mencap, as a charity, is no exception. The development of policy and strategy, while leading the executive team and supporting them, is key. This is where my business experience comes in, for Mencap is a hugely complex organisation and the task of the Chairman is to ensure coherent, sensible areas of activity, which requires allocating resources according to priority and ensuring accountability and responsibility for managing outcomes against targets and budgets. That is why Mencap is such an interesting organisation, a caring charity (in the original and best sense of the word) *and* a business where financial management and strategy are so important.

That summarises the formal role of Chairman. There is another and, in my view, equally important one, which is best described as 'coach'. Adding value to an outstanding Chief Executive and management team is always my aim and, speaking personally, far from being onerous, this is the most attractive and rewarding part of the Chairman's function at Mencap.

On becoming Chairman of Mencap, though, I quickly realised that my job was also about a mixture of short, medium and long-term considerations – today's cashflow, tomorrow's funding and then even longer-term viability – always remembering the reason the charity exists – for people with a learning disability, their parents, families and friends. The job of a chairman, in this light, is never done . . . you never reach your destination for it's a continuous journey. I was fortunate to inherit a well-run, efficient and financially robust organisation. Not every chairman can say that!

On a changing world

The major challenge for Mencap is to reach its strategic goals at a time when we operate in a world of discontinuous change – more volatile and more unpredictable than I have ever experienced before in my business life.

What sort of changes?

- An ageing population, older members, parents and carers.
- Changing ethnic mix, bringing to the forefront the need to understand and work with a variety of cultural backgrounds.
- Technology is developing exponentially, bringing amazing, positive opportunities for the disabled, but making the outlook for those less technically literate an additional burden.
- Changing attitudes to donations – a more competitive environment with corporates apparently seeking to measure their charitable investments as they do all others.
- Dramatic increase in the number of mothers needing and/or waiting to have full or part-time jobs.
- The increase in legal and other challenges and constraints.

Anticipating and then managing these and many other factors become the principal concerns of trustees and managements in any organisation, while the journey for the learning disabled becomes harder and even more complex. The journey as I have described it is a long one – impacted by the fact that about 200 children each week are born in the UK with a learning disability and about one-third will have special and complex additional needs.

On the 1998 constitutional change

This was undoubtedly the catalyst for many of the big changes which are still taking place at Mencap. But it has also posed some tough challenges – democracy has some downsides! We have to make it work more for our local societies to invest at the grass-roots level, but now is still not the right time to make any further major changes. After all, the really successful organisations in the world are the ones which can evolve – not go through revolutions every few years – i.e. keep internal change at the same pace as external change. On this note, it's vital that we also engage more with ethnic minority groups, children (and their families) and people with profound and multiple learning disabilities.

On the changes in the fifteen years I've been involved with Mencap

I was first introduced to Mencap through meeting Brian Rix at a Lord's Taverners charity cricket match where he was bowling slow off-spin (and I thought he was rather good). Then I remembered he is a Yorkshireman after all and once, in his youth, played as a fast bowler in the Yorkshire League! When I met him he'd been closely involved with Mencap and learning disability for some twenty-odd years and he encouraged me – as Chairman of the Lord's Taverners – to get the charitable aims of this sporting charity aligned to those of Mencap.

Of course we have achieved a great deal since then, but in my more depressed moments I sometimes wonder how much. But then Brian helps me understand that things really have changed for the better, for he speaks as the recently bereaved father of a daughter with Down's syndrome and as the grandfather of young Robbie who has the same condition. He maintains that the difference between the attitudes prevalent in 1951 and today are staggering, but this must never blunt our efforts to improve all aspects of our work.

On the rising aspirations of people with a learning disability

This is just how it should be ... that they should have – and be encouraged to have – higher aspirations. Education is absolutely vital for this to happen, encouraging people to go into tertiary education. And it's also about the whole system recognising the different skills people with a learning disability can bring, focusing on what people can do, not what their disability prevents them from doing.

On the balance between business and charity

This is vital for Mencap to get right, and in all honesty it will be a continuous challenge. We have to keep looking at how governance is changing, in terms of the rules for aspects such as accounting, health and safety, employment and personal behaviour. And it's a testament to Mencap's recognition of this aspect that we have a Governance Committee specifically charged to ensure that we demonstrate best practice in all these areas.

On the future

I have just been elected Chairman until 2009. What do I aim to see achieved and then hand on to my ultimate successor?

1 A shift in attitude in recognising the responsibility we all have to contribute to the lives of the disabled and the disadvantaged. I am appalled that in 2006 we need to be concerned with issues of bullying and harassment of people with a learning disability. I also want to receive no more letters or complaints about a housing project for one of our homes which the locals object to on the grounds that their property will be devalued.

2 To see Government, national and local, devote more resources in the area which affects our members. We need to be higher up the list of priorities. A great deal is being done, and more money is being injected into services, but we need to do our part by demonstrating we offer exceptional 'value for money' – which we do – for this will again justify a higher level of priority for learning disability.

3 To continue to press for changes in our tax system which give greater benefit to the donors – corporate or individual – as well as the beneficiaries.

4 To develop closer links with other organisations and to act as facilitator where direct involvement is not cost-effective.

5 To give even more priority to education at all levels, including the development of our own excellent colleges.

6 Sport, leisure and the arts offer wonderful opportunities for learning

disabled people. We need to work with other organisations in these fields to widen and develop our involvement.

7   To increase the level of training and development for our extraordinary group of managers and staff at Mencap.

8   To embrace science and technology to seek meaningful advances in the improvement of skills within the world of learning disability, especially for those with profound difficulties.

The establishment of the Rix Centre as part of the excellent University of East London will be a major move forward for Mencap and other disability organisations. Led by the previous Chief Executive of Mencap, Fred Heddell, the centre has made encouraging progress in its stated intention of improving the lives of people with a learning disability through the use of new media techniques. Mencap will play its part in ensuring the success of the venture.

The last word

It is an honour and a privilege to serve Mencap and people with a learning disability and their families, carers and friends. That things have improved in so many ways for people with a learning disability over the last sixty years is indisputable – but still many of them do not have access to equal rights or chances in life, to a decent place to live, to a job or daytime activity which suits them, and the opportunity to learn and develop. What is more, their families and carers do not enjoy the support they need. Mencap is here to change all that and I am committed to continuing involvement in all the Society's efforts to achieve its goals.

Chairman of Golden Lane Housing
Chairman of the Governance Committee

Roger Galletley   Roger and Susan Galletley's second child was born on 13 February 1968 at St David's Hospital in Cardiff. He was a boy, Shaun David, and he had Down's syndrome. The news was broken to the proud mother and father in the usual brutal way, prevalent in those days, and the Galletleys were left, like so many parents, to deal with matters as best they could. It was three years before Mencap got in touch with them – for the Society had no means of discovering which parents had a learning disabled child – and as Roger says in his story, told in Chapter 17, 'this is when our lives really began to change'.

Roger was soon in the thick of it, being appointed to the National Executive Committee of the National Federation of Gateway Clubs, serving as Vice-Chairman of the Federation from 1984 to 1987 and as the Chairman from 1987 to 2000. He also served as the Secretary to the Usk and District Gateway Club from 1994 to 2005. Before all that, in 1975 he had been elected to the National Council on which he served until 1999. In those days, if you were a National Councillor you were also a trustee – a system which changed when the new constitution was enacted and the trustees were reduced in number, being elected by the new National Assembly, or being nominated as an independent appointee. Not altogether unsurprisingly, Roger was elected and remains a trustee to this day. As the heading above indicates, he is Chairman of Golden Lane Housing and of the Governance Committee, as well as being the Chairman of Trustees of the Renton Foundation, which supports leisure activities and Gateway clubs.

As if this wasn't enough, Roger has been on the Usk Town Council from 1979 to the present date, Chairman of the Usk Town Council Finance Committee from 1986 to 2004, Mayor and Chairman of the Usk Town Council on three occasions, 1982–3, 1987–8 and 1999–2000, as well as serving on the Usk Twinning Committee from 1979 and being the Committee's Chairman from 2001, also to the present date. In spite of being born an Englishman, he is a rabid, renegade supporter of Welsh rugby, wildly cheering – along with his son Shaun – any of their victories or bewailing their defeats at Twickenham or the Millennium Stadium in Cardiff. However, the growth and development of Mencap in England and Northern Ireland is just as important to Roger Galletley as Mencap Cymru. That far-off February date in 1968 has provoked a lifelong commitment to learning disabled people which can hardly be matched by anyone.

Chairman of the Finance and General Purposes Committee
Patrick Slater MBE   His son Malcolm was born in 1966 and, like Roger Galletley and the majority of parents at that time, he and his wife were told separately – and in a perfunctory manner – that their child was

a mongol. The Education Act came about when Malcolm was five years old and he was thus able to go to school, but the only one available was in the grounds of Borocourt Hospital. This led the Slaters to join the Parents' Association and as Patrick was a banker he soon became the Treasurer and retained this role until the hospital closed in 1993. Patrick's first contact with Mencap was through the Parents' Association and its affiliation to the National Society for Mentally Handicapped Children, but soon the Slater family moved from Reading to Taplow and joined Maidenhead Mencap, where Patrick took on the job of Secretary. During that time he became a member of the Mencap Southern Division Executive and attended his first meetings at Mencap's HQ in Golden Lane. In 1982 the family moved to Newbury and, shortly afterwards, Patrick became the Chairman of the extremely hard-working local society, now known as West Berkshire Mencap, running services for all age groups, including leisure activities, an employment and training venue in a splendid new building provided by the Greenham Common Trust, a respite bungalow for six adults and a purpose-built centre which HM The Queen opened in 1998. Patrick retired from the NatWest Bank in 1992 and founded the West Berkshire Citizen Advocacy Service with one office in Newbury and another in Wokingham. He became a National Councillor and trustee of Mencap in 1993, serving on the Finance and General Purposes Committee, becoming Chairman in 2003. He was a founding Director of Golden Lane Housing and is a Governor of the Mencap National College. Patrick was awarded the MBE in 1999. He says: 'It is important for Mencap to continue its campaigning role alongside the development of high quality and innovative services. This should provide a lasting legacy for the work of Lord Rix and so many others following in the footsteps of the original founders of the organisation.'

At this stage, in listing the efforts made by people connected with Mencap, it would seem desirable to mention the first two Mencap trustees to be appointed under the new constitution, each having a learning disability. The first, Simon Cramp, was elected by the National Assembly in 2000 and retired from that office in 2004. His successor, elected in 2005, is Andrew Hoof.

Simon Cramp   Simon has been involved with Mencap at a local level in Chesterfield since he was sixteen or seventeen years old, when he was a student at a further education college on a special needs course. He first came to the attention of the Mencap hierarchy when Lord Rix, Roger Galletley and Fred Heddell visited the area to debate the proposed constitutional changes in 1998. Simon continues the story:

> There was a meeting at the Chesterfield Hotel [which Lord Rix mentions in 'Genesis 1'], when I got up to speak and surprised everyone when it was revealed I had a learning disability. This was followed, in October 1998, by the EGM when Lord Rix spoke to me beforehand and said that he was planning to invite me to speak – to deploy me as a 'secret weapon' – to persuade people of the need for people with a learning disability to get the chance to become much more involved in strategic decisions about Mencap [i.e. on the National Assembly]. So I spoke at the end of the debate and told the audience that they had to give people with a learning disability a chance to prove themselves, otherwise they'd never see that it could work. This completely changed the mood of the occasion and I think was a key factor in winning the argument . . .

After the constitutional change in 2000, Brian Baldock, Mencap's Chairman since December 1998, recognised that Simon – who by now was serving on the new National Assembly – had exceptional qualities and suggested he might wish to become a trustee, if elected. Simon writes:

> Then, somehow and from somewhere (I'm not sure how or where), the idea started going around that maybe I could even become a trustee. I 'ummed' and 'ahhed' about it a lot, because I wanted to do it, but was very worried about the level of commitment I might need to make. But in the end I thought it was too big an opportunity to let go by. When I was then elected, it was a great shock, and I was delighted.

Simon served the Society well as a trustee for four years before many other outside commitments – all connected with learning disability – made it impossible for him to continue. However, he is still a great supporter of Mencap and attends all the relevant and important meetings, including those held by the All Party Parliamentary Group on Learning Disability.

Andrew Hoof Simon's successor as a trustee was elected after Mencap's AGM in the autumn of 2005. His family have been involved with Mencap for over twenty-five years, his father being the Chairman of Telford Mencap since 1999, while his mother continues as an enthusiastic and successful fundraiser for the same local society. Andy was educated at Bridge School and Telford College and became a member of the South Telford Gateway Club when he first left school. He is also involved with the self-advocacy group and serves on his local Learning Disability Partnership Board, while continuing to attend day services and the local college of further education.

Andy became involved with the constitutional change in Mencap and was elected to the District Committee for Shropshire and Telford in the year 2000 and was re-elected in 2003. He has made an outstanding contribution during his time as a committee member and has campaigned successfully against reductions in day-service provision and has been leader of the local anti-bullying campaign. He was elected to the Mencap National Assembly in 2004 and became a Royal Mencap Society trustee in October 2005. He is a firm believer in partnership and sees Mencap as the organisation which can work with learning disabled people *and* family carers to achieve the aims set out in *A Vision for Change*.

Andy made the concluding speech, after Lord Rix, Brian Baldock and Jo Williams, at the St James's Palace Reception on 24 January 2006 in the presence of HRH The Countess of Wessex, to celebrate Mencap's Diamond Jubilee – emphasising how far people with a learning disability have progressed since those dark days in 1946.

One final name should be entered on this roll of honour: **Di Lofthouse,** who became the first and only person with a learning disability to sit on Mencap's National Council, the predecessor to the National Assembly. Her story is told in Part III Chapter 8, but let it be stated here that it was her presence and her wise interventions which encouraged Mencap to adopt its new inclusive constitution in 1998.

Joint Chair of the National Assembly

Steve Austin   Steve is a parent with a learning disability. Steve has served on the National Assembly since 2002 and became the Joint Chairman, along with Mary Oliver, in 2003. Steve says:

> I was delighted to have been elected to this post. It was a really big achievement for me. I think the National Assembly works really well and the support that I and other National Assembly reps with a learning disability get is brilliant. It means that we have a voice and that Mencap is listening to what we have to say. After all, that's what Mencap is all about – the voice of people with a learning disability, and I want to use my position of influence to get Mencap to campaign for local authorities to provide really practical advice and support to parents like me who have children. However, I think we are making good progress at Mencap on all the big issues – transport, respite, children and so on – but there's still a long way to go.

Joint Chair of the National Assembly

Mary Oliver MBE   Mary has worked for thirty-seven years within the education system for special needs, first as a teacher and now as special needs officer with Conwy Local Education Authority. She first became involved with Mencap through the Gateway Federation in 1972 when she became Leader of the Llandudno and District Gateway Club and, thirty-four years later, is still a member. Mary moved to the Gateway National Executive Committee and the Training Committee in 1983, and in the nineties she became a governor of the Mencap National Colleges, a member of the Children's Committee and a member of the Organising Committee for Mencap's fiftieth anniversary. Currently she is Joint Chair of the National Assembly, alongside Steve Austin, and is the chair or member of at least seven more Mencap committees.

Mary Oliver received her MBE in the 2004 New Year Honours for her services to people with special needs in England and Wales and now serves on the Education Panel Honours Committee reporting to the Cabinet Ceremonial Secretariat. She writes: 'I joined Mencap to help to give people with a learning disability more opportunities with their lives. I have witnessed huge changes within the organisation over the years and feel proud to have played – and still play – a part in helping Mencap become what it is today, the leading learning disability charity.'

Tribute should be paid here to the first Chairman of the National Assembly, **Joe Steen**, who retired from that office in 2004, having served Mencap and Liverpool Mencap for over thirty-five years. He worked for social services in that city and was the originator of many new ideas for projects concerning people with a learning disability in the North-West. He was inspired to do this work for he is the father of two sons, both with differing forms of learning disability. This, plus the fact that he came from Liverpool, made him an extremely effective – albeit argumentative – member of the National Council and then, after 2000, the National Assembly, when he chaired a group of over fifty people, many of them with a learning disability. Here, briefly, is how he describes his time at Mencap:

> It was hard work and there were times when it was a bit bitter and they got annoyed with me, but that was my role. It was basically playing the conscience in the organisation, asking the awkward questions to try and make people think about where we were going and why we were doing it, and also to try to bring some new thinking in from outside . . . if there was an important issue at a meeting and everyone wanted to speak, when Brian Rix was Chairman he would always go around from his left to his right, so if you wanted the last word you sat on Brian's right. I almost always managed to be seated there!

CHAPTER 3

George Lee OBE

Secretary-General 1957–80

This chapter – and the next three – contain the stories of the four Chief Executives who have had the greatest influence on Mencap's progression throughout the last sixty years. The first, George Lee, writes as follows.

Since the following recollections will be regarded as coming from the 'dark ages', you are asked to forgive the terminology of those days. Enlightenment did follow.

In 1957 I was Secretary-General of what was then called the British Council for Rehabilitation which was formed to alleviate and solve the practical problems associated with physical disability. As a member of the Society of Friends, I had entered the voluntary organisation world by first working for the Council of Refugees, finding homes for refugee Jewish children from Nazi Germany at the beginning of World War II, resulting in the formation of the Council for Christians and Jews and the Save the Children Fund.

I was told that the National Society for Mentally Handicapped

Children was looking for its first Secretary-General, having until then been administrated by an Executive Committee consisting mainly of parents of mentally handicapped children. After the formation of the National Association for Parents of Backward Children inspired by Judy Fryd, local societies had sprung up all over the country and funded the national body, but there was little formal national or regional structure. My interview was conducted in a room borrowed from the National Association for Mental Health (now MIND) and I formed the impression that someone was needed to interpret, coordinate and undertake the understandably urgent desire of frustrated parents to fill the existing void of the lamentable provisions and attitudes.

Upon my appointment I inherited two and a half rooms in a very decrepit building in the Strand owned by King's College and soon to be demolished. Office furniture, of which there was little, tended to move along the sloping floors and the one lavatory was shared by several other offices. But we did own the inevitable Gestetner duplicating machine. In those days we had a welfare officer, a publications officer and two wonderful women to look after our office needs. But everyone had to turn their hand to anything.

My first task was to gain the patronage and support of nationally organised figures to establish the Society in the public eye and to impress Government departments, health and local authorities and, hopefully, donors. Without a creditable letterhead one's approaches tended to be put in the waste paper basket. My quest for a prestigious Chairman gave me an interesting glimpse into people's reasons for being unable to be associated with what was an unknown charity. But the unforgettable Lord Longford (then Pakenham) came to my rescue. Since quarterly meetings of the Executive Committee were held on Saturdays, he was understandably reluctant to return to London and so it was arranged that members from all over the country were conveyed to Tunbridge Wells near his home. It was eventually his appointment as a minister in the Wilson Government that necessitated his resignation as Chairman.

We, luckily, had a ready made Hon. Treasurer in Lord Grenfell, who was a pillar of support. During the passage of the first Mental Health Act in 1959 he was the first person to speak in the House of Lords as a parent of a Down's syndrome daughter and it was he who later negotiated the royal patronage of the Queen Mother. He continued as Hon. Treasurer until his retirement in 1978, with Lady Grenfell always at his side.

When I joined the Society there existed one paid regional officer (as they were then called) in the North-West Region based in Manchester. In that region a home for severely disabled children, Orchard Dene, had already been opened, initially under the auspices of the National Association for Mental Health. Gradually professional officers were appointed to each of the eleven regions throughout the country in suitable rented or purchased premises. Thus the work of the National Office was widened and strengthened. Although all the regions, of course, had equal status, it did seem a landmark when the Northern Ireland region became our twelfth region with Lord Segal as its President, and it was always heartening to see how mental handicap brought together people from all sides of the political divide.

The Archbishops of Canterbury and Westminster, the Chief Rabbi, the Moderator of the Free Church and the MPs Sir Derek Walker-Smith and Christopher Mayhew agreed to become patrons and I now felt that we presented a 'respectable' face, with a voice in the Houses of Lords and Commons. During my tenure I felt fortunate to serve under three further Chairmen – Lord Stonham, Lord Segal and finally Lord Renton – all of whom gave me their unfailing support and encouragement.

So what were our principal challenges? They are presented in no particular order, for they were all pressing.

Raising public awareness of the difficulties faced by parents and children because of the lack of provision and the non-acknowledgement of special needs. Don't forget that in those days you were lucky if your child was accepted for any sort of training, let alone education. An elementary day centre in a hospital was all that was available. Even the diagnosis of a Down's syndrome baby – then labelled 'mongol' – was often postponed or mishandled.

Providing examples of excellence It was not our goal to build up an empire of facilities, but to inform local authorities what they should be providing. We financed a research project by Professor Jack Tizard who demonstrated that mentally handicapped people did not have to sit around the walls of a room being 'fed and watered' with a television as diversion. From this rose the Slough Training Centre and Hostel, opened by our Royal Patron, the Queen Mother, and directed by a man of vision, James Cummings. We were also greatly influenced by visits we had made to Holland, which was leading the way in the provision of varied facilities. There was obviously much to be gained by investigating how other countries were developing their services and being in touch with parents and professionals abroad. As now, the exchange of information and experience was provided by international conferences and in 1960 we were presented with an ideal vehicle by the inauguration of World Mental Health Year for which we organised an international conference at County Hall, London. I well remember the problems presented in the early years of simultaneous translation. There then evolved the idea of a European League of Societies for the Mentally Handicapped and Dr van Dijk from Holland, Tom Mutters from Germany and I got together to put flesh on the bones of this idea. We had an enthusiastic response and eventually that organisation developed into the International League of Societies for the Mentally Handicapped which continues to thrive and expand under the title Inclusion International.

The Slough Project was essentially geared to employment being provided by industrial contracts (an innovation in itself) but an opportunity presented itself to acquire a property – Lufton Manor in Somerset – which would lend itself to development as a residential centre for training in horticultural and agricultural skills. There was also a need demonstrated for a holiday centre to which local authorities could send their children in care and thus came about Pirates Spring in Kent. Its opening in 1963 by Valerie Hobson, in her first public appearance since the scandal which had engulfed her husband, John Profumo, is described in the next chapter by Brian Rix, who by then had become the Chairman of our first Special Functions Committee, whose money-raising efforts contributed to the holiday home's purchase price. It was a singularly brave appearance on Valerie Hobson's part, for she had to face the biggest gathering of the world's press we had ever managed to interest in one of our events.

Dilston Hall in the North-East, Pengwern Hall in North Wales and Pembroke Road in Bristol were all residential training projects established to demonstrate the varying ways of recognising the potential of mentally handicapped persons. How did we pay for their capital cost? Local societies' increasing ability to raise money from the public, support from our bank and eternal optimism that money would come from somewhere!

Raising money inevitably had to be a preoccupation and although it was local society subscriptions which financed our initial activities, we had to supplement their generosity. As already mentioned in the Mencap diary, Doris Drown, whose husband was a founder member of the National Society and who was a driving force in so many spheres of developments for the mentally handicapped, introduced us to Frank Kerry, who had just formed a company called Ivory Cards, later Webb Ivory Ltd. Having started as stationers, Webb Ivory were intent on building up a national scheme for the sale of Christmas cards, and we were the first national charity they had approached. Their brilliant selling point was that the cards would be supplied on a sale or return basis to local societies and that they would be completely responsible for handling the scheme. Profits on sales would be divided between local societies and the National Society. Obviously, we had a ready made corps of sellers. For many years we were Webb Ivory's biggest success story due to the enthusiasm of local society sellers and the service which Webb Ivory gave, resulting in the sale of cards reaching into the millions every year. Later, sales of gifts by catalogue were included.

As now, there were many facets to raising money. We had a fruifut contract with Green Shield Stamps (remembered by some older readers?). Actor-manager Brian Rix, famous for his Whitehall farces on stage, film and television, chaired our Special Functions Committee, Roger Moore, then known for his role as 'The Saint', helped and encouraged us and we had an annual spring ball for many years at the Grosvenor House Hotel, London, supported by many stars of stage and screen. The children's TV programme *Blue Peter* chose us as their charity one Christmas (as I believe they have done again in the recent past), while the response to radio appeals was always heart-warming, bringing in much-valued thousands of small amounts from the less well-off. The Show Biz Car Club was for many years sponsored and chaired by that doyen of vintage cars, Lord Montagu of Beaulieu.

Sponsorship of research was a particular reason for wanting funds.

From the start, we had financed the production of the *Journal of Mental Deficiency Research* (now *The Journal of Intellectual Disability Research*) with an eminent board of editors. It was the beginning of the discovery of the cause of hydrocephalus and the Society helped to finance the development of the Spitzholter valve which alleviated or cured the condition. We were only able to offer small grants to pioneers like James Hogg, for instance, but research was high on our list of ambitions.

The expansion of activities and responsibilities of the NSMHC had long outgrown the two and a half small rooms in the Strand. We were always constrained by having to make the books balance and so our change of premises was necessarily governed by our ability to pay larger rents for more space, though it now almost sounds like the bailiffs were chasing us. Rooms at the top of a building in High Holborn (with sloping ceilings instead of sloping floors) were followed by a house in Bulstrode Street (and the wartime HQ of General de Gaulle, which we discovered when the GPO came to install the telephones). Then there were the premises in Newman Street (since demolished) and a house in Pembridge Square which we managed to persuade our understanding bank manager we could raise money to purchase. Finally, Alan Phillips, our wizard manager of buildings (among other things), found an old warehouse in Golden Lane which was ripe for conversion into offices. When I retired I was delighted to be given framed lithographs of all those premises which, to a certain extent, charted the development of the Society.

Conferences and seminars provided the opportunity for parents and professionals to widen their horizons and learn from one another and now this, of course, includes people with a learning disability themselves who at last have a voice of their own. In those early days residential weekend schools were welcomed by parents to enable them to meet one another, National Society staff and specialists in various fields.

Publications, films – one of which, *Concrete Steps*, won an award – and *Parents' Voice* (a regular magazine edited for many years by Judy Fryd) all played a part in disseminating information to parents and children.

For those parents unable to look after their children at home, hospitals were then the only alternative. We campaigned hard and long for the adoption of group homes or, at the very least, hostels with the goal of independent or assisted living in flats, etc. The concept used to be that mental handicap was a matter for health experts and psychiatrists but we pressed that it was the educational experts who should be mainly involved. Many of our parents had children who were then termed 'educationally subnormal' and we worked closely with the Guild of Teachers of Backward Children. The *Warnock Report*, which we helped to launch, came out in favour of the inclusion of children with specialist needs into mainstream schools rather than special schools. I think that most people are now agreed that multifaceted provision and choices are what is needed by the parents, children and adults concerned. Incidentally, our title was changed to the National Society for Mentally Handicapped Children and Adults because those pioneering parents, mainly of young persons, were now confronting the issues posed by adolescents and maturity and many of the residents in the hospitals were now even reaching old age. With the advent of more user-friendly titles we chose Mencap as our everyday acronym.

The growing awareness of the rights of disabled people and the need for more national coordination and provision was reflected by the Government appointing Alf Morris MP (now Lord Morris) as the first Minister for the Disabled. He was (and is) a tireless campaigner and a staunch friend of the NSMHC, as was Jack Ashley (now Lord Ashley). Inevitably this sounds like name-dropping but so many public figures of the day helped to bring us to the attention of the general public. Harold Wilson's wife, Mary, donated the proceeds from the publication of her poems, Elizabeth Taylor attended one of our functions (although the press were more interested in her new Richard Burton diamond ring) and the Guild of Toastmasters under Ivor Spencer arranged star-studded events in our aid.

I could not be accused of being anti-feminist, as my first staff was entirely composed of women and was joined in 1960 by a PA, Marie, whom eight years later I was to marry. My first male assistant was Trevor Riches, followed by Tudor Davies, and a couple of years later by Ken Solly as Deputy Secretary-General. Alan Phillips then came as Assistant Secretary-General. Both had been working as Regional Officers in the South Wales and Metropolitan regions respectively and both happened to be Quakers. So, considering Brian Rix went to a Quaker school, one could say that the Society of Friends proved a good training ground for persons involved in voluntary service. Ken Solly, Alan Phillips and Harry Neal (later recruited) were all appointed OBEs for their innovative work.

After losing Marie as a PA, I gained a superb replacement in Loretto Lambe (now Jim Hogg's wife – we were quite a good marriage bureau!). I think you could say that in those days before the luxury of specialisation, every member of staff had to be versatile. Ken Solly had a gift for words and personal relationships and imaginative thinking. Alan Phillips' forte was for getting down to the nuts and bolts of day-to-day administration and handling a growing staff and property portfolio. They both had the overall improvement of life for mentally handicapped people and their families as their goal, which they nursed into existence and of which they were the guiding forces.

I apologise for the many episodes, developments and people I have not mentioned who played such a large part in my time with the Society. I retired in 1980, to be followed by an explosion of publicity with the appointment of Brian Rix as Secretary-General and all the transformations of attitudes towards people with special needs.

So many memories, but my abiding admiration is for parents who inspired and worked for the immensely changed way of life that people with special needs can now enjoy and participate in. It was a great privilege to be part of the journey which still continues.

(I am very grateful to George for penning his story. We share a birthday – along with Mozart and Kaiser Wilhelm II – on 27 January. The difference between us is ten years, for George was born in 1914 and I arrived in 1924. BR)

CHAPTER 4

Brian Rix (The Lord Rix Kt CBE DL)

Secretary-General 1980–7

I have tried to keep my contribution at arm's length, as it were, by recounting the following narrative as though being interviewed. This method is used in other chapters of the book, when the interviewers are either Tim Segaller or Justine Williams.

When did you first come into contact with learning disability?
When I was a young boy living in the comparatively wealthy village of Hornsea in East Yorkshire. The well-to-do businessmen in Hull had houses at this small seaside resort (famous later for Hornsea Pottery and Hornsea Mere, a great favourite of the RSPB) and, as might be expected, everyone knew everybody else's business, both in Hull and in the home. My father was a shipowner so my mother had a great deal of time on her hands and became a great charity worker. One of the charities she supported was known by the typically forthright Victorian label – The Poor Brave Things. These poor brave things were in fact kids with cerebral palsy, some with a learning disability, and their holiday home

was a pretty miserable house near the LNER railway station in New Road. In contrast, another charity supported by my mother, was the Sailors' Orphans' Holiday Home which was a massive late nineteenth-century pile on Hornsea's north cliff. I was used to seeing The Poor Brave Things wheeled or hobbling into church every Sunday morning (where I was taken as a matter of course by my mother) while the Sailors' Orphans used to march there with drums beating and fifes squealing. All this happened during the chilly, east coast summers and, frankly, I thought little of it. I just knew my mother helped to support them all and some of them looked a bit funny.

Surely something must have registered?

Well, when I was at the local prep school, St Bede's, we all had to dress in a school uniform of blazer, shorts, long socks and school cap. During those halcyon years I used to see four other 'boys', dressed in similar uniforms, wandering round the village with ladies who looked like their nannies. They were, in fact, young men disguised as schoolboys by their parents in the vain hope that their 'backwardness' would not be noticed by the locals. It was then that I first heard the dread word 'mongol'.

So when did you hear it again?

At six o'clock on the evening of 5 December 1951. Our first daughter, Shelley, had been born two days before and the gynaecologist, Mr Searle, had asked to see me in his rooms in Harley Street. My wife, Elspet, and I worried greatly about this, but were assured that he liked to see all fathers after their first child was born. So, I went. His first words to me recalled those far-off days in Hornsea. 'Have you ever heard of mongolism?' he queried. I mumbled that I had, with my stomach dropping through the floor. 'Well, I'm sorry but your daughter's a mongol. Please tell your wife.' Of course the inevitable questions followed: 'Why?' No explanation. 'What do we do?' 'Find a good home for her and try again.' 'Will it happen to any more of our children?' 'Most unlikely,' and so on for several totally unproductive minutes. Then it was off to perform at the Whitehall Theatre in *Reluctant Heroes* – tears shed in actor-playwright Colin Morris's dressing-room, a large slug of brandy to steady the nerves and I was on – to make people roll in the aisles at my gormless recruit, Gregory, suffering endless insults from our bullying sergeant about my mental capacity and, perhaps worst of all, lines like, 'I dare say they'd leave your kids alone if they took a second look at them'. It was not a happy performance.

Did you tell Elspet?
Of course. The next morning – but by then she already knew in her heart of hearts that all was not as it should be.

What happened next?
Well, the usual advice: 'Put her away, forget her and start again' – or words to that effect. I think breaking the news to our parents was perhaps the worst part. Their incomprehension, their shock, their unhappiness for us was heart-breaking. But there were several stalwart friends who tried to cheer us up – actor John Slater, who played the sergeant in *Reluctant Heroes*, was particularly bullish, even buying a pair of Japanese buttons made into cufflinks, displaying cranes taking the place of storks, so that Elspet could give them to me as a memento of the arrival of our first-born. I have them to this day. The most practical help, though, came from George Jeger, the MP for Goole and one-time LCC Councillor. In those days MPs either had to have a private income or work for their livings, so poor was their recompense from the House of Commons, and George's morning job was as the General Manager of the Whitehall Theatre. Being an MP, who had once served on the LCC, meant he could introduce us to everyone who was in a position to offer us 'advice and guidance' and he put me in touch with the Ministry of Health, whom I contacted some two months after Shelley was born. In their written reply, full use was made of the dire descriptive terms laid out in the 1927 Mental Deficiency (Amendment) Act, while nothing appeared to have changed for the better since the original 1913 Act, two world wars and four decades of 'progress' and, of course, it hadn't. The letter soon made that all too clear as I had, apparently, been 'enquiring about the services available for mentally defective children' and, to heap Pelion on Ossa, the writer dictated that 'the mongol child you referred to [our daughter!] will not be capable of education under the education system, and will therefore have to be dealt with under the Mental

Deficiency Acts'. The services available were chiefly characterised by *not* being available, consisting of a right to fund a place myself without any state help, in a 'private home approved for the reception of mental defectives, feeble-minded high-grade imbeciles and helpless idiots'. However, these homes were full and had waiting lists. The alternative was a NHS placement in a NHS institution, but again there was a lengthy waiting list for each and every one. The letter concluded: 'If we can be of any further assistance, we shall be pleased to hear from you.' I often wonder if the bureaucrat who composed that letter was aware of the irony of that concluding paragraph. About five years later George helped us to make it possible for Shelley to enter the top-of-the range hospital of Normansfield. That meant that Shelley had to be 'certified' and again this was arranged by George through his contacts at the LCC. By then Shelley was nearly six – and still unable to walk – for she had been born with congenital dislocation of the hip and the doctors always said it was almost impossible to correct this – not absolutely true, of course, although it is difficult. I've often wondered if the medics considered it to be a waste of money to try to correct Shelley's condition as she had a learning disability. That has certainly been true for quite a number of well-publicised cases in the last few years and Shelley could possibly have been one of them. In fairness, though, I must say that when Shelley died on 19 July 2005 at the age of fifty-three, the medical and nursing staff in the West Middlesex Hospital could not have been more helpful and caring, in complete contrast to the two female doctors at County Hall in 1956 who cross-examined Shelley to certify she was 'ineducable'. The memory of that visit will haunt Elspet and me till we are no more.

Then did Shelley go to Normansfield?
Yes, in 1956. It was quite small – as opposed to some of the other huge, dreadful places we had seen with thousands shambling round the grounds – and still run by the grandson of the founder, Dr John Langdon Down, who gave his name to Down's syndrome. His grandson was Dr Norman Langdon Down, the kindest of men. He tried to keep up all the activities started by his grandfather, referred to by Professor Conor Ward in 'Doctors Who Cared: The Victorian Beginnings', but the paucity of

his financial support from the NHS made it increasingly difficult. Eventually, just after Shelley moved in, we formed the Friends of Normansfield and, over the years, provided a school (our children were still considered ineducable), a magnificent holiday home at Selsey Bill (our sons and daughters were not welcome at ordinary holiday accommodation), a shop, a clubhouse, a toy library, and support for the unique private entertainment hall built by Langdon Down in the 1870s and now fully refurbished and flourishing today as the Langdon Down Centre and housing the Down's Syndrome Association. Then there was the large hydrotherapy pool with all the necessary hoists and equipment for those with both learning and physical disabilities and the money raised for this was almost entirely due to our daughter, Shelley. Elspet and I, although publicity conscious in theatrical terms, had decided never to drag Shelley into the publicity 'inspired' by our press agent. When it came to the television appeal for the pool, I was deputed to do it. The producer wished to use Shelley at the end of the appeal but Elspet and I resisted, so he suggested we shoot it two ways – our preferred ending and his. We reluctantly agreed and the last shot was of an eleven-year-old Shelley running, as best she could, out of Normansfield's front door, flinging her arms round me and then – freeze frame – end of the appeal. The producer had his way, the money poured in and Shelley alone paid for that hydrotherapy pool. Today, of course, there is no Normansfield Hospital, just a splendid housing complex, the Langdon Down Centre and the entertainment hall. But the memories remain. More than that, for Elspet is a trustee of the Centre, while I take a back seat as the Patron.

Why didn't you join Mencap?
In the early fifties it was still the Association of Parents of Backward Children and nobody in our neck of the woods had even heard of it. At first we joined the wrong society, The Stars' Organisation for Spastics (SOS), and I became the first treasurer and the third chairman, following Wilfred Pickles and Vera Lynn. Our main task was fundraising, as it was in 1956 when we formed the Friends of Normansfield, shortly after Shelley went to live there. Eventually George Lee, the General Secretary (this title was later changed to Secretary-General and then Chief Executive) of what was then the National Society for Mentally

Handicapped Children, tapped me on the shoulder and reminded me that Shelley's support should really come from his society as well as from the Friends. Would I become the first chairman of the newly formed Special Functions Committee?

Although I was already involved with the Friends, the SOS, the Lord's Taverners and SPARKS (Sport Aiding Medical Research for Kids), I accepted and shortly afterwards I was chairing meetings on the stage of the Whitehall Theatre between the Thursday matinées and the evening shows, scantily clad in my dressing-gown, and hearing suggestions for all sorts of weird and wonderful ways of raising money: the inevitable ball, of course, at Grosvenor House, a never-to-be-forgotten Sunday evening at a Soho strip club, a day's racing at Kempton Park (with many big show-biz names as owners for the day), an evening at the dog track, cricket matches – and so on, *ad infinitum*.

The first big project we funded was the large holiday home called Pirates Spring at Dymchurch, which was opened in 1963 by Valerie Hobson. Like so many of us, she had a good reason for making that appearance as she had a learning disabled son by her previous marriage to Anthony Havelock-Allen and had been an early member of the Association of Parents of Backward Children. Before this event, though, George Lee had asked me to tell a packed house in Central Hall that I was the father of a 'mentally handicapped' daughter. After much debate with Elspet I agreed to do it, en route to a five o'clock Saturday matinée of *One for the Pot*. It was the most difficult speech I have ever had to make – as you can imagine – and next day pretty well all the Sunday papers carried the banner headlines BRIAN RIX CONFESSES . . . BRIAN RIX ADMITS . . . That summarises better than anything the lack of regard felt in those days for parents and children with a learning disability and the 'disgrace' attributed to the situation. It was a very miserable weekend.

And then there were all the other charities in which Elspet and I were involved: organising balls, not only at Grosvenor House but at the Dorchester Hotel, the Hyde Park Hotel, the Park Lane Hotel, even at Wandsworth and Ealing Town Halls, cadging tombola prizes and raffle prizes, selling tickets, drawing up table plans, persuading all the stars of the day to do the cabarets, the midnight matinées, the Drury Lane matinées, the fashion shows, the art exhibitions, as well as busking or selling programmes at the annual SOS Record Star Show (the forerunner of the pop concert) – the list was endless. Furthermore, when I wasn't appearing eight times a week at the Whitehall Theatre, or Elspet wasn't having another baby, both of us seemed to be learning lines and rehearsing for the hugely successful television farces, or making a film, or chasing all our friends and acquaintances to do us a favour. In those days, practically everyone did.

Where was Shelley all this time?
Living at Normansfield. By now our other three children – Louisa, Jamie and Jonty – had arrived, or were arriving, and Shelley used to come home at weekends, high days and holidays to complete the family circle. We lived on the borders of Richmond Park and Normansfield was just across Kingston Bridge, so it was very close. Shelley never seemed to mind going back, largely, I believe, because she was somewhat spoilt. Until her last years she always had an ebullient personality, with a touch of theatricality thrown in. I will never forget compèring a show at the Commonwealth Institute in Kensington. The place was packed with people who had learning disabilities, including Shelley, as well as their parents and carers. A splendid jazz trumpeter from Jamaica had just finished his session and was being followed by a steel band from a nearby Borstal. Most of the players were huge young men and as I announced their act I also told the audience that it was Shelley's birthday. The jazz trumpeter started to busk 'Happy Birthday to You', the steel band provided the rhythm backing and there was a great shout of 'that's me' from Shelley as she came stumping up to the stage, limping the while, kissing me affectionately, bowing extravagantly to the audience, grabbing the nearest steel-band drummer and sweeping him into a rather wild dance, made even wilder by her gammy leg and her gigantic partner's height. Immediately the stage was filled with excited members of the audience dancing away to the steel band and the trumpeter, transformed into the Pied Piper. It was a wonderful birthday treat for Shelley and, frankly, everyone there . . .

So was it Shelley who made you give up the theatre and go to Mencap?

Well, yes, I suppose if it hadn't been for Shelley, I can't think I would have had such an interest and personal involvement in the subject. But there were other factors, too. The importance of politics in relation to learning disability was borne in on me way back in the early sixties when George Lee asked me to go and see Enoch Powell, who was then the Minister for Health. Knowing how unsuccessful my first encounter had been with that department, I didn't exactly relish the encounter but agreed. It was then that I came to realise how comparatively easy it was for a well-known actor – me – to contact and be seen by a Minister. I merely telephoned the department and was almost immediately invited round to Enoch Powell's house for breakfast, simply on the strength of my success at the Whitehall Theatre. Unfortunately that success was not replicated over coffee and toast with Enoch. I had been briefed by George Lee to report that there were now many local NSMHC societies in England, Wales and Northern Ireland who would be glad to offer help and support to any parent who gave birth to a baby diagnosed with 'mental handicap'. Could the department circulate this information to all the health authorities?

Mr Powell nearly choked on his coffee. 'The NHS is not a postal service,' he spluttered, 'and, furthermore, there is no need to offer help and support. All doctors, midwives and maternity nurses are fully conversant with all the facts and know exactly how to deal with the situation.' To underline his point, he opened up a couple of already marked tomes sitting on the table and quoted some totally inaccurate information. But then he'd always been a great believer in statistics, rather like the person in Scottish writer Andrew Lang's quotation: 'He uses statistics as a drunken man uses lamp-posts – for support rather than illumination.' Remember his 'rivers of blood'?

Yes, but one encounter with Enoch Powell couldn't have convinced you to give up the theatre.

Absolutely right. It did remind me, though, that there were many battles ahead to ensure that people with a learning disability took their rightful place in the political scheme of things. An Act of Parliament does not necessarily change the public's attitude immediately, but over the years it does have a remarkable effect. The 1970 Education Act enabled children with a learning disability to go to school, as a matter of right, for the first time. To begin with, this was greeted with incredulity by most of the teaching profession but, over the years, the majority have come to believe in the principle of inclusive education. Parental choice, on the other hand, seems to be split between mainstream and special schools and will remain so until true inclusive education in the mainstream becomes a reality, with all the flexible support programmes for both disabled and non-disabled children in place.

You still haven't answered my question.
I apologise. As the years rolled by and I went on night after night at the theatre – 12,000 performances in all – I began to realise I was getting bored with the task and that if I was getting bored, then it wouldn't be long before the great British public followed suit. John Slater used to love playing the leading parts on tour, but now he had gone into BBC TV's *Z-Cars* it was my task to tour the plays when they finished in London and I loathed being away from home for weeks at a time. So, in the mid-seventies, I began to cast around in my mind for some fresh venture away from the theatre and at that time I was presenting the first-ever television programmes for people with a learning disability on the BBC, *Let's Go!* Mencap and Enable (Mencap's Scottish equivalent) were involved in the distribution of the programmes around schools and training centres, so I was therefore in regular contact with them, as well as Fred Heddell who was writing the notes (and, eventually, the programmes), and various groups and individuals taking part in the programmes of which, over the years, there were forty-two in all. This started me thinking that I ought to do more than just raise money; I could raise the profile of Mencap and learning disabled people as well if I was in charge. An amazing thing then happened. Mencap's long-serving Secretary-General, George Lee, decided to retire. The job was advertised, I applied and was turned down, even though I already had a CBE for the work I had done for the cause over the years. Happily, the man who was selected as Secretary-General designate had problems with the headquarters staff and was persuaded to concentrate on Mencap's regions. The job was offered to me until I reached retirement age. After

consulting Elspet and the family, I unhesitatingly accepted, took a considerable cut in income (thank goodness Elspet was working!) and soon realised it was the best decision I had made for years, ever since I had determined to bring *Reluctant Heroes* to the Whitehall Theatre on 12 September 1950. I had twenty-seven years as an actor-manager in London – doing voluntary work in my spare time – and by Mencap's actual sixtieth anniversary date in November 2006, I will have served the Society more directly for the same length of time, first as Secretary-General, then as Chairman and now as President. The only way they are going to persuade me to give up this job, though, is when the final curtain falls. There is still so much to do . . .

This book should make that clear. What did you do when you went to Mencap as the boss?
A great deal can be learnt from the Mencap sixty-year diary in Chapter 1 where I have been careful to refer to myself in the third person. Can I concentrate on some of the highlights?

Of course.
I first had to overcome the natural suspicions of a staff, a National Council and a membership at an AGM in Manchester that I wasn't just an actor who lost his trousers for a living, but a man who could lead the Society to bigger and better things. I was sure I could – after all, being a successful actor-manager does sharpen your wits – and I was greatly helped by the Chairman, Lord (David) Renton, and the Treasurer, Neville Thompson, who, as the senior Honorary Officers of the Society backed up all my early decisions and pronouncements. Our Royal Patron, too, weighed in with a message via Sir Martin Gilliatt, her Private Secretary, which also helped: 'Queen Elizabeth asks me to tell you how delighted she is to learn that Brian Rix is to be appointed as successor to George Lee. This is a most imaginative appointment . . .'
I held my first senior staff meeting on the day I took over. I had already been touring the regions and local societies so I knew quite a bit about the internal organisation, which gave me a certain amount of confidence. Even so, I didn't appreciate that twenty-seven directors-of-this and heads-of-that would crowd into my office, so it was obvious that

a degree of rationalisation would have to take place. This was achieved in fairly short order, without too much bloodshed, and interesting new jobs were created for those who might well have been facing redundancy. For instance, the Education and Employment Department had an excellent Director, James Cummings, who had a Deputy, Rolf Hermelin, who sat in his office all day, smoking himself to death for want of something to do. I enquired if Rolf was interested in politics. As a pre-war German refugee with a legal training, he was. So I created the first post in Mencap of a Parliamentary Officer. Over the years, Rolf – who, at the age of sixty-four became a rather elderly research assistant in the Commons so he could get a pass – was an invaluable help in our political endeavours and his one-man band was the forerunner of what is now one of Mencap's most effective and important departments, Campaigns and Policy. Headed by an ex-MP, David Congdon, its work reaches out all over the country and is not confined to Westminster and Whitehall alone.

You are not going to go through every department, surely?
No, no, of course not, although some of our activities have chapters of their own as we proceed through the book. I was merely illustrating that change is almost inevitable when new brooms sweep clean. Fred Heddell, in turn, had his creative ideas as did, and does, the current Chief Executive, Jo Williams. However, I think it would be remiss of me not to pay tribute to some of the staff members George Lee had recruited over the years, who continued to serve with me. They were a splendid lot, and had toiled away for the cause, with little reward, for considerable lengths of time. Many of them are no longer with us but I would like to name them, all the same, if you will permit me.

Yes, of course. They are part of Mencap's history, after all.
First, then, was George Lee himself, who genuinely dragged the Society into the realms of respectability, by sheer doggedness and determination. For this, he was awarded the OBE. Two others, who were also awarded the OBE, assisted him most ably. Ken Solly, now deceased, the Deputy Secretary-General and Alan Phillips, the Assistant Secretary-General (who became my deputy, for Ken had retired just before I joined), were incredible jacks-of-all-trades, who not only controlled the regional

activities of the Society, but the administration, the finance and Gateway, the leisure arm, as well. Weekend after weekend, year after year, the three were stumping the country with no suggestion of overtime or time in lieu or any of the other emoluments which generally go with such activity, and their devotion to duty was not caused by any personal motivation, like mine. Three singular men, all of them Quakers.

Others who had served for many years were the aforementioned James Cummings, in charge of education, brought into the Society to run the Slough Project in which those more severely disabled were given consideration and education, possibly for the first time, by the Society itself and by society as a whole. James was then succeeded by my colleague from the *Let's Go!* series, Fred Heddell, who eventually became the Chief Executive and whose story follows mine. Then there was Harry Neal, who supervised the formation of the Mencap Homes Foundation, along with two National Councillors, Ron Miller and Herbert Bradfield. James Ross was responsible for welfare, addressing himself wholeheartedly to the mind-boggling complexities of the social security system and fighting many battles on behalf of our members. Together with Janet Campbell, he also controlled the Trustee Visitors' Service, which provides support for our offspring when we, as parents, are no longer around to cope. Rolf Hermelin became Head of our Parliamentary Affairs and was eventually succeeded by Mary Holland, an American with a surprising knowledge of our parliamentary system. Nowadays, David Congdon is Head of Policy and Campaigns with Dr Tom Holland as Mencap's Parliamentary Officer. In 1980 the newly created legal department was originally run by Gerald Sanctuary, then by Michael Whelton, who was besieged by parents of learning disabled people anxious to know how to word their wills and form their trusts before it was too late. Mencap now has a Wills and Trusts Service with Aarti Puri as the in-house solicitor, heading a team of four who, every year, advise over 2,500 parents and carers. There is even the Mencap Trust Company Ltd, a company that manages discretionary trusts, as some people choose to appoint a company rather than an individual to act as trustee of their trust. Marketing and communication were in the flamboyant hands of Alan Leighton, who joined the Society just before me, from television and radio in the Midlands, where he was the original agony uncle, as well as offering sound advice in the newspapers. Leisure, through the medium of Gateway, was run by John Oliver and is fully discussed in Chapter 17. Finance and administration were controlled by the omniscient Alan Phillips who, in addition to all his other duties, seemed to be a practical handyman around the building, even repairing the ancient refrigerator in the kitchen on the very day I arrived. Of course, many others were responsible for much while I was Secretary-General, otherwise the small conference-room wouldn't have been full to overflowing on that first day: Peter Pascoe (also in Chapter 17), Marjorie Peacock (succeeded as Head of Personnel by Jill Tombs, now one of Mencap's senior directors), David Reid, Vicki Shennan, Tudor Davies, to name but five, plus our twelve Regional Directors (soon to be reduced to seven Divisional Managers), the principals of the training establishments, the matrons of the residential homes and the fantastic secretarial support staff in my outer office headed by Loretto Lambe. Without her, it's doubtful if I would have been able to find my way through the administrative labyrinth of the Society, nor to see ways round the log-jam of logistics affecting parents and staff. Loretto was with me for four years, before moving to Manchester to run our newly formed Profound Retardation and Multiple Handicap Project, as it was entitled in those days, and was succeeded by Nikki Gavin, who more or less took over where her predecessor left off. She eventually ran our ever-enlarging conferences and finally left to start up her own successful businesses. Leigh Banks then took over as the Committee Clerk and is still going strong today. Two more names to mention and then I'm finished. Marion Young, like Loretto Lambe, came up with the rations, so to speak. In other words, she was a part-time secretary to George Lee. Gradually, though, her job changed, and she is now the Legacies Officer responsible for negotiating the final details of the legacies left to Mencap. Matty van Rooden became my personal secretary about two years before I left and is now responsible for Mencap's membership office. As you might gather from her name, she is Dutch, but speaks and types English perfectly, although not when she first arrived. She was always entering dates in my *dairy* – until we bought her a word processor. I began to feel like a milk-maid.

What was in the first letter you had to answer?

Frankly, it was nothing short of an ultimatum, a threat of UDI by our North Wales members who no longer wished to be attached to their English colleagues in the North West. Nor, for that matter, did they wish to be attached to their fellow-countrymen in South Wales either. This was a problem which took me nearly two years to solve, but the melding process was eventually speeded up by the Welsh Office's announcement that it would shortly be bringing forth its *Strategy for Mental Handicap in Wales*. As this strategy would be looking for a coherent and cohesive cohort in the Principality, it was my job to effect this amalgamation as soon as possible. With a great deal of travelling and a great deal of diplomacy (and a great deal of support from our Regional Director, the late Langdon Doidge) I was eventually successful and in 1982 Mencap yng Nghymru – now Mencap Cymru – Mencap in Wales came into being. So did Mencap in Northern Ireland but, despite the Troubles, that was an easier task, thanks to the work of yet another splendid Regional Director, Evelyn Greer.

What else in 1980?

In December we held a conference with the deliberately provocative title 'Better Services for the Mentally Handicapped – When?' Note that it still did not refer to 'the mentally handicapped' as 'people' for the title was taken from the original Government document, published in 1971, with only 'When?' added. However, from time to time in the book – particularly in the years I am now describing – I will be using the term 'mental handicap' for it was then the official label, used by Mencap and Government departments alike. The current label 'learning disability' came later, but no doubt that, too, will change in time. Anyway, the Secretary of State for Health and Social Security, the Rt Hon. Patrick Jenkin MP (now Lord Jenkin) was the principal speaker and when it was all over I had occasion to write to him in the following way: 'I would be less than honest if I did not convey to you the deeply felt disappointment which was unanimously expressed by both parents and professionals, during and after your visit.' The rest of the letter listed all the problems voiced by speakers following the Secretary of State's departure from the conference and ended: 'On a personal note I would like to thank you for your obvious interest and concern and believe that you would do more if only times were different. Unfortunately this generosity of spirit is not easy to share with parents of mentally handicapped people who are often in desperate need. It would be a sad reflection on society if in 1990 we are still asking the question, "Better Services for the Mentally Handicapped – When?"' I regret to say that in 1990 we still *were* asking that same question, and in the millennium year, 2000, as well. The White Paper *Valuing People* – which did chart a way ahead – was published in 2001 twenty-one years after that original conference and thirty years after that original White Paper. Perhaps this illustrates better than anything why the first Chairman of the National Society for Mentally Handicapped Children – Frederick Ellis (then the Financial Editor of the *Daily Express*) – was so hopelessly wrong in his fervent wish to do the Society out of a job in his lifetime. That was in 1954, and still the end is not in sight.

It sounds as though you had quite a busy inauguration.
Well, frankly, it's been like that ever since I became Secretary-General. Even when I retired in 1987 I was only put out to grass for six months before becoming the Chairman. In that 'fallow' period, I wrote *Farce About Face* which explained my transition from an actor-manger to charity worker. It was written in a conversational style and detailed all that went on in the world of learning disability in the eighties and now, in 2006, I'm at it again with this book.

Can you give us some of the highlights?
Of course. The International Year of Disabled People (IYDP) in 1981 was the first time, as far as I'm aware, that people with a learning disability were bracketed along with all the others who had physical or sensory disability. At last we were allowed a peep outside the ghetto and, as Secretary-General of Mencap, I sat down at the same conference tables as the Directors of RADAR, RNID and RNIB, plus all the others, without feeling the least bit inferior. Not that I felt inferior anyway – but you know what I mean.

Also early in 1981, along with David Renton, I met with the Secretary of State for Education, Mark Carlisle (now Lord Carlisle), and managed to persuade him to accept a number of important clauses in the forthcoming Education Bill. Soon after that I was in Birmingham to record a BBC television programme for Pebble Mill, telling the tale about my change of occupation, and during one part of the recording I met with a journalist, Mary McCormack, who asked me what Mencap was doing for those who, like her child, had profound and multiple mental and physical disabilities. I had to confess that I thought we were doing very little – ever since our residential experiment in Slough nearly twenty years before had finished – and I would look into it as a matter of urgency. That's how our PRMH (Profound Retardation and Multiple Handicap, now PMLD – Profound and Multiple Learning Disability) project started some three years later. It took that time because I had to raise quite a large sum of money to fund the project, which was in association with the Hester Adrian Research Centre at the Victoria University in Manchester and Piper Hill School in the same city. The founder members – Loretto Lambe and James Hogg – tell their story in Part IV Chapter 14, with James interviewing Loretto – now his wife.

Anything else in 1981?
In May of that year I was involved in a bit of excitement, for I was invited to address a group of parents in Dublin. It turned out to be the day of the funeral of IRA hunger-striker Bobby Sands and there were demonstrations going on all over the place. I was literally smuggled out of the airport, round the outskirts of Dublin, hurriedly shoved into the hall and told to get on with it. I did, to a packed house, and when it was over the whole process was repeated and I was once again smuggled back to the airport and back to London, whence I came. The next day I had to fly to Belfast, where the process was more or less repeated, although I was allowed to sleep in a fortified hotel – not conducive to a good night's rest!

A month later, back in my own bed in London, there was our annual conference which was addressed by Professor Joan Bicknell, holding the first-ever Chair of Psychiatry of Mental Handicap, St George's Hospital Medical School, University of London. Joan was then succeeded by Professor Sheila Hollins, who appears in Part IV Chapter 12 and, of course, other universities now have departments devoted to the cause of learning disability. Would there were more. Shortly after that conference, though, Nigel Evans produced a television documentary for ATV (later Central) called *Silent Minority* which purported to show life at St Lawrence's 'subnormality' hospital at Caterham. It was quite horrifying, although it was later alleged that some of the scenes had been, as it were, stage-managed. Whatever the truth of that accusation, the media took a great interest in the programme and there were parents' meetings, friends' meetings, staff meetings – even health authority meetings – and much abuse hurled back and forth. Mencap and I were piggy-in-the middle and when the interest died away, we were left feeling somewhat battered and bruised, wondering if *Silent Minority* had achieved its original purpose and made the great British public sit up and take notice about the lives of people with a learning disability and their families. Unfortunately, the GBP seemed to be singularly uninterested and 'mentally handicapped' people and their parents felt as excluded from normal society as ever.

A much happier occurrence was the production of *Fundamental Frolics* (Mencap was not responsible for the punning title!) at the Apollo Victoria in London's West End, in aid of Mencap's college at Lufton Manor. Organised by Jane Tewson (who went on to produce many other well-known charity events, including Red Nose Day), Jane Charlton and musician Nico Ramsden, it was both a financial and an artistic success. Not altogether surprising, for the cast included Rowan Atkinson, Elvis Costello, Ian Dury, Griff Rhys Jones, Chris Langham, Alexei Sayle, Pamela Anderson and the two directors of the show, Mel Smith and Nico Ramsden.

The beginnings of other pet schemes of mine showed the first signs of life in 1981: the Mencap City Foundation (now the Rix-Thompson-Rothenberg Foundation) and the Mencap Unit Trust, to mention but two, while David Renton and I managed to have the Royal title added to the Society's name and the National Council instructed me to begin our first housing project, Homes Foundation. However, these and other events are all well covered in the diary or elsewhere in the book – so we move on to 1982 – and I promise, from now on, only events not already mentioned or about to be mentioned will be included in my answers.

Splendid! So – briefly – what else is there to report?

Well, the 1982 Mencap conference, entitled '16 . . . and then what?', which alluded, of course, to continuing education for learning disabled young adults. The key speaker was the Secretary of State for Education, Sir Keith Joseph, who, as is usual on these occasions, told us little that was new. When he had finished I asked how soon the two major departments – Health and Education – might collaborate a little more effectively for the benefit of people with a learning disability. Sir Keith was not minded to answer and decided to cut the question session short and make his escape. Unfortunately, the conference was being held in Cinema 1 in the bowels of the Barbican Centre and any reader who has tried to effect egress from there in a hurry will know that it's no easy option. Sir Keith blundered up and down the stairs, stood cursing by the lifts and was generally in a tizz by the time the driver of his car had finished racing round the building, trying to pick up his puffed-out passenger. It was not a fortuitous climax to our conference and I never did get to know if he spoke to his opposite number in Health. Somehow I doubt it.

It was in 1982, of course, that the Lord Mayor of London, Sir Anthony Jolliffe, made Mencap his charity of the year. This meant that Elspet and I had to attend the Lord Mayor's Banquet when the Chancellor of the Exchequer, Sir Geoffrey (now Lord) Howe, was speaking. Apparently he had mislaid his trousers on a train the previous week so Frank Johnson in *The Times* chose to report him thus:

> Sir Geoffrey has entered history as the Chancellor who lost his trousers. Pretty soon people will believe he lost them in the presence of Mrs Thatcher, or at a cocktail party for visiting heads of central banks, or even in the chamber of the Commons itself. Eventually it will be said that he does it all the time, enlivening Cabinet meetings thereby. He will become the Brian Rix of monetarism. In the esteem of the British people his future is assured.

As well as the money raised by the Lord Mayor's Appeal, the sales force of Hambro Life – soon to be Allied Dunbar – contributed from their sales commission no less than £150,000 to ensure that one of our colleges, Dilston Hall, became ours. Since then the college has gone on to bigger and better things, only made possible by the generosity of an enlightened workforce of insurance salesmen. And remember, this was in the days before there were any tax advantages to such a donation.

1983 began with a metaphorical splash, for it took place in the seaside town of Teignmouth. Regrettably, some of their senior residents, particularly certain members of the local Chamber of Commerce, became bitterly opposed to the use of one of their best hotels, the Royal, as a favourite watering hole for disabled people in general and learning disabled people in particular. Of course, it's true that by then Mencap was against the mass take-over of any building for holiday purposes – that's why we had got rid of our holiday home, Pirates Spring, and turned others into colleges – but the things that were being said and written about our sons and daughters with a learning disability were pretty grim. One civic dignitary said that they were 'eroding the seafront' while another wrote in the *Teignmouth News*, suggesting a rationing system:

> The handicapped could holiday in a hotel on the edge of Dartmoor where acres of ground will give them boundless pleasure and privacy. Once or twice a week they could hire a coach and come to Teignmouth and relax on the beach and splash at the water's edge. The organisers could fetch them gallons of ice-cream and drinks. Come teatime, they could return to the tranquillity of the moor undisturbed, refreshed, and leaving others unperturbed.

The owner of the Royal, Paul Bourge, was threatened with the removal of his drinks' licence and it was even alleged that Teignmouth District Council was considering an enforcement notice to stop Mr Bourge accepting disabled people as guests. All this over a total occupancy of less than 22 per cent who had a learning disability.

I gathered together the leaders of several disability charities and we descended on the town, breathing fire and brimstone. The media joyfully joined in on our side, led by the *Guardian*; the Minister for the Disabled, Sir Hugh Rossi, lent Government backing – both financial and practical – to our protestations, a Liaison Leisure Officer was appointed, people of goodwill came forward and the whole absurd affair fizzled out. But it was pretty nasty while it lasted.

THIS TABLET WAS ERECTED
IN GRATEFUL MEMORY
OF
THE REVᴰ ANDREW REED.D.D.
THE FOUNDER OF THE
LONDON ORPHAN ASYLUM
BY
THOSE WHO HAVE BEEN EDUCATED IN THE INSTITUTION.
A.D.1863.

THE METHOD OF DRILL,

The Gymnastic Exercises,

AND THE

MANNER OF TEACHING SPEAKING,

USED AT

ESSEX HALL, COLCHESTER,

FOR IDIOTS, SIMPLETONS, AND FEEBLE-MINDED CHILDREN.

BY

P. MARTIN DUNCAN, M.B. (Londin.)

LONDON:
JOHN CHURCHILL, NEW BURLINGTON ST.;
COLCHESTER: EDWARD BENHAM.
1861.

Above: the Revd Andrew Reed, a philanthropic Nonconformist who initiated services for people with learning disabilities in the mid-nineteenth century

Above: the title page from Martin Duncan's revolutionary book for helping children with a learning disability

Below: Essex Hall, Colchester – an early Victorian asylum

ASYLUM FOR IDIOTS.—ESSEX HALL, COLCHESTER

Above: John Langdon Down after whom Down's syndrome was named

Above: Mary Langdon Down, who set up her own training programme

Earlswood eventually housed over 500 residents

Normansfield and its remarkable theatre (below)

Above: *Parents' Voice* – the magazine founded by Judy Fryd

Above: Judy Fryd who set up the National Association of Parents of Backward Children, the genesis for what would later become Mencap

Below: Michael Sangster, Joey Deacon and Ernie Roberts – three friends who worked for eighteen months to produce Joey's book *Tongue Tied* which Mencap published in 1974

Twenty-five years of the NSMHC commemorated

Above: an early Gateway club outing

Left: Gateway marks its Silver Jubilee

Top: a Gateway group, with volunteer helpers, climbed the 18,478ft Mount Elbrus in Russia. The achievement was given official United Nations 'Climb for the World' status

Middle: for the International Year of Disabled People 1981, Gateway clubs combined to provide and install water pumps in a number of African villages to support the United Nations' Water Decade

Bottom: John Langdon Down's grandson, Norman, with Elspet Rix (centre) and Norman's cousin, Stella, Lady Brain

Top: Brian Rix receives encouragement after receiving an honorary degree from the Open University

Bottom: The Queen Mother opened the workshop at Golden Lane in 1981

Could it happen today?
Not really, The Disability Discrimination Act is in place and the Disability Rights Commission is on the ball. Even so it's pretty pathetic that people stop being as prejudiced as that only because the full weight of the law is against them. Oh for the day when such biased opinions really are a thing of the past.

Did the National Development Team not help to put such matters right?
No, no. You will find further references to the team as you go through the book, but in my case I was involved in a cloak-and-dagger operation with David Hencke of the *Guardian.*

Tell me more.
Well, it all began on 16 March 1983 when I met David for lunch at La Rochetta, an Italian restaurant, which might well be thought to be a suitable venue in which to hatch a little plot with distinct Sicilian overtones. Ever since I had joined Mencap as the Secretary-General I had become increasingly irritated by the fact that the NDT (National Development Team) reports on conditions surrounding the lives of people with a learning disability were largely kept secret by the health authorities commissioning them. Only occasionally would one be en-lightened enough to go public. Furthermore, those outsiders who joined the team (my wife, Elspet, being one) were made to sign the Official Secrets Act so they could not disclose anything they had seen, even if it was pretty dire, which it generally was. Hence the Cosa Nostra lunch.

Now David Hencke at that time was the social services correspondent (now the Westminster correspondent) of the *Guardian* and over our lasagne verdi and verdicchio we agreed on a campaign to have the NDT reports published and for the voluntary members of the team to be able to avoid signing the Official Secrets Act. David went to work and reports were whisked off desks before they had even been read, smuggled to King's Cross or Euston or Paddington, photographed and returned without anyone being any the wiser. Senior members of staff seemed to be only too anxious to talk, as did members of health authorities and David was able to compile a most damning set of documented evidence. Remember this was in the time before 'leaks' and 'spin doctors' became a part of Government policy and was investigative journalism at its best, for it was a just cause and the *Guardian*, too, must be congratulated on allowing so much space and editorial comment over a four-day period. David Hencke's initial article began:

> Appalling and inadequate conditions for thousands of mentally handicapped people living in isolated hospitals have been uncovered by a national team of health experts over the last seven years. Confidential reports covering fifty hospitals and thirty homes reveal widespread instances of overcrowding, understaffing, custodial attitudes to patients, fire risks and the denial of the basic human dignity of toilets with doors, adequate washing facilities and personal furniture and clothing for many 'patients'. In isolated cases the reports reveal evidence of unexplained cruelty and neglect and squalid ward conditions such as urine-soiled carpets and dirty beds.

The ghastly list continued with actual damning quotes from reports being cited and a final hard-hitting comment from me, which ended: 'The Minister [Kenneth Clarke] seems to speak with forked tongue. He has been spending his life suppressing reports on these hospitals yet claiming that "the mentally handicapped" are a priority.' The following day there were more examples of shameful conditions and a further long article from me, which began:

> Since 1944, there have been twenty-four Acts and thirteen or more sets of regulations affecting the lives of people with mental handicap. Other important DHSS references include such high-flown titles as *Better Services for the Mentally Handicapped* (1971); *Mental Handicap: Progress, Problems and Priorities* (1980); *Care in Action* and *Care in the Community* – both issued in 1981. Yet this impressive panoply, erected by successive Governments and constantly referred to by those in authority, has crumbled to dust when set against the melancholy, shameful and degrading list of conditions pertaining in many mental handicap hospitals and local authority areas, as chronicled in yesterday's *Guardian*. Were these revelations the work of some irresponsible ghoul, intent on polluting the ear of a desipient

journalist, seeking yet another shock-horror story for his yellow pages? Indeed, they were not. They came from reports compiled by the National Development Team for the Mentally Handicapped – an eminently respectable group of professionals and parents working in that particular field.

Later in the article I wrote:

The fact that so many reports have become readily available to the *Guardian* makes a mockery of this whole secrecy procedure. Even the members of the Team have to sign the Official Secrets Act before commencing work. You would think the DHSS guarded our most precious defence secrets and, God knows, enough of those have been leaked.

Of course, the proverbial hit the fan in no uncertain way. I was hauled in to the BBC by Sir Robin Day to the *World at One* to talk to the Minister most concerned, Kenneth Clarke. To be fair, I don't think Kenneth had any idea what was going on and genuinely didn't know that people like Elspet had to sign the Official Secrets Act. He promised to look into matters immediately – and did. We never heard another word about the Official Secrets Act. It just vanished from the NDT's remit.

In 1985 there was another story leaked to the *Guardian* which had a less happy outcome for Mencap. It read:

The Secretary-General of Mencap, Brian Rix, should thank Christopher Whitehouse, a militant moral majority campaigner, for a letter he will receive this morning from Cardinal Basil Hume, Archbishop of Westminster. The letter says that Hume can no longer be a patron of the Society and his name must be removed from the stationery. Mencap is lobbying MPs to vote against the Unborn Children (Protection) Bill and favours the Warnock Committee's proposals to allow limited research on embryos to detect handicap, whereas the Catholic Church is unequivocally against Warnock. Whitehouse, who works for the husband-and-wife team of right-wing Tory MPs, Nicholas and Ann Winterton, made it his business to pester the Cardinal about Mencap and has now got a result.

Not a very happy way to learn of a Patron's resignation. I replied to the Archbishop:

> . . . may I express my disquiet to see that your letter was leaked to the *Guardian* yesterday, on the very day it was posted to me, and to read of the overt pressure which has been brought to bear on you by Christopher Whitehouse, the so-called 'militant moral majority campaigner.' It seems unfortunate, to say the least, that this pressure could be construed to have affected your decision – and this can only be deplored.

Despite this brouhaha, the Warnock White Paper formed the basis for future legislation, whereas the Unborn Children (Protection) Bill was stillborn.

I'm glad to report that, despite the Cardinal Archbishop's resignation, Mencap once again had a record-breaking year, as far as revenue was concerned, and our services continued to grow exponentially. But can I lighten the narrative for a moment and tell a personal story, describing how my knighthood in 1986 nearly ended up as undelivered mail. A tatty brown envelope arrived in the post in the second week in May containing what seemed to be a returned postal package. This turned out to be an even tattier white envelope with 'On Her Majesty's Service' gummed on the flap and a label indicating that it had been OFFICIALLY SEALED IN THE POST OFFICE, with an upside-down crown on the rear. Looking at it closer, I saw that the address through the scratched and almost obscured transparent window was for a house we had left ten years before. Furthermore, the postal district was wrong, indicating that we had lived in SW14 whereas it should have been SW13. Some joker had pencilled in '–1'. The letter had obviously hiccuped around a number of mythical addresses for a mass of hieroglyphics stated 'gone away', 'unknown at this address', 'undelivered for reasons stated', 'return to sender' – the sender being the Prime Minister herself. Some post operative in the sorting office had ignored 'Personal', slit open the envelope and worked out who I was and where I lived, but in so doing he knew, before I did, the letter's contents: 'The Prime Minister has it in mind etc.' I was requested to accept, or otherwise, my proposed knighthood *by return of post* and the damn letter was already almost a fortnight late in arriving. Had I been stripped of my knighthood before I'd even bent the knee? I tore to the post with my acceptance, still in my dressing-gown, causing all my neighbours – or rather the ones that saw me – to think I had reverted to my Whitehall farce days, *sans-culotte*. But I hadn't, and by the time we held Mencap's fortieth anniversary reception at St James's Palace, in the presence of HM Queen Elizabeth the Queen Mother, the Kt was mine. I was delighted about this, not just for personal vanity, but for the fact that such an honour reflected a distinct change in the way that politicians and the public had begun to view people with a learning disability, as well as Mencap itself. Incidentally, at that reception the Queen Mother, who was meant to be with us for an hour, stayed for two-and-a-half, even though it was the hottest day of the year. The Chairman, Lord Allen, and I were stretched to the utmost, trying to keep up with her and remember everyone's name at the same time. But it was all worthwhile, for many people with a learning disability were present and the Queen Mum sought them out, which caused much excitement and delight.

We now come to your last year as Secretary-General.
Quite right. I completed seven years as I had always said I would and expressed my interest in taking over as Chairman after a suitable period of absence. It's all in the Mencap diary, but I left at the end of October 1987 and succeeded Philip Allen as Chairman the following spring. Not before a final flurry of excitement and controversy, though. The excitement came when Elspet and I were invited to go to Australia and New Zealand to see how those two countries operated their intellectual disability services. We spent four weeks in the Antipodes and it was marvellous. At that time the services in Australia seemed to be somewhat fragmented, with each state taking its own line, but New Zealand, under the leadership of J.B. Munro, was quite a different kettle of fish. I thought that many of their services were better than ours in the UK but now, by 2006, I'm sure that has changed and we are all on level pegging. I don't suppose, at my great age, I'll be invited again to find out! Mind you, I did make two further trips abroad as Chairman of Mencap. The first was to India – again with Elspet – at the request of the British Council and then to New Zealand on my own, for Elspet was working,

when I was invited by the Government to fulfil the totally unexpected role of a 'living treasure'. Audrey Hepburn was there at the same time as me, representing UNESCO, while I was there for intellectual disability and the theatre. All these tours were pretty hectic, but in my dual role as a 'living treasure' my feet hardly touched the ground, for I was doing theatre workshops in Auckland, Wellington and Christchurch and the rest of the time attending lunches and dinners to speak about learning disability. Still, I had a minder, a butler and a driver supplied by the Government, my suitcases packed, my transportation worked out to a 'T', presidential suites in all the hotels, so now I know how it feels to be a Head of State. But for me, alas, it lasted precisely two weeks and then it was back to cleaning my own shoes, pressing my own trousers, laying the table and loading the dishwasher. How are the mighty fallen . . .

You mentioned 'controversy'. What was that about?
In the Mencap diary you will see that I was involved in an issue concerning sterilisation. I will expand on that a little. The Court of Appeal ordered the sterilisation of a seventeen-year-old girl with a learning disability who was, to quote, 'showing signs of sexual awareness and sexual drive'. On my way to the BBC Television Centre to give an interview about Mencap's reaction to the case, I was determined to find a phrase to put in our press release which would make people sit up and take notice of the moral issues involved. I found it and ended my written statement thus: 'In the nineteenth century early educationalists assumed that all people with a mental handicap were capable of some improvement, even if they could not be cured. They did, however, keep alive the possibility that they might not be truly human. Frequent comparisons were made with animals. I cannot help wondering, is the girl in this case to be spayed like a bitch?'

That closing phrase made headlines throughout the land. The girl in question became a *cause célèbre* with a vengeance and the topic of many, many articles and leaders. Here is but one extract from, yet again, the *Guardian*:

There was little talk about basic human rights in the Appeal Court this week and the law is now weaker for it. The decision to sterilise is bad for several reasons. It is bad because it asserts that the courts really can divide the population into those who are fit to reproduce and those who are not. That is a very large claim, against which most mental health law and policy in the last thirty years has rebelled. It is bad because its finality denies the possibility of change or improvement in the person to be sterilised. This is not a question of future miracles – although some people will take that possibility seriously. It is a question of preventing unwanted conception through counselling and protection, in much the same way as you would do with a child or as is already done with patients suffering from hereditary handicaps. It is bad because it is a judgement with more than a hint of expediency about it, the expediency which says that there aren't enough social workers to go round to care for such people any more and she'll be eighteen in a couple of months' time anyway, and thus outside the court's jurisdiction.

Exactly. My point was (and is) that the human rights of – and community presence and participation for – people with learning disabilities demand legislation guaranteeing respect and protection for all. In opposing compulsory sterilisation I am clearly not writing about a right to have babies where a woman is so severely disabled that she is unable either to consent to intercourse or understand her own body or care for a child. But surgery as an admission price for community care seems to me to be even more unacceptable than the old practice of locking up 'feeble-minded' women in case non-feeble-minded men should get them pregnant, or the practice for many years of the segregation of the sexes in large and small institutions alike so that intercourse – both social and sexual – was quite out of the question.

The *Sunday Times* offered me their 'Platform' columns and my contribution appeared under the eye-catching headline: THEIR FINAL SOLUTION. It wasn't the final solution, of course. The Official Solicitor took the matter to the House of Lords but the Court of Appeal ruling was upheld and the girl in question was sterilised.

All this, and the revelation that the Queen Mother had a number of learning disabled nieces caused further ructions – as did the speed (or otherwise) of hospital closures – and I approached my farewell speech as

Secretary-General at Mencap's AGM with a certain degree of trepidation. Here it is, with my apologies, yet again, for using the term 'mental handicap', which was still in vogue in those days:

> I came to this great movement some seven years ago, believing that I could achieve something for people with a mental handicap and their families because of the theatrical fame I had enjoyed for many years. This, perhaps egotistical, belief was backed up by the value I had seen stemming from the *Let's Go!* programmes and from the very personal belief that I owed a great deal to my Down's daughter, Shelley, and the tens of thousands like her.
>
> Over the past seven years I think much *has* been achieved. More Acts of Parliament affecting the lives of people with a mental handicap have been enacted in that short time than in the previous thirty-six years. Hardly a week or a day goes by without some positive aspect in the lives of people with a mental handicap becoming known to the world at large, while local authorities and central Government dare not move without giving some consideration to their rights and just demands. And I'm happy to have been part of that general progress.
>
> But, of course, there are doubters and bigots always waiting in the wings. By an extraordinary twist of fate these last few weeks have seen a series of events which have caused the media some joy and parents much fear. Are our hospitals being closed too quickly, allowing discharge without regard to become a horrifying fact of life? Are the general public as uncaring and unhelpful as they were in days of yore? Should sterilisation be allowed? Has the Queen Mother been party to some unfortunate cover-up? There are some who believe that all this may be so. Their letters to me go to prove this. And they cause me much unhappiness and many a sleepless night. But there are others, many others, who believe the opposite and that the dignity and quality of a person's life must at all times be pre-eminent, even at the risk of personal vilification. I am one of those believers.
>
> The other day I stood in Westminster Hall at the grand lobby organised to support the implementation of the 'Tom Clarke Act' – the Disabled Persons (Services, Consultation and Representation) Act

– and I met, again, the very people I am talking about. This afternoon we go across to the Festival Hall to see thousands of people with learning disabilities – some mild, some severe, some profound – taking part in a heart-stopping, heart-warming exercise in love and life and laughter – the Gateway Festival.

Those very people are the reason for Mencap's existence. We must never give up in our efforts to eliminate for ever the use of the word 'madhouse', to eliminate the myth that our sons and daughters are second-class citizens and should be put away out of sight and out of mind and never be allowed to have a recognition of their own worth and value.

I'm glad to say that this was greeted with a standing ovation. I felt somewhat better after that, and able to contemplate the months ahead with a little more tranquillity. Actually, it was only six months before Lord Allen retired as Chairman, succeeding Lord Renton as President – who then became the Immediate Past President – while I came out of purdah and assumed the role of Chairman, completing more than ten years in this particular honorary office. At the end of 1998 I retired as Chairman and am now in my eighth year as President. Rather than detail all those eighteen years – which would tire you and me – I believe the next two chapters by Fred Heddell and Jo Williams cover most of the major happenings and bring matters up to date, while the contribution by Brian Baldock, the current Chairman, plus the Mencap sixty-year diary, complete the picture. I am happy to have been around in the wings for most of the time and, since 1992, have been able to play a much-needed role as a cross-bencher in the House of Lords, speaking up or negotiating for people with a learning disability, and Mencap, in all areas of legislation. For me, it has been a remarkable fourteen years, and I trust there are more still to come. I have made some close friends and found ministers and politicians of all parties (and none) lending a sympathetic ear and giving practical support to my endeavours, while the expert advice and help I have received from Mencap's staff has been quite remarkable. I owe them all a great debt of gratitude.

At the time of writing this chapter of the book I found myself involved, once more, in the question of 'labels'. This argument has raged for centuries but especially in the last sixty years of Mencap's existence, as people with a learning disability have gradually taken their rightful place in society and, quite understandably, are sensitive about the 'label' which applies to them. Some parents, too, are equally sensitive, but in the opposite camp, for they believe that the less powerful (I hesitate to use the word 'offensive') the label describing the condition, the less will be the services provided. As I say, it is an unresolved conundrum which can cause great anger and distress to many.

I made reference to this is my maiden speech in the House of Lords on 12 Tuesday May 1992 and ended with these words:

> When I first went to Mencap as Secretary-General in 1980 I was very fond of quoting a certain Dr John Langdon Down, who gave his name to Down's syndrome and who voiced these sentiments well over a century ago: 'Today we have to provide the highest possible culture, the best physical, moral and intellectual training, and open out fresh realms of happiness for those who have the strongest claims on our sympathy.'
>
> Maybe time and political correctness have overtaken the use of such Victorian language, but I am sure your Lordships would agree that the underlying message should always be uppermost in our thoughts, governing all the relevant legislation which this and any subsequent Parliament chooses to place on the Statute Book, particularly that opening statement, 'Today we have to provide'. Such a phrase allows no room for tentative guidelines, for lack of resources, for wishful thinking.
>
> The words 'Today we have to provide' are unequivocal. We should always remember them, not only today but tomorrow and the day after tomorrow. People with a learning disability, irrespective of their current label, together with their families and friends, deserve no less.

CHAPTER 5

Fred Heddell CBE

Director of Education and Employment, 1985–1990
Secretary-General, then Chief Executive, 1990–2003

I first started working with people with learning disabilities around 1964 when I volunteered in what was then a junior training centre (JTC) in Stratford, East London. A friend had recently been appointed as the supervisor at the newly opened John F. Kennedy Centre and as teaching children with learning disabilities was very much a woman's world, she was anxious to involve a few men to cope with the bigger boys.

JFK was probably the best JTC in the country with fabulous facilities, including a proper swimming pool, a teaching flat, superbly equipped craft and teaching workshops as well as a fully equipped special care unit which would be the envy of many schools even today.

After a couple of years of volunteer work, the Medical Officer of Health for the Borough of West Ham persuaded me to accept a full-time appointment. I don't think it would be acceptable today, but in order to attract me (a man) he offered me almost twice the salary my female colleagues were earning.

Thus started a career that has lasted over forty years. The London Borough of Newham paid my salary, initially through the two-year training course for teachers of mentally handicapped children and latterly on a one-year Postgraduate Certificate in Education so that I became a fully qualified teacher when the responsibility for the education of children with learning disabilities moved from Health to Education in 1970. It was in my initial training in 1968–9 that I first crossed paths with the Rix family when I taught Shelley during a short teaching practice at Normansfield Hospital.

After I qualified I moved across the London Borough of Newham to help set up a new school and then to Thurrock in Essex as a Deputy Head Teacher.

During my time in Thurrock I became involved with the BBC, working with Brian Rix on the production of the *Let's Go!* series. My initial contact was at a preview of some pilot programmes. Rosemary Lee, the BBC Education Officer, was getting a very rough time from teachers who really could not see the potential in pilot programmes that left much to be desired. I suggested to her that, as they were designed for young people with a learning disability, it might be a good idea to show them to some of the target audience rather than teachers. As a result I was given the pilots on video tape (half-inch open reel tape – long before VHS) to try with fourteen- to eighteen-year-olds in schools, colleges and centres in Thurrock. The work on using the programmes as part of an overall teaching package both shaped the design of the *Let's Go!* programmes and changed my career for ever.

I was later commissioned by the BBC to write the back-up notes and subsequently the script outlines for all three series, forty-two programmes in all. This also brought me into contact with Mencap and what was then known as the Scottish Society, for these two organisations paid for much of the back-up material, including slide sets used in classrooms all over the country.

Looking back it is difficult to imagine the impact and influence of *Let's Go!* The programmes were broadcast just as the concept of care in the community was gathering momentum. Its amazing now to think that the combination of Brian Rix – a well-known and very popular actor – on the BBC, promoting the ideas of people with a learning disability going on a bus, going shopping and generally moving around their communities freely and independently was radical thinking, so radical in fact that the BBC actually withdrew one episode because it showed people with a learning disability being encouraged to cycle and the volume of complaint from the general public was deafening. Things have changed a great deal in the last quarter of a century, although we often forget how much.

The success of *Let's Go!* was amazing, with almost all the schools, centres and colleges throughout the UK providing for people with a learning disability using the series as the basis for their inclusion into the community programmes. Mencap's role as a central partner with the BBC (and departments of Government) in the promotion and dissemination of the series was a crucial part of this success, and promoted the movement away from hiding people with a learning disability from society towards genuine inclusion.

At the same time as the *Let's Go!* programmes were being produced, I was appointed as Head Teacher at Warren Special School in Lowestoft, Suffolk. While I was at Warren I continued working with the BBC, not only on the *Let's Go!* programmes, but also on several other series both about and for people with a learning disability. I also worked on the BBC micro-electronics programme, ensuring that the needs of disabled people were fully included.

The school at Warren was a very valuable experience. Until then I had always worked in urban settings but most of the children at Warren came from rural backgrounds. Although the school was modern it was not well respected locally so the whole process of developing a curriculum which really met the children's needs, involved the families and raised the profile was a major challenge. With hindsight, many of the lessons I learned stood me in good stead for the later work at Mencap.

It was while I was at Warren that I become closely involved with local Mencap. Although I had had contact at the schools I had worked at in the past, my involvement at Warren was much deeper as I became the local society Secretary. I also represented Lowestoft Mencap on the County Group and attended Mencap meetings all over the country.

In parallel, following his success on *Let's Go!*, Brian Rix had become Secretary-General of the Royal Mencap Society, so he gradually drew me into the voluntary structure of the national organisation and I guess it was inevitable that in 1985 he finally persuaded me to accept the appointment of Director of Education and Employment at the Royal Mencap Society. This involved a move of home from rural Suffolk to nearer London and a countrywide role dealing with the Mencap Employment Services, the colleges and campaigning for improvements in education.

It was something of a blow when just three years later Brian retired as Secretary-General and, though I applied to replace him, a retired Vice-Admiral was preferred.

I think this was probably the most difficult period in my whole working life. The Vice-Admiral was not well equipped for an organisation like Mencap and despite strenuous and loyal efforts to support and advise him, the organisation was clearly declining quickly, not only financially but equally importantly in its work and reputation.

It was with a very heavy heart that by the end of 1990 I had decided that I had had enough and was about to leave to take up a post as the CEO of another charity. The morning of the National Council meeting in November 1990 was one of those never-to-be-forgotten occasions. I was aware of rumblings among the trustees (they often rumbled) but I did not realise that they were about to act, or that the Secretary-General was about to leave. When I was asked to take his place on a temporary basis that Saturday morning I was confronted with a major dilemma. I already had another offer which would certainly have been easier and probably safer. However, having been given assurances by the trustees of support and a real chance to be offered the job permanently if we succeeded in overcoming the immediate problems, my commitment to Mencap and people with a learning disability meant that I really had no choice but to go for it.

The few weeks at the end of 1990 and the first couple of months of 1991 were traumatic – it even snowed in early January just to make things harder.

I needed to act quickly; we had already had some representations from the Department of Health making their concerns about Mencap clear. The withdrawal of their financial support would have been critical and they called us to account for our husbandry one snowy January morning and only Brian Rix (then Sir Brian and the Chairman of the Society) plus newly recruited Roger Smythe managed to battle through the snowdrifts and persuade the Department to extend their support. It was glaringly obvious that the first priority was to stabilise the financial situation; the second, but just as urgent, was to clear out a weak senior management team while at the same time regenerating the confidence of our staff and members as well as our partners outside the organisation. Sacking colleagues whom I had worked with for several years was not an easy task.

However we were very lucky with a small number of committed and competent colleagues: Roger Smythe, who joined us as a temporary Finance Director; Jill Tombs, who had been appointed Director of Personnel about three weeks before the change; Lydia Sinclair, our Legal Director, who sadly died a few years later; and Brian McGinnis, whose wisdom was so invaluable, were key figures in head office. Around the country the Divisional General Managers like Martin Gallagher, Richard Capewell, Jean Taylor, Neville Short and Deven Pilay in England, Maureen Piggot in Northern Ireland, Rex Hewitt in Wales, all of whom had been so dissatisfied by the previous regime, were crucial in helping to dig us out of the biggest hole in Mencap's history. It is easy to take the credit for the success of the early nineties but it was very much a team effort with everybody making superhuman efforts, often despite the criticism of members and staff alike.

As I have already written, the first and most important task was stabilising the finances. Mencap had not managed the enormous growth in Homes Foundation very well and we were faced with a serious cash-flow problem. The basic issue was our seeming inability to collect the money due quickly enough to meet the obligations of a growing monthly salary bill. In the early months we simply concentrated on systems to ensure that invoices were sent out on time (or even a little early). However, it soon became clear that many of the contracts with local authorities and housing associations, which had been drawn up quickly, were inappropriate and often committed Mencap to billing three months in arrears. This was fine when Homes Foundation was small but impossible as we grew into the largest provider of housing services to people with a learning disability in the UK. The renegotiation of these contracts was a task that went on for several years, but most were satisfactorily settled in time.

Inevitably the changes at Mencap had seriously undermined the confidence of many of our partners and members. Above all the confidence of the members and trustees had been severely dented and it was high priority to reassure them that everything was under control and problems were being resolved. The value of Sir Brian Rix's trips around the country to local societies and member groups, together with significant trustees such as Roger Galletley, Barry Ockwell and Leslie Wooster was vital as part of this process, and I am delighted to say that the improvement over a few short months was dramatic.

It was not just the members whom we needed to convince that we were in control. Those who provided our funds at all levels were crucial. Government, both central and local, were top of the list, but major donors were equally important. After that snowbound meeting in January between Brian Rix, Roger Smythe and the Department of Health they continued to support us – with their fingers firmly crossed – but they insisted on a number of further meetings, for they were convinced that we were heading for bankruptcy and were anxious to cover their backs before it happened. Fortunately Roger Smythe as our temporary Finance Director was both effective and convincing. He has a background of trouble-shooting in the commercial sector and although his measures to make us efficient, effective and cut our costs did not make him the most popular person in Mencap, they did convince most of those with whom we dealt that they need not panic. Barrie Davis, the Treasurer at the time, spent several days each week working with Roger, despite the pressures of his own business. Looking back it's amazing just how much we achieved in the first six months of 1991 which set the stage for the period of the most rapid growth in Mencap's history.

In planning for the following three to five years in Mencap it was clear that we needed a great deal more money which was not tied to particular projects and gave us the opportunity to develop our general support services and advocacy work.

In the early 1990s the whole concept of advocacy in its various forms, particularly self-advocacy was becoming the underlying philosophy in working with people with a learning disability. This meant ensuring that we listened to what people with a learning disability themselves were saying, not only about controlling their own destiny, but equally ensuring that they had a part in developing and running Mencap. It's easy, fifteen years on, to see the wisdom of the self-advocacy approach but in the early nineties there was a great deal of opposition from those who believed that our role was to care for people rather than giving them the opportunity to develop and control their own lives. It has always been controversial in Mencap as to whether we should pitch our approach towards those with the most severe disability rather than recognising that many people are able to make decisions about many aspects of their lives, and somehow getting the balance of these two necessary approaches is always difficult.

In the early nineties there was a fundamental issue about the image of Mencap. There were those who believed that as the terminology was changing from the use of the term 'mental handicap' to 'learning disability' the name of the organisation should also change. I was very concerned that the experience of other organisations that had changed their name suggested that the drop in public recognition was always accompanied by a severe drop in income – something, that with all our other problems, we simply could not afford. For me and many of our trustees there was a very difficult balance, on one hand ensuring the stability of our services, our help for people with a learning disability and their families and, of course, the people we employed, and on the other hand not offending the very people we were working for. Overall the feeling was that nobody would thank us if we had to make serious cutbacks in our work for the sake of being politically correct.

In order to create a new image we did decide to modernise and update our logo and the style we presented to the world. The 'Little Stephen' logo had been around for many years and at least one of our significant senior members vowed that it would be changed 'over my dead body'. I felt very strongly that the pathetic Little Stephen image was not appropriate in an age where we were beginning to recognise that people with a learning disability were people like everyone else and not just the objects of charity. Mencap's role was to listen to those we worked with and work towards their full inclusion in our society, and we needed an image to portray this objective. I think the whole organisation is particularly grateful to Steve Billington, who by that time had become our Director of Communications, for his very clever idea of keeping a very similar style but replacing Little Stephen with a series of photographs of real people with learning disability. The intrinsic message said all the right things. It demonstrated a new modern approach; it suggested that we were about real people doing real things. The five images chosen portrayed people with a wide range of disability and ethnic background and the fact that the great photographer that Steve had found was Caroline Cook, Brian Rix's daughter-in-law, all added up to a new image that was right for the time, widely praised and mostly popular with the members.

Together with the new image there was an urgent need to raise more money, a lot more money. We had several initiatives underway which were proving very useful. Probably the most valuable was the affinity credit card which had been started a few years earlier with the Leeds Building Society, later taken over by Halifax. By the early nineties it was producing over £250,000 a year reliably and with very little effort or cost.

We were also extremely fortunate that John Major had become Prime Minister. Norma Major had been a long-standing supporter of Mencap in their Huntingdon constituency, and she was anxious to use her role as the Prime Minister's wife to benefit Mencap nationally. Our first event with the Majors was a dinner at No. 10, an event which not only raised a great deal of money, but also opened the door for one or two of us to talk to Mr Major about Brian having a seat in the House of Lords. We were all convinced that as a cross-bench politician he could have a great influence on the shaping of legislation for people with a learning disability. The rest is history. Brian became Lord Rix in 1992 and his influence on legislation to benefit people with a learning disability over the next fourteen years has been immense.

Dame Norma tells the tale of the incredible events which raised money at Chequers and Downing Street later in this book (Chapter 15), and it has already appeared in the Mencap sixty-year diary as well as being trailed by Brian Rix in the profiles of our Vice-Presidents. However, as I was greatly involved with the Challenge Fund when it came to fruition, I feel I must pay my tribute here, even at the risk of repetition. After the original event at No. 10, we were very fortunate to be able to hold four extremely lucrative and high-profile opera evenings and several lunches at Chequers, the official country home of the Prime Minister. This was the first time that Chequers had been used in this way and Mencap not only benefited from several million pounds of income which we used for the Challenge Fund, but also the people we met created contacts and links that we were able to turn into long-term support. Although Norma was the influence behind the events and opened the opportunities, much of the fundraising was undertaken by Pauline Harris (now Dame Pauline Harris) who worked so hard to persuade people to attend and contribute very large sums of money. Norma and Pauline's contribution to Mencap in those difficult recovery years cannot be overstated.

The Challenge Fund was created from the funds raised, particularly at the Chequers events. The idea of the Fund was to distribute the money to local groups all over the country who had been raising funds for their local projects but who inevitably found the second half of the money much more difficult to raise than the first. The Fund ran for nearly ten years and distributed more than £2.5 million. And when you realise that is only half the money raised – for the Chequers' trustees insisted, quite rightly, in another charity being involved at every event – you begin to understand what a staggeringly successful operation it was.

The fiftieth anniversary of the founding of Mencap in 1996 created a great opportunity for a major fundraising appeal. Along with the people we serve, the staff, members and our many partners, we finally decided to use the appeal to develop a new information service, together with a network of staff to deliver the service directly to the people with disability and the families who needed it. The target was to raise more than £10 million to develop the new Family Advisory Service (FAS) and the information database to back up this project.

We retained Marion Alford, who had led the phenomenal Great Ormond Street Wishing Well Appeal, to advise us on what we decided to call the Blue Sky Appeal. Following her guidance, we asked Sir George Bull, then the Chairman of Grand Metropolitan, to be Chairman of the Appeal and gather around him an influential committee which would be able to open doors to the support we needed to raise the £10 million. George was very ably supported by Brian Baldock as Vice-Chairman of the Appeal Committee. Little did Brian realise at the time that this would lead to his becoming much more involved in Mencap and eventually succeeding Brian Rix as the Chairman of the entire Society.

We also managed to recruit some of the best-known figures in business, advertising, promotion and technology to join the committee. Through these links we were able to approach donors and supporters from all sections of society and eventually, after a great deal of blood, sweat and tears we did manage to raise more than the target, though occasionally some creative accountancy helped to take account of some of the contributions which were in kind and not just simple cash.

For me, one of the most important aspects of the anniversary year was the conference celebration in Cardiff at the end of August. More than 2,000 people attended and we filled the massive Cardiff International Convention Centre. It was both celebrating fifty years and a launching pad to meet the challenges of the future. It was probably the first major Mencap event which was truly inclusive, with people with a learning disability, their families, as well as people with a professional interest, all equally involved in every aspect of the conference. It marked the official launch of the Blue Sky Appeal for the Family Advisory Service. We even broadcast the Sunday *Songs of Praise* television programme from the conference with a massive open-air gathering of people from all sections of Mencap in the grounds of Cardiff Castle. Inclusion International and Inclusion Europe held their annual gatherings in conjunction with the conference, so we had guests and representatives from the world of learning disability from all over the world. Credit has already been given elsewhere in this book to Alan Hill and Nikki Gavin for all the work they put in, ensuring this conference was a huge success, but I would like to add my tribute here.

The Family Advisers were gradually absorbed into the expanded general Advisory and District Officer services which Mencap provides all over the country. The information database has now become the extremely successful Ask Mencap advisory service which has been supported by the Government to provide the information needs envisaged by the *Valuing People* White Paper.

From the incredible conference in Cardiff and others which followed, it became clear that the structure of Mencap needed to change to become a truly inclusive organisation. The traditional structure, where the members of Mencap came from the 450 local societies who each nominated a member to speak and vote on their behalf, tended to preclude people with a learning disability from becoming involved. In many ways even more inequitable was the fact that the 550 Gateway clubs had very limited influence on the parent body.

After much deliberation it was agreed that we should look for a form of one member one vote, so that genuine inclusion would be backed up by real democracy. Predictably the organisation as a whole was not ready for such a radical move.

The original aim was to present the change at the AGM in 1997 but it was clear that at that time there would not be the necessary 75 per cent of votes likely to be cast in favour by the existing local society members. We decided to put the vote off for a further year, a year when we mounted an almost military operation to ensure that the issues were debated the length and breadth of Mencap. We identified a task force of staff in each region who had all the information they needed and who were charged with identifying supporters and opponents so that we could target appropriately. Lord Rix and Roger Galletley spent most of the year on the road addressing often hostile local gatherings to try to persuade them that it was not only right in principle that Mencap should have a formal process to ensure that the voice of people with a learning disability should be properly heard, but in the days when disability organisations were becoming led by people with disability themselves, the world of learning disability needed an organisation which was a genuine inclusive partnership between those with disability and those who supported them, both in the family and professionally.

At a specially convened EGM in October 1998 it was time for the vote. The tension would not have been out of place on television for, although we had proxy votes cast beforehand, many local societies sent representatives to vote, so the outcome was not known until the votes were counted. I must admit that I was uncertain and having staked so much on being Chief Executive of an inclusive organisation, I wondered if I would be looking for a new job on Monday.

In the event there was an 88 per cent vote in favour of the change, a highly appropriate decision as we entered the twenty-first century and a decision of which I am immensely proud as I genuinely believe that this change made Mencap the leading inclusive organisation for people with a learning disability anywhere in the world.

Implementing the change with the new governance system was not an easy task. Creating the membership system and encouraging the members who had been members of local societies and Gateway clubs was difficult, and even now not as successful as we would have hoped, although more than half the members are people with a learning disability. The first new National Assembly, with at least one-third of its members people with a learning disability, had to be voted in and, in turn, they had to elect the new trustees. Systems of working with the appropriate paperwork, the use of supporters for members with a learning disability, time out for consideration and even the best room format were all major challenges. I think everyone involved in those early National Assembly meetings would agree that that they were tough, and nobody was really satisfied with the outcomes. Many people, particularly Joe Steen who had been elected as Chair of the Council (a different role from the Chair of Trustees), had great vision, and were prepared to persevere, try new ideas and change when it was clear that things were wrong, resulting in a system that, although hardly perfect, worked well enough. Constant development and further change has meant that over five years the process has developed and is a real example of inclusive democracy in practice which is copied by people all over the world, even though it's still not perfect.

The 1990s were a time of massive growth and development in all aspects of the Royal Mencap Society. Not only was our underlying philosophy changing to become more inclusive for people with a learning disability, but we were also providing more services and more support that ever before. Indeed, between 1990 and 2003 the Royal Mencap Society grew by almost ten times its original size with expansion across almost every aspect of our work, though not the same level of growth in every area.

The development of our residential services was undoubtedly the largest and probably the most difficult. In 1990 it was the cash-flow problems in Homes Foundation that almost caused the downfall of the organisation. However, having sorted out the short-term problems, the stage was set for rapid development which eventually helped provide homes for over 5,000 people. By the end of the decade the demands were changing, and I am very proud of the way that we were able to respond to these changed demands. When Homes Foundation was established the focus was very much on the provision of community-based group homes. These were often established to provide an alternative to the traditional long-stay hospitals and the residents were moved from one place to another, often with little choice or option. By the end of the decade the success of the philosophy of independence was clear. Many of our residents wanted to move, often into a more independent setting and sometimes with a partner they had chosen rather than the house mates that had been selected for them. This put new strains on the system and demanded a different approach. Equally, families wanted to get involved in choosing the house and many were prepared to become financially involved. The answer was Golden Lane Housing, a very imaginative new approach which used joint ownership and in some cases gave the residents the chance to own a portion of their own property, just like everyone else in modern Britain. Clearly one of the greatest challenges for the future of modern Mencap is the ability to develop and change as demands change.

A particularly difficult area in residential development was the traditional children's homes that we had in Hampshire and Norfolk. In Norfolk we had a twenty-four-place home for people with profound and multiple disability. The original home was a fairly modern but unsuitable building, right on the North Sea beach. It had been provided by local subscription so the process of closing it and moving the residents, many of whom had lived there most of their lives, was difficult. The plan to buy an existing house and develop three other small units in the same village proved to be popular in the end so now we have a very happy community living in small family-sized accommodation.

The home in an old manor house in Hampshire has proved to be much more difficult but again plans are now well ahead and one of the sixtieth anniversary achievements should be modern and appropriate houses for the very severely disabled people and staff who have struggled in unsuitable accommodation for so long. The superb Dolphin Court opened, in fact, on 5 June 2006.

The colleges, Dilston, Pengwern and Lufton, also had to change significantly during the nineties. They had started life almost by accident with large old houses being given to Mencap by different routes during the sixties and seventies. Pengwern and Dilston had both started life as holiday centres, and Lufton was bought through a high-profile (though not very successful) fundraising appeal. They had gradually changed to being residential training centres working on similar philosophies to the original Slough Project, which emphasised the vocational training needs of young people with a learning disability.

By 1990 the right to continued education beyond the age of sixteen for people with a learning disability had been accepted and the colleges needed to become proper further education establishments, inspected and monitored by the Department of Education and Science rather than local social service authorities. This created a massive pressure for change. Most of our staff were not qualified teachers and we were not well geared to delivering the formal curriculum to meet national requirements. Staff changed, including some of our long-standing and loyal staff, who found the process very painful.

The proof and value is best judged by the excellent inspection reports which all three colleges have received in recent years. Demand for places is up and for the first time in twenty years there are waiting lists. The students themselves enjoy the courses, and there is no doubt that they are better prepared for adult life when they return home.

Our employment services also strengthened during the same period, though growth in this area was much slower and competition from other organisations greater. The Pathway Employment Service was ground-breaking when it was launched in the late seventies. The direct, on-the-job training and support which Mencap provided was undoubtedly the most successful way of helping people with a learning disability into the employment market, and is still recognised as the best method even today. It was so successful that it was frequently copied and other organisations sprang up using similar approaches. Some of these were specifically employment agencies and by the end of the nineties had overtaken Mencap as major providers. Employment remains hard to get for people with a learning disability, though it is a little easier today than twenty years ago. Mencap's employment services remain an important provider, but these days are only one player among many.

The philosophy of genuine inclusion which Mencap both responded to and led during the 1990s was widely endorsed among the forward-thinking families and professionals. It was almost thirty years since the publication of the *Better Services for the Mentally Handicapped* White Paper in 1971. The philosophy of care in the community which it contained was a major spur to the development of community-based services during the ensuing period, but it was clear by the mid nineties that thinking had moved on and a new direction from the Government was needed.

The team at the Department of Health was conscious of the climate which Mencap and many others had played a great part in creating. They were both inspired and brave in their recognition that any new direction would need to come from the very broad spectrum of interest in learning disability, which must include people with a learning disability themselves, so the consultation process was long and intensive. It wasn't universally applauded, as some parents and professionals felt it would be dominated by people with a mild degree of disability at the expense of those with more profound handicaps. To the credit of the planning team they did not waver from the ideal of making sure that all voices were heard and views taken account of, even though in the end not all opinions could be satisfied. I am very proud that Mencap at both national and local level was a major contributor to what is widely regarded as a world-leading document.

The *Valuing People* White Paper broke new ground in Government policy papers for people with a learning disability. It really took on board the 'nothing about us without us' philosophy which had been a key feature of the consultation. The resulting policy, which emphasised the concept of providing services for what people want rather than what someone else believes they need, is truly ground-breaking and has subsequently been copied all over the world. Included in this is the process of person-centred planning which means that the person with a learning disability should be at the heart of the process and, wherever possible, in control.

Inevitably the implementation has been a lot slower than the rhetoric and some frustration has crept in, both about the lack of resources available and the resistance of many professionals and families to new approaches. However, in terms of White Paper implementation it is still very early days; after all, it took nearly thirty years to feel the full value of the 1971 version.

For Mencap, one of the major challenges which had been bubbling for several years but which came to a head as a result of the internal changes and the White Paper concerned the name of the organisation. The name Mencap had clearly developed from the term 'mental handicap'. The term 'mental handicap' had been largely rejected and represented the attitudes of the past with the abuses of exclusion and separation. However, the Mencap brand had been well established over many years and the very strong advice from several professional brand image consultants was that we should not risk the change under any circumstances. The new National Assembly considered the issues several times over more than a year before coming to the conclusion that we should stick with the Mencap name. Market research suggested that the public saw the word Mencap as a word in its own right and the majority had no idea of its origin. It was agreed that we should modernise the logos and style and probably more importantly drop the long name (The Royal Society for Mentally Handicapped Children and Adults) in favour of a shorter title – The Royal Mencap Society. As Brian Rix has pointed out, there is now a new Mental Capacity Act in place so, for anyone still concerned, Mencap can be an acronym which salutes an Act which presumes all people have capacity, unless it is proved otherwise. It is interesting that the original proposal of Royal Mencap did not meet the approval of our Royal Patron, the Queen Mother, and 'The Royal Mencap Society' was, in fact, her suggestion. How could the National Assembly not agree?

By 2002 it was clear that the continued development and growth of Mencap meant that we had to consider further administrative changes. I had been through this disruption countless times, so I decided that after twelve years it was probably time to consider my retirement. I was also anxious to get back to direct work with learning disabled people rather than the administrative role as Chief Executive of an organisation now topping £150 million a year. The trustees were generous in their support, both for my desire to move on and to establish a new initiative aimed at taking learning disability issues into the twenty-first century. The process of identifying a new Chief Executive was started. I was very pleasantly surprised by the volume of applications for the job; it clearly showed how far we had come in the twelve years since I became CEO, for Mencap was now seen as one of the most prestigious jobs in the charity sector. After an exhaustive process, Jo Williams was identified and agreed to accept the post. I know that David Scott-Ralphs, who had been our very successful Director of Marketing and Communications, was extremely disappointed that he did not get the job but I fully understand that the combination of Jo's experience, dynamism and charm was unbeatable. I also think it was a good choice to have someone very different so that the organisation could move on and develop its identity to meet the needs of the early 2000s. I retired and Jo took over the reins at Easter in 2003. A major change and the end of an era for me.

The Rix Centre

I have been convinced for many years that modern computer technology has the potential to help people with a learning disability overcome some of their handicaps. I am equally convinced that unless we make sure that the technology is made accessible for people with a learning disability it will increase the barriers and potential exclusion.

Mencap had already developed some small projects at the University of East London, but when I retired there was a clear opportunity to make an impact on the exploitation of the technology for people with a learning disability and, at the same time, establish a centre in Brian Rix's name in recognition of his life-long contribution to people with a learning disability. Brian has been the very popular Chancellor of the University for more than nine years. The proposal that we should develop a research centre at UEL was greeted with great enthusiasm by the University governors and management team. The aim was to research the use of multimedia technology, to help develop accessible material and software, where necessary making sure that suitable hardware was available and, especially important, teach people to use it.

The Rix Centre was formally launched in April 2004 as both a charity to help raise the resources and a research centre to do the actual work.

Early developments have been the creation of a computer-based personal profile system which provides an extremely valuable platform for person-centred planning. This is linked to a repository of learning materials which helps to find ways to turn the person-centred plan into an action programme to make things happen.

This will provide the first 'branch' of what has become known as the Big Tree, an Internet portal which aims to make access to the five million or more references to learning disability and associated conditions quickly and easily accessible to all those who need them. The five million doesn't include all the important and associated pieces of knowledge so the aim of the Big Tree is to bridge the gap between the millions of sources of knowledge and those who need it, and the early 'branches' will focus on education and learning. By its nature the Big Tree has global value and appeal and simply by using the technology to share and use this vast reservoir of knowledge we can help improve the lives of millions of people all over the world.

I must pay tribute to the trustees of the Rix Centre, for they are already overburdened with work for people with a learning disability. They are chaired by a newcomer to the scene, Rudi Mueller CBE, who has turned out to be what is known in common parlance as a 'gem'. He is as adept at raising money for the trust as he is in chairing our deliberations. His fellow trustees are Brian Baldock CBE, the current Chairman of the Royal Mencap Society, John Alderson, who supervises all the accountancy matters, and Jonty Rix, Open University lecturer, son of Brian Rix and father of Robbie, who has Down's syndrome. Then there is Tony McClellan, just appointed, and he, like Jonty, is also the father of a son with Down's syndrome as well as being a businessman who will be of great help to the trust. I am both a trustee and Chief Executive of the charity, while Andy Minnion and his supporters at the University of East London do all the work at the coalface. I am very fortunate to have each and every one of them working to make the Rix Centre the success it deserves to be, for the hope and dream is that in the next ten years it will meet the needs of people with a learning disability, their families and those that work with them all over the world – an appropriate legacy to Brian's lifetime work.

Inclusion International

As already described, in the mid sixties, George Lee, the Secretary-General of Mencap, along with Tom Mutters, the Director of Lebenshilfe in Germany, worked together to start the International League of Societies for the Mentally Handicapped, a worldwide network of organisations like Mencap. They quickly joined with others from the United States, so that in a few years most of the Western European countries together with countries such as Canada and New Zealand had become involved. By the early nineties there were around 200 member organisations in 120 countries of the world.

Initially the four-yearly congresses were designed to build the network and share experience but gradually the organisation has also become involved with campaigning as part of the wider human rights movement. In 2000 the organisation changed its name to Inclusion International to reflect its campaign for the right of every person with a learning disability to be included as a respected part of the society in which they live. Inclusion International is now recognised by the UN and its constituent parts and has participant status in many an important global forum.

In 1988 the European members decided to create what has become known as Inclusion Europe. It has to be admitted that the prime motivation was to form partnerships for the growing European funding programmes. The early instigator and first President was none other than Tom Mutters, who was one of the original founders of the league over twenty years earlier.

Inclusion Europe has also grown and now has members across the continent in both west and east. It has a number of major successes including provision for people with disability in the terms of accession for new member states of the European Union. A recent valuable piece of work, which shows its status as one of the most respected Europe-wide NGOs, is the report on remaining institutions across the whole of the EU. The study was controversial and the recommendations very challenging, not only for the new member states from the east but for the larger countries of the west as well. Overall, Inclusion Europe's role in making sure that people are no longer shut away and hidden from society is crucial.

CHAPTER 6

Jo Williams CBE

Chief Executive 2003–

When Brian Rix asked me to contribute a chapter on everything Mencap wants to see change for people with a learning disability – and to do it in around 5,000 words – my immediate (private) reaction was mild panic. To sum up, in such a short space, the situation today and what we want to happen is a tall order indeed.

But this personal challenge is not unlike the one that Mencap faces: on the face of it very daunting, but not unachievable. And what is that challenge for Mencap? It is to fight for a world where people with a learning disability, their families and carers get equal rights and chances in life, and where they get the support they need to participate in society as full citizens. We do this in two ways. We campaign for change; that is, we say how things should be done, and we provide services in housing, education, employment and leisure and show by example how things should be done. In this chapter I want to concentrate on our campaigning agenda.

But first, I must pay tribute to Mencap's indefatigable president, Lord Rix. Quite simply, if it wasn't for him, Mencap wouldn't be the powerful force for change that it is today. I don't need to say more about this here, because this book – impressively compiled by Brian – provides a comprehensive account of how Mencap, in sixty years, has grown from a fledgling parents' support group to one of the UK's largest and most influential charities.

Brian also asked me to say something about myself and how I came to Mencap. Here is the potted CV. I joined Mencap as Chief Executive in March 2003. Prior to that I had worked for more than thirty years in social services departments, for the last ten years as a Director (five years each at Wigan Metropolitan Borough Council and Cheshire County Council). Rather than going into any more detail about my career history, I'd like to focus instead on two life experiences that helped shape my passionate belief that society must ensure the meaningful inclusion of all people with a learning disability.

So, the first experience: as a young, impressionable student at Keele University I visited one of the old 'subnormality' hospitals (I cringe now in recalling the terminology). The sheer inhumanity of the treatment of the 'patients' there left a strong mark on me. I remember distinctly thinking that no one, regardless of their disability, should be treated this way – as a lesser human being.

This belief endured throughout my career at social services, which brings me to my second formative experience. In the 1980s I managed disability services in south-east Cheshire. At the time, many of the large, long-stay hospitals described elsewhere in this book were being closed down, presenting us with the challenge of rehousing people with a wide range of support needs. I saw this as a wonderful opportunity to try something radically new: supporting people with a learning disability to live at the heart of their communities rather than being shut off from the real world. So we bought up a variety of local properties, each to house a handful of people. We appointed community workers to set up and run these new-style 'supported living' schemes. Crucially, we also recruited volunteers to spend time supporting people to get out and about and do normal everyday things in the community – like shopping or going to the cinema. The project was a huge success and was replicated elsewhere. My most vivid memory from this time was when a group of people who could not speak showed their delight at their new-found independence by waving their house keys at me!

For me, this was confirmation of my belief that the more control we can give people with a learning disability over their own lives, the greater quality of life they experience. And this belief lies behind Mencap's *raison d'être*: to ensure that people with a learning disability (no matter how severe that disability) get the support they need to play an active and equal part in society. So, how far off this goal are we as a society? What are the particular challenges ahead? And what would Mencap like to see happen? These are the questions I want to address now.

Let's start by taking a look at the bigger picture, at what rights people have and what the Government is doing to champion them. The first thing to recognise here is how much things have changed since Mencap was founded, and this is shown in detail in Brian's excellent history of Mencap. The most notable highlights in this are: the 1970 Education (Handicapped Children) Act (which deemed that no child should be considered 'ineducable'), the 1990 NHS and Community Care Act, the 1995 Disability Discrimination Act and the 2001 *Valuing People* White Paper on the future of learning disability services.

Bringing this up to date, there has been a raft of public policies and strategies recently that also promise to have a big impact on the lives of people with a learning disability, their families and carers. These include: the Prime Minister's Strategy Unit's report *Improving the Life Chances of Disabled People* (which sets the year 2025 as a target for all disabled people to have equality in society), the Department of Health's White Paper on adult health and social care, *Our Health, Our Care, Our Say*, and the Disability Rights Commission's *Shaping the Future of Equality*. Also, as from December 2006, the Disability Discrimination Act will include a duty on all public bodies in England and Wales to promote equality for disabled people.

This book is not the place for a detailed analysis and critique of these far-ranging proposals and strategies. What I can say is that Mencap welcomes this package of measures, in principle, as a means of ensuring that people with a learning disability get the support they need to live as equal citizens. It shows that there has been a much-needed paradigm shift in social policy away from the old welfare model of getting support if you can't do things to supporting people to do things for themselves.

But there's a big difference between policy and action and we still have some major concerns about things actually getting done. Most significantly, it often seems that people with a learning disability get forgotten about among the wider disability population. The Government also still seems to have a silo mentality towards providing services, with a lack of joined-up thinking and effective read-across between its various departments and strategies. The challenge here is to find innovative ways to use resources to meet needs, pooling them where necessary. We'd also like to see much more evidence of how the Government is going to involve people with a learning disability in planning and testing services. And Parliament should spend much more time scrutinising progress made in the aftermath of legislation and policy directives.

I don't mean to be overly critical; the direction of travel is good. But the bottom line is that policies alone don't change anything. In fact, the biggest single thing that needs to happen in order for people with a learning disability to have equality is a marked shift in attitudes across the board, all the way down from Government to the man on the street. In practice this means people with a learning disability need to be much more visible in our communities and the media so that there is a common understanding about what learning disability really is. Everything should stem from this shared understanding. The Government can't, of course, achieve this single-handedly, but it can certainly take a lead.

So societal attitudes are the key factor in the reality of life for the 1.5 million people with a learning disability in the UK. At the top end, they affect policy, and at the bottom end, they affect people's everyday experiences. So let's now look in more detail – across a range of loose topic headings – at what these experiences are and the challenges they present to both the Government and Mencap.

Where better to start than the beginning of life – children and their families. I wish I could say that there have been dramatic improvements over the years in the support they get. And while there have been some positive changes, many families still tell us that they have to fight for everything, that they don't get the services they need automatically and that they find other people's attitudes towards them when they are out and about offensive and unhelpful. These attitudes even sometimes extend to the friends and relatives of families with children with a learning disability. It's as if the families have to live in a totally separate world, outside the networks of support that exist for other families. The fact that you have a child with a learning disability can effectively define your whole family unit as different and 'to be avoided'. As one mother put it: 'I come from a family of immigrants, but never have I experienced such discrimination'.

It's something of a paradox. At Mencap we will keep raising the needs and rights of children as an 'issue' that the Government must have on its social agenda; yet ultimately our aim is to show that, as long as the right support services are in place, having a child with a learning disability doesn't really have to be such an 'issue' (as in a 'problem') at all. And if this was the case – if there was widespread acceptance and inclusion of children with a learning disability and their families in every section of society as a given – everything else would fall into place. Parents wouldn't have to worry that their child's long-term future is secure (an anxiety that often transfers to the children themselves as they pick up snatches of fraught conversations about what school they'll be going to, whether their transition plan is in place or whether the local authority will pay for this or that service). Indeed, mainstream schools would have the facilities and staff training in place to include children with a learning disability in a meaningful way (making the whole mainstream versus special school debate redundant). Children with a learning disability would be able to form lasting friendships with their non-disabled peers, rather than spending the majority of their time with their parents and this would be major step in bringing to an end the appalling bullying that many children with a learning disability still face on a daily basis.

So what can we do about all this at Mencap? Well, we can't change things on our own. But we can harangue, influence, persuade and provide useful information. It's all about keeping up the pressure on the Government and our public institutions to ensure that their laudable aims for meeting the needs of children generally (and disabled children specifically) – as set out in legislation and policy – really do include children with a learning disability. We want them to recognise that services that meet children's and families' needs are not a luxury that parents should have to be grateful for but their right.

Perhaps the most disadvantaged group of people in society, however, are those with profound and multiple learning disabilities. It goes against the grain to lump anyone into a group – at Mencap we like to think about people as individuals. But there is a good reason, in this case, to think of a group, as sometimes that's the only way to get their needs recognised. What people in this group have in common is their need for extensive support, often round-the-clock care. This also means we have to think about the needs of the people who care for them, usually parents or family members, for whom caring can be a full-time job – unpaid, of course. And the reality is that this group, who are in the greatest need, often get the least support from the authorities. At Mencap we hear of case after case of a shocking lack of services, as documented in two recent hard-hitting reports, *No Ordinary Life* and *Breaking Point*. Some of these stories beggar belief.

Part of the reason for this situation can be traced back to a shift in service provision for people with complex needs. Traditionally, where it was provided it came from the NHS, but ever since the long-stay hospitals started to shut down (a good thing in itself) local social services have had to step in. As a result there is something of a postcode lottery for services, and in some areas people with profound and multiple learning disabilities end up in totally inappropriate places, like psychiatric assessment units. Meanwhile, the families who do manage to get some services still face so many barriers to 'normal' life on a daily basis – unable to use public transport, or to find a public toilet anywhere that has the special facilities they need (a changing bench and lifting hoist).

In short, Government and local authorities tend to despair when trying to plan for the needs of this group. But if they really want to ensure that everyone with a learning disability is able to participate in society they will have to be much more imaginative and innovative in how they support people with profound and multiple learning disabilities. At Mencap, this is exactly what we have been exploring in the past few years. The key phrase here is 'meaningful representation': finding ways to meet, on their own terms, people who can't speak or use other conventional forms of communication. Recently we have run a pilot scheme in multimedia profiling, which uses a range of technologies, including videos and cameras, to build up a picture of a person, their likes and dislikes, their choices and preferences.

Ultimately, it all comes down to rights and values. And what I find so extraordinary in this day and age is that when it comes to people with profound and multiple learning disabilities not only do we have to argue for the support and investment that will ensure their dignity and quality of life, we actually have to argue for the right to life itself. Recent high-profile cases, like baby Charlotte Wyatt, have brought this home all too clearly. That's why I'm absolutely committed to ensuring that Mencap continues to champion the rights of people with profound and multiple learning disabilities very publicly and very vociferously.

In some ways it's much easier for us to champion the rights of people with milder learning disabilities. That's because the changes we are arguing for are, on the face of it, more achievable and in line with the Government's social welfare agenda, particularly when it comes to employment.

Currently people with a learning disability are the most excluded group of people in the workforce – only one in ten has a job (of people with a learning disability known to social services), compared to five in ten for disabled people generally. The reason for this is a fundamental misconception among employers and Government that people with a learning disability can't work, which itself stems from ignorance about what learning disability actually is. Many people who do work are exploited, doing mundane jobs for as little as £1 an hour in so-called work preparation schemes. Government programmes are often highly inflexible to the needs of people with a learning disability. For example, people have to work sixteen hours or more to access funding support under its Workstep programme. Yet many people with a learning disability find the progression towards sixteen hours much harder than those with other disabilities. We want the Government to find ways for people to get into the world of work – and off benefits – without having to work sixteen hours straightaway.

Recent proposed reforms to incapacity benefit and welfare provision are certainly a step in the right direction, recognising that many disabled people want to and can work. But we are concerned that there just isn't the right support in place to make this happen for people with a learning disability. Indeed, with the rollout of its Pathways to Work programme the Government appears to be mainly concerned with people whose health conditions can be 'managed' or 'cured', which totally misses the point as far as people with a learning disability are concerned. There is a real danger that all people with a learning disability will be considered too disabled or sick to work and just left to rot.

We know from our own experiences running our Pathway Employment Service that it doesn't have to be like this. People with a learning disability just need a bit more support getting a job and then learning how to do it, but once they're in it, they do it as well as anyone else, and on average stay in it three times longer than other people. Encouragingly, the private sector is beginning to understand that this isn't about charity but business, pure and simple. We've demonstrated this clearly through our WorkRight programme, a best practice model for the kind of workplace changes employers need to make to help progress people's careers. It aims to get 500 people with a learning disability into work by 2008. We're now extending the programme to local authorities, potentially opening up thousands of jobs. And, to be fair to the Government, it appears our message is getting through: the *Valuing People* Support Team recently published a set of guides for employers and employees about changes that can be made in the workplace.

As ever, the biggest potential stumbling block to rapid progress is a lack of funding. This affects our own education employment and services. For example, we run three residential colleges teaching young people with a learning disability aged sixteen to twenty-five the essential skills for a successful transition to adult life. Most of the students' accommodation costs are paid for by the Learning and Skills Council (LSC). But it's likely that the LSC will soon expect funding to come from elsewhere, meaning Mencap may need to partner with other organisations. Limited funding streams are also putting a squeeze on our Pathway Employment Service. The Department of Work and

Pensions is downsizing, which means funding for JobCentre Plus is becoming more competitive and schemes like Access to Work are in a state of flux. Notwithstanding these concerns, we are still extremely hopeful that the employment revolution we dream of for people with a learning disability really can happen. But we may have to be patient.

Things look much less positive, however, when it comes to housing and community care. I should, perhaps, have dealt with this topic earlier, because the place where we live is the base from which we build our lives, and this applies to people with a learning disability as much as anyone else. Thankfully, most of the long-stay hospitals have now been closed down. When this process started in the 1980s, people began to move into residential care homes, ordinary houses in the community. This was a huge step forward at the time. Things have moved on now. There has been a welcome trend away from services provided by the NHS towards services provided by or purchased by local authorities. And there is growing recognition that a group of people with a learning disability don't necessarily all need the same kind of support. Different people want different things and everyone wants to be able to choose how to lead their life – hence the move towards supported living schemes, like those pioneered by my social services team in Cheshire in the eighties. Schemes like this are on the increase, and organisations like Mencap – and our sister charity, Golden Lane Housing – are leading the way in providing them.

But it's all too easy to gloss over the fact that still today the vast majority of people with a learning disability don't benefit from the freedoms and opportunities that supported living can deliver. There are an estimated 40,000 people with a learning disability living in residential care homes and a variety of NHS campuses and units, some of which, alarmingly, still hark back to the old-fashioned institutions.

An even bigger concern is the fact that around 50–60 per cent of adults with a learning disability still live in the family home. Almost 30,000 of these are cared for by a parent over the age of seventy. Local authorities simply don't view them as a high enough priority for housing. Their view tends to be: 'If someone has a roof over their head, then what is the problem?' Indeed, the whole system of assessment for 'community care' is cumbersome and restrictive, and tends to be used as a rationing device. We want to see a much simpler assessment system, based on entitlement, giving people the right to live where they want with the support that allows them to have the greatest possible independence and control over their lives.

It all boils down to attitudes: people with a learning disability just aren't seen as worth investing in. The absurdity of this is that local authorities would save themselves a lot of money in the long run if they planned ahead for people's housing needs, as they would avoid crisis situations requiring expensive solutions. The thrust of Government thinking on this issue does finally seem to be changing now, albeit slowly, but the jury is still out on whether it will deliver what it promises.

We're much more hopeful that we'll see the changes we want on our campaigning agenda for health. Our 2004 *Treat me right!* report highlighted the poor quality healthcare services people with a learning disability often get. People with a learning disability have poorer health than the rest of the population. Though in some cases this is due to medical conditions (e.g. chest problems or epilepsy) that can be linked to the person's disability, it's also due to people's lifestyles and circumstances (e.g. whether they have a job and are active in society, their diet, etc.). And this gives us a clue as to the real root of the problem: ignorance and prejudice. The majority of medical professionals simply don't understand learning disability because they haven't had the right training. In many cases, they attribute people's presenting conditions and symptoms to the learning disability. In short, professionals often take the approach that people with a learning disability don't warrant the same attention as other people and, in the worst cases, this attitude can lead to premature, unnecessary death.

Our *Treat me right!* report was a big wake-up call to the Government and we're pleased that it has agreed to carry out a feasibility study into a confidential inquiry into premature deaths. But it's now vital that this is backed up by a range of other measures and Mencap can play a big role in making these happen. We want healthcare staff to have better training about learning disability. People with a learning disability themselves can provide this training, working alongside medical students. We can contribute to this process through our links with consultation forums, like the GMC's Patient and Public Reference Group.

It's also about strengthening the patient's voice, which is a welcome trend currently in the health service, away from paternalism and towards more shared responsibility. Mencap can give a lead on this, thanks to our expertise in developing communication tools that allow people who cannot speak to express themselves. Linked to this, we also want to see more accessible information and advice about health in surgeries and hospitals. And we want annual health checks to be offered to everyone with a learning disability. On this point, it will be interesting to see how the Government's proposals for regular health MOTs for all UK citizens will be applied to people with a disability in general.

Behind everything on our wishlist lies one fundamental need: for medical professionals, families and carers to have much higher expectations for the health and well-being of people with a learning disability. We are, in fact, optimistic that the Government's strategy, as set out in its proposals for adult health and social care, is heading in the right direction. Mencap is now ideally placed to be a key partner in putting this strategy into practice.

Thanks to our network of local groups, Mencap is also in a good position to lead the way in developing advocacy services. Advocacy is a relatively new concept, having sprung out of the rapid rise of the disability rights movement. In a nutshell, it's about supporting people to express their feelings and choices and to have a greater say in running their own lives. Some advocacy services empower people to speak up for themselves; others act as mediators for people who cannot use language. But the key common factor that all successful services must share is total independence. In other words, the aim of the service must be to allow people's views to be known, without these views being adulterated or interpreted in any way.

Because of this crucial need for independence, some people question whether Mencap – as a provider of other services, particularly residential care – should really be running advocacy projects at all. We are at risk, the argument runs, of running into a conflict of interests. This is a valid concern, but it doesn't mean Mencap should avoid getting involved altogether. There is, undoubtedly, a massive need for advocacy services across the country. And truth be told, the Government has not yet developed a robust strategy for delivering or funding them. In light of this urgent need, Mencap has a real contribution to make to the advocacy movement: we can pass on to others what we have learnt in the recent past from running many successful projects. That's why we want to support organisations and groups in setting up a range of advocacy services across the country. Once we have helped them get up and running, we can let them be fully independent.

We shouldn't underestimate the huge difference that effective advocacy can make to the lives of people with a learning disability. But there are some major challenges ahead. In particular, advocacy services must be integrated into mainstream provision so that a much higher proportion of people with a learning disability can access them. There is also a huge need for both paid staff and volunteers who are prepared to commit to being advocates on a medium- to long-term basis – particularly for people with profound and multiple learning disabilities. In this case, effective advocacy relies on innovative approaches such as 'intensive interactive training', where the advocate spends a great deal of time with the person, earning their trust and getting to understand them through a range of techniques, such as mirroring their behaviour. This kind of intensive advocacy support requires significant investment, and it remains to be seen where this might come from.

Lack of funding has been a common theme throughout this overview of the main issues facing people with a learning disability and their families and carers. This funding problem is a result of the poor attitudes generally held towards people with a learning disability. And these poor attitudes are the strongest unifying factor in all the main obstacles identified here to people with a learning disability having equal rights and chances in society. If people with a learning disability were truly valued – as having just as much to offer as anyone else – then we wouldn't have to keep fighting for the right services and support. It's as simple as that.

In this sense, Mencap's campaigning message is very straightforward: we want people with a learning disability to be properly valued. But we're not complacent about the challenges that lie ahead for us as an organisation.

One of the main challenges will be how we can work best with our network of local groups and members. We mustn't forget, after all, that the national organisation grew out of local activism.

We currently have more than 13,000 members, including people with a learning disability, their families and other supporters. It's important that we get a good balance between each of these groups, both locally, through our groups and district committees, and nationally, at the National Assembly (which is like Mencap's parliament). Since the last major change to our constitution in 1998, at least one-third of its members must be people with a learning disability.

Today, in fact, half the elected positions at both national and district level are filled by people with a learning disability, which has been an important change in ensuring that people with a learning disability are at the heart of Mencap's work. But we must allow the voices of families to be heard as well – and we are particularly keen now to draw in more parents and engage them in our work. It's also vital that everyone elected to our district committees and National Assembly gets the support they need to fulfil their role. This is about effective, meaningful represent-ation. It should apply throughout Mencap – to our campaigning, and to the services we provide.

As for our 700 or so local groups, our challenge is to continue to develop strong partnerships with them, sharing knowledge and expertise in how we campaign and provide services. This is very much a two-way process. So, we must work in a coordinated way, with each partner's roles and responsibilities clearly defined and agreed. In some cases we will encourage smaller groups to join together in partnership, allowing for very localised activity to continue but supported by a stronger infrastructure. The key driver here is the need for flexibility: Mencap is a big organisation, but we have to be able to adapt to the varying needs of people in different parts of the country. It's for this reason that we recently changed the way we provide community support in England, setting up teams in each region to focus on key areas, such as children, people with profound and multiple learning disabilities and family carers. We also aim to strengthen our local networks of arts, leisure and sports projects, which have traditionally been provided by Gateway.

There are some other tough challenges for us in the future. We want to embrace new technologies that can support people with a learning disability in a variety of ways. We must ensure that we support families and carers as effectively as we support people with a learning disability themselves. This is so important because of the interdependence that exists for many families, particularly those where the parent-carers are in old age. And, as the public debate continues about what role the voluntary sector will play in future welfare provision, we're going to have to make some difficult decisions about the extent to which we get involved in running services ourselves or in partnership with other like-minded organisations.

Some tough challenges indeed. But I'm confident that we will rise to them, with the same determination that has enabled us – in the past sixty years – to bring about major change for learning disabled people. We won't rest until we see the further radical changes we want. We are at the beginning of a long and exciting journey. I can't predict when we will reach its end. But I can promise that I will bring all my drive and energy in leading Mencap in the right direction.

Acknowledgements

I'd like to thank the following colleagues who helped me put this chapter together:
- Angus Baldwin, [former] Parliamentary Officer
- Susan Boddy, National Employment Officer
- Val Brittin, Head of Community Development
- Lesley Campbell, National Children's Officer
- David Congdon, Head of Campaigns and Policy
- Beverley Dawkins, National Officer for Profound and Multiple Learning Disabilities
- Theresa Gorczynska, [former] Information and Research Officer, Profound and Multiple Learning Disabilities
- Carol Herrity, Campaigns Manager
- Alison Sargent, Director, Education and Employment Business Unit
- Tim Segaller, [former] Campaigns Officer
- Alison Shea, Assistant Director, Housing and Support Business Unit
- Neville Short, Director, Community Support
- Jan Tregelles, Director, Housing and Support Business Unit
- Matty van Rooden, Membership Secretary

I am fortunate to be surrounded by professionals with exceptional knowledge and expertise.

PART III

*People with a Learning Disability
Speaking up for Themselves*

CHAPTER 7

Nothing About Us Without Us

In the past few decades many people with a learning disability have been given the opportunity – denied them in years gone by – to speak up for themselves and tell their own stories. Part III of this book is devoted to that theme and that's why the title of this first chapter is 'nothing about us without us', which has become something of a catchphrase in the disability world. The phrase encapsulates a vital trend in the recent history of people with a learning disability, recognising that the best way to support people is by giving them as much of a say as possible in determining their own lives. In a sense, this is the lesson that the history of people with a learning disability teaches us.

In this section of the book we'll hear from people with a learning disability connected to Mencap in a variety of ways, as well as a couple of abridged articles, already published, by Lloyd Page (a member of the National Union of Journalists) and Paul Annear, telling his very personal story about love and marriage. Gus Garside finishes Part III by recording the achievements and ambitions of a selection of artists with a learning disability. But first, it's worth tracing the origins of this welcome trend towards allowing people to use their own words to describe their histories, thoughts and feelings.

It all started with Joey Deacon. His is quite a remarkable story.

Throughout his life many people assumed Joey to be 'mentally subnormal' (to use the terminology of the time). But Joey was intelligent, something he was able to prove conclusively when, with the help of friends at the long-stay hospital where he lived, he wrote his own life story, *Tongue Tied*. The book, published by Mencap in 1974, has had a massive impact on the public's understanding of learning disability in particular, and of disability in general.

Joey Deacon has, in fact, become something of a legend. A Google search on his name throws up a huge amount of material celebrating his life and his book. However, it's almost impossible to find any direct quotes from that book. And in the spirit of this section of Mencap's history – which is about allowing people with a learning disability to speak for themselves – we must allow Joey's own words to come through. So the following account of his extraordinary story will include some direct quotes from *Tongue Tied*.

'May the twenty-fourth, nineteen-twenty . . . Camberwell. This is where my life began.' Joey was born with cerebral palsy, caused by an accident: '. . . my Mum fell down the stairs before I was born'. This left him with problems with his arms and legs. 'When I was about four years old my life in hospital started . . . they operated on the backs of my legs. The operation wasn't successful.' Joey used a wheelchair for most of his life.

Joey couldn't speak: 'I used to go to school . . . They turned me down because of my nerves. I could not talk.' But his mother was convinced that he was intelligent, and she could prove it. '. . . every morning my Mum used to put me outside the front door. She used to ask me how many motors had passed and I used to answer by blinking my eyes . . . once for every motor that passed. My Mum understood this.'

After Joey's mother died of tuberculosis when he was six, he lived with his grandmother. Two years later, after more operations, he was admitted to Caterham Mental Hospital, later known as St Lawrence's Hospital, where he lived for the rest of his life.

In hospital Joey was again able to prove his intelligence: 'I was asked the difference between triangle, oval shape and round ring. I pointed [at] the figures with my nose and I got them all right . . . The doctor told [my Dad] I was a very intelligent boy.' But Joey often found it frustrating that he couldn't make himself understood: 'It was a battle when I tried to say something . . . All I wanted to do was talk. I used to think to myself a day will come when I will be able to talk.'

Joey suffered this frustration for many years. Then, in 1941, a newly admitted patient, Ernie Roberts (who also had cerebral palsy) was able to 'interpret' the sounds Joey was making: 'When I wanted something or to tell him something I made some noises to make him understand. It was not easy at first but Ernie did not give in. He tried very hard until he began to understand me.' A few simple tests proved to the hospital staff Ernie's ability to understand Joey.

This discovery was a key moment in Joey's life: 'That's how it all began. This was the first time I started to talk a little . . . Ernie was very good.'

However, it was many years before Joey would get round to telling his life story. In 1958, the seed of thought was planted in his head, when a nurse told Joey about another patient with cerebral palsy who had written a book using his toes to hold his pen. He suggested to Joey that he might want to do something similar. Then, one day twelve years later, Joey told his friend Ernie he wanted to write his story.

What then happened was an extraordinary, painstaking process of collaboration between Joey, Ernie and two other patients they had become close friends with, Tom Blackburn and Michael Sangster.

Ernie 'translated' Joey's sounds and Michael wrote the words down in longhand. Once Michael had done this and the script had been proof-read by hospital staff, Joey read the corrections back – letter by letter – and as Ernie 'translated' again, Tom typed them out. Tom couldn't read or write, but he'd taught himself to use a typewriter, using one finger of each hand. It took the team of four a whole day to get three lines typed. The resulting forty-four-page book took them a year and a half to complete.

Little could Joey and his friends have known at the time quite what an impact their work would have, and in many different ways.

First of all, it had a big impact on Joey, Ernie, Michael and Tom themselves. Impressed by the collaborative dedication of the four-man team, readers across the world raved about *Tongue Tied*. The book sold extremely well and was translated into French, Dutch, Swedish, Italian and Japanese. With the book royalties and other donations, Joey and his three friends were able to move to a bungalow in the Caterham hospital grounds in 1979, allowing them much greater independence. They also had holidays in France, Switzerland and Holland. Joey had often said that two of his greatest ambitions in life were to travel and to move from hospital into a proper home. He had achieved both ambitions.

Joey's story did, however, have one particular negative impact on people with a learning disability, though perhaps only in the short term. In 1981, the International Year of Disabled People, Joey became the focus of a fundraising appeal on BBC's *Blue Peter*. He was presented, quite rightly, as an example of a man who had achieved much in spite of his disabilities. But young viewers learnt to imitate Joey's distinctive sounds and movements and his name quickly became a label of ridicule in school playgrounds across the country. This was, undeniably, very regrettable. But it can be seen as unfortunate collateral damage in the context of something much more important: the public exposure of the reality of life for many people with a learning disability still living in old-fashioned institutions.

This brings us to the most important impact of Joey's story. And for this, we can learn a lot from the opinions of the staff of St Lawrence's at the time of the book's publication. In his introduction to *Tongue Tied*, consultant psychiatrist Geoffrey Harris recognised that: 'It should . . . help us to appreciate that those who live in such institutions have a point of view of their own . . . feelings and aspirations which not only do they have the right to express but have very often the capability of so doing if they have a fair chance.'

For the mid 1970s, this was an extremely progressive, even revolutionary, approach to people with a learning disability. Indeed, Geoffrey Harris goes on to consider what Joey's achievement should mean for learning disability services in general: 'The day must surely come when we do listen to what is said by those who depend on us . . . for care; when we take them into our planning and even our conferences, since it is for them and their needs.'

Geoffrey Harris's comments are prophetic. They point to the way to today's widely held view that it's only by listening to what people with a learning disability have to say that we can give them the most effective support. In this sense, the publication of *Tongue Tied* paved the way for the whole advocacy and self-advocacy movement that is so flourishing today. The stories and comments from people with a learning disability in the following two chapters are testament to this. They are part of a tradition – of people with a learning disability telling their own stories – that has its roots in *Tongue Tied*. People with a learning disability who are able to speak up for themselves and their rights today owe a great deal to Joey Deacon.

The last words in this introduction should go to Joey himself. He, too, recognised the debt he owed to others in enabling him to tell his own story. And this is the thought with which he ends: 'In this book my friend Ernie has taken the words out of my mouth, and with the help of Tom and Michael and some of the staff put them on paper. This is the end of my autobiography. I am very grateful to all the people who helped to make it possible.'

CHAPTER 8

Me, Myself and Mencap

Compiled by Tim Segaller

*Without the help and support offered by Mencap
I just wouldn't have had the opportunity to be involved.*
Paddy, a Mencap volunteer

T his chapter belongs to people with a learning disability. It is about the part Mencap has played in their lives, how they have got involved in Mencap's work, and how these experiences have shaped their views on the future for people with a learning disability – all in their own words.

The selection of people quoted represents a fairly wide cross-section of the people who are supported by, and involved in, Mencap's work. But it is worth noting a necessary omission: people with more severe learning disabilities who do not use language. This is not to say that they cannot communicate their views and feelings, and Mencap is leading the way in developing technologies that enable people without language to do this. But this was beyond the scope of that chapter.

Mencap is, of course, here to support not only people with a learning disability themselves, but also the people around them – families, friends and professionals. We must always remember the huge part that they play in the lives of people with a learning disability. And we hear from many of them elsewhere in this book.

In what follows, we will hear the voices of people who have been involved with Mencap for many years, and those who have only recently made contact with us. We'll come across a variety of people supported by Mencap's services in housing, education and employment, leisure and the arts, and advocacy. And we'll meet people who are closely involved with Mencap's work today, either as the 'public faces' of Mencap, or working at Mencap's National Centre in London.

First, let's hear from two people whose involvement with Mencap stretches back many years: Di Lofthouse and Mabel Cooper. Di talks about her work for Mencap and other learning disability organisations. And Mabel gives her views frankly about the future for people with a learning disability and Mencap.

Di Lofthouse Di came across Mencap when, aged twelve, she started to go to a Gateway club in Ripon. Here she had her first opportunity to speak out for herself. Ever since, Di has been a passionate advocate for the rights of people with a learning disability.

Lots of the Ripon Gateway members wanted to do something different from our usual day trips. And so the Gateway leader asked if we wanted to have a committee members' meeting. I became the chair. This is how it all started. I found these meetings good fun – at long last people were listening to what I was saying.

Then I joined Harrogate Gateway and got voted on to the members' committee. Very soon I got to be chair of this club as well. Then we got a regional members' forum going – we wrote to all the committees for other clubs in the area asking if they wanted to join us.

We ran a workshop to show the people down in London how to run regional forums. From this came the idea to start a national forum . . . I thought this was a great idea. Then someone suggested I should put myself forward to go on to Mencap's [then] National Council. Nobody with a learning disability had been on this before. The first time I was asked to go as an observer, but they told me not to say anything. This was really frustrating because I was bursting to say things. After this first meeting they said next time I could speak.

At the first meeting one of the big issues was whether we should close down one of Mencap's national colleges. The argument being put forward was that Mencap is a big business and has to make tough decisions sometimes. I said that they shouldn't and that Mencap is also a charity as well as a business. I think I helped persuade some people to agree with me.

When I first joined the National Council there were some people who weren't very nice to me and thought I shouldn't be there. One woman wrote to me and said that 'people with a learning disability are just that – people with a learning disability'. But there was someone there who looked after me and talked through everything before and after the meetings. Lord Rix was also very good to me. At the end of a Mencap conference one year, he asked me to speak up about myself and my work. So, for the next three or four years, I helped run workshops at the conference that gave people with a learning disability the chance to speak out.

I went to Brussels to speak about disabled women being abused and I spoke about my own experiences which I found really helpful. A lot of the women came up and told me that they had similar experiences and they were so glad that they had a chance to speak about it with other people who understood.

I also went to the World Congress in Amsterdam. This was the first time that people with a learning disability had a right to vote on world issues. I also spoke at Inclusion International and ran a workshop on my own about people with dual diagnosis (learning disability and mental health problems). I was asked to speak at the closing ceremony because I'd done so well!

It's not just about speaking up for myself, but also for others who find it a lot harder. A lot more people are now speaking up for themselves than before and this makes me feel very good and proud of myself. Speaking up for myself has actually given me a life.

There are more people today who care about people with a learning disability and understand more. It's easier to speak up than it used to be, to say what you do and don't want. But people's attitudes generally haven't changed that much – the people you come across in everyday situations. That's why it's so important that people get better education at school about things like discrimination and bullying.

Mabel Cooper We've already heard from Mabel in the prologue to this book: she told us about life inside one of the old institutions that housed many people with a learning disability. Here Mabel talks about her experiences as an advocate, and speaks openly about the direction she thinks Mencap should take.

I've done a lot of advocacy. I've gone into schools to speak to children and explain how bad it is to bully people who are different in some way. I started up a People First group in Croydon. Now I go to a consultative group [affiliated to Mencap]. We discuss what we've all been up to and any problems we've got and try and help each other out.

I think Mencap still has a lot of work to do to make sure it is representing people with a learning disability and not just their families and carers. In particular, it should focus on people with a learning disability who don't have a family. The only way to do this is by employing more people with a learning disability.

I've not had much of a family life. I only really saw my Auntie in Bedford and she's passed away now. Friends are more to me than families. Because of my life experiences, I think that it doesn't matter how severely disabled someone is, they should never be put into an institution. If someone decides to have a baby after the age of thirty and the child is disabled as a result they should be made to look after their child. But they should have the support they need. If they can't cope, they should put the child up for adoption.

When I first came out of the institution, Mencap was really for families only. People with a learning disability didn't go to any of the conferences or anything like that. But then some groups of people with a learning disability started up and things started to change slowly. Mencap needs to be able to confront some parents and tell them that their child can do more things than they think, otherwise their child won't be able to do things later in life.

Children with a more severe learning disability should go to special schools where the teachers can give them the support to learn. The teachers need to have the right skills and qualifications for this to work. But children with mild to moderate learning disabilities should go to mainstream schools. In an ideal world children with a severe learning disability could also go to mainstream schools, but if they go there and are separated from non-disabled children then this would be worse than being in special schools.

I do feel like I have the same rights as other people now, but still a lot of people are frightened of learning disability and don't understand it. And in practical terms, sometimes people don't get the same rights because the support just isn't there.

'I think it is a good thing for more people with a learning disability to go into supported living, as long as they get enough support. But if they don't, then it can be cruel to make someone live by themselves, especially if they've spent years in institutions with everything done for them. And I think that sometimes Mencap and other people encourage people to go into supported living without realising what it's going to be like for them.

People who have benefited from our services

Mencap is the biggest provider of services that support people with a learning disability and their families and carers to live their daily lives. Its direct services – in housing, education and employment – support more than 8,000 people. And through its work in the community, it supports some 70,000 people to speak up for themselves and their rights, gain confidence and take part in activities that really interest them. Let's hear from some of them now.

Getting into work . . .

Tom Jeanes was the first person to find employment through WorkRight, a Mencap scheme for employers who want to follow best practice in employing people with a learning disability. Tom works as a postroom assistant at Pitney Bowes: 'I love my job here. This is the chance I've been waiting for. I'm finally off benefits and in a job that I know I can do well. Now I'm saving up so I can leave home and get my own place. It's brilliant!'

Michelle Kenton found her job with support from Mencap's Pathway Employment Service: 'When I was looking for a job, the Jobcentre suggested I got in touch with Mencap. They first got me a job at a baker's. This didn't really work out, because the manager didn't really understand about my learning disability. I really wanted to get a job that suited me better. Mencap then found me a job working in the canteen at a London police station. I do lots of different things there, like cleaning the tables, collecting and washing the plates, and restocking the fridges. It's just right for me, the other staff are very supportive and I get to chat about things regularly with my Mencap supporter. When I found out that I'd passed my training, I was so happy because it meant all my hard work had paid off.'

Finding a place to live . . .
Roy Langrish, Joyce Muggleton and **Geoffrey Hussey** live in a Mencap supported-living scheme: 'We all love living here. It's a really nice house in a lovely area. We get a bit of support from Mencap, but we look after ourselves the rest of the time. We get on well with our neighbours – we have an "open house" day every New Year's Day, and we're really good mates with the local stationmaster. We were the first people with a learning disability in Hampshire to go on to the "Direct Payments" scheme. So instead of just going to a day centre, we get to choose what support services we get. We've had woodwork, arts and crafts lessons, and the support to get out and about to do the things we want in the community. Life is just great for us now!'

Leanne, from Darlington, lives in a house run by Mencap's sister charity, Golden Lane Housing: 'I like it here! The living room is my favourite place. Everyone always sits there together especially at the weekend. There is loads of space here. There wasn't much where I used to live. I have more choices too. I like to go to the club with everyone and bowling. My favourite time was the house-warming party and loads of people came. We're going to have another at Halloween!'

Learning new skills . . .
Graeme Chandler was a student at Mencap National College: 'I made lots of new friends at Mencap National College and did lots of different

things. Staff helped me to look after my room and myself and be more independent.'

Paddy Harland volunteered at Mencap's Unlocking Potential project in Northern Ireland: 'I volunteer once a month at Cabinhill, a residential home for older people. I play all the old tunes that the people like to sing along to. The people at Cabinhill enjoy it and it pleases me to know they look forward to me coming. I also volunteer with conservation volunteers: I water plants, cut leafings and grow vegetables and generally keep the area nice and tidy. I have learnt new skills and more importantly become more confident in myself as I realised I can contribute and make a difference. Without the help and support offered by Mencap I just wouldn't have had the opportunity to be involved.'

Speaking out . . .
Amy Forgacs has been involved in an action group of people with a learning disability in Cambridge elected to represent their peers at a 'service users' Parliament': 'It makes a difference to people's lives, giving them a chance to contribute to decisions about the services they receive and making them realise they do have choices.'

David Chapman has been part of an advocacy project in West Kent: 'The scheme has made a massive difference to my life. It's given me freedom, choice and the confidence to deal with life's problems. Plus I've been able to give something back, by showing the way for other people who are afraid to speak out.'

Getting into sport and the arts . . .
Sarah Newman is a keen photographer: 'Photography is really important to me. It gives me the chance to capture many aspects of life – the highs, the lows and all the bits in between! It's also a brilliant way for me to prove what I'm capable of, despite my learning disability. So I was thrilled when I won a prize in Mencap's *Snap!* photography competition in 2003, which went on show at the Victoria and Albert Museum. It was an even bigger honour to be chosen as a judge for the 2004 competition. I hope that what I've achieved with my photography will encourage

other people with a learning disability to take more photos and have the courage to share them with the rest of the world.'

Greg Harwood, from Manchester Mencap, was part of the prize-winning *Hidden Voices* project, which gave people with a learning disability a unique chance to express, through art, their experiences of having lived in institutions: 'I enjoyed doing *Hidden Voices*. It gave me a chance to tell everyone what it was really like in the institution.'

Trevor Lemon was one of seven outstanding talents to feature on 'Like a River Flows', a ground-breaking album, conceived and produced by Mencap: 'I've always loved singing. So it was wonderful to get this chance to have my talent recognised. I really hope it can help me pursue my singing career.'

Mark Jeffries was the goalkeeper in Mencap's national Gateway football team, which played in an annual European football tournament for people with a learning disability: 'It was great to take part in the tournament. I love football and really enjoy playing in a team with my mates.'

Getting out and about . . .

Jeffrey was supported by a Mencap travel training scheme in Newcastle: 'I find it hard to understand and do some things. I used to need help to do everyday things that most people take for granted. But then I found out about Mencap. They help people with a learning disability like me do lots of things, like learning how to use public transport. I learnt about using the ticket machines, reading maps and recognising my stop. We spent lots of time practising. It's brilliant – now I can do it on my own. It's opened up a whole new world for me. In fact, I've got a job interview next week and I'm travelling there all on my own.'

Being in the know . . .

John Marley got invaluable support from one of Mencap's helpline services: 'My wife Mary and I support each other – I've got a learning disability and Mary is visually impaired. She helps me by reminding me about my appointments. And I help her by reading out things to her. One day we got a letter about "Direct Payments". It said we couldn't keep getting our pension money by cashing our order books at the local post office. Instead, we'd have to use a new machine with a PIN number. But Mary can't use this because of her visual impairment. So we called the Wales Learning Disability Helpline for help. Since then, Mencap has sorted everything out for us: we're still able to get our pension using our order book and Mencap is on the case to make sure that this can still happen. Little things like this can make such a big difference to our lives. We are so grateful to Mencap.'

Five public faces of Mencap

Leading from the front ...
Simon Cramp was the first person with a learning disability to be elected as a Mencap trustee (see Genesis 1 and Chapter 2). Here he speaks about what it meant to him to have so much involvement in Mencap's work, and what he thinks Mencap should learn from his experiences: 'I wanted to put something back into the local community and to help others who weren't as articulate and clued up as me. It wasn't just about personal gratification. It was such a fantastic experience and I have learned so much about myself and what you have to do to get things done. In the future, I think Mencap has got to try and get more people with a learning disability into top jobs. This has to happen for Mencap to grow and mature. For it to happen there would have to be a lot more support, and I believe that Mencap is really trying to make this happen now.'

Andy Hoof followed in Simon's footsteps in getting elected to serve as a Mencap trustee (see also Chapter 2): 'This is a great opportunity for me to help other people with a learning disability. As a trustee, I will be looking at all the big issues like housing, money and jobs. I want to work with the other trustees to decide the most important things Mencap should be doing. I've already got experience of doing this kind of work from partnership board meetings and as chairman of a local advocacy project, where I have to make sure we are doing all the right things.

Having these responsibilities makes me feel very good about myself. I have learned so many new skills and become much more confident. Mencap has played such a big part in my life and I think the support they have given me has been great.'

In the media spotlight . . .

Lloyd Page is a volunteer for Mencap in London (see Chapter 9). He is also a media spokesperson for the charity. He was the first person with a learning disability to become a member of the National Union of Journalists. Recently, he conducted a wide-ranging survey on the representation of people with a learning disability in the media: 'I think people with a learning disability are under-represented in the media. I don't see people with a learning disability reading the news, or on soaps or game shows. If I see people with a learning disability it is often as negative stereotypes such as mentally handicapped or retards. This is not fair or accurate to people like myself. I would like to see people with a learning disability in a positive light, represented in the same way as everybody else.'

Paula Sage is a successful actress and Mencap's first celebrity ambassador with a learning disability (see Chapter 15). Of her role as an ambassador, she says: 'It's brilliant. Fantastic! I'm doing it because it might help people who have what I've got realise what they can do.'

Keith Shortman is a Mencap member and another media spokesperson for Mencap. He uses this platform to speak out against the bullying and discrimination of people with a learning disability. And in the last seven years he has been doing high-profile work with the Chief Commissioners of the Metropolitan Police in London, advising them on how to treat people with a learning disability. He co-wrote the guide *Stay Safe* for people with a learning disability: 'I did it because I got kicked and punched to the ground and nothing was done about it. So I spoke to people at the Camden [Mencap] Society and told a support worker. He went with me to speak to the local council at the liaison group and they decided to do something about it. The police should work with people with a learning disability to make sure they get a better service if they are attacked or are victims of bullying. There should be more police on the beat so that people with a learning disability feel safer. I hope that my work with the police can help them to understand and stop people with a learning disability from being bullied. I also hope that the *Stay Safe* booklet will help everyone, including people with a learning disability, to feel safe at home and in the community.'

Four people working at Mencap today

There are eighteen people with a learning disability working today at Mencap's National Centre in London in a variety of jobs in communications, campaigns, fundraising, finance and human resources. Fourteen of these eighteen sit on a panel that interviews prospective candidates for jobs at National Centre. We held a group interview with four of these panel members.

Ismail Kaji has worked for Mencap for eight years and is a campaigns information assistant. Before coming to Mencap he was at college during the day, and did voluntary work with people with a learning disability for Barnardo's in the evenings.

Ciara Evans is a part-time celebrity research assistant and part-time receptionist. She has been at Mencap National Centre for two years. Prior to this she worked at one of Mencap's Pathway services and was a library assistant at a local library.

Lorainne Bellamy has been at Mencap for twenty-three years and is now a communications assistant. Before working at Mencap she did voluntary work in a day centre for old age pensioners in Islington.

Lloyd Page, who also appears in the next chapter, works as a volunteer as a cards and gifts administrator. He's been at Mencap for ten years. Before this, he volunteered for the self-advocacy organisation People First.

We asked all four to explain what kind of support they get to do their jobs, whether they feel this support works for them, what they like and don't like about their jobs, and what they think Mencap should do in the future. The following is an edited transcript from the group interview.

What kind of support do you get to do your job?
Ismail: I get twenty-two hours' support per week on the Access to Work scheme. If my supporter, Wayne [Wayne Walker, Mencap Campaigns Officer] sees I'm getting better, my hours will drop down. I used to work on the helpline before I worked in campaigns. Campaigns was new to me, like doing spreadsheets, going to college to do more of my course and also doing WorkRight presentations. Wayne gives me guidance to do my tasks, he sees how I do it and how I need to improve, so he'll tell me straightaway if it's wrong. He made me a folder to break my job into different categories. Also each morning we do lists and I've got a timetable for Monday to Friday. I've improved a lot since I had the support from Wayne and Access to Work.

Ciara: I get support from both of my managers. When I'm on reception, that's Matt, the Facilities Manager. I work with Dawn there and if I have a problem I can ask her. I also see Marsh [Marsh Stitchman, Employment Support Manager] once a month and he tells me what the managers have said and asks how I think things are going. So that's really good. And when I'm in my celebrity job Neal Alexander, the Celebrity Co-ordinator, supports me on that.

Lorainne: The Communications Office Manager helps me on the computer. The main thing I have to do is invoices: I have to put them on spreadsheets and then they have to go up to the accounts department every fortnight to be paid. I also order stationery on my computer. I also go to college – Ismail and I are studying PowerPoint at the moment. And I passed my Excel exam and got a certificate. I also see Marsh once a month to discuss if I have any problems at work and how I'm getting on.

Lloyd: When I work in Fundraising I get support from my line manager, Michael, and from the whole Individual Giving team. When I'm in Human Resources, I get support from my line manager, Marsh. My main job in Fundraising is sending calendars, diaries and Christmas card competition packs. I do the entire database for the card competition list and I'm also one of the judges.

Do you think that this support is enough for you?
Ciara: When I first started here in my celebrity job, because I've grown up knowing about the media, I said to my manager that I don't feel I need support right now. But there are times when I feel maybe I should ask, but I can't quite pluck up the guts, because I've got quite big pride ego. But sometimes I go to Marsh and I ask if I've understood something right, and he'll say to me, 'Well, you need to do this or that' and I'll say, 'I'll take that on board and learn'. There have been a few things recently I know I need to improve on and Marsh helps me. That's been really good. I can also talk to my managers. The level of support I get right now is perfect. I know I can ask for help which is really good because if I don't, I know I'll come to a point where everything will go wrong. The greatest thing is that recently I felt that I couldn't do things and then I did them! I've always been told in the past the two words 'I can't'. Well, actually, with the right help I can.

Lloyd: I think I get lots of support – as much as I need. If Katie tells me what job to do and if it gets too difficult I'll call her over or Emily or Emma or whoever. They can help me to do it.

Lorainne: Yes, I think it's just right for me. I don't mind having a go at new things, but I don't like asking people for help. But I do ask when I have to.

Ismail: When I worked at the helpline, my manager and all the advisers were really busy and didn't have the time for me when I needed help. But since Marsh started at Mencap, it's changed a lot and I really appreciate that. And the same goes for everyone with a learning disability. Then I moved to Campaigns and then Marsh found out that I could get support from Wayne under Access to Work. It's been a big change for me and I really feel that now I'm getting the right support. Marsh also gives me a lot of support; he works together with Wayne as a team.

Do you think you get challenged enough in your job to do things for yourself and to learn new skills?

Lloyd: I think in previous years I needed lots of support but I don't need so much now. There's no way we're going to be wrapped in cotton wool, are we? I'm absolutely grateful to Emily and Katie because they have definitely pushed me further to do my own projects: sending out the calendars, the Christmas cards and Christmas competition packs. Marsh has pushed me further as well and so has everyone in Fundraising. It's fantastic.

Ciara: When I worked at Mencap's Pathway Service in Sutton, my manager was very good in this way. I could go and talk to her and if she felt that I was being a bit idle, she'd pull me up and make me improve. It was great. I'm a totally different person now. When I first came to Mencap I always felt I was stupid because that's what I was always called at school. Now I know that I can achieve things – I just need to ask for the right help. And I've realised in my jobs here at National Centre that when I ask for help and I do things right, it might sound like a small achievement, but to me it's big.

Lorainne: My job is very different to the ones I've done here before. I used to work in Mencap's flower shop here. There were only three people there and two managers. Then in Mencap Office Services, there were loads of us and sometimes it got too hectic because there was so much work we didn't have time to get it all done. I thought it was a bit too childish for me; it was like being in a factory. But I think it's changed quite a lot for me because I can do a lot more things now. I never used to go to college. Now I do.

Ismail: Marsh often talks about encouraging people to do new things. It's a good thing; if he didn't do that we wouldn't move ahead. It makes me quite frightened at times, but at the end of the day you feel that you've gained something. I've still got more to learn, like when I help with the WorkRight training for companies who want to employ people with a learning disability. I want to get more involved with this. I enjoy all the work I do overall. Without this support, it just won't work. Also with the course that I'm doing at college which I used to do in the evenings by myself. I tried my best but it was difficult without the support. Now Wayne comes to college with me and he guides me and shows me what to do and then I do it. Marsh, myself and Wayne, and Jane (my line manager in Campaigns) plan together about the changes in my job. Hopefully I will be able in the future to do a job similar to Wayne's and then I'll be able to support someone else with a learning disability myself.

What do like most in your job?
Lorainne: It's having friends. I also like the new stuff I'm doing for the Mencap Visiting Service, which Marsh supports me with. I'm helping a lady called Pamela at the moment, taking her out, doing things she likes. I haven't got the confidence to start going there on my own. I can travel all right on my own and do things with her. But I'm a bit worried in case something happens to her, I'd be a bit panicky and I wouldn't know what to do. I also really like doing editing for *Mencap Matters* [Mencap's newsletter for donors, written and edited by people with a learning disability]. I find it a bit hard but I'm learning. Also, I like going to college.

Lloyd: The thing I like best is doing the presentations. That's because I love meeting people and getting to know them.

Ismail: I like everything! I like WorkRight: getting involved in presentations and training. And I like my work in Campaigns: doing spreadsheets, sending out publications and getting involved with customers. It's good talking to people with a learning disability about their rights, and how to make things change. I can be very busy, because I have loads of emails every day, and it's hard but I enjoy it. I like getting involved in interviewing people for jobs at Mencap, and doing the training for this as well.

Ciara: In the celebrity research post, I love the celebrity gossip. I'm like a total dictionary celebrity gossip right now. I'm actually quite lucky – not many people get to read celebrity magazines and get paid for it! And on reception, I love meeting new people. And learning. You can never stop learning, so that's what I love about Mencap. With both of my jobs, I really love the new challenges that come every day. In the past, because I was badly bullied, I was always told, 'Oh no, you can't do this'. So coming to work at first I was like, 'Can I really do this?' I've learnt that I've got to learn, take things on board and improve. Plus, I've made lots of friends, not only work friends but they can be sociable friends as well. When I was moving into my flat, the whole of my team got together and brought me some nice things for my new flat. It's really nice knowing that people care about you.

What do you like least in your job?
Lorainne: I really don't like meetings, both one-to-one meetings and team meetings. That's because I find it hard to know what to say. One thing I don't like about my job is people calling me names. It still happens, not people at Mencap, but people outside. I do get irritated by this.

Ismail: There's nothing I don't like, because if I didn't like something, then it's pointless me being here! But sometimes I just worry too much about unnecessary things, when I'm not clear about what to do. So I talk to Marsh, Wayne or Jane and that always helps a lot.

Ciara: Some days can be difficult and when I go home I think I don't want to come back tomorrow. But then I say to myself, 'Hold on! If I give up, that's it. Tomorrow's a new day, a fresh start, so get on with it!' I have to challenge myself to do things but when I've done them it's a completely different story.

How can Mencap give the best support in the future to people with a learning disability?
Lloyd: Mencap should encourage more people with a learning disability to do what I do: speaking at conferences and events and to the media. That way, more people will understand about learning disability and people will get treated better.

Ismail: I'm very lucky to get the support in my job. In the future I hope to keep getting it. I also want to teach other people with a learning disability what I've learnt. We're all here to help each other; it's all about good team work. So, I'd like to see Mencap supporting more people with a learning disability in the way that they support me.

Lorainne: Mencap has changed and I've changed a bit as well. Mencap is going the right way. It's having more people with a learning disability working here and helping more people with housing, employment and education. So I think it should keep up the good work!

Ciara: I think Mencap should help more people like me to challenge themselves to learn new skills and do all sorts of different jobs. I know from my own experience that when I put my mind to it, I can do lots of things I didn't think I could do before. I think there are lots of other people who would find the same thing, as long as they got the right support and encouragement.

And finally . . .

It's very tempting to draw out all kinds of conclusions and common threads from people's experiences and views as quoted above. But that would be against the spirit of this chapter – namely, to allow people to speak for themselves.

However, there's a rather neat parallel here – this reluctance to speak on behalf of someone else who is perfectly capable of speaking for themselves is exactly what the Mencap of today is all about.

So perhaps we can, after all, admit one conclusion from all this: Mencap is here to enable people with a learning disability to have a voice and a choice, and in giving people the chance to say what they think, that's exactly what this chapter has been about.

Acknowledgements

Many thanks to all the people interviewed and quoted in this chapter, and their supporters. A big thank you also to Josie Scantlebury, who typed up the transcripts of the group interview with Mencap staff.

CHAPTER 9

Representing People with a Learning Disability in the Media

Lloyd Page

As the first person with a learning disability to have joined the National Union of Journalists (NUJ), I am delighted to be writing this article for *British Journalism Review* and delighted to be taken seriously as a journalist. In researching this article, I asked Alison Peebles, actress and director of the film *Afterlife*, why she thinks it is important for people with a learning disability to be represented in the media. She answered that people with learning disabilities are part of society and the media should reflect that. I agree with Alison and I think people with a learning disability are under-represented and misrepresented in the media industry.

The name's Page . . .

Let me tell you a little about what I've done in my work in the media over the years. I have been a personal assistant and researcher to Donal MacIntyre for over four years and I have worked at the BBC and several other production companies during that time. I have also recently been a researcher on a Channel 5 documentary on abuse in care homes which was reported by Donal MacIntyre.

> I was introduced to Lloyd Page, my assistant, at a Mencap conference. Lloyd is forty-five, has learning disabilities but he is probably the most efficient assistant I could ever have. He is brilliant at remembering things and the most reliable assistant I have ever had. He fully deserved the on-screen credit he received on one of my Channel 5 care home investigations. Lloyd is breaking down barriers all the time. Donal MacIntyre[1]

I write and lecture on learning disability in the UK and Europe and was the European Vice-President of Inclusion Europe for three years. Occasionally I have my own column with the *Worcestershire Weekender*.

I volunteer for the UK learning disability charity, Mencap, and my work includes writing as the political correspondent for their celebrity *BIZ* magazine. At *Learning Difficulties Media*, which promotes and supports people with a learning disability in the media, I am a media consultant researching and looking for publications and websites. I have been nominated for an award for Volunteer of the Year in 2005.

Laying the groundwork . . .

I came to do the survey on how people with a learning disability are represented in the media when I was asked to do some research by Donal MacIntyre. During the second half of 2004 I posted out surveys to people who work in the media. Eighty-five per cent of the media professionals questioned thought broadcasters have a responsibility to represent people with a learning disability in the media better. This was an interesting answer and I decided to take this further by asking more broadcasters and journalists for their views on this subject.

The turning point . . .

I spoke to Alison Peebles again. *Afterlife* starred the actress Paula Sage who has Down's syndrome. I asked Alison if she thinks that there should be special programmes for people with a learning disability or should people with a learning disability be integrated into mainstream programmes.

She told me, 'I'd love to see people with learning disabilities and physical disabilities in all kind of programmes: dramas, soaps, comedies and game shows. I don't think they should be ghetto-ised.'

The bad . . .

I wrote to Endemol pointing out that there are no participants with a learning disability selected to appear on the *Big Brother* show. I asked them to let me know if there is an official policy on this. So far, I haven't heard from them. I'm also waiting for the BBC press office's response as to why there is no one with a learning disability on *The Weakest Link* or *Eastenders*. I look forward to their reply.

By not seeing people with a learning disability in mainstream television and in newspapers and magazines regularly, audiences will think of people with a learning disability as stereotypes, such as retards and spastics. This is not fair or accurate to people like myself.

The good . . .

I asked Marion Janner of *Learning Difficulties Media* about the possible reasons why people with a learning disability are not represented in the media She told me:

> You cannot generalise all media as one and the same. In terms of news, this is very specific. Main news stories centre on controversy and debates, and having a learning disability alone does not equate to a news story. However, premature babies who are severely disabled open up a wider debate which then becomes a news story. Having said this, regional newspapers do offer surprisingly good coverage. The best are the articles about people's sports successes.
>
> In terms of dramas and stories there is very little inclusion of disabled people. A television company did some research and one of the programme makers said there was a general nervousness about doing the wrong thing in portraying minority groups and so not involving them is a lot easier.
>
> I think a good way forward is to help the media in the way they want to be helped. So rather than giving them a long list of do's and don'ts, they tend to prefer to have, first, access to great stories and,

second, access to great contacts, like BAFTA-winning actress Paula Sage.

We established *Learning Difficulties Media* out of *Mental Health Media*. *Mental Health Media* has been doing work with people with learning disabilities for some years. It wanted to separate its mental health and learning disability work. Also, it wanted to have a sharper focus on its learning disability work. We work to help people with learning difficulties make better use of the media as consumers, creators, contributors and in terms of content.

I am encouraged by the work of Marion and her thoughts. Changes are happening slowly. Print media is also beginning to recognise this change.

I believe there are a few examples of good practice in the national media, such as recent articles in *Press Gazette*[2], *Evening Standard*[3] and the *Guardian*[4]. I have picked these three examples because they have all portrayed me and people with a learning disability in a positive light. I picked the *Guardian* because there was an accessible summary. By being accessible the *Guardian* could reach more people and include people with a learning disability in its readership.

The not quite so ugly . . .

Another area of good practice seems to be in films. *Afterlife* is a definite example. Christopher Eccleston came to public attention starring as Derek Bentley in the film *Let Him Have It*, in 1991. This was his first film about learning disability issues. *Flesh and Blood*, his second, is a story about a man discovering that his real parents have learning disabilities. Like *Afterlife*, this film starred real learning disabled people, Dorothy and Peter. Christopher Eccleston said of *Flesh and Blood*:

> I was attracted by the idea of working with non-actors who were learning new skills. This was the case with Dorothy Cockin and Peter Kirby who play Joe's mum and dad in the piece. I thought it was an admirable impulse on the part of Pete Bowker [writer] to want to include people who are so often excluded. It was not just an acting job for me. I had other responsibilities. Along with Julian Farino, the

director, I had to help to coax the performances and I really enjoyed that extra responsibility.[5]

When I asked Donal MacIntrye about other people with learning disabilities getting into the media, he said: 'There is no reason why there shouldn't be a learning disabled assistant working in every newspaper in the country. My journalistic team are learning disability aware, there is no excuse.'

The final take . . .

Kati Whitaker, award-winning broadcast journalist, news presenter and reporter, worked on Radio 4's live programme *Does he take sugar?*. This programme offered people with a learning disability the opportunity to have their voices and views heard about issues in the world around them. Sadly this programme finished in the late nineties.

Kati recently ran a media training course for Mencap's spokespeople with a learning disability. I attended the course. Kati said:

> Throughout my work over twenty-odd years with the BBC, I have been acutely conscious of the lack of representation of people with learning difficulties in the media. In the ten years or so that I presented the Radio 4 disabilities programme *Does he take sugar?* I had some fantastically lively and impressive people with learning disabilities as guests on the programme Their contribution was always telling and apt and yet they often complained that they were rarely heard on mainstream programming. Things are now changing but still very slowly. It's absolutely vital that people with learning difficulties are given all the help they can to present themselves in a way that will encourage the media to invite them to participate.

Conclusion

I know that people with a learning disability can be positive images to television companies, newspapers and a wide range of audiences. I felt there was some positive feedback from Christopher Eccleston, Alison Peebles, Donal MacIntyre, Marion Janner and Kati Whitaker, but as individuals they cannot speak on behalf of the whole media industry.

Things are starting to change though and inclusive media is definitely the way forward.

There is some progress being made in print media and in film but not enough is being done in mainstream television. This is a shame because mainstream television is the most accessible and often influential media type to the public. Society is lacking in knowledge because of this, and this is degrading to people with a learning disability.

I would like to see everyone getting together at a conference or a meeting to thrash these problems out to result in people with a learning disability being seen working in television and appearing on programmes such as dramas, game shows and soaps.

Acknowledgement

Mencap wish to thank the *British Journalism Review* for permission to publish this abridged version of Lloyd Page's original article.

References

1   'Me and My Charity' (*Evening Standard*, 16 May 2005)
2   'Give jobs to autistic' plea to employers (*Press Gazette*, 24 June 2005)
3   'Me and My Charity' (*Evening Standard*, 16 May 2005)
4   'The Fight for Rights' (*Guardian*, 22 June 2005)
5   Drama Interviews (www.bbc.co.uk/drama/interviewchristophereccleston)

CHAPTER 10

My Relationship with
Andrea Kellett

Paul Annear

I was born on 29 June 1960 in Norwich. I know this because it says so on my birth certificate. These small details are all I know for sure about the beginning of my life.

In those days people with Down's were not treated as they are now. We weren't expected to get jobs or fall in love. Instead we were expected to spend our lives in institutions and homes. We were not allowed to have ambitions or dreams.

It was very sad.

I don't know much about my mum. The file is very slim. She was probably very scared when she realised her baby was going to be different.

I can't know for sure but I reckon she thought she wouldn't be able to look after me. I was fostered. I went to live with a Mr and Mrs Agate. I called them Granny and Grandad Agate. I liked living with them. They were kind and I felt safe there.

But when I was thirteen Grandad Agate died. Granny Agate couldn't manage on her own. A social worker came to see me. She said: 'I've found somewhere new for you to live. It's a big place and you'll be with lots of other children. It's called the Ormerod Home.' [It was owned and run, ostensibly, by Mrs Don Gittins. I say 'ostensibly' because our North-West Divisional Director was her husband and seemed to spend quite a lot of time there! BR]

The Ormerod was in Blackpool, around 200 miles from Norwich. I was excited and scared all at once. I didn't want to leave Granny Agate but the decision had been made. So I made the best of it. I knew I had to be brave.

I went to live at the Ormerod with fifty other children. It was noisy and busy and I was scared at first. I missed Granny Agate. But I soon got used to it. I even started to like it. I made lots of friends and I became close to a little girl called Andrea Kellett. She was younger than me and I looked after her. She had Down's too.

When the Ormerod closed down we were separated. We cried. But nothing could keep us apart. I travelled across Blackpool and found her. After that we were always together. We fell in love and defied the sceptics by getting married, as we described in *Take a Break*. We were supported by our friends and workers at the Ormerod Trust.

We were very happy and I reckoned I had almost all I wanted – except one thing. I still wanted to find my birth family. It would help me to understand where I had come from. It would make me feel more complete.

Nobody knows where my mum is now. I think about her a lot. What did she look like? What did she sound like?

Sometimes I wish that things could have been different.

On the other hand, if I hadn't gone to Ormerod House I would never have met Andrea. And I wouldn't be so happy now.

Mum, if you are reading this, I hope you feel proud of me. Do not blame yourself for putting me into foster care. I have a happy life, a job and a home. And I have a wonderful wife. As I say, I am happy–sad.

Acknowledgements

Mencap wishes to thank Paul Annear, Louise Baty and *Take a Break* for permission to reproduce this article. We agreed to place the following notice which accompanied the original article:

Can you help Paul Annear find his birth family? Write to Louise Baty, Take a Break, FREEPOST LON12043, H Bauer Publishing, London NW1 IYU. All letters will be treated in confidence until we have permission from those involved.

CHAPTER 11

The Arts

Compiled by Gus Garside
National Arts Development Manager, Mencap

The last two decades have seen an amazing growth of learning disabled artists and arts organisations around the UK. Companies like Mind the Gap, the Shysters, the Lawnmowers, Heart 'n' Soul and Anjali are now well-established and newer companies are emerging all the time, such as the Unlimited Company and Firebird Theatre. More arts events are being run by people with a learning disability, the Oska Bright Film Festival and Mencap's In the Frame conference and exhibition at Tate Modern. But despite this display of new creative talent that has introduced new languages and experiences, learning disability arts continue to struggle with lack of funds, resources and mainstream recognition. As a result, some companies, including the pioneering Strathcona Theatre Company, have been forced to close down or downsize.

To get some sense of the state of play I took the opportunity to interview a number of learning disabled artists and performers about their work.

I met painters **Andrew Apicella** and **Louella Forest** who have recently completed a three-year visual arts course, Access to Art, at Sussex Downs College in association with the University of Brighton. Both are keen to continue to exhibit and sell their work and are part of a new Arts Council-funded artists' group called A2A Rockets. As Louella puts it, 'I want life and a future, to do and sell more paintings'. They had both been through well-structured training and I became interested to know how other people got into the arts.

For **Jon Tipton** it merely took the experience of seeing others perform and he immediately immersed himself in drama at school before joining a theatre workshop project. This led to an audition for a group that was later to become the touring theatre company the Shysters. He said, 'I've been in the Shysters now for roughly eight years and I've enjoyed every moment of it. It's been fantastic and since those eight years my skills as an actor have developed rapidly and we're now classed as a professional theatre company.'

Jon has performed alongside Matthew Kelly in a version of *Don Quixote* at Birmingham Rep Theatre. Prior to this he had played Bottom in *A Midsummer Night's Dream* at Coventry's Belgrade Theatre. Other members of the Shysters performed as the various rude mechanicals in this main house inclusive production, which Jon describes as 'the best thing I've ever been in. It was a goal that I had set for a long time that I'd reached and achieved – getting on the main stage at the Belgrade in a full-scale performance piece and that is what I wanted to do. It was the biggest goal I've reached.' It is clear that Jon received a lot of encouragement at school and, although he found school boring, it helped him set clear goals for himself. 'Oh, I've got a very clear path ahead of me. I want to have a full career acting, full wage, go on mainstream stages all over the country and get myself an agent. That's my focus at the minute.'

He continues to work with the Shysters and is committed to using theatre to say something to the world about learning disability. He described one of their shows to me:

> Basically it's about people with special needs who travel by bus to day
> services. And the message that we're getting across to them is that

they can make their own choices. For instance, when they go to the day centre they can come and go as they want. They don't have to go by the bus if they don't want to. 'Cos they're saying special needs people need more help and they need to be constantly looked after twenty-four hours of the day. We're saying this is what we want to do with our life. We want to do other things than sit on a bus all day long, going to a day centre every single day. I want to get the message out that [people with special needs] are human beings born a little bit different . . . that doesn't matter because they breathe, they eat, they do the same . . . it doesn't matter that that person was born slightly different . . . and people who can't accept them, well then there is something wrong with them . . . It's them that's got the problem and that what we're trying to get across with these shows.

Becoming a professional actor has changed how Jon sees himself, 'Well, me and Sunny [Patel Jones, who was also with the Shysters] feel we've grown out of our learning disability . . . we've only just very slightly got one now'.

Sunny Patel Jones was with the Shysters for seven years as an actor, director and company assistant before going freelance to seek work as an actor and stage manager. There are other similarities in the encouragement he received at school and in his determination to say something about how people with a learning disability are perceived. 'We may be labelled as a learning disabled performer or artist or person but we can do things just as well as anyone else. So don't look at us as if we're aliens from another planet cos we're not.' He went on to tell me that he 'would like to see more learning disabled people on TV, more learning disabled people on stage, more learning disabled people in professional shows'.

Professionalism was an important theme. Both Jon and Sunny were clear that they considered themselves professionals. **Mark Barber** of Anjali Dance Company felt 'it's all that commitment to dance and to stay professional. I like being professional and you could say my body has changed, I am more flexible, fitter and more confident and easy going.' **Robin Meader**, from the Somerset-based Unlimited Company, considered that he was working to becoming a professional storyteller. He put it beautifully when I asked him how he would know when he was a professional. He replied, 'Audiences will listen to me . . . to my stories and what I have to say'.

Robin Meader and **Brian Marshall** are both part of a group of storytellers who mix traditional tales and personal narratives. As Brian says, 'It's telling people what it's like to have a learning disability. It helps me and it helps people to listen. They feel opened up. I hope it helps people come out their shell and gets them to learn what it's like to have a learning disability.' I asked him if learning about people with a learning disability might encourage people to treat them better? 'It might and it might not. It's like with this Government, it's one step forward and one step back, isn't it?' Finally I spoke to **Jez Colborne** (aka **JC Jamma**). Jez is an actor (with the national touring company Mind the Gap). He has played lead roles in *Don Quixote*, *Cyrano de Bergerac*, *Pygmalion*, *Of Mice and Men* and *Jekyll and Hyde* as well as touring his own one-man show *On the Verge* about his travels across America. He is also an accomplished musician and songwriter and last year played his first live jazz gig at the Banqueting House to celebrate Brian Rix's eightieth birthday. He was joined on stage by Kenny Ball, Terry Lightfoot and John Dankworth – jazz legends, indeed – and the result was a wonderful jam session, with Jez leading the group magnificently. The audience were both moved and exhilarated, with Jez proving what a musician with a learning disability can accomplish if he has the inborn talent and application.

Jez was one of five students selected to be part of the first Staging Change course. Funded by the Learning and Skills Council as part of their Dance and Drama Awards, this is the first major attempt to embed training for learning disabled performers in mainstream drama colleges. It is run by Mind the Gap Theatre Company in collaboration with four drama colleges (Arts Educational, Oxford School of Drama, Guildford Conservatoire and Mountview). I asked Jez if Staging Change was the first time he'd had an opportunity to do some training in a mainstream drama college. 'Oh yeah. It was amazing, we learnt so many things about posture, about attitude towards acting, about the way you act, about the way you breathe. We looked at *Animal Farm* and Shakespeare. I had no qualms about it, I just got on and did it.' I asked him if he was a professional. 'Yes, I think of myself as a professional because I don't think like an amateur; I don't think, "Hey this is cool, I'm going to do this" and then "come on guys". You know it's a really professional warm-up, get myself ready, get myself focused for playing a part or for playing what I'm going to play anyway. And that's how to be professional.' Many of Jez's songs are about the politics of disability. 'People have of a lot of ways to say, "Hey I've got a disability, you know, this is who I am, what I am". But I found a lot of barriers, so I wanted to stop all the barriers by writing. "We've Got to Fight", that was the first-ever song I wrote. And then "Got to Have a Revolution" that was another song I wrote; you know it's all about people getting together that's got a disability to just enjoy what they are, who they are. And that was the kind of stuff I was going through, you know. "Leave Me Alone", for instance, is about someone telling you what to do all the time, not giving you a chance to be yourself.'

The above are all relative success stories of people with a learning disability working in the arts, though few of them can earn money from their work. But for many opportunities like these to develop their skills and take up careers in the arts are all too few and far between. There are some real barriers that have yet to be overcome. Most of the artists I spoke to had been recruited into a particular company and received their training there. Staging Change and the Access to Art course in Brighton, both mentioned above, are rare examples of mainstream training for learning disabled artists or performers. Despite the full implementation of the Disability Discrimination Act, many colleges still view inclusion as fitting people into existing practices rather than developing new approaches. But it's hard for colleges to get excited about inclusion when there are major barriers to employment for people with a learning disability. It is difficult for people with a learning disability to take the leap from benefits to employment without a safety net if they need to stop working or, as is the case for many in the arts, when the periods of employment come in relatively short bursts.

While the demand for learning disabled actors is increasing, it is still small. Despite the fact that people with a learning disability are less institutionalised than in the past, soaps and dramas still insufficiently reflect their presence in society, with some highly successful exceptions such as *The Bill* and Scotland's *River City*.

There is still a lack of agents, and the like, promoting learning disabled talent. Though some work is being undertaken into new ways of establishing groups, such as social enterprises or community interest companies, which may aid the development of new companies and the continued nurturing of the uniqueness of learning disability arts, it still sidesteps the inclusion agenda.

There has always been a worry about the quality and the critical appraisal of learning disability arts but the criteria of originality, honesty, surprise, challenge, excitement, range, variety, depth and intention apply equally well to the work of artists with a learning disability as they do to non-disabled artists. I recall not so long ago witnessing a company of professional non-disabled actors playing characters with a learning disability, a practice I thought belonged to the past. I was reminded how shallow such portrayals are in comparison with the resonance of such performances by actors with a learning disability.

There is also the issue of who this work is for. Some of it is specifically for audiences of people with a learning disability but much of it should play to a wider audience and this needs sophisticated marketing.

These should be the concerns not merely of those who work in the learning disability arts field but of everyone who works in the creative industries. It is about aiming for a major cultural shift. It's about understanding who we are through understanding difference. That's what the arts are all about.

As Jon Tipton says:

> I'm hoping that they can get more disabled actors getting more work and getting the message across. I'm hoping they can make more disabled theatre groups. That they can tour anywhere round the world. The fears are that people aren't listening to our messages. It's going in one ear and out the other. My fear is that they will discriminate and put these people down and put them off . . . if people aren't going to listen, people will give up trying to get the message across. That's my fear.

In Jez Colborne's words, 'The worst thing is facing barriers, you've got to really be strong about it, cos if you cave in everything stops. And I don't want everything to stop, I want to be strong and say, "Hey this is me, give me a chance, I want to do what I can do to show you that I can do it".'

PART IV

Some Mencap Initiatives

CHAPTER 12

Families and Healthcare:
Reflections from
parental and professional perspectives

Professor Sheila Hollins FRCPsch, MBBS, MCPCH
President, The Royal College of Psychiatrists

Reflecting on the first sixty years of Mencap is thought-provoking for me as I prepare to celebrate my own sixtieth birthday! When Lord Rix invited me to contribute to this history of learning disability, he asked me to say what had inspired me to become involved with people with a learning disability, and to share my views on their healthcare – past and present – and on how I teach medical students about their health needs.

Although I grew up near a small 'mental handicap' hospital and used to go to tea with the matron (a friend of my parents), and play in the grounds, no one ever explained why the residents were there, and it seems that I probably didn't ask or perhaps accepted whatever I was told uncritically. One of my mother's friends had a child whom we perceived as troublesome, and I later learnt had been autistic, and my parents used to talk about her 'poor' mother. Again I never asked why. My parents were ambitious for my three siblings and for me and we were encouraged to go to university, although my mother was doubtful about my wanting to be a doctor. I didn't have very competent science teaching at A level and would have done much better doing arts subjects. Somehow I scraped through and applied to VSO to teach as a volunteer in Africa, probably the most formative part of my education for life. Again there were no disabled children in my school or village but I had a holiday job working in a leprosy settlement that also housed a rehabilitation centre for blind people. I was given the task of accompanying the centre manager to rural villages to help assess visually impaired children for their suitability for rehabilitation. While he chewed nuts with the village elders and persuaded them of the value of rehabilitation and negotiated their contribution to the ongoing support of the child, I meanwhile assessed the child's dexterity and finger sensation. Back at the centre I was involved in teaching the pupils practical skills that would eventually earn them a living. I remember later visiting a 'graduate' of the centre who was working close to my village, and still have a woven bag made by him.

Returning to London I commenced a five-year medical course at St Thomas's. Here I had little teaching about learning disability, except in paediatrics where we learnt about the physical characteristics of Down's syndrome from a textbook, and were taken on what we later considered a rather voyeuristic trip by coach to Queen Mary's Hospital, Carshalton. Here we were shown many children with 'syndromes', without any discussion of how these children and young adults had come to be there. There was no consideration of their social or emotional needs or family relationships. Many students found the visit aversive and would remember the experience for the rest of their careers – an experience that would unfortunately lead them to avoid any contact with people with a learning disability, even when care in the community led to more people being referred to ordinary services.

Thus it was that my first real introduction to someone with a learning disability was when my own son was diagnosed in his second year of life. I knew about deafness and visual impairment, but not learning disability. My husband Martin and I learnt the hard way, or perhaps it was the best way in reality, because we didn't have too many preconceptions about what to expect. We have recently written a book for parents in which we tried to distil some of what we have learnt ourselves from our own experience as parents, from other families and from our professional work. Our key message is for parents to trust their own judgement and knowledge of their child; to remember that they are the real experts about him or her. This expertise is hard won and in our book we suggest how parents can further develop their skills in this area.[1]

Suffice to say that we slowly discovered that doctors and teachers were often wrong about our son and that we were going to have to be very patient to find things out for ourselves as he developed. And to be his staunchest allies.

By this stage I had decided to move from a career in general practice – the career for which I thought I had studied medicine. I had discovered that I was ill prepared to understand the social and psychological needs of my patients and decided that a period of training in psychiatry would better prepare me. From the start I loved psychiatry, particularly the chance to spend more time with each person and to work with skilled professionals of many disciplines. Psychotherapy training was offered and I found I had an aptitude for both group and one-to-one therapy and had a chance to complete a three-year training in psychodynamic therapy alongside my psychiatry training. Child and family psychiatry seemed to offer the best setting for me to practise in a multi-disciplinary team and to work as a psychiatrist and psychotherapist. My son was now well established in a special primary school and his severe communication difficulties were improving with the help of the school-based speech therapist. But his behaviour was at times challenging and there were family issues that we knew other families like ours were also facing. It seemed to me that families with children with a learning disability might benefit from the skills we were using every day in the child guidance clinic. However, my colleagues in child psychiatry did not recognise how they could apply their skills in these circumstances and I found that disabled children referred to the clinic were rarely offered appointments. This is how I came to work in this field. Gradually I started to accept referrals that would otherwise have been rejected, until by the end of my two-year placement, my whole practice was with disabled children and their families.

At around this time I heard Joan Bicknell speak and learnt that she had been appointed to the first Chair in the Psychiatry of Learning Disability in the UK, and possibly the world. She took up her new post in 1980, and I arranged to meet her to tell her about my experience in the child guidance clinic, and to ask why more community-based work such as this was not happening. I had made enquiries about any special services for children and adults with a learning disability and been shocked to discover that virtually all services were based in long-stay hospitals. It seemed that if a family couldn't cope with their child's physical or emotional needs or their behaviour then they might be lucky to have occasional respite care. Otherwise, if they were at the end of their tether, then long-stay admission to hospital was still the only viable option. This was shocking to me, but as the mother of a now primary school child with a learning disability, I had discovered that rather than a child with special needs getting extra help to support him, he was more likely to get less help and fewer services and opportunities than his siblings. It was relatively easy for Joan Bicknell to persuade me to join her at St George's Hospital Medical School (now just called St George's) in the University of London and I became a Senior Lecturer and Consultant Psychiatrist in Learning Disability in 1981.

So now I was a doctor specialising in learning disability and I had to try to bring together what I knew as a parent and what I had learnt as a doctor. To integrate these very different trainings was certainly going to be a challenge, but it was an exciting time, and Joan introduced me to people such as David Towell, Oliver Russell, Philippa Russell, Alan Tyne and Linda Ward. My perspectives were being challenged and developed during this period. I became involved with Elspet Rix and Mencap Homes in a small-scale housing project, and then found myself in a management role at Normansfield for a short period. Making changes was not proving very easy and a new visit by the National Development Team (NDT) was helpful in moving things along. My clinical leadership was primarily concerned with developing community teams for adults with a learning disability who also had mental health or behavioural problems. I was able to bring my family therapy and psychotherapy skills into my work and that of the multidisciplinary team. However, my work and interests were necessarily broader than just mental health, and I found my early training as a GP very useful. People who referred themselves to the community team seldom had just one health problem; in general their physical health was poor and few people had any regular health surveillance. My research and service development initiatives mainly focused on health, including mental health; teaching for postgraduate psychiatrists was on mental health, but my teaching focus for undergraduates aimed to bring a psychosocial approach to their understanding of people's physical health.

One of our main objectives at St George's over the last twenty-five years has been to prepare the doctors of today to provide excellent healthcare to people with a learning disability regardless of their particular area of medical practice. Joan and I wanted students to be inclusive in their approaches, but we were sure that their attitudes and their communication skills would be key to the success of our aspirations. The first task was to cancel the various trips to long-stay hospitals being organised by the paediatric and genetics departments. We knew that these simply created negative attitudes and would do nothing to help our students recognise the whole person they were seeing. From the start we wanted the teaching to be very practical and person-centred. We wanted the students to learn from good examples, not to tell them how badly doctors do things, something some parents' groups seemed determined to tell them. So we invited parents and carers of people living in their own homes – just as the majority of people with a learning disability always have lived at home – to come and talk to small groups of students. In 1982 our social work colleague Edna Wallace saw the Strathcona Theatre Company perform at the South Bank in London, and was so impressed she invited them to run an interactive session for all of our teaching and clinical staff. I signed the company up for termly drama workshops with students and these continued in one form or another until the company was wound up in 2005. In recent years first Strathcona and more recently the Baked Bean Theatre Company, part of ACT II at Merton Abbey Mills, have been working as simulated patients in both our teaching sessions and our clinical examinations. It is inconceivable to me that any medical school could consider their curriculum complete without such a rich experience of learning disability being brought to them by the people themselves and their families.

How well were people's health needs met in the past? The majority of people with a learning disability have always lived at home with their families, and many family carers were very dissatisfied with the poor health care their disabled relative received, although every so often a carer would report that their child had received a first-class service and effective advocacy by the family GP. One of the arguments by doctors who were in charge of some of the old hospitals for retaining them, at least in part, was that 'ordinary' doctors would never be able to meet the complex health needs of people with a learning disability. In fact the health status of many patients in those hospitals was also poor. When I first became a consultant in 1981, I had medical responsibility for 200 people living in seven run-down wards in a long-stay hospital in Surrey. I was concerned about the general health of the residents and started by looking at their dietary intake. Most were underweight and needed a soft diet, which I discovered was provided in bulk as a cook-chill meal. They did not have fresh fruit and vegetables, there was no hospital dietician and the catering manager was unable to tell me about the calorific content of a meal. I then discovered that patients in mental handicap hospitals had less spent on their food each day than any other category of patient in the NHS. I requested orange juice for my patients but this was discontinued after three months on the grounds of cost. I was not convinced at all that the hospitals should be kept open in any form and still hold that firm view today. I have no personal experience of the quality of care in the period from 1946 to 1980 but from what I have read I have not been persuaded that there was ever a golden age in institutional care.

So how has the challenge to achieve better health for people that Joan and I and others were concerned about in the early 1980s been dealt with in practice? Are doctors adequately prepared to be inclusive and effective in their approaches now, or are they still discriminating against some people? Unfortunately, a lot depends on where you study medicine, as some medical schools still do not include a relevant course in their curriculum. However, I would not attribute all progress just to what is formally taught. Students learn much in their own lives that contributes to their knowledge of people, and many will have had a more enlightened exposure to people with a learning disability than I had as a child. For example, many will have had disabled siblings, cousins or neighbours who have been supported to live at home, and they may have got to know someone at school or in an after-school club who has a learning disability. Many students have voluntary experience while still at school and frequently this will be with disabled children. So changing attitudes in society are being helpful in developing more inclusive attitudes in our medical and other healthcare students.

I do consider that the Government White Paper *Valuing People*[2] has had an impact on health services and has raised the expectations of people with a learning disability and their families. I was involved with many others in the health subgroup of the Minister's Advisory Group under the leadership of Dr Oliver Russell when *Valuing People* was being written, and was a contributor to the recommendations about the potential value of health action plans, and also the recommendation that the Government should launch a confidential inquiry into avoidable mortality in people with a learning disability. These initiatives are still being introduced, so it is too early to know how effective they will prove to be.

Perhaps the work of the Disability Rights Commission to challenge discrimination in healthcare, particularly with its inquiry into health inequalities, will prove to be the most important and effective lever to change professional behaviour and service provision. Sometimes the move to open ordinary services to all, whether health or other public services, has meant throwing out the old specialist service before the new inclusive services have got it right for people with a learning disability. This hasn't worked in the past, so I believe that sustained advocacy and the relentless pursuit of excellence for people like my son will be needed for the foreseeable future. Much of this advocacy will come from family members, as Brian has so rightly recognised and encouraged. I do still hope that education of healthcare professionals will increasingly involve family carers and people with a learning disability as teachers. One plan announced by the Royal College of Psychiatrists in 2005 requires that carers and users are both employed in all postgraduate training programmes for psychiatrists, and as President I am pleased to support and monitor the introduction to this new initiative.

I would like to end this piece with congratulations to Brian Rix for conceiving this project, but especially for being such a strong advocate for better health for people with a learning disability for the past sixty years. I hope that his inspiration will continue to encourage so many of us to continue in our chosen work for years to come.

References

1   Hollins, S. and Hollins, M. *You and Your Child: Making Sense of Learning Disabilities.* London. Karnac. 2005

2   Department of Health. *Valuing People: A New Strategy for Learning Disability in the 21st Century.* 2001

CHAPTER 13

Treat Me Right!

David Congdon
Head of Campaigns and Policy, Mencap

Everyone has the right to good-quality healthcare. The NHS was founded on this principle. All the arguments that rage today about how exactly healthcare should be provided still take this basic human right as their major premise. Many people would, in fact, argue that our healthcare system is not meeting the needs of large parts of the population. This may well be true, and may well call for the Government to make some radical changes to ensure equality of treatment for everyone. But regardless of this, we can say with absolute certainty that there is one group of people who are being let down in a big way by our healthcare system – people with a learning disability.

I want to look at how and why this is happening, and at how Mencap believes things can and must change. I'll be referring to the key findings and recommendations from Mencap's 2004 *Treat me right!* report on healthcare for people with a learning disability, which Jo Williams also speaks about in her overview of Mencap's campaigning agenda (see Chapter 6). *Treat me right!* has already had a major impact on the

Government and our healthcare system and I'll also be explaining why we are hopeful that they are beginning to take this issue as seriously as they must.

First, I'd like to set out plainly and simply our irrefutable thesis about the inferior healthcare treatment which people with a learning disability receive.

The starting point is that people with a learning disability have poorer health than the general population. Indeed, they are much more likely to die before the age of fifty. They are three times more likely to die from respiratory disease. They also have higher rates of coronary heart disease, gastrointestinal cancer and stomach disorders.

There are a variety of reasons for this general poorer state of health, and it's important to unpick them carefully here.

In some cases, people have conditions or problems that can in some way be related to their disability. Some examples include epilepsy, cardiac problems, thyroid problems, sight and hearing problems and a variety of mental health problems. But the higher incidences of such conditions do not alone explain the poorer-than-average general health and life expectancy for people with a learning disability.

The argument here is that people with a learning disability are not valued as equal citizens in society and that this leads to them getting poorer-than-average healthcare. There are two widely accepted premises to this argument. First: people from disadvantaged backgrounds have more illnesses and shorter lives than those who are well off. Second: people with a learning disability are disadvantaged in society – they often live apart from mainstream society, and are generally poor, living on benefits or a low income. As a result, people with a learning disability generally lead unhealthy lifestyles; fewer than 10 per cent of adults with a learning disability eat a balanced diet, while more than 80 per cent do less physical activity than is recommended.

As these social factors are, undeniably, major contributors to the poorer-than-average state of health of people with a learning disability. However, they still do not tell the whole story. But they do point us in the direction of the whole thrust of our thesis: that our healthcare system is letting down people with a learning disability. This is due to, at best, ignorance and, at worst, negligence and discrimination. Either way, it

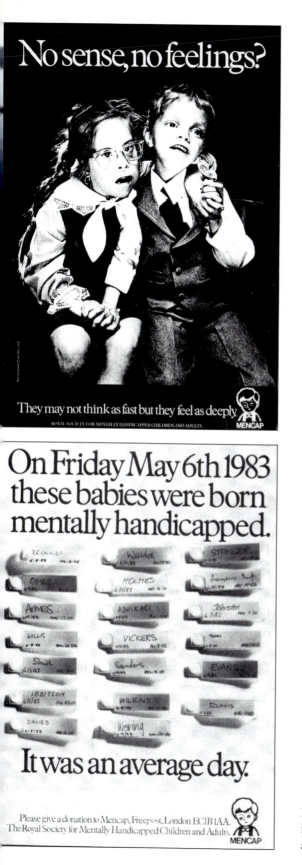

Hard-hitting Mencap advertisements in the eighties aimed to raise public awareness of learning disability

Horticultural and agricultural courses are available for people with learning disability at Lufton Manor Rural Training Unit

Above: a young man with learning disability taking part in a fundraising event

Below: a learning disability group make their voices heard

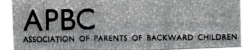

APBC
ASSOCIATION OF PARENTS OF BACKWARD CHILDREN

MENCAP

**Royal Society for Mentally
Handicapped Children & Adults**

mencap
making the most of life

mencap

MENCAP
Understanding learning disability

Mencap branding has changed over its sixty years:

Left: a sequence of logos

Right: three of Caroline Cook's powerful images taken to promote the Society

Left: a man with Down's syndrome proudly shows a photograph of himself as a child in a sailor suit

Below: a father shows the strong bond between parents and their children who have Down's syndrome

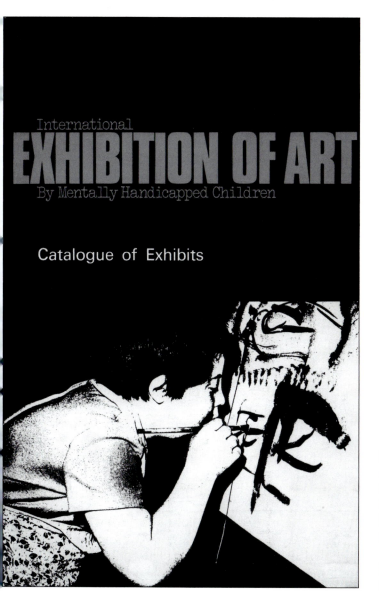

Left: catalogue for the eighth edition of the International Exhibition of Art by Mentally Handicapped Children, 1970

Below: drawings from the exhibition

Catalogue number 70

Catalogue number 54

Above: Ken Solly

Right: Alan Phillips

Below, right: Brian Baldock, the present Chairman of Mencap

brings us back to the argument, that people with a learning disability are not valued as equal citizens.

Before we examine how exactly people with a learning disability are being let down by the healthcare system, it's worth tracing the root of the problem. Traditionally, the healthcare of people with a learning disability was provided by 'specialist' learning disability services, namely the long-stay hospitals that thirty years ago housed some 60,000 people. As a result, mainstream health services did not see people with a learning disability as their responsibility. Most of these hospitals have now closed. But it seems that many of the mainstream services haven't caught up; many healthcare professionals simply don't understand much at all about learning disability. As I will show, this results in a generally poor overall quality of service. In some cases it can result in a refusal of treatment, as in one recent example of a woman with a learning disability who has cancer. In yet other cases it can even lead to early, unnecessary deaths.

Let's now look in some detail, with a few examples, at what's going wrong. First, there's the problem of accessing GPs and other primary healthcare practitioners. In research commissioned by Mencap for *Treat me right!*, 75 per cent of GPs had received no training to help them treat people with a learning disability, while 90 per cent felt that a patient's learning disability had made it more difficult for them to give a diagnosis. This has inevitably resulted in people with a learning disability – and their families and carers – not feeling confident that they will get effective treatment. So, many don't even go to their GPs to report illnesses or symptoms. And even when they do, there can be further problems.

In some cases, doctors wrongly believe that a presenting problem is as a result of the learning disability and that not much can be done about it. An example of such 'diagnostic overshadowing' was of a man who was scratching his face and seemed to be very distressed. His mother, believing him to be in pain, took him to the GP, who told them: 'That's the way they are sometimes. Just take him home.' It turned out that the cause of the pain was an abscess, which was treated successfully by a dentist. In another case, a woman went into hospital for an emergency operation. Her support worker went to visit her after the operation and raised her concerns to a nurse that she wasn't speaking. The nurse, looking surprised, replied: 'Can she speak?' The woman could indeed speak before her operation. In fact, she had had a stroke after the operation and it had been completely undetected.

Clearly, therefore, medical professionals sometimes make dangerous faulty assumptions about people with a learning disability, thus revealing an overall lack of training and skills in understanding the condition, which can lead to misdiagnosis, inappropriate treatment or no treatment at all. Indeed, some of the medical conditions known to be associated with having a learning disability can be prevented, and most can be successfully treated. But this depends on health services being vigilant in diagnosing them. Research by the National Patient Safety Agency (NPSA), for example, revealed a lack of awareness among health and social care staff of the symptoms of aspiration pneumonia and the risk of death caused by swallowing difficulties. Problems with eating and drinking can be life-threatening. They can lead to respiratory tract infection, which is a leading cause of death for people with a learning disability.

Lack of understanding among health professionals about the different ways that people with a learning disability may communicate can also be a major problem. People with a learning disability may find it hard to communicate their symptoms and to understand what they are being told. As a result, some people have to put up with a great deal of pain and discomfort before they get the right treatment. And in some cases it can lead to serious, irreversible consequences. In one example, a man told his mother that he could see 'a funny black thing'. She took him to the optometrist, but they weren't taken seriously. On their fourth visit, the man said, 'black blob bigger' – prompting the optometrist to at last make a proper examination of the back of his eyes. He found two detached retinas. The man has now been registered blind.

People with a learning disability also sometimes experience very poor quality of care in hospitals, again due to a lack of understanding among staff. Some people are simply neglected because they are unable to tell staff that they are in pain, or that something is going wrong with an intravenous drip. Indeed, there are particular problems around feeding, resulting in some patients not getting food or drink. There are also examples of a lack of attention to epilepsy and a failure to prescribe appropriate medicine. Another major problem is that parents and care home staff often feel they have no choice but to provide basic care themselves, otherwise their son or daughter might starve or come to harm. The hospitals should really be doing this; they have a legal duty to all patients while they are in their care. In the worst cases, the consequences of this lack of understanding and due care can be fatal. In one example, a thirty-year-old woman went into hospital suffering from chest problems. The hospital was aware that she had severe epilepsy and that she needed medication to control her fits. After a few weeks, she was put on an intravenous drip. The hospital staff forgot to include her epilepsy medication in the drip feed. As a result she had a violent and prolonged fit and died.

In everything I have drawn attention to so far the common theme is a lack of understanding and appropriate training among staff leading to poor quality healthcare. That this happens may point to generally poor attitudes in society towards people with a learning disability. However, there are some cases where such poor treatment could be as a result of pure discrimination, when healthcare staff make value judgements about the worth of people with a learning disability. Such cases are notoriously hard to prove, but the body of evidence is significant enough to suggest that discrimination does happen. In one example, a mother of a seventeen-year-old boy with Down's syndrome was wrongly told that her son's heart condition was inoperable. In another, the mother of a thirty-three-year-old woman with profound and multiple learning disabilities who was about to have a kidney scan overheard a doctor say: 'That's not coming in my room. It will destroy the equipment.' There are other cases where doctors appear to question parents' decisions to allow vital surgery to go ahead. And in the most extreme cases, doctors deny treatment by putting 'do not resuscitate' notices in patients' notes or by failing to make life-saving interventions.

Such tragic cases of premature death are the worst consequences of the generally poor attitudes and understanding of healthcare staff towards people with a learning disability. So, what can be done to improve this situation so that people with a learning disability get healthcare treatment that meets their needs?

In our *Treat me right!* report, we set out a number of clear recommendations that would go a long way to addressing the problems outlined above. Mencap was given the opportunity to put these recommendations firmly into the public domain when we gave evidence to the Disability Rights Commission's (DRC) formal investigation into health inequalities experienced by people with a learning disability or mental health problems. And we are delighted that the recommendations for action mirror our own in *Treat me right!*.

At the heart of the DRC's report is the vital recognition that the inequalities in physical health and primary care services experienced by people with a learning disability (and/or mental health problems) require positive, urgent and clear action from all organisations with a role in the provision of health services. The recommendations for how this should happen centre around five key areas. First, healthcare services must ensure that people with a learning disability know their rights in relation to their physical health and the services and support programmes on offer. Second, such services must be made much more readily accessible to people in whatever setting they live (in the family home, in residential care or in supported living). In connection with this, GP practices should make any 'reasonable adjustments', such as longer or more flexible appointments; plus people should be offered regular health check-ups. Third, healthcare services should give people better, more accessible information, advice and support on healthy living, including diet, exercise and the risks around alcohol, drugs and smoking. This and other useful information should be available – in an accessible format – in GP surgeries and other primary healthcare services. Fourth, primary care staff should get comprehensive training in learning disability, involving people with a learning disability themselves. And fifth, the planning of services for people with a learning disability should take much greater account of their physical health needs. In connection with this, people should have 'health passports' linked to individual health action plans.

As I explained, these key recommendations closely match those in our *Treat me right!* report so I need not set these out in full. However, there are a few additional measures we would like to see. In particular, we want secondary healthcare services (i.e. hospitals) to fulfil their legal duty of care and provide appropriate levels of support to patients with a learning disability. It's also important that all health screening programmes ensure that people with a learning disability have the same access rate as other people. Plus health records should also show clearly if someone has a learning disability.

So, where does all this leave us? What impact will the DRC's report on health inequalities have on the Government and healthcare services? And will things really change for the better?

Well, in a sense, we've already been here. Previous reports by Mencap and others have highlighted all the problems outlined above. And the Government has made the right noises in response, acknowledging the barriers that people face in getting the services they need. Indeed, it has been NHS policy for many years that people with a learning disability should have equal access to mainstream services. But there can be a huge difference between policy and action.

However, there is cause for us to be hopeful, albeit cautiously. Already one of our key recommendations in *Treat me right!* has been acted upon: the Government has agreed that the National Patient Safety Agency (NPSA) will carry out a confidential inquiry into the premature deaths of people with a learning disability. They have also agreed the principle of health checks for people with a learning disability. We will also keep pressing both the Healthcare Commission and the Department of Health to have rigorous performance indicators to ensure marked improvements in the quality of care provided and we note that the *Valuing People* Support Team is already doing good work on this front, and we will help whenever possible.

There are other reasons for optimism. Under the Disability Discrimination Act 2005 there is a new Public Sector Duty requiring all public sector bodies to produce disability equality plans. These plans will certainly have to address how health inequalities can be reduced. This should have a major impact on the quality of healthcare services for people with a learning disability.

In fact, the general trend of Government thinking on healthcare provision seems to be heading in the right direction. There appears to be a commitment to tackle the problem of health inequalities (although we are concerned that its only focus is on inequalities due to socio-economic background as opposed to disability). Meanwhile, the White Paper on health and social care services in England, *Our Health, Our Care, Our Say*, aims to give people with a learning disability much greater control of their own well-being through the introduction of individual budgets. It also makes crucial reference to the need for regular health checks for people with a learning disability, as well as making a commitment to closing down the remaining 3,000 places in NHS residential accommodation and campuses. And it proposes to bring forward a review of the Carers' Strategy, stating that local authorities will be required to provide emergency short-break support for carers of people with profound and multiple learning disabilities.

While we welcome the plans set out in this White Paper, we are concerned that it does not explain where the necessary funding will come from, in particular in relation to individual budgets and regular (not only emergency) short breaks for family carers. However, it isn't all about funding. Indeed, the vast majority of the changes recommended by both the DRC's report and *Treat me right!* need not cost a penny extra. Rather they are about attitudes towards people with a learning disability. If people with a learning disability were valued as equal citizens, they wouldn't experience discrimination and a poor quality of service from our public institutions. This has been the recurring theme throughout my argument. It is also, perhaps, the recurring theme throughout the history of people with a learning disability – and, indeed, this book.

Treat Me Right!
2

Neal Kinsella

Neal Kinsella, thirty-four, from Finstock, near Whitney in Oxfordshire, is a member of Whitney and District Mencap. He is very involved in a range of different campaigns for the group, such as day services and transport. He was also a Mencap National Assembly representative from October 2002 until June 2006. He enjoyed his role hugely, but decided to step down to allow himself enough time to concentrate on a computer course he is currently taking through Learn Direct. He hopes to get a job working with computers at the end of this course. Neal currently works part-time for the self-advocacy group My Life My Choice in Oxford. He has worked there for seven years. Prior to this, he worked for ten years in a local delicatessen shop. Here, Neal tells his story about his experiences in hospital.

On 23 March 2004 I was admitted to the John Radcliffe Hospital in Oxford with pneumonia on my lungs. I was given morphine and oxygen and taken to intensive care. I felt strange but I was very well looked after. I don't remember anything about being in intensive care, because I was heavily sedated.

My mum and dad came to see me every day. They talked to me about my friends and family and put all my get well soon cards up for me. They put up a photograph of me so that the staff could see what I looked like before I was a patient. The doctor and nurses arranged for a bed to be brought in especially for me; it had air cushions and a cooling blanket and it could roll me over! It was a real Rolls-Royce bed. My mum wanted me to be treated with homeopathic medicine, which the hospital helped her with. I wasn't able to eat anything so the medicines were rubbed on to my wrists.

When I came round after seventeen days in the intensive care unit, I wasn't sure where I was. I felt relaxed but drowsy. My mum and dad were both there. After three weeks in intensive care I was allowed to go up to the medical ward. I was given a lot of attention on the ward; the nurses really looked after me. I was given physiotherapy because I needed help to start walking because my legs felt like jelly but I soon got the hang of it.

After two weeks in the ward I was allowed to go home. I had to rest for five weeks so I had to use a wheelchair if I went out so I wouldn't get too tired.

In June 2004 I had to go back to hospital to see the consultant. He gave me the all-clear but made an appointment for me to see him again because of the hole I have in my heart. I was called back to the hospital for many investigations in January 2005. They wanted to use a tiny camera to look at my heart but decided not to because it would be too distressing for me. So an MRI scan was arranged for 13 April. This involved being put in a big chamber which gave the doctors a moving picture of everything that's happening inside me. Unfortunately, they still couldn't see exactly where the hole was so they asked me to go to the coronary clinic in July.

My condition is not life-threatening and the doctor suggested that I might think about having surgery to mend the hole in my heart. This would involve minor surgery – inserting a little spongy double-headed umbrella into my heart, which would block the hole. They use a little camera to do this. The operation means I would only have to go into hospital for one day. I had an appointment in July 2006 to see the specialist again so I had some time to decide if I wanted to have the operation or not.

I'm feeling a lot better now. It has been a roller coaster of a ride for me but, thankfully, one with a very happy ending!

Postscript

Since Neal wrote this story in summer 2005, his medical condition has been under continuing investigation. It has not yet been decided if he will have an operation to block the hole in his heart.

CHAPTER 14

Profound and Multiple Learning Disability

I am honoured to be the President of the Roy Kinnear Foundation. For two years, from 1967 to 1969, Carmel Cryan, a bubbly, red-headed Irish actress, was in my company at the Garrick Theatre when we were romping through a very funny farce, *Let Sleeping Wives Lie*, by Harold Brooke and Kay Bannerman. Others in the splendid cast were Leslie Crowther, Andrew Sachs, Leo Franklyn, Derek Farr, Bill Treacher, Anna Dawson, Dennis Ramsden, my wife Elspet (Gray) and me. It was a jolly time and it was in those halcyon days that Carmel and Roy Kinnear began their relationship. A year or two later they married and the story of their first child follows.

Karina

Carmel Kinnear
Founder of the Roy Kinnear Foundation

Karina, the first of our three children, was born on 4 October 1971, after a twenty-one-hour labour and forceps delivery. The professor who was supposed to attend the birth was unfortunately unable to be present so a rather inexperienced young doctor was put in charge of the delivery. When the waters broke there was green meconium, which can indicate that the baby is in distress. However, as my pregnancy had been trouble-free, the staff were told to continue with a normal delivery and listen to the foetal heart every thirty minutes. (Nowadays, having a foetal monitor on the mother's stomach for the full duration of the labour and delivery is standard.) Despite the green meconium, which was cleared from Karina at birth, she did not appear to have any problems. She looked beautiful and healthy, and Roy and I were overjoyed. Four hours after Karina was born, she had a cyanotic attack, which we were told later was like a small epileptic attack. She was taken to the special care unit as a precaution but flourished very quickly, breast feeding and reacting to stimuli. Three days later, we went home very happy.

After a few weeks, it was noted that Karina was not gaining weight. She was then put on to milk formula which resolved this problem, but I began to notice other differences between her development and other friends' children born at the same time. She always kicked to one side of her body and did not seem to respond well to visual stimuli. At four and a half months, Karina was diagnosed with cerebral palsy due to a lack of oxygen at birth. When I went to see the professor, he was amazed. As if in some way to explain what had happened, he said, 'Of course, in retrospect, I should have given you a Caesarean, but green meconium does not always mean a child will be a spastic'. He then ordered foetal monitors for his obstetric department.

You are so shocked when something goes wrong with your first child, you really cannot believe it has happened. Through the emotional haze of that time certain things stick out. After we were told of Karina's disability, which was not yet really apparent, one of the paediatricians asked if we could come and speak to a group of medical students to tell them how we felt the next day. Still reeling from the news and unable to think straight, we agreed, initially unaware of how insensitively we were being exploited. We would have benefited from a little time to build up the necessary strength for this ordeal.

Karina was under the care of the Child Development Centre at Charing Cross Hospital, which had just been built. This was an excellent centre with doctors, physiotherapists, speech therapists and psychologists all in one small building, like a family home. Karina attended two or three times a week for physio and any other help we needed for feeding, change of medication and general reassurance. It was a lifeline for which we were so grateful. A wonderful physio called Nancy Finnie, who wrote the excellent book *Handling the Cerebral Palsied Child*, worked skilfully and lovingly on Karina's body every week. She gave us such hope, love and support and was like a member of our family, remaining a dear friend until her death a few years ago.

We had been informed that Karina might at some time develop epilepsy, and when she was seven months old she had her first epileptic attack. We phoned the hospital straight away but her paediatrician was in a meeting and could not be disturbed. So we were told to go straight to our GP's surgery. What followed, just like the professor's absence the weekend of Karina's birth, proved to us that sometimes in life you're just powerless to change the dice you're thrown. Our GP was leaving the surgery as we arrived, supporting a patient. 'Roy, Carmel!' he said. 'I'm so sorry: this man is having a heart attack. If I don't get him to hospital right now he will die! Wait for me – I'll be back in ten minutes.' Roehampton Hospital was very near so we waited in the surgery for his return. Karina did not seem to be in much distress as she seemed to be twitching only a little in the corner of her mouth, but neither of us had seen someone having an epileptic fit before. We thought it would be much more dramatic if it was serious. When our GP returned, he phoned Karina's paediatrician again. As the latter was still busy, our GP was told to phone another paediatrician at a different hospital. Our doctor phoned three other paediatricians before he found someone who was able to tell him the correct dosage of Valium to inject into her. (If you give too large a dose, the patient can go into a coma.) All of this wasted valuable time. We often regretted not having gone to Charing Cross Hospital straight away. Karina was definitely far more damaged mentally after this episode and had to go on sedation.

Karina did not sleep at all well, resulting in years of sleepless nights for us. We took it in turns to attend to her at night. Roy always said he loved it the night it was his turn to attend to her because he knew the next night he could sleep right through!

A few years later Kirsty was born. It was a joy to have a child walking around the house and speaking. Even when she was very small, she was very protective of Karina. As a parent you are aware of how disability affects the rest of the family but you are united in your love and enthusiasm and you carry on with all the energy you have inside you. We truly felt that if we worked on Karina with physio and stimulation twelve hours a day she could get better.

A few years later Rory was born and I was so delighted for Kirsty that she now had a normal sibling to play with, like her other friends. Kirsty was always worried about Karina's health and Rory tried to find new ways to make her laugh.

Karina used to go to a day centre in Earlsfield from the age of three. She was taken every morning by the ever cheerful Peggy and Jim, who took such care of the young children in the bus.

When Karina was four years old, Cheyne Walk Centre for Spastics was recommended to us as an excellent junior school. We knew Karina would have to be assessed as the young people were supposed to have a mental age of two before they were accepted and there was no way Karina had this mental capacity. We taught her some skills we thought would impress: taking hoops off a pole and putting them on to a table, banging a bell with a little hammer, and several other little tricks that she learned through repetition and praise. Having actor parents obviously helped for her first big audition. She was accepted. We could not have been more overjoyed if she had got a double first at Oxford or Cambridge. We foolishly thought all our problems were solved.

Everyone at Cheyne Walk was so knowledgeable about all the young people's disabilities. The physio was excellent; as were the drama and music facilities – all under one roof. So much time was spent teaching them to eat and drink properly and toileting, in order to prepare them for as independent a life as possible. Sadly, this wonderful centre was closed about three years ago. All that expertise was disbanded and that centre of excellence lost for ever.

We were also lucky to find a wonderful girl called Hilary who lived with us for several years, allowing us both to work when we wanted (I didn't get asked as often as Roy did). Hilary could not have loved Karina, Kirsty and Rory more if they had belonged to her own family. Before Karina went away to school, we did not have any respite care. Roy's family were in Scotland and mine in Ireland, so Hilary was very important in our lives. When Karina went to boarding school, though, Hilary left to train as a nurse, but she was one of the first people through the door after Roy's death in Spain. She and her lovely husband had driven through the night from Mansfield.

Karina was now having great difficulty with her feeding. Taking up to two hours to eat, she was sometimes sick afterwards, sending us back to square one. A very bad chest infection followed, which required her to be suctioned through her nose twice a day. We were getting exhausted and depressed, resigned to the fact that her condition would never improve much. A weekly boarding school in Hindhead was recommended and, having visited several times with Karina, we reluctantly sent her there, with fear and trepidation in our hearts. We had many sleepless nights worrying about this massive decision. The guilt, and the feelings of abandoning her and missing her, were overwhelming. We would take her back to her school after a weekend with us and then cry all the way back home on the A3. Roy nicknamed us 'The Blubbers'. In the end, since we were unhappy with the level of care she was receiving and the increased frequency of her chest infections, we had to take her away.

We heard from the staff at Roehampton Hospital that Tadworth Children's Hospital was building a small house for ten young children in their grounds, next to St Margaret's School. This would have all the medical expertise which we required, along with schooling, physiotherapy, speech therapy, swimming, etc. all on site. We hurried down there that day, as eight of the places had already been taken. We were delighted when she was accepted. Karina used to come home every other weekend and for school holidays. She remained at Tadworth for five years. During this time, because she was being fed orally (she is now fed by peg tube), sometimes the food would go down the wrong way, due to a poor swallowing reflex, causing her to develop a chest infection. There were quite a few occasions when we would have to drive to Tadworth in the middle of the night, hearts in our mouths, when she had suddenly been admitted to hospital with a chest infection. Whenever this happened after Roy died, I had to leave the other children at home on their own. I remember thinking while driving that Karina would have to attend somewhere nearer to our home after the age of nineteen, the age when she would have to leave Tadworth.

Roy died in 1988, while rehearsing a scene in Spain for the film *The Return of the Musketeers*. His horse slipped on cobbles that did not have sufficient sand on them to make the ride safe. He fractured his pelvis, but it was internal bleeding over the next twenty-four hours which caused his death. All he needed was a blood transfusion. He had been moved to three different hospitals. I was with him for his final hours when the consultant kept trying to reassure me with the words, 'Bueno, no haemorrhage!' The autopsy would reveal that he had lost five pints of blood.

Karina was sixteen at the time and the impact on all our lives was, naturally, catastrophic. Roy and I had a blissfully happy marriage for eighteen years and throughout our married life had shared the emotional and physical strains that came with having a disabled child. Sometimes we felt lucky for the effect Karina's problems had in strengthening our relationship to a depth that some couples could never reach. With Roy's support, love and ability to share the problems all now ripped away from me, I felt as if my life support had been switched off. After a long period of misery, I began slowly to emerge from the darkest days of my life, with the help of family, friends and neighbours. I was at least surviving, helped by the responsibility of having to look after three young people whom I loved desperately and who needed me as much as I needed them,

Directly after the accident I had to find a lawyer to begin legal proceedings against the film company and their insurers for allowing the fatal horse ride to go ahead. I originally commissioned D.I. Freeman, but after four years without any real progress and ever-increasing costs, our wonderful actors' union, Equity, took over the case, leading to a successful conclusion in the High Court in 1994.

One year after Roy's death, Karina underwent a major operation to have two Harrington rods inserted in her back because the scoliosis in her spine was deteriorating rapidly. Unfortunately, she suffered a lack of oxygenated blood supply to some of her nerves during or after the operation, resulting in her becoming paraplegic from the waist down. The one thing that you could say about bereavement while looking after a seriously ill child is that you're certainly not allowed to wallow in grief.

It really was sink or swim. I had been so lucky to have all those years of Roy's support. I have met many mothers, some of whom have had two disabled children, who have not had that privilege and have had to cope entirely on their own for many years.

Throughout this time, I still had the huge dilemma of where Karina would live when her educational funding ran out at nineteen. An unfortunate consequence of the operation was that Karina now needed to be catheterised, which required nursing intervention. There were so many meetings about potential future residential placements, but none of them had any nursing care. Despite several years of desperately searching I, along with health authorities and social services, was unable to find anywhere suitable near London that didn't have a sterile hospital environment. I visited quite a pleasant nursing establishment in Norfolk but, living in London with two children who would be taking major exams in the future, this was completely impractical, especially in the event of emergencies. The notes on the case merely reported, 'Mother refused placement'.

Tadworth continued to take care of Karina. They had a hospital on site and she enjoyed the hydrotherapy pool, drama, music and the interaction with all the young people. By the age of nineteen and a half, she could not stay any longer and came home as nowhere else had been found.

I continued looking while Karina was living at home again, initially without any day-care services. Eventually the Delarue College in Tonbridge offered her a place as they had twenty-four-hour nursing care. The euphoria was short lived. Karina was only there for a year before it closed down. Once again a unique centre of expertise was broken up, with the staff moving to other organisations. The headmistress who had been so kind in taking Karina – by far the most disabled young person they had ever had there – moved to run a school for the blind. I do hope the wonderful drama teacher is helping some other group of disabled young people to enjoy life as Karina did in her classes. Karina came home and I started my search for a future placement all over again.

This eight-year period in which Karina lived with us again was obviously full of stress, struggle and sheer hard work. But it had its rewards as well. She is so important in our lives and I believe it has given all of the family a deep relationship with her, which we might not otherwise have had. In some ways it has given both my other children a sense of perspective about what is important in life. Despite her disabilities she continues to a offer a great deal to people who meet her. Karina needs total care in her daily life; she is in a wheelchair, does not speak, has severe asthma, a hiatus hernia, impaired vision, osteoporosis and is fed by peg tube. Amazingly, though, she still has a happy life. Her favourite activities are music, swimming, going for walks, circuses and musical shows, wheelchair dancing, story-telling. In the last few years, she has even acquired the art of using some computer pro- grammes by employing a specially adapted large yellow button that she bangs at intervals, producing sounds and music and various amusing images on the screen. In spite of all her problems, she has a joyous personality with a laugh that touches everyone. Mentally, she is like a young baby but when one considers what she has been through – the endless hospitalisations, suctioning, physio, injections, drips, wheel- chair fittings, scans, etc. – her incredible determination to live is enormously inspiring.

Roy and I had often said we would one day like to build the definitive centre for the young disabled and I was now aware of the fact, with nowhere suitable nearby, that I would have to do it myself. David Kernan, who had been in a popular TV series, *That Was The Week That Was*, with Roy many years ago, was now helping to produce and present shows. He suggested that we organised a gala concert to raise money to build or purchase a house for Karina and other young people to live in. In 1994, I made an appointment to see Richard Eyre at the National Theatre as Roy had worked there in several plays the year before he died. I thought it would be a large enough venue to make a decent profit as a deposit for a house. I remember being quite terrified meeting with Richard and about twelve other important people around a long table, giving them a list of the artists who would be performing and the sort of programme that could be expected. In fact, the only person who had agreed to perform at this stage was Dame Judi Dench. In the end, it was an amazing evening with an international cast, including Helena Bonham Carter, Tim Brooke-Taylor, Barry Cryer, Frank Finlay, Charlton Heston, Eddie Izzard, Brian Murphy, Peter O'Toole, Michael Palin, Victor Spinetti, Peter Ustinov, Richard Wilson, Michael York and a host of other wonderful theatre friends. We made about £50,000 from the show.

However, I realised £50,000 was not enough money to do anything with, so I organised a fundraising committee, headed by an amazingly enthusiastic woman called Roma Hooper. I also engaged a secretary with whom I started writing to trusts and foundations that donated money specifically for people with learning difficulties and disabilities. Many local charities were incredibly generous. We were amazed and so grateful for the kindness of so many of these organisations. We arranged a lunch at the House of Lords, hosted by the President of the Roy Kinnear Foundation, Brian (Lord) Rix, and one at the Garrick Club, hosted by Dame Judi Dench, which brought in considerable funding. Roma and her committee continued to organise balls, marathons, fashion shows and many other fundraising events.

In 1997 we purchased a lovely house in Twickenham, which had four bedrooms, good downstairs accommodation, a very large old garden and ample room for a large extension at the back of the house. By this time I had acquired the considerable talents of a gentleman called John Rice, who came to work for us two and sometimes three days a week for absolutely nothing except his petrol money. John had been recommended by a company called Reach, which provides charities with retired executives who still have a great deal of brainpower but are no longer in full-time employment. I shall always be grateful to John for his continued help over seven years and, as he put it, 'you needed someone to keep your feet on the ground.' We had eight personally chosen trustees who helped very much with the building programme over the next few years.

We decided to name the building Roy Kinnear House and the charity the Roy Kinnear Trust (later becoming the Roy Kinnear Foundation), as it was because of Roy's name, initially, that I was able to succeed with the fundraising. During this time we also won our court case against the film company and the hospital. This ended six years of yet another struggle, fighting for a sense of justice over what had been an horrendous and unnecessary casualty of poor safety practices on a film set; as well as an appalling standard of medical care at the last two hospitals tending Roy. Ironically, we settled the case in the High Court on Karina's birthday, 4 October 1994.

During this time, Karina was still living at home and going for day-care services, after much negotiation, to Ravenswood village in Crowthorne. We had funding from Health and Social Services for a full-time nurse from 8.30 am to 6 pm. The nurse would travel with Karina to Crowthorne and stay with her during the day. There was at this time no other alternative other than the Neurodisability Hospital in Putney. This arrangement continued until 2000, when Karina at last went to live at Roy Kinnear House.

Over this period, Karina's funding was reduced on several occasions and I ended up having to pay more for the nursing each year myself. Often I was shouted at over the phone in an abusive manner and received unpleasant letters about Karina's funding costs. This sometimes reduced me to tears, but I certainly would not have let them know about it. It is such a relief not to have to go through this deliberately degrading procedure now, since I am no longer involved in those negotiations. So many parents have to go through similar experiences that involve con-stant fighting for the rights of the people who cannot speak for them-selves. In June 2000 Judi Dench kindly opened Roy Kinnear House. In her welcoming speech, she said, 'I have known Carmel for thirty-two years and for thirty of those she has been fighting for disability'.

We have had to change the house considerably. We built on a large extension at the back, where there is a lovely garden with a big pond, waterfall and fountain. We had to fit special bathrooms and an extra bedroom and hoists. It would have been an advantage to have more land with the property but London is not known for wide-open spaces and, although it would have been cheaper outside the capital, the purpose of the house was to have somewhere for people who live in London. Our young people see their parents very regularly and this creates a warm, extended family feeling in the house.

When we were fundraising, we applied to the Mencap Challenge Fund, and we have had two or three special grants since then from the Mencap City Foundation (now the Rix-Thompson-Rothenberg Foundation) for which we are so grateful. So many groups of parents are now arranging to build similar houses for their children. Once the building has been provided, health authorities and social services will usually provide the ongoing costs of care. There is still a long way to go at Roy Kinnear House. Some people are mentioning the idea of Roy Kinnear House 2, but first we need to provide two other bedrooms at this house to make it financially independent so we do not have to keep fundraising.

When we opened the house in 2000, we had another organisation providing the care but this was not a satisfactory arrangement and the Foundation now provides the care for the house. We have an excellent experienced Head of Home with a nursing background, five qualified nurses, two care assistants, a secretary and visiting speech therapists, physios, dieticians, reflexologists, masseurs and music therapists. The young people go swimming every week in the local hydrotherapy pool, they attend a sensory centre and we have just had two large pine-log cabins built in the garden to provide more day-care services ourselves.

Roy Kinnear House is a facility that was desperately needed in the community. All of our young people need nursing help at certain times of the day and there are so few places that provide this care. We still need to improve and move on: hopefully our day-care services can expand and extra physiotherapy can be acquired. Originally the house was built as a centre of excellence, which it continues to be, and I hope any future Roy Kinnear houses will be, too. We must not be complacent and we have to look out for new ways of improving the quality of life for the young people who live at the house.

As a young actress with dreams and ambitions this was a world in which I never imagined to find myself; a world I was thrust into by the fickle hand of fate and kept in by a parent's instinct to care for her child. I can't say I would not have wanted it any other way but, through the good people it has brought me into contact with – the helpers, the selfless givers of time, the other parents fighting for their children's right to a quality of life – it has shown me that in the darkest of times and situations there are still great, warm, life-enhancing shafts of light. Throughout I have been grateful to everyone who has shone some of this light on me, and hope it continues to shine on our charity long after our story has been forgotten.

The Story of Mencap's PRMH Project

Loretto Lambe

Tell me about the origins of the PRMH Project.
Brian Rix has already told the story about setting up the project in the Mencap diary and in his own story in Chapter 4. To recap briefly, shortly after Brian became Mencap's Secretary-General he was interviewed in Birmingham for BBC Pebble Mill and a mother in the audience, Mary McCormack, asked Brian what Mencap was doing for people like her son who had profound mental handicap and multiple disabilities. Brian replied that he didn't know (he'd only just taken over the organisation) and thought that we did very little and he'd go away and find out.

And what did he find out?
Just what he'd expected – very little was done for this group – and as we subsequently discovered, very few families caring for a daughter or son with profound disabilities had any contact with Mencap. His response to this was to bring together the relevant people in Mencap, such as the Chairman of the Education and Training Committee, Peter Wildblood (the Head Teacher of the largest special needs school in Birmingham, if not in the country); the Director of Education and Training, James Cummings; Ann Allen, another mother of a son with profound and multiple learning disabilities; myself and, from outside the organisation, Dr (now Professor) James Hogg from the Hester Adrian Research Centre (HARC) at Manchester University, one of the few people who had at that time undertaken research with this group, plus Fred Heddell when he, too, was still the Head Teacher of a special school. Others who joined an advisory committee, chaired by Peter Wildblood, were Dafydd Wigley, then an MP, Leader of Plaid Cymru and the father of two disabled sons, Jean Willson, yet another mother who had worked miracles with a profoundly disabled daughter, and the Secretary-General, Brian Rix. The project was given the label PRMH, which stood for the wording used in those days, Profound Retardation and Multiple Handicap.

Why James Hogg and why a centre in Manchester?

At the time, the Hester Adrian Research Unit was the largest research unit in Europe working in the field of what we would now call intellectual disability research. James had undertaken some of the earliest research in this field, as well as writing two seminal books with Judy Sebba on the education and therapy for people with profound intellectual and multiple disabilities. It was agreed by the advisory committee that the new project – the PRMH Project, as it was then called – would develop a model of support for families caring for someone with profound disabilities which could then be used by those working for Mencap throughout England, Wales and Northern Ireland. Because of the possibility of working closely with the HARC, it was decided, in the mid eighties, to locate the project in Manchester.

Were you based at Manchester University?

No. After much to-ing and fro-ing we were fortunate to find offices in Piper Hill Special School, one of the five Manchester schools for children with intellectual disabilities run by Manchester City Council. Over one-third of the pupils had profound and multiple learning disabilities (PMLD) and being located there brought us closely into contact with families and professionals. We had unstinting support from the Head Teacher, Sue Fagg, and her staff.

How did you go about setting up the project?

From the outset we were determined that the work we did would be based on the needs of parents and people with PMLD (you will note that I am now using the initials preferred by Mencap), rather than being imposed from the top down. We undertook a huge national survey which yielded several hundred returns to a very long questionnaire which gave parents and professionals the chance to say what were their needs and aspirations. We also met with groups of parents and discussed with them how best the project could support them.

And the upshot of this consultation exercise?

This confirmed, first, how extensive were the demands for someone with PMLD. Families provided, on average, seven and a half hours in direct care activities each day and did not receive the professional support they needed.

What were the areas in which they needed most help and were there any surprises?
Given the very high level of physical and sensory disabilities, some of their needs were only to be expected. They wanted support for what has come to be called 'physical management' and help with understanding and improving communication, as well as practical, day-to-day issues. Other areas of concern were more surprising: for example, the poor quality of oral health care their daughters and sons received and the absence of suitable and/or accessible leisure opportunities in the home and community. Remember that in those days no one was talking about leisure and PMLD, a situation that has changed markedly in the subsequent twenty years. Families were also in need of personal and emotional support as they coped with the undoubted stresses they experienced. However, their overriding concern was 'what will happen when we [the parents] are no longer here?'

How did the project set about meeting such a multiplicity of needs?
We did this in three principal ways. First, we offered individual support to help families deal with a range of practical and emotional difficulties they encountered. This led to some very close relationships and I'm still in touch with some of these families twenty years later and some four hundred miles apart. Second, we offered information to enquirers – information on rights and entitlements, availability of therapies and so on. We began to develop a very comprehensive information resource on which families and our small staff could draw. Third, we developed a programme of training workshops for families addressing the very issues raised by them.

What topics did you deal with?
Some I've already mentioned: oral health care, improving knowledge about non-verbal communication, physical management, as well as understanding the benefits system, understanding and managing epilepsy, supporting a daughter or son with challenging behaviour and so on. Most of these workshops ran for three days in successive weeks and

often involved individual follow-ups where parents could consult with the course tutors about their individual problems. The course tutors were always the top people in their field, and they gave their time unstintingly because they found such close contact with families helped their own understanding.

I've always heard professionals say that they find it near impossible to get hard-pressed family carers to come to workshops like that. What was the trick?
There was no trick. Again we consulted with family carers as to what would enable them to attend the workshops, for the main issue was who would look after their son or daughter and their siblings while they were out of the house. So, we initially held the workshops in schools during the holidays and provided parallel leisure schemes, which were fully inclusive, for the children and young people who attended. We tailored the hours to families' needs and we provided transport where this was required. Translation was provided for families for whom English was not a first language. The whole event was made a thoroughly enjoyable day out, with a good lunch and often a glass of wine. Parents were given the chance to talk together, as this always provided an important part of the day.

Were the workshops successful?
Very successful. We evaluated them very carefully and where improvements could be made, we did so at subsequent events. The whole programme was written up, together with the evaluations, in what became known as our 'red books', on account of the Mencap red covers. Parents were also given a very comprehensive participants' pack which covered all the workshop material and local services. Some parents referred to these packs as the 'Bible', and when I did home visits I would often see them prominently displayed.

Was the 'Bible' available to non-Christians?
Of course. In a multi-ethnic community like Manchester we had many people for whom English was not their first language and we provided individual interpreters and translations of the packs.

You mentioned earlier that the intention was to develop a model of support and then use this more widely throughout Mencap's services. Is that what happened?

Mencap subsequently made attempts to start this by making commercially available packs which would enable others to put on the workshops we had run. For example, packs for potential trainers based on the workshop on oral health care and on communication were prepared and published. The difficulty was that the support structure I described above, which enabled us to put on the training workshops, was simply not available outside Manchester and, as you said, it is notoriously difficult for parents to attend training events – without that support, I would say almost impossible. The trainers' packs never had the intended impact.

So staff teams, like Mencap's Manchester team, were called for elsewhere?

Undoubtedly. We developed a plan that would progressively roll out our project's model across the Mencap regions. This was prepared and costed, but sadly never implemented. At this stage Brian Rix's successor informed us 'that the word "project" means "project", that is, it has a beginning and an end'.

In other words, you were to be terminated.

Yes, after only five years of honest endeavour which was bringing forth much comfort and understanding for those with a profound and multiple learning disability, we thought the project was to come to an end and the wider dissemination of our work would not be carried through.

And is that what happened?

Not quite. James Hogg and I felt that this unique project had achieved so much that we were not prepared to see the end of it. We set about developing an independent voluntary organisation which would continue to focus on the needs of people with PMLD and their families. This led to the development of PAMIS (Promoting A More Inclusive Society) with support from Derek Adams of Barclays Bank Charitable Trust, Colin Whiteside of (then) PriceWaterhouse, plus two stalwarts from the old advisory committee, Dafydd Wigley MP and Jean Willson. PAMIS was registered with the Charity Commission in 1992.

Were you able then to roll out the project model as you intended?
Yes, but not in England and Wales. James and I (married by this time) moved to the University of Dundee in Scotland. We immediately received funding from the Scottish Office to begin regional development supporting work for people with PMLD and their families. Over the past thirteen years we now have coordinators and development workers in a quarter of Scottish local authorities with the same three aims as we had for the Mencap Project: individual support, provision of information and workshop programmes on topics of the parents' choice. We have also developed a whole range of inclusive leisure projects across Scotland. We have twenty-four staff members working exclusively with families with a relative with PMLD, but also working closely on policy development with the Scottish Executive and MHS Scotland. PAMIS parents sit on all the major national intellectual disability committees and stakeholder groups. PAMIS has established a PIMD (we use the term Profound Intellectual and Multiple Disability to the one preferred by Mencap, Profound and Multiple Learning Disability) network of parents and professionals with a bulletin board dealing with key issues and supported by core funding from the Scottish Executive. PAMIS, too, has become a unit within the University of Dundee's Faculty of Education and Social Work.

Where can I learn more about your present work?
We've an excellent website. Visit us there: www.dundee.ac.uk/pamis

And Mencap?
Mencap currently has a National Officer for Profound and Multiple Learning Disabilities (Beverley Dawkins) and PAMIS works very closely with her, as indeed we now do with several European and international groups involved in PMLD. At present Mencap and PAMIS are jointly working on a national campaign, Changing Places, to provide fully accessible toilets in public places, a campaign originally started by PAMIS. This is a very good example of voluntary agencies working together to achieve common goals.

What have you personally taken from over twenty years of such intensive work with people with PMLD and their families?

My real experience began at the start of the Mencap project when a mother with two daughters with very significant and complex disabilities invited me to spend a series of days in her home. I was overwhelmed and moved by the intensity of care she provided and the way in which it was only possible to cope by organising her whole life around them. I learnt, too, of the pressure this put on the girls' brother and the isolation he uncomplainingly bore. Later there was the sadness of attending each of the girls' funerals. I've been very, very privileged to meet and work with so many families who contribute so much in extreme situations with such incredible good humour. James and I often come home at night and say quite simply: 'We haven't got any problems'.

Mike Powderly
Former Head of Life Chances, Mencap

Life for people with profound and multiple disabilities remains extremely hard. They are often isolated, poor and without the range of services required to meet their complex needs. Often difficult to diagnose and even more difficult to support, people with profound and multiple disabilities are the least well served by health services, social care and education. It is almost always their families and carers who remain responsible for ensuring that they are supported and cared for on a daily basis, year in year out, often without regular respite care.

We know that short-term breaks and home support is under-provided. In a *Panorama* programme in 2003 we saw examples of six families struggling to live their lives because of inadequate support. In one case a profoundly disabled young women and her family were assessed as needing only six hours of support a week. And in the event, this was not provided because the local authority claimed that it was unable to recruit suitable staff.

Where people with profound and multiple disabilities do receive day-service support this is often provided in segregated and isolated settings wholly inconsistent with being able to live a valued life as part of their community. People with profound and multiple needs are often unable to access their community. Transport is not available, shops and town centres are not designed to meet the needs of people, there are few changing facilities to meet the needs of those with continence problems, restaurants and food providers are often unable to meet the needs of their profoundly disabled customers.

Families of people with a profound and multiple disability often bear a heavy burden of responsibility. They find themselves in a position of conflict with decision makers. Family relationships become strained and life becomes unbearingly difficult. With the right support and help, Mencap aims to ensure that families get the opportunity to live better lives.

We will be working with the families of people with a profound and multiple disability to ensure that they receive better services more often; to make local town and city centres more accessible; to raise awareness of the needs of this least well-served group.

We will work directly with people whose lives are challenged, learn from those experiences and develop resources, skills and methods of support to let people know that they are not alone and that together we can make a difference.

CHAPTER 15

Fundraising

Dame Norma Major DBE
Vice-President, Mencap

When I was a child I remember that Peter always seemed cheerful, always found something to laugh about. I know now that when the door closed on our visit his parents, my great aunt and uncle, had little to laugh about. For Peter was spastic, they were elderly and trying to cope with the disability of a grown man. We don't use the word 'spastic' any more. Peter suffered from cerebral palsy and we now know far more about the condition than we did in the 1950s. It is distressing to realise that he probably had a greater understanding of what was going on around him than was evident at the time.

In every field of disability there will always be more that can be done, and we must strive to do it. With 1.5 million people in the United Kingdom with a learning disability, all needing more help and support than Government can provide, there is a perpetual need for more money, and supporters of Mencap are full of ingenuity about how to raise it. Fundraising is never easy, but it is infinitely worthwhile and when the money is wisely spent it can make a real difference to the quality of life in all its aspects, for those with moderate learning difficulties as well as those with profound and multiple disabilities, and their families and carers.

I was introduced to the work of Mencap in Huntingdon, by Lord Renton, when, after thirty-four-years in the Commons, he announced his retirement and John was selected as his successor. It was the start of a long and close friendship.

David and his wife Paddy had an adult daughter with a severe learning disability, and it was this circumstance and David's role, at that time Chairman of Mencap, that prompted my involvement with the work of the Society. The Huntingdon Society was active in the provision of group housing, training and respite care and in the support of the families of those with a learning disability. In due course, with the help of friends, awash with exciting ideas, we began to fundraise with a specific project in mind – a purpose-built respite-care home for children in Peterborough. Local people and businesses were hugely supportive, contributing sponsorship, buying tickets for balls and race days, attending the antiques fairs we organised and coming to opera performances at historic Elton Hall, made available by the generosity of Sir William and Lady Proby.

The opera evenings were particularly successful and when John became Prime Minister I decided to stage them at Chequers, his official country residence. With the help of Lady Harris – surely one of the most innovative fundraisers of all – and a dedicated committee, several such evenings were held. It was hard work for all involved, but it was fun and, most important of all, it raised, as Mencap's share, around £2.5 million. It was with this sum that we established the Mencap Challenge Fund with a view to initiating activity over and above the excellent work that Mencap already did.

During those privileged years we also staged a cricket match at the Oval, when professional and amateur players joined together for a wonderful afternoon of cricket. On a balmy, sunny Sunday everyone performed creditably on this hallowed pitch. My son-in-law Luke was 'man of the match', and my son James hit two sixes, a four and a couple of singles, and caught and bowled out members of the opposing team. John and I hosted a dinner at No. 10 to round off a day that significantly boosted the Challenge Fund account.

Groups under the Mencap umbrella, many of them endeavouring to get imaginative projects started, were invited to make an application to the Challenge Fund. The Fund has been able to help people across the whole range of learning disability from children on the autistic spectrum and those with profound special needs to young adults and the elderly. Up and down the country the Challenge Fund has contributed to a variety of initiatives, from the provision of sensory rooms and special equipment to the expansion and development of arts and sports projects, and projects which encourage people with a learning disability to become part of a wider community and make the most of all the opportunities that the rest of us so often take for granted.

Meanwhile, in Huntingdon, our fundraising continued. Local supporters of Mencap, like the indefatigable Steve Moss who did battle on our behalf with planners and builders, have been a rich source of ideas. An annual cricket match instigated by David Pilling at Alconbury has become a local tradition in which David English brings his all-celebrity Bunbury team to challenge all comers. Now in its sixteenth year it has provided some memorable days, hugely enjoyed by everyone.

We have tried to use the money raised wisely and where there seemed to be the greatest need. In partnership with the Axiom Housing Association, we built a residential home in Huntingdon so that ten people with a learning disability could be encouraged and enabled to live their life as independently as possible. We named the home Renton Court in honour of Lord Renton's lifetime of work for the charity. Since then we have been able to contribute to the opening of a further group home and a respite-care home, this time for children with a learning disability who are also acutely ill. Most recently in partnership with a hugely successful project in Littleport, Cambridgeshire, called Branching Out (the brainchild of Terry Brook), a redundant funeral parlour was transformed into a state-of-the-art training and education centre which runs in conjunction with Huntingdonshire Regional College.

Although fundraising is crucial, it is not our only purpose. We are concerned also with raising awareness of the extent of the work that Mencap does, as well as the needs of those with disabilities; how to support them as members of the community; how to encourage and train them for employment; how to offer respite care for their families, who so willingly take on the burden of caring. Anyone who has ever cared for a sick relative or friend will know that, however much love is involved, the task is demanding and exhausting. When care is required on a permanent basis, I believe that respite is essential and we help to provide it.

In the past sixty years great progress has been made in understanding disabilities of all kinds and in the provision of funding. We have found ways of enabling a measure of independence once thought impossible and there are now opportunities for those with a learning disability to have a say in the decisions that affect their daily lives. In the realms of care, education and housing, the services and facilities that are available have been greatly enhanced by the work of the voluntary sector. All of these developments have improved the quality of life for those with disabilities and, for this is important too, for those who care for them.

Our work will never be finished. We who are fortunate not to have any disability have an obligation to help provide as much of a normal life as possible for those less fortunate who have often been treated cruelly by fate. They have a right to dignity, a right to choose and the right to enjoy some of the good things of life. It is our privilege and – if it is not an old-fashioned concept – our duty, to help.

The world today for fundraising and communicating

Vanessa Longley
Head of Fundraising, Mencap

The fundraising landscape has changed a great deal since 1946. Charities have had to become increasingly professional in their approach, and it has brought rewards: in 2004, UK donors gave around £6 billion to charities (BACS 2005). However, an ever-increasing number of charities are jostling for public support; figures from the Charity Commission in December 2005 suggest there are now around 170,000 charities, but just 8 per cent of this number receive 90 per cent of the total annual income recorded,

Mencap has always tried to innovate in order to generate income, some of that through good planning, and some through happy accidents.

When in the forties one of our local group members first bought surplus Christmas cards from Frank Kerry, who later went on to found Webb Ivory, she probably wasn't aware that she was helping to found a charity Christmas card industry that's now worth more than £100 million.

And who would have thought that only fifty years from then, hundreds of people would each raise thousands of pounds for the privilege of getting dirty, dusty and dishevelled on one of our challenge events?

Mencap has also been recognised by some of the largest events which take place in the UK, and in 2000 we were adopted as the official charity of the London Marathon. In total a dedicated team of 650 people ran for Mencap, including Jamie Rix, the elder son of our President. We also used this special year as an opportunity to set aside twenty free running places in the marathon for people with a learning disability. Mencap provided the team with accessible training materials and specialist training support and invited other Mencap runners to 'buddy' them. The event was a great success, raising £750,000 for Mencap.

The Mencap Special Events Committee – revived in 1997 – has been an integral part of our fundraising activities ever since, helping to raise vital funds to support Mencap's work. Their most successful event to date was a Bollywood-themed ball which was held at the Hurlingham Club on 15 September 2005, raising over £175,000. However, the committee always strive to devise unique fundraising events in an ever-demanding charity market, and their endeavours have resulted in a ladies' fashion show lunch at the Mandarin Oriental Hyde Park, and 'From Russia with Love', a themed Russian party at One Lombard Street in London.

Many of the committee members have strong reasons to support Mencap, including Gilly Yarrow, who has a son with a learning disability and who recently stepped down as Chair. Gilly and the committee have achieved fantastic results. We cannot thank them enough.

In this, our sixtieth year, Mencap's fundraising activities aim to provide enough interest and excitement for anyone who wants to support our work, from themed balls, with glamour and glitz, to our school Spellathons, which aim to teach literacy and philanthropy hand in hand.

But increasingly, it's a local or personal connection which determines whether someone lends their support to a charity and in 2006 Mencap is trying to respond to this with the reintroduction of regional fundraising teams, setting up fundraising offices in four regional locations which will allow Mencap to work more closely with its local groups, and will help show donors how the money they give to Mencap makes their community better.

Working with partners has become increasingly important, with our grants team leading on collaborative partnerships across Mencap and our large local groups to secure long-term strategic programme funding. Our corporate partnerships team are always looking for ever more innovative ways for charities and companies to work together for their mutual benefit. In 1999, Mencap entered a new partnership with Transco, launching the Health and Safety Challenge which aimed to create a safer working environment for the company, preventing the potential disability caused by accidents at work. By tying donations to Mencap to the spotting, reporting and fixing of hazards, Transco reduced their lost time injury rate by 80 per cent over five years and spotted 40,000 hazards. Mencap received £2.5 million from this partnership and saved the company £5 million. This idea won the Institute of Fundraising's 'Most Innovative Corporate Partnership' Award in 2001 and was shortlisted for the BITC Healthy Workplaces Award in 2005. Since then Mencap has rolled out the challenge with other companies, including Northumbrian Water and Skanska.

Throughout, Mencap has tried to put people with a learning disability at the centre of their fundraising, ensuring that we never forget why we are working so hard to raise money. And we will continue to provide opportunities for people with a learning disability to be more involved in our work, and communicating that to our supporters. Recent editions of *Mencap Matters*, our supporter newsletter, have been written and edited solely by people with a learning disability.

Like all teams across Mencap, we're trying to practise what we preach. Ten staff with the campaigns, communications and fundraising team have a learning disability, a figure we hope to increase.

Putting people with a learning disability at the centre of our awareness-raising activities is important too. While many charities, including Mencap, have successfully used celebrity power to help them get their message across, increasingly we're looking for ways to help people with a learning disability themselves to be role models and take the limelight. The appointment of Paula Sage, an actress with Down's syndrome, as our latest celebrity ambassador, is a fine example.

Paula, star of the critically acclaimed film *Afterlife* and BBC Scotland's *River City*, made movie and soap history by becoming one of the first actors to land leading roles playing characters who, like herself, have a learning disability. Traditionally such parts have gone to actors without disabilities, like Dustin Hoffman in *Rain Man* and Daniel Day Lewis in *My Left Foot*. Paula joins five other official Mencap celebrity ambassadors who devote much time to supporting Mencap's causes, and their stories follow. We are so very grateful for all their support and encouragement.

Mencap Ambassadors

Thank you for the Music

BBC Radio 1 DJ and Mencap ambassador Jo Whiley talks about her sister Frances and how their mutual love of music has created a bond between them

My sister Frances has a learning disability and, when I was younger, I was a member of a group called SIBS. SIBS was set up by Mencap to help people who had brothers and sisters with a learning disability and my mum and dad were very keen that I go. It was kind of helpful, but I never really felt that having a sister with a learning disability was a problem. My parents were obviously very worried that I was being affected by my situation, but I wasn't. I was fine. I was always fine with it really.

Music has definitely helped create a bond between Frances and me. For as long as I can remember she has listened to the chart show religiously. Every week she writes down who she thinks is going to be number one and the entire family have to join in the game and make a prediction too. 'Family' covers a list of about thirty people. Everyone from me, my mum and my dad to the dog and the goldfish! Frances will then listen to the chart countdown, ticking things off as she goes along. When the DJ eventually announces who's top of the charts Frances either cheers or cries. It's so funny.

Frances has her favourites. For example, if Will Young is number one for a couple of weeks, and he drops down to number two, she will have hysterics. She will literally cry, scream and throw tantrums on the floor. But if someone like Chico gets to number one, then she will jump up and go 'Yay!' She likes the big cheesy songs, as much as I try and steer her in a different direction.

Frances can spot a hit a mile off. She likes anything with a massive chorus, so whether it's ABBA, the Spice Girls or 'Show Me the Way to Amarillo', she'll say, 'This is great!' The number of CDs she has got through in her lifetime is just unbelievable. She's so careless with them. I'm always saying, 'Look after the CD; put it back in its case.' And she'll say, 'Yeah, yeah,' and then I'll find it strewn on the ground, scratched to pieces and I'll have to try and get her another one. That's one lesson I can't teach her.

I get a real kick out of DJing with Frances at events like the 'Learning Disability Today' conference, which we try to get to every year. It's just great to meet people and see people with a learning disability having a great time and talking to them. It's something that Frances really looks forward to and when she's there she takes it incredibly seriously. Initially I didn't realise quite how seriously she would take it, but for her it's a proper job and quite often what happens is that while she's putting the records on, lots of people are queuing to get my autograph. I end up just standing there signing, while Frances puts on the CDs.

There have been a number of times when Frances has raised a laugh. When I was ten or eleven I used to swim competitively at a national level. Frances and I used to go to galas together. I'd be standing there on my box, the entire swimming pool completely hushed, and someone would say, 'On your marks, get set . . .' Frances would always shout 'Go!' as the gun went off, but on more then one occasion there was a slow start and Frances would shout 'Go!' too early. I'd be standing on the block, mortally embarrassed, but looking back it was really funny.

Frances was my bridesmaid when Steve and I got married. We walked up the aisle, started the service and got to the vows, but instead of going back to sit in her chair, Frances didn't budge. She stood right by our side, between us and the vicar, for the whole ceremony. It was brilliant. It was exactly where she should be.

Taking Centre Stage

Actor and Mencap ambassador Christopher Eccleston first became properly aware of learning disability in the late eighties when he did extensive research on the subject for his first major film *Let Him Have it*

Christopher played Derek Bentley in the true story of a teenager with a learning disability who was hanged for a murder he didn't commit. More recently, he did *Flesh and Blood*, part of BBC2's disability season, about a thirty-eight-year-old adopted man who finds out that his biological parents both had learning disabilities. Here he talks about his experience of working on both dramas and why he thinks people with a learning disability should be more visible in the world of film, drama and television.

How aware were you of learning disability before you encountered the subject through your acting work?
Only in the way the ordinary man in the street is acquainted with it. I'd had no specific contact. Nobody in my family had a learning disability. Nobody in my close social circle. But I was brought up very well by my parents not to be frightened of people with a disability and always to see the positive in them.

Your first film role was playing Derek Bentley in Let Him Have It. *What kind of research did you have to do for that role?*
I had two things to confront with Derek. He was nineteen and, at the time of the crime, had an estimated learning age of eleven. He also had epilepsy. So my research involved meeting people who had both conditions, getting a feel for them, spending time with them and observing how they dealt with their lives.

How did that research influence your portrayal of Derek?
At the time I remember having quite a tussle with the directors and filmmakers about not portraying Derek as an 'idiot savant'. I felt that they were taking a sentimental approach to both his working-class background and his learning disability. It was very clear to me that there

was a dark side to Derek's condition, which was to a certain extent exploited by the young men he was running around with but also, most horribly, by the authorities. Derek was framed for a murder he didn't commit. It was very easy to present him as unsociable and aggressive in a courtroom situation, because basically he didn't know what was going on. I felt that if one is going to present learning disability in a drama, one has got an obligation to present it in all its reality – its positive and its negative sides. Otherwise you're just hitching a ride.

Did the film change your perception of learning disability?
Of course. It showed me both the advantages and disadvantages of having a learning disability. Derek's openness to suggestion led him into terrible trouble, but alongside that was a tremendously open nature, which is a positive thing. When I was speaking to his mother, Iris Bentley, who fought for many years to have his name cleared, it became obvious that Derek was a very sensitive and emotional person.

How did you get involved in Flesh and Blood?
Flesh and Blood was the most collaborative, enjoyable and most enriching experience of my life. I had worked with the writer Peter Bowker previously, on a drama called *The King and Us*. He told me he'd been a special needs teacher and had in mind a drama called *Flesh and Blood*. I arranged for Peter to meet with Nicolas Shindler at Red Productions and the project grew out of that.

Was it always Peter's idea to involve actors with a learning disability?
It wasn't actually. At one point Peter had scripted actors down to play the roles of my parents, but then a brilliant director called Julian Farino came on board and said, 'I feel if we are going to represent these people, we should let them represent themselves'. So the original script for the actors playing my mother and my father was scrapped and Julian started contacting lots of theatre groups for people with a learning disability in the area; obviously it's useful if the actors have got some acquaintance with drama. And that's how we found the extraordinary Peter Kirby and Dorothy Cockin. Peter, who plays my father, and who carries the drama as much as I do, was found through a Rotary Club event I think.

Dorothy had acted before. Indeed, I will be performing with her again soon in a production of *Romeo and Juliet* at the Lowry Centre.

Not having worked with actors with a learning disability before, did you have any preconceptions about Peter and Dorothy as performers?
I had very high expectations, but again that's partly to do with the way I was brought up. I'm not frightened of people with a learning disability. I expected the very best and I got more than that. There's an openess to both Peter and Dorothy's nature, which is ideal for acting and drama, and is very much in line with the way I work. I've always been collaborative on projects. The best actors are always the ones who are most open to what the other performer is giving them. Peter and Dorothy were very open to me and the way I work. They played into my hands that way. Obviously there were considerations. At times the line was blurred for Peter. We had to explain certain situations to him, like when we were going to do something that was potentially upsetting. We had to prepare him for that. Not Dorothy though. Dorothy always knew that we were making a drama.

Was there a lot of improvisation involved?
There was a certain amount. All my dialogue was scripted, but Peter was allowed to react and come up with his own responses, and occasionally lines of dialogue. Dorothy, on the other hand, was much more familiar with drama. There is no doubt that there are different considerations when working with actors like Peter and Dorothy. We had to prepare things differently on the day, but why the bloody hell shouldn't we? The rewards were huge. You could not have got performances out of Daniel Day Lewis, or anybody else for that matter, as good as Peter and Dorothy's. And the amount of experience it gave them was invaluable: the break from the routine, the chance for them to be centre stage and for Dorothy to hold a child for the first time. Not to mention what it gave to the crew. I mean we had big hairy electricians who had to go to a social event on the four Tuesdays that we were filming. They couldn't wait to get back to the set! Everybody came out on a high because all you got from those two performers was openness, which in the television industry is extraordinary and rare.

Why do you think there are so few actors with a learning disability working in film, television and theatre?

I think it's an old prejudice. There's still a certain amount of fear attached to people with a learning disability and a 'can't be bothered' attitude. I think you can see that across drama. Minorities are not well represented on mainstream television and that seems extraordinary to me. If you look closely at any community, which is what the soaps are claiming to represent, you will see people with a learning disability at the centre of family life. And as *Flesh and Blood* showed, incorporating learning disability into storylines can make for a very powerful, commercial drama. *Flesh and Blood* won the Pre Europa Award, which is the biggest drama award in Europe, beating over 600 other entries. Even today, I'm stopped in the street and asked about *Flesh and Blood*. I've been in the industry for twenty years and I've done a lot of high-profile television dramas, like *Doctor Who*, and it's always *Flesh and Blood* that people want to talk to me about.

Do you have any future ambitions as a Mencap ambassador?

I'd like to increase the visibility of people with a learning disability in drama. Back in the late eighties I saw a friend of mine working on a production of *Androcles and the Lion*. He was the only actor without a learning disability in the entire production and I'd like to do something like that in the West End. About four years ago I went to see a show by Celebrity Pig, a Manchester-based theatre group for people with a learning disability. It was one of the greatest things I've ever seen and I remember sitting there thinking to myself, 'Yes, this is what it's all about'.

What do you get out of your work for Mencap?

It's a feeling of well-being. To be honest with you, I get more out of it I think than the people I'm supposed to be helping. I work in an industry where little can be trusted, particularly people's motives. When I attend a Mencap event, I'm on a high for a couple of days afterwards. All I get there is a welcome and an acceptance of who I am. Everyone is pleased to see me and that, for me, is immensely comforting.

Tackling Prejudice Through Pop

Singer and actor Will Young talks about why he's committed to Mencap for the long term

You must have been approached by a large number of charities when you won Pop Idol. *What made you choose Mencap?*

I hadn't really heard of Mencap before, so the fact that it was new to me was probably one of the first things that grabbed my attention actually. Initially I wanted to support an education charity. I felt that I was very lucky in the education that I had. I had some great teachers and I got a lot out of school. Also, I've always been very interested in breaking down people's prejudices and I thought that Mencap tied those two things together very well. I liked the fact that Mencap helps to empower people by giving them their own home and enabling them to work so they don't feel so helpless and victimised.

Did you know much about learning disability before you began working with Mencap?

Not really, but I think in a way that aided me. It made me aware of my own narrow-mindedness.

Shortly after you won Pop Idol, *a woman who had a son with autism contacted you.*

That's right. A woman wrote to me and said her son was autistic. He was quite high up in the spectrum and couldn't really communicate at all. He required a lot of care and only slept three hours a night. This woman was on her own and hadn't had a holiday in two years. She wrote that one day when she was playing one of my songs around the house, my second single I think, her son started communicating with her in a way he had never done before. Then my third song came out and he did it again. It was just such a beautiful letter.

And then you decided to pay her a visit?

Yes. At the time I was about to go on tour, so I went to see her in Manchester. I saw her a couple of times actually and we kept in touch. I really felt for her. It was so frustrating for her knowing that her son couldn't really project his love back to her. I think that must be devastating as a parent.

One of your first project visits was to Lufton College, one of Mencap's colleges for students with a learning disability. How did you find the experience?
I loved visiting Lufton College because it was something very new to me. I was slightly nervous going down to the college, but my first impression was how well behaved the students were compared to other schools I've been to where the pupils don't have learning disabilities. It was a very loving atmosphere and the students got so excited. I love the fact that people with a learning disability can be so uninhibited with their emotions. They show you this inordinate amount of love and, for me, being very middle class and British, that's very refreshing.

Why do you think there is so little representation of people with a learning disability in the media?
People are very ignorant and don't want to hear about issues that aren't 'sexy'. If something isn't the 'norm' then people often feel uncomfortable. I think that's one of the problems in trying to raise awareness about subjects like learning disability. It's very hard to get those kind of stories printed in the papers, but I think that Mencap deals with that side of things very well.

What do you think are the benefits for charities associating themselves with celebrities?
As I see it, the two key things I can help with are raising awareness and fundraising. As someone in the public eye, I can relay to people how they can help. I can add that element of 'up-to-dateness' for people and pull in their attention, which is what we need. It's one of my key roles as ambassador, I feel, to keep pulling in that kind of attention.

What do you get personally out of your work with charities like Mencap?
Events like the carol service are great. A lot of the things I'm asked to do in my job are fairly meaningless, so when I can take time to do things that are far from meaningless, it's worthwhile.

Do you have any future plans with regard to your role as a Mencap ambassador?
I feel I'm very much in this for the long term. I'd like to continue to help break down people's misconceptions and prejudices about learning disability and want to reach as many people as possible with my work with Mencap. I have no qualms about turning up to an event and having my photo taken to publicise something so worthwhile. I see myself as a bit of a whore in that respect.

What's the best thing about being an ambassador for Mencap?
Meeting the individuals with a learning disability. Like that wonderful girl, Alyson Heppell, whom I met at the *Snap!* photography exhibition at the V&A. She was such a bundle of joy. And naughty too. She pinched my bum! Things like that remind me of my own narrow-mindedness before I became an ambassador. I guess I didn't really know how to treat people with a learning disability before. Now that I know a lot more about the subject, I feel very relaxed with it.

A Tribute to My Uncles

Singer Lisa Scott-Lee sees her role as a Mencap ambassador as a tribute to her two uncles, Alex and Andreas, both of whom have learning disabilities

My dad's brothers, Alex and Andreas, have been a massive part of my life. When I was growing up, they lived five minutes away from me with my grandparents in Rhyl. The fact that they were 'different' only really became apparent when I started school, when my uncles would come to watch me in shows and sports days. The attitudes of some of the other schoolchildren towards them really used to upset me, but I always stuck up for them. I loved my uncles and I felt that other people didn't see them the way that I saw them, as the wonderful, caring people that they are.

I used to see my uncles a few times every week. We did everything together. Christmas and birthdays were always really special occasions. There was so much laughter in the house. Every year at Christmas my dad had this little ritual where he would dress up as Santa Claus and try to trick my uncles into thinking he was the real thing. Andreas obviously knew that it was my dad under the beard and as soon as 'Santa' walked in the door, he'd shout, 'Tony, Tony!' My grandad would say, 'No, it's Father Christmas', and Andreas would say, 'No it's not, it's Tony!' And then Dad would rip the beard and hat off and we'd all laugh.

Some of my fondest memories of my uncles are going to their college Christmas parties with my grandparents and brothers. Alex was a bit older than Andreas, so he would often have a lager or a cigar at the party as a little treat. He doesn't really smoke, so he'd often be sick afterwards, much to my nana's disgust!

My grandparents never had much in the way of support, but if it was difficult for them, we never knew about it. They have coped remarkably well and I have so much admiration for them. They always made it seem very much like a normal family and I think it's all credit to them that they brought Andreas and Alex up the way that they did.

When I talk about Andreas, I'm talking in the past tense because sadly he died a few years ago of a heart problem. He was only thirty-three. It came as a real shock, as the boys had never been to hospital in their lives, or had any illnesses. Alex and Andreas had a wonderful relationship. They looked after each other. Alex would make Andreas sandwiches and still sets the dinner table for him, just little things. Andreas loved the group Steps. He was our biggest fan. He used to come to all the concerts wearing a bright yellow jumper, just so I could see him in the crowd.

Alex still lives at home with my nana. I think it's so wonderful that she's cared for her sons, not only through their teenage years, but into adulthood. It really is a lifetime job and I'm not sure that many people realise that. Obviously I can only speak from my own experience, but I imagine it's a similar scenario for other families.

These days Alex goes to a day college. Nana walks him to the bus stop every day and he gets the bus to college and comes back at five, so my nana gets a bit of time to herself during the day. She likes to have Alex there; it's company for both of them.

As a Mencap ambassador I try to go to as many events as possible. The last one I attended was the private view of the *Snap!* photography exhibition at the V&A Museum in London. It was so lovely to see people with a learning disabilty being given the chance to show that they are talented and creative.

I also enjoyed visiting Pengwern College for students with a learning disability in Wales. The students and staff were so welcoming; in fact, they didn't want me to leave. My dad came along with me and we went to the students' Christmas disco. They took us on a tour of the college, showing us where they live and work. They had helped with organising the food for the event, even down to the DJing. It was really lovely to see them enjoying themselves.

I get a lot of personal satisfaction working with Mencap. Andreas and Alex have given me a lot of love over the years, so in a way I see my role as a Mencap ambassador as my personal tribute to them. Learning disability is still a taboo subject in the media, so obviously one of the main things I can do as a 'celebrity' is raise awareness and help create a greater understanding, which is the key to things I think. A greater understanding.

Making a Difference

Investigative journalist, Donal MacIntyre first became involved with Mencap through a controversial programme he made about the abuse of a group of people with learning disabilities living in a care home

My father's sister – my Aunt Caline – has a mild learning disability. She wasn't allowed to go to school as a youngster because of her disability, and was taught at home instead. When I was growing up in a small village in Ireland, where my family still live, my aunt used to come to stay with us. She was tremendous fun, much more fun than most of the other adults around me, and she was always up for playing games.

In our village there was a home for people with a learning disability, which was run by St John of God, an Irish charity. They were, in fact, the largest employers in the village, so it was considered normal to have people with a learning disability working in the local shops and pubs. We never knew any different so, from childhood, we grew up accepting that people with a learning disability were no different from anyone else.

My upbringing gave me a passion for learning disability issues, which I have since been able to channel into my work as a journalist and campaigner.

My involvement with Mencap came about through a documentary I made for the BBC, which was an undercover investigation into abuse at the Brompton Care Home in Kent. The programme, which I view as my most important, showed shocking incidences of abuse of people with a learning disability by staff in the home. The police found five assaults in just twenty-one days of filming. Over seven million viewers tuned in and a record number of viewers rang the helpline. The film changed Government policy and is used as a teaching and training aid across the industry.

Subsequent police criticism nearly derailed my care campaign, as the Kent police inexplicably said that the programme's allegations were false. With the support of Mencap, I sued the Kent police for libel to defend journalists' rights and the rights of the learning disabled before the law, winning a heralded victory in the £750,000 libel action which included damages, all legal costs and a full and total apology. I gave the five-figure damages award to three charities for people with a learning disability.

My work as Mencap ambassador is fun and very special. It involves meeting and talking to people, supporting people, offering a campaigning profile and promoting issues. Mencap is a great charity and is continually working to involve more people with a learning disability in its management, which is very important.

I ran the London Marathon and the Disney Half Marathon for Mencap two years ago, raising a few thousand pounds in the process. I remember hating being overtaken by an eight-foot mobile phone, a heavily suited rhinoceros and then having Buzz Lightyear attempt to give me a 'high five'!

My most memorable moment so far as an ambassador for Mencap has been the *Snap!* awards, a photography competition for people with a learning disability, at the Victoria and Albert Museum: watching the joy on everyone's faces, seeing the winners celebrate what was their Olympics. Everyone has their own Olympics in their lives, such as GCSEs, going to university and so on. *Snap!* was theirs. To see them celebrate – and see the celebrity ambassadors like Will Young and Christopher Eccleston share and engage in this – was a very special moment.

My goal as a journalist is to try to make things better for people with a learning disability, which is exactly what Mencap is doing. As journalists we can make lots of noise but we often don't achieve very much. Together with Mencap we can make a difference in this area.

Standing up for ourselves

Bafta Award-winning actress and Mencap ambassador, Paula Sage talks about life after *Afterlife*

I don't worry too much about having Down's syndrome, though sometimes it does get me down when people call me names or judge me, which has happened sometimes. I can't remember much about when I was a child so I don't know if my disability has affected me differently at different times. At school I got on with everybody but there were one or two occasions at the high school when others pupils made fun of me.

I have an older brother Mark and an older sister Marie-Louise. They have always supported me with my mum and dad and this has brought us close to each other. Having Down's syndrome I had to work very hard in my acting to show I could do it. Being in *River City* has been a bit easier because I had already done a film. By doing well at acting I can show other people that people like me can do lots of things.

I also enjoy sport, especially netball which I do every Tuesday. I play for Scotland West team and we got a silver medal at the Special Olympics, which was fantastic. I like playing in the team and being with the other players.

I got involved with Mencap and Enable because I was asked to do so. Brian Rix came to see my film *Afterlife* in London and he liked it. He met me after the film and said I was good. I will go to conferences and other events and make speeches for Mencap and Enable. I will try to tell other people with learning disabilities that they can do lots of things if they try hard. I want to encourage them.

Lots of people still think people like me can't do much but we can. We have to stand up for ourselves. People with a learning disability should have opportunities to try things and use their skills. I was lucky to get the chance to join the One in a Hundred drama group in Cumbernauld; the film producer and director came to see the group and I was chosen for an audition. The auditions were hard but I managed to get through and get the part.

I work hard at learning my lines; I sit in my bed at night and read them through all the time. In the film I had some help from Julie Austin, who was my coach, and also from the director and the other cast members. I love acting. It gives me a buzz. I like the other actors and we get on well. I got into *River City* because of my part in the film *Afterlife*. The pop star Darius recommended me to the *River City* people at the Great Scot Awards when he gave me my award. I sang the hit song 'Colourblind' with Darius on stage too.

Since I have been in *River City* everybody knows me and I get stopped in the streets for autographs and photos. I like being recognised but sometimes it's hard when strangers come up and talk to you. Being an actress has made me more confident. I was really surprised at getting a Bafta but it was great to get it – it was awesome. I didn't know whether to laugh or cry.

Angel of the North

How Newcastle celebrity Donna Air has been raising awareness and funds for Mencap in the North East

Around 20,000 children in the North East have a learning disability and one in two of their families live in poverty.

Newcastle-born actress and TV presenter Donna Air's relationship with Mencap began in January 2005, when she agreed to front an awareness campaign to help increase public understanding of learning disability in the North East. Since then, she has been involved in helping to raise awareness and funds for Dilston College in Corbridge, for students with a learning disability. The college has been raising the final £35,000 to pay for a kitchen rebuild and refurbishment, to which Donna and her partner, Damien Aspinall, kindly agreed to make a donation, following Donna's visit to the college in October 2005. In January of this year she attended a reception hosted by HRH The Countess of Wessex at St James's Palace to launch Mencap's birthday celebrations. More recently, she returned to Dilston to see how the kitchen rebuild was progressing and to catch up with the students again.

'I always enjoy my visits to Dilston College,' says Donna. 'The students there are lovely. They have a great sense of humour, just like everyone I know up here. They always make me feel really welcome and it is great to see them getting so involved with the local community, whether that be through the organic vegetables which they grow on the farm here, or through the café on the college grounds, which is staffed by the students.'

'The students are always so excited to see Donna,' says Alma Devine, North East Area Fundraising and Communications Manager. 'She's really down to earth and makes the day really special for everyone. She takes a genuine interest in the students' lives. We are extremely delighted that she agreed to be North East ambassador for Mencap. She is so popular here that her support will make all the difference to our Mencap Diamond Appeal to give 20,000 children with a learning disability in this area a better quality of life.'

CHAPTER 16

Westminster Watch

The Rt Hon. Tom Clarke CBE JP MP
Co-Chairman of the All Party Parliamentary
Group on Learning Disability

It was 1985 and I had only been a member of the House for a few years and my first experience of Private Members' Bills came as a big surprise. I was waving goodbye to a constituent at Westminster tube station when a young woman stopped me and congratulated me. 'Congratulations on what?' I asked. 'I'm from the Commons Library,' she said, 'you've just drawn first place in the ballot for Private Members' Bills.'

It was as well that I had this notice. When I returned to the Commons the scene was chaotic. Journalists queued up to hear what I was going to do; fellow members were just as inquisitive; and voluntary organisations and lobbyists pleaded with me to use my good fortune to promote a cause dear to their hearts.

In truth I was never in any doubt about what I wanted to do. My Bill would be about people with a learning disability and their carers. Apart from some limited family experience of many of the problems faced, during my time in local government before I came into the House I had a great deal of interest in social services, and I saw this subject as a big priority.

How to start? The obvious thing to do was to telephone Brian Rix at Mencap, and that's exactly what I did. Shortly afterwards I was having coffee in the Pugin Room at Parliament with Brian and his formidable parliamentary assistant at that time, the late Mary Holland. Our aims were clear: people with a learning disability should be protected from discrimination. There should be access to education, to transport, to the NHS, as well as to public and private services. Above all, advocacy was at the heart of all we sought to achieve.

In the weekend that followed I was persuaded to extend the Bill to other aspects of disability and a very pro-active group quickly gathered together. Their task was not just to advise me as the Bill made its way through both Houses, but to campaign in the country so as to encourage MPs to turn up and support the Bill at its various stages.

The coordinator of the campaign was a young man called John Healy, then working for MIND and now MP for Wentworth and currently Financial Secretary. Sir Brian Rix (as he became during the passage of the Bill) and Mencap were pivotal to everything that followed.

However, as the Bill made its way through the labyrinthine processes, there were good times and there were bad ones. At its January 1986 second reading it was hardly inspiring to hear that the Government Minister Barney Hayhoe (now Lord Hayhoe) explain that the front bench position was one of 'sceptical neutrality'. But we were nevertheless past the first hurdle of getting that vital second reading.

Even before the Bill went to committee I travelled around Britain and this was a fascinating experience. I met many local councils, health authorities and others, and their responses were far from uniform.

But the most compelling support and the most inspiring anecdotal witness came from individuals and their own experiences. I met with young people, their families and their carers. On numerous occasions I had a familiar discussion with parents as they posed the question: 'What happens to our offspring after we are no longer able to cope?' And that issue of 'no longer able to cope' was a big one. How often I was told that as the disabled person grew bigger and stronger, the parents became more frail. There were times when people gave so much of themselves that both the carer and the person they cared for became hospitalised. It was imperative that there should be an assessment of the needs of disabled people, but it was just as important that carers should be able to have an assessment of their own needs.

Above all, the absolute relevance of advocacy was paramount. There were some excellent examples of best practice, but my supporters and I dearly wanted to see advocacy becoming the norm. Against all the odds, Mrs Thatcher's Government agreed that the Bill would have its third reading on 11 April 1986. In the Lords it was sponsored by Baroness (Sue) Massam, speaking from her wheelchair, and ably supported by her colleagues. The Bill received Royal Assent in early summer of that year, and became the Disabled Persons (Services, Representation and Consultation) Act 1986. But for many the battle was just beginning. I was to learn that it was not enough just to sponsor an Act of Parliament successfully; one must campaign for its full implementation.

True, a great many resources have been spent by successive Governments in introducing parts of the Act, but even today it is far from being fully implemented. Mencap led campaigns and lobbies of Parliament, especially on anniversaries of the passing of the Act. The fight for its full implementation has been raised in numerous debates in both Houses, and that battle goes on.

It is a privilege for me to serve with Brian – Lord Rix – as co-Chair of the All Party Group on Learning Disabilities. Demanding the implementation of the remainder of the 1986 Act is a major priority among the other goals which the group has set itself.

Westminster Watch
2

David Congdon
Head of Campaigns and Policy, Mencap

If it hadn't been for Mencap . . .

Mencap has played a huge part in bringing about major changes in the law that have benefited thousands of people with a learning disability, their families and carers. David Congdon picks out the highlights and assesses Mencap's role as a force for change in its sixty-year history.

I make no claims to be a great historian. I am also aware of the dangers of playing the 'what if' game with history. But I'd like to pose a simple question: what would life be like today for people with a learning disability if it hadn't been for Mencap and the changes it has helped bring about in society?

In all probability, hundreds of thousands of children with a learning disability wouldn't be able to go to school, thus missing out on the opportunity to learn the skills that equip them for the adult world. Thousands more adults would still be living in terrible conditions in out-dated institutions – away from their families and friends – deprived of the right to live as independently as possible in the community. Many could even find themselves being held against their will in hospitals.

It may come as a shock to imagine this kind of world. But these are just some of the many ways in which things could have been very different had it not been for Mencap's steadfast campaigning since 1946. In this chapter, I'd like to take an overview of our campaigning achievements. This won't be a comprehensive account, as Lord Rix has already provided that in his diary history of Mencap in Chapter 1. Instead, I'd like to concentrate on five key 'rights' that Mencap has helped enshrine for people with a learning disability: the right to education, the right to live in the community, the right to liberty, the right to equal rights and opportunities and the right to services that meet people's needs. My main focus will be on the first three, as they take us back to Mencap's earliest days. I'll deal with the last two much more briefly, as more recent history.

First, though, I'd like to remind readers that Mencap is now, and always has been, a campaigning organisation first and foremost – a force for change. It's easy to overlook this because the charity has become so involved in the last three decades in providing a range of services, particularly in housing and employment. But these services would never have come into being had it not been for changes in the law and the corresponding shift in attitudes.

Indeed, Mencap has its very roots in campaigning. As Lord Rix recounts in the prologue, it all started when Judy Fryd wrote a letter to *Nursery World* expressing her concern about the lack of educational provision for her daughter, Felicity. She suggested that other parents in her position could get together to fight for the fundamental right to education for their children. Hundreds of parents responded and Judy put them in touch with each other in their local areas. So it was that Mencap was born on a campaigning agenda.

But it was another twenty-four years before Mencap's long fight for the right to education bore fruit with the 1970 Education (Handicapped Children) Act. To get a true picture of how momentous this piece of legislation was, it's worth painting in some background. (The terminology that follows in describing what we now call 'learning disability' reveals much about the attitudes of the time.) Under the 1944 Education Act children had to be tested, from the age of two, for 'mental deficiency'. Schools had to notify local authorities when any of their pupils who had been classified as 'defective' were due to finish their education. Such a notification was obviously very stigmatising and so, in an effort to soften this blow, new regulations substituted the labels 'educationally subnormal' or 'maladjusted' in place of 'mental defective' – all unacceptable terms today. Among the children thus classified some were able to go to school and others were not. The key test to decide this was IQ: 'educationally subnormal' children with an IQ of 50 or more were able to go to state-run special schools. Those with an IQ below 50 were considered to be 'ineducable'. A small number of these attended 'occupation centres' instead of school, where they carried out a variety of monotonous tasks. But in the vast majority of cases, their parents had to keep them at home or – if they could afford it – find private education for them.

This was largely how things remained until 1970. The Education Act of that year changed things radically. Not only did it give all children (in England and Wales) – regardless of their disability – an absolute right to a full education, it also made a huge difference to where and how they were brought up, and to the lives of their families. That's because prior to the Act, many children with a learning disability were segregated from society in large special hospitals. It was, indeed, official policy to fill up these institutions, in particular with adults and children with mild learning disabilities. Many of these people looked 'normal' and so – according to the unenlightened logic of the time – were thought to pose a greater threat to the community. As a result, parents were often put under a huge amount of pressure to give up their children to these hospitals. The whole system conspired to make this happen because there simply weren't enough support services to enable parents to bring up their children in the family home.

So it's easy to see, in this context, what a massive impact the 1970 Act was to have: not only did it give all children the right to an education, but it also represented the beginning of a major shift in attitudes towards people with a learning disability, away from segregation towards inclusion at the heart of community life.

This brings me on to the next key right that Mencap has helped win for people with a learning disability: the right to live in the community. The starting point here is the publication of a report in 1957 by the Royal Commission into Mental Illness and Mental Deficiency, in the run-up to the 1959 Mental Health Act. This report made a distinction between 'mental illness' and 'mental deficiency', a crucial point to which I'll return later. In making this distinction, the report also suggested, for the first time, that 'mentally handicapped' people should be cared for in the community rather than in hospitals. As it turned out, the 1959 Act stopped short of making such community-based services compulsory, and failed to provide funds to encourage local authorities to use their enabling powers.

However, the seed of thought about this vital change in policy had been sown. This would dominate Mencap's campaigning activities for the next three decades, as many parents, through their local Mencap societies, fought tirelessly to get better services for their children. But the campaign to move people out of hospitals and into community care really came to life only when the general public's attention was drawn towards a series of scandals of ill treatment in long-stay hospitals. Most memorable among these was Maureen Oswin's book, *The Empty Hours*, which showed the extraordinary deprivation suffered by children in hospital.

This was backed up by the Government's own findings in its 1971 White Paper *Better Services for the Mentally Handicapped*. The Government also set up the National Development Team (NDT) to investigate services in individual authorities. This is where Mencap played a crucial role: the NDT reports were rarely published. But Brian Rix was determined to get the issue into the headlines. He persuaded the *Guardian* to run a campaign and published his own damning article in the newspaper. Eventually the Government caved in: the reports were published, revealing often extreme squalor in mental health hospitals. The attention this drew to the issue would set in motion the long campaign for the right to live in the community. In 1979 the Jay Report advocated community living with support from non-medical caring professions, a radical move away from the medical model of care. The 1981 report *Care in the Community* added weight to this. Further campaigning by Mencap and others kept up the pressure, and the Government slowly started to respond positively, recognising that community care could be the way forward.

Responding to the shift in public policy, Mencap took the lead in setting up residential care homes in the community in the 1980s. By showing in practice how much better community care was for people with a learning disability than long-stay hospitals, Mencap was building further momentum for the campaign to shut down the hospitals for good. The 1990 NHS and Community Care Act accelerated this process and the vast majority of hospitals are now no more. Of course, times keep changing, and now there is a trend away from residential care in group homes towards supported living where people have much more say in how they live their lives. But history will surely record that residential care homes were a vital step along the way towards today's ideal model of independent living.

History will also record that – thanks to pressure from Mencap and others – society has eventually come to recognise that people with a learning disability have a fundamental right to liberty, the third key right in my list of five. This brings me back to the 1959 Mental Health Act. Mencap and others were hugely disappointed when the Act failed to take up the recommendations of the 1957 Royal Commission report to distinguish between 'mental illness' and 'mental handicap'. As a result, people with a learning disability continued to be bundled together with mentally ill people and so could be forcibly detained in hospital. This is a stark reminder about the kind of attitudes and treatment that Mencap was fighting against less than half a century ago when people were deemed to be a threat purely because of their disability.

This is an issue that, shockingly, today is still not completely resolved. But there have been developments in the right direction since 1959. In its 1981 White Paper *Better Services for the Mentally Ill*, the Government again made the key distinction between mental illness and handicap. The subsequent 1983 Mental Health Act failed to remove the powers of compulsory hospital detention and guardianship of people with a learning disability, which Mencap had been fighting against. However, the Act marked a clear shift in public policy: in future only those 'mentally handicapped' people who suffered from 'abnormal aggressiveness' or 'serious irresponsibility' would be subject to compulsory detention.

Bringing things up to date, Mencap is among many pressure groups that have recently expressed serious concerns about proposed new mental health legislation. The Government has responded to these concerns by shelving plans for a completely new Act. Instead, it intends to amend key sections of the 1983 Act. Mencap will be campaigning hard to ensure that these amendments finally bring an end to the forced detention of people with a learning disability who pose no threat to society.

Alongside this right to liberty sits the fundamental right to equal rights and opportunities, the fourth right in my list of five. This is what Mencap – along with other disability organisations – turned their attention to in the 1990s. Here is not the place for a detailed account of the painstaking efforts of campaigners to see this right enshrined. Suffice to say that the Government was initially resistant, but that eventually the 1995 Disability Discrimination Act (DDA) was passed. Although this did not go as far as many would have wanted, it was the first anti-discrimination legislation for disability. It has been progressively implemented over the last decade and Mencap has been fighting hard to ensure it reflects the particular needs of people with a learning disability, as opposed to disabled people generally. Along with others, Mencap has also campaigned for the DDA to be strengthened, culminating in the DDA 2005. This includes a new public sector Disability Equality Duty (DED), which is one of the most important things ever to have happened for disabled people. It says that all public bodies must ensure their services meet the needs of disabled people – both as customers and as employees – rather than just dealing with problems to do with discrimination as they come up. This means they must think about the needs of disabled people in *all* their decisions and activities, and they must do this when they start planning anything new.

At Mencap, we hope to use the DED to make a real, practical difference to the everyday lives of people with a learning disability – in how they are treated by our public institutions, and in the quality of services they receive. Indeed, people with a learning disability should have this right to services that meet their needs – the last in my selection of key rights that Mencap has fought for. Indeed, in a sense, everything that Mencap campaigns for is directed towards this right: when people get the services they need, then they are able to play a full part in society; and when public bodies can provide these services, it shows that they have the 'right' attitude towards disabled people. It's in this context that the 2001 White Paper *Valuing People* was such a seminal moment in Mencap's campaigning history. It was the first Government strategy specifically on learning disability since the 1971 White Paper. *Valuing People* sets out the Government's plans to improve services for people with a learning disability based on the vital principles of rights, independence, choice and inclusion. Mencap played a major part in the work leading up to its publication, and has pushed hard since for it to be properly implemented. We are still concerned about the lack of funds to pay for the things it recommends. But *Valuing People* was a major milestone: it laid the foundations for people with a learning disability to have, for the first time ever, a real voice and a choice in how they lead their lives. Thanks to the service user forums and local Learning Disability Partnership Boards that *Valuing People* recommended, people with a learning disability now have a seat at the decision-making table. They are listened to rather than ignored.

This is not to say that people with a learning disability now have all the same opportunities in life as other people. Mencap's campaigning days are far from over. We are still fighting for equal treatment on a whole range of issues: children, education, healthcare and employment, to name but a few. I need say no more about this here, as Jo Williams has dealt with these campaigning challenges in detail in Chapter 6. All that I need say is this: much has to change if Mencap is to achieve our vision of a society where people with a learning disability have truly equal rights and chances in life. But I remain hopeful that we can emulate Mencap's great campaigning achievements of the last sixty years – as set out in this chapter – and translate this vision into reality.

Mencap and Diversity

Aarti Puri
Solicitor, Mencap

Mencap's vision is for a world in which everyone with a learning disability has an equal right to choice, opportunity and respect. For sixty years we have successfully campaigned along these lines, fighting to change the social landscape and end discrimination against people with a learning disability. However, a careful examination of Mencap's work reveals some variation in the degree of impact which we have had on the lives of people from different communities. As the UK population has diversified over the years, some groups have unintentionally been left behind. This is true not only for Mencap, but also for the wider learning disability community.

The Government's White Paper *Valuing People* recognised in 2001 that people from black and minority ethnic (BME) communities are often overlooked when it comes to service provision. Indeed, it is estimated that less than a quarter are even known to social services. They receive diagnosis at a later stage and less information and support. They also experience greater stress and social exclusion, exacerbated by language barriers and racism.

The social model of disability attributes disability not to physical symptoms or medical diagnoses, but to the construction of society in a way which puts certain people at a disadvantage. This also applies to other minority groups who are 'disabled' by their differences. For example, in the UK, we – not unnaturally – use English to communicate, putting non-English speakers at a disadvantage, virtually excluding them from the rest of society.

This is clearly contradictory to Mencap's values. We believe that every person has equal value in society regardless of their background or life circumstances and, therefore, is equally entitled to choice, opportunity and respect. This forms the premise of everything we do at Mencap. We want to ensure that people who may be different from the majority are given opportunities to shape the social world we live in so that they are less disadvantaged or 'disabled' by it. At a Mencap National Assembly workshop in October 2005, the majority opinion was that we need to promote diversity and equal opportunities because it is right so to do.

When it comes to challenging discrimination, Mencap's focus has clearly been on redesigning aspects of our society which present problems for people with a learning disability. We have made some attempts to challenge other forms of discrimination, but we know that we need to do more. In *A Vision for Change*, our strategic priorities for 2004–09 include a commitment to increase our work with specific groups, including BME communities, who may have been left behind in the past. In our corporate plan for 2006–07, we have identified one of our goals as including more people from different backgrounds and encouraging them to use our services and support.

Diversity is not, however, a stand-alone priority. It runs through all the work we do to meet our other priorities as well. For example, in order to give people information that is really useful to them, we will have to evaluate individuals' diverse communication needs, including content, language and format preferences. Similarly, providing truly supportive services requires flexibility in accommodating different needs and preferences, including cultural and religious ones. We also want to encourage more people to join the Mencap community, and critically examining what we can offer people from minority ethnic backgrounds will provide a new basis for working with whole communities of people who have previously felt that Mencap is not for them.

The term 'black and minority ethnic communities' is used differently by different people. It always refers to people who identify themselves as having a non-white or mixed ethnic background, and sometimes (but not always) includes people from a white non-British background.

In the 2001 population census, approximately 8 per cent of the UK population identified themselves as having a non-white ethnic background. About half of the minority ethnic population describe themselves as Asian (Indian, Pakistani, Bangladeshi or Other Asian), and just over a quarter describe themselves as Black (Black Caribbean, Black African or Other Black). The rest had Chinese, Mixed or Other ethnic backgrounds.

With the prevalence of learning disability higher in some Asian communities than the general population, we can safely assume that the proportion of people with a learning disability in the UK who are from BME communities is higher than 8 per cent. Moreover, this figure is likely to continue increasing with the growth of the total BME population, which expanded in size by 44 per cent between 1991 and 2001.

For Mencap, this means that a growing proportion of our potential client base of people with a learning disability has a non-white ethnic background, and there is a real and intensifying need for us to engage with these communities.

Much external research has been conducted on the barriers that people with a learning disability from BME communities and their families face in accessing services. Within Mencap, various pieces of research have also looked at these issues and, specifically, at what is preventing these communities from becoming involved with Mencap. Here are some of the key issues that are particularly relevant to our organisation:

- Lack of awareness of Mencap and learning disability;
- Anticipation that Mencap cannot provide for diverse language and cultural needs;
- No established channels for communicating with BME families;
- Perception of Mencap as a 'white organisation'.

Various initiatives have aimed to address the under-representation of people from BME communities in our organisation and the wider Mencap community. These have been developed in a somewhat ad hoc manner in response to the perceived need in a particular service, an individual staff member's interest and commitment to this work or the availability of specific funding. Here are some examples from current projects and local groups.

Ethnic Minority Access and Participation Project (EMAPP)

Mencap now has a Community Support Group and EMAPP can be seen as their pioneering project working specifically with BME communities. It was set up in 2003 following a piece of research into the needs and experiences of families affected by learning disabilities from BME communities in Ealing and Hounslow. Staff provide information, advice and general advocacy to parents and carers through regular focus groups, consultation forums and information days. Professionals are also invited to the information days so that parents can discuss issues such as housing, respite and transportation directly with them. The aim is to build family networks and help families gain the confidence to speak out about their concerns and to ask for better services. All forums are run by bilingual staff who are fluent in Hindi, Punjabi, Urdu, Somali and English.

Birmingham Mencap

Birmingham Mencap has a Black and Minority Ethnic Development Worker who works with organisations and individuals in BME communities to assess the needs of people with a learning disability and their carers, and to make Birmingham Mencap more accessible to these communities. The insights gained are also used to inform the development of appropriate, relevant and culturally sensitive services in the Birmingham area. Birmingham Mencap and the Royal Mencap Society also jointly commissioned a research project entitled *Reaching Out*, which will be launched in September 2006. This research describes the experiences of individuals, carers and professionals who work with them. It also highlights many of the cultural and social factors that make it difficult for people from these communities to make use of existing statutory and voluntary services, and suggests ways in which such organisations can work better with these communities.

The Wills and Trusts Team at National Centre

The Wills and Trusts Team, already referred to in Brian Rix's description of his first day as Mencap's Secretary-General, works with organisations and individuals in BME communities to talk to parents and families about the importance of planning for the future of their child with a learning disability. This is achieved through dedicated seminars being held by bilingual staff and/or with the assistance of translators and the provision of information and free legal advice to parents. The aim is to encourage BME parents to discuss their concerns about the future of their child with a learning disability within their families and with professionals, and to take steps while they are alive to secure their child's future.

The Diversity Steering Group

Mencap has also developed a Diversity Steering Group to coordinate and monitor all projects and to develop our strategy and action plan for BME communities. Our aims over the coming years are to achieve:

- Greater understanding of learning disability within BME communities;
- Greater awareness about Mencap and our services within BME communities;
- Greater involvement of BME communities in Mencap as staff, members, service users and volunteers, so that as an organisation we reflect the diversity of local communities;
- An organisational culture that makes people from BME communities feel understood, supported and valued;
- Better understanding in the general population of how learning disability affects people from BME communities;
- Planning processes that incorporate diversity considerations at all levels, and lead to flexibly designed projects and services;
- A perception of Mencap as a diverse and inclusive organisation.

For a long time, a lack of knowledge and understanding of the implications of ethnic diversity and the fear of 'doing the wrong thing' seemed to paralyse organisations, including Mencap. More recently, we have started to break this cycle by undertaking research projects and consultations aimed at understanding what we need to do to reach out to BME communities. Now is the time to turn knowledge and commitment into action. Now is the time to reach out. We probably won't get it all right at first, but in the words of William Hickson, 'If at first you don't succeed, try, try again'. That we most certainly will!

PART V

Mencap Initiatives Outside Golden Lane

CHAPTER 17

Mencap Cymru

Liz Neal
Director, Mencap Cymru

Dr Roger Banks
Royal College of Psychiatrists

Simon Smith
North Wales District Representative of the Mencap Cymru Committee

In 1955, the year in which the Warsaw Pact was formed, Winston Churchill was succeeded by Anthony Eden, the National Association of Parents of Backward Children changed its name to the National Society for Mentally Handicapped Children and Cardiff was proclaimed capital of Wales. Cardiff is today the home of the offices of Mencap Cymru, located on a busy industrial park in Llanishen, a suburb to the north of the city and providing a focus for the people with a learning disability in this Celtic nation of almost three million citizens. A nation in which there is considerable social and geographical variation, from the densities of urban and industrial populations of Cardiff, Swansea and Port Talbot along the south coast to the coastal strip of Conwy, Llandudno, Rhyl and Deeside in the north which merges with the populations of north Cheshire and Merseyside, from the hills, mountains and sparsely scattered farming communities of Gwynedd and Powys to the strong former mining communities of the valleys of Glamorgan.

Early days

Today there are thirty-three local societies and forty-four Gateway clubs in Wales but the history of Mencap in Wales has much smaller beginnings in the early 1960s, when there were local groups in Cardiff, Bridgend, Swansea and Usk. The first director of Mencap Cymru was the orchestral dance band leader Langdon Doidge whose widow, Peggy Doidge, writes:

> I am delighted that twenty-five years later the Langdon Doidge Trust Fund is still of interest to children with a learning disability in Wales. The Langdon Doidge Arts Award was launched at the National Eisteddfod for Wales in 2005, a very successful exhibition took place in the Museum of Welsh Life in St Fagans and the outcome of the Christmas Card Competition was announced at the National Assembly for Wales.

Most of the activities of the society at this time were focused on mid to south Wales, although a few groups were beginning to form in North Wales, such as Pwllheli and a parents and teachers group in the Llandudno area. A characteristic of the geography and population of the north-east of Wales, where the majority of North Wales residents are concentrated, has been its tendency to look to the north-west of England, Merseyside and north Cheshire for its links and support and for some time it was uncertain as to whether Mencap links would follow the same pattern.

Mencap Cymru activities in these early days included the St Athans' Fun Day for Children with Learning Disabilities and day trips to Barry Island. The Cardiff Chameleons Swimming club and Swansea local society provided some of the only sports and leisure activities for children with a learning disability; the registration of the Cardiff Chameleons, originally formed in 1959, led to the establishment of the Special Olympics in Wales. It is interesting to note that sports and leisure have continued to be a strong theme in Wales; the appointment of a Gateway Award and Leisure Officer has allowed promotion of activities throughout the nation. As a result, in 2005, sixteen people from Wales went to England to take part in trials for the Gateway football team and three successful players were selected to join the fifteen-man squad in Geneva.

Education was a key campaigning issue for Mencap from the very start of the Society in the 1940s. Members such as Judy Fryd and Langdon Doidge (who had been inspired by education he had seen on a visit to Israel) exposed the exclusion from school of many children with a learning disability. Sustained campaigning by members of the Society throughout the 1960s finally led to the Education (Handicapped Children) Act in 1970.

The history of the Pwllheli Mencap is one illustration of the diversity of Mencap in Wales. The Society was formed forty years ago by a group of older parents who were concerned about what would happen to their learning disabled children after they were gone. Bryn y Neuadd Hospital had not opened at that time and they wanted their children to live locally and were looking for a hostel or house. They established the Gateway club and called it Clwb Ni – Our Club. It had twelve members and was different from other societies in that the society and club were one body (most Gateway clubs are independent). At that time children with a learning disability in the local area had few if any activities outside the family home other than going to school if they were able (most were at mainstream schools and there were no day centres). Clwb Ni provided a new opportunity every Monday for two hours when children were collected and driven to the club by volunteers. In addition to activities in the club, there was the chance to go on holidays to Pengwern and Bala Colleges.

The Urdd Gobaith Cymru, a Welsh youth movement that promotes sporting and cultural activities, hosted a week for the 'handicapped' (*sic*) every year and Pwllheli Mencap Society supported and paid for people with a learning disability to attend. The children were involved in all kinds of sports, including tobogganing, horse riding and swimming. A holiday at the Urdd Camp in Llangrannog widened the children's horizons and made a significant improvement in their quality of life.

Clwb Ni now has twenty-five members, meeting every Monday for a range of activities, including boccia, darts, pool, arts and crafts, singing and playing in the club band. Members will be attending the North Wales games as they have done for the past few years. The age range is from fifteen and they have just lost their oldest member, who died at the age of seventy.

Dark days

In July 1967, the *News of the World* exposed allegations of misconduct on the part of some members of the staff at the Ely Hospital in Cardiff. Ely was originally established as a Poor Law Industrial School for Orphaned Children; in 1948 it was linked with Whitchurch Hospital and was classified as a psychiatric hospital in 1959. In 1964 there were a total of 614 beds of which 192 were designated for mental illness and 422 for 'mental subnormality'.

The subsequent NHS inquiry, the first of its kind, found the substance of the allegations to be justified and described a culture that was isolated and inward looking with poor clinical leadership, inadequate management structures and systems and poorly resourced. As a result of the high-profile findings of this inquiry, there was a social and political resolve to move away from institutional care and a new emphasis on community living and the planned closure of long-stay hospitals.

All Wales Strategy for the Development of Services for Mentally Handicapped People

At a conference in Cardiff in 1981, convened by the then Secretary of State for Wales, Nicholas Edwards (now Baron Crickhowell), those involved with the care of people with a a learning disability pointed to a lack of progress in community care in the ten years following the publication of *Better Services for the Mentally Handicapped* in 1971. Statutory service provision was still concentrated in large hospitals, often far away from the individual's origins and family. Those people with a learning disability who remained in the family home, and this was the majority, had access to very little in the way of support and thus institutional care often remained the only option when families were no longer able to cope. Integrated, comprehensive and adequately funded services were required together with a shift towards the provision of social care. An All Wales working party was established involving statutory providers, professionals and representatives of service users; this group produced its report in July 1982. Following wide consultation, the report was published as the *All Wales Strategy for the Development of Services for Mentally Handicapped People*, with a projected timescale of ten years and the commitment of funding that would rise to an additional £26 million per annum. It was clear, and borne out by retrospective analysis, that both the timescale and the amount of the investment would be inadequate to achieve all the intended outcomes of the strategy. Fundamentally it was expected that three main principles should be at the heart of the development and evaluation of services for all people with a learning disability regardless of the severity of their intellectual and physical impairment:

- Mentally handicapped (*sic*) people should have a right to normal patterns of life within the community.
- Mentally handicapped people should have the right to be treated as individuals.
- Mentally handicapped people require additional help from the communities in which they live and from professional services if they are to develop their maximum potential as individuals.

The All Wales Strategy provided both a broad direction and specific guidance for the development of a range of services. Underpinning the strategy as a whole was the emphasis on developing 'new patterns of comprehensive services' and the move from institutional living to staffed homes in the community using 'local housing stock'. The needs of the family were also to be given pre-eminence through access to 'short-term relief' that was local and responsive and provided through a range of domiciliary services. The strategy could be said to be ahead of its time in its emphasis on equality of access to the same range of health and other services as the rest of the members of the community. The delivery of these new services was to be driven not by attempting to fit people into existing resources but rather by a process of focused assessment and planning centred on the uniqueness of each individual. Were the aspirations to have been realised in full, people with a learning disability would have been liberated from the chains of an institutional and segregationist model of 'care' to an integrated role in society using inclusive local resources and networks of support.

In 1994, updated guidance on the All Wales Strategy was issued which emphasised the need for care to be coordinated through lifelong planning that accurately represents the needs and choices of the individual: 'The dignity and self-respect of individuals often depends on their ability to make everyday decisions and to feel that they are not only consulted but that they are listened to before decisions are made for them. Good quality care must not only meet the needs of the people it supports, but must also reflect their wishes and preferences.'

Over the following decade, however, the close working alliances between social and health services, with the local authorities being given the lead role, was eroded by a number of factors, including the inadequate funding for the strategy and the restructuring of services and the relationships between providers and purchasers within statutory authorities. Agencies that had previously worked together, hand-in-glove, were, by the turn of the new century, generally disconnected from each other and among professionals and public alike it was being said that the All Wales Strategy was dead.

At the end of 1999, aware of the growing sense of disillusionment, the Welsh National Assembly drew together a Learning Disability Advisory Group to review what progress had been made on the strategy and to 'prepare proposals for a framework for services for people with a learning disability' that would clarify what services and support people with a learning disability, their families and carers are entitled to receive. The report of this group was entitled *Fulfilling the Promises* and it provided a wider picture than that of health and social services, addressing also education, leisure, training, employment and housing. The report noted the progress in areas such as residential and day services, domiciliary services and family support but also that this had been uneven across Wales and the vision of the 1983 strategy had not been fully achieved.

Fulfilling the Promises in itself constituted neither strategy nor policy; the response of the Welsh Assembly to the report indicated that the All Wales Strategy was still alive in principle yet required consultation and initiatives across a number of policy areas and also new life and direction breathed into existing services, including the non-statutory sector. It stopped short, however, of committing the funding that would have been required to accomplish the aims of the All Wales Strategy in its original form. The Assembly response, emerging as it did amid the high-profile strategic developments in England (*Valuing People*) and Scotland (*The Same as You?*), noted that spending per head of population in Wales on health and social services for people with a learning disability was greater than in these other countries as a direct result of the All Wales Strategy but that the funding being committed to the English and Scottish strategies might reduce that advantage. What did emerge, however, from the response to the report was:

- The establishment of a Learning Disabilities Implementation Advisory Group to monitor the recommendations and actions from the Assembly's response to *Fulfilling the Promises* and to continue to advise on relevant issues for people with a learning disability.
- Section 7 guidance to health and social services on 'service principles and responses' against which authorities were required to audit their existing services, prepare costed and prioritised action plans and bid for a share of new funding to implement these.
- Three years of funding for the development of advocacy for people with a learning disability throughout Wales through an advocacy grant scheme (subsequently administered by BILD).
- The issuing of guidance on person-centred planning.
- A commitment to review the strategies for carers and older people and the National Service Framework for children to ensure that they were in line with the requirements of learning disability strategy.
- A public consultation on an updated policy and practice document. The updated statement of policy and practice is intended to build on the section 7 guidance and provide clearer standards for authorities to follow and to inform people with a learning disability and their families.

Mencap Cymru has had a strong influential role throughout the All Wales Strategy development and beyond. In recent years this has included the Director participating in the advisory group that wrote *Fulfilling the Promises* and being part of the Learning Disability Implementation Advisory Group as well as campaigning for the closure of all long-stay hospitals by 2006. This brought forward by four years the original timetable for closure. The year 2006 will also see the introduction of regular health checks for people with a learning disability, following Mencap Cymru's *Treat me right!* campaign.

Mencap Cymru today

Mencap Cymru has always been committed to the principles of the All Wales Strategy and continues to embody these in its work every day. It provides local services including supported living, short-term care and supported employment and is committed to helping people with a learning disability and their families to get the support they need to develop to their maximum potential.

In 1999 Mencap Cymru was commissioned by Carmarthenshire County Council to provide support to six individuals who had been resident in a long-stay hospital in South Wales. After supporting them through a difficult transition period they eventually moved into two houses in Llanelli owned by a housing association.

The success of this project gave Mencap Cymru the confidence to tender for more services. They were awarded three supported-living schemes in Ceredigion in 2001 and also developed a partnership with Flintshire County Council to provide supported-living services to twenty individuals in their own homes.

In total Mencap Cymru provides support to sixty-five individuals throughout Wales to live in their own homes with their own tenancy agreements. We also support around fifty people in a registered respite service in Conwy County.

Helping people to find and keep employment has been a long-term concern of Mencap Cymru and our Pathway services span nearly three decades. Initiated in south-east Wales, there are now services in Carmarthen, Pembrokeshire, Ceredigion, Llanelli and Wrexham and over the years we have supported over 500 people into employment.

The Wales Learning Disability Helpline was launched on 28 March 2000 in Cardiff and gives callers direct contact to Mencap Cymru, where they can obtain independent support and information on subjects such as employment, housing, health, support, education, services, membership and campaigns.

The Welfare Benefits Advice Service (WBAS) started in October 2002 and is funded by the Community Fund (Big Lottery). The lottery grant stated, 'Recent research has shown that the costs to families of supporting learning disabled family members can be up to three times higher than those incurred by families without similar care responsibilities. However,

Mencap research has shown that people with a learning disability are among the lowest claimants of welfare benefits'. The Welfare Benefits Advice Service aims to enable young people between sixteen and twenty-five with a learning disability, their families and carers to gain access to benefits advice and support. They offer free, confidential and independent benefits entitlement checks, help to complete claim forms and access to general benefits advice. Importantly, WBAS can assess the benefit entitlement and 'knock-on effects' for the whole family unit and not just the young person. Between January 2003 and January 2006 the WBAS has increased the benefit incomes of people with a learning disability, their families and carers in Wales by over £400,000.

During 2000 the Board of Trustees of Mencap asked that a regional committee be set up in Wales as a link between the Board, the Mencap membership and the National Assembly for Wales. The first meeting of this committee took place in December 2000 and comprised eleven people. Since then there have been sixteen further meetings spread across Wales. From 2005, committee members will be elected for a period of three years.

Ensuring that people with a learning disability have normal patterns of life is fundamental to Mencap Cymru's approach. An example of this is our link with the Lesotho Society for Mentally Handicapped People. In 2000 two people with a learning disability were supported to visit Lesotho and a return visit occurred in 2002. Another visit is currently being planned, with committee members raising the necessary funds.

What will the next sixty years bring?

It is an exciting time to be living and working in Wales. The National Assembly for Wales is still in its infancy and the effects of the devolved structure are only just beginning to create a difference in policy direction and outcomes. The history of the All Wales Strategy means learning disability services are ahead in this process and some differences from England and the other parts of the UK are already apparent. As well as the money that was used to create change, people with a learning disability and their families have been very much involved in the statutory planning processes and have therefore enabled decisions on what was important to them. The impact of the Assembly gaining further devolved powers and the long-term effects of different policy routes will only become apparent over the next sixty years.

Despite the different policy directions and culture of diverse influences for bringing about change, people with a learning disability in Wales tell us that what they want to see is:

- More people with a learning disability getting jobs, being paid and having careers.
- More people with a learning disability having more friends, being in a committed relationship and looking after their families.
- More people with a learning disability being able to live in their own home with the support they want.

Employment

Here is Gary's story.

Gary is thirty-three years old and lives on the Isle of Anglesey in North Wales. On leaving college almost ten years ago, Gary decided that he would like a job. After his case manager provided a referral to Anglesey Social Services, Gary received an interview for a job at Penrhos Tea Rooms in Holyhead; this is a social services initiative for people with a learning disability. Gary had this to say about his job:

> I work three days a week – Tuesday, Wednesday and Thursday – from 10 am to 4 pm. I help in the Tea Rooms by doing the following jobs: take orders and serve customers, clear tables and brush the floor, take rubbish to the wheelie bin, stack and unstack the dishwasher, peel potatoes and carrots, butter bread, prepare toasties, etc. I get paid 80p per day for my work. This is rubbish; it is not nice, and who else would work for that? They should pay me more!
>
> I have a free bus pass so it costs me nothing to go to work. I get paid if I am on holiday and if I am off sick. I get provided with aprons from work but no other clothing. The café is closed at the weekends in the winter months.
>
> I enjoy my job. I think I do a good job and it makes me feel good going to work. I like meeting people and chatting to them. I always get to work on time unless the bus is late. I like working with my friends; we get on well together.

Last year the local authority proposed introducing a charge for services. For providing this service to Gary it would cost him approximately £75. Gary strongly disagreed with this charge:

> I wrote to all the county councillors; there are thirty-two or thirty-six councillors, I can't remember how many. I got seven replies by letter and two phone calls. I am still awaiting a reply from the portfolio holder for social services. I also wrote to Ieaun Wyn Jones, Welsh National Assembly Member for Anglesey; he was very good, as was Albert Owen, MP for Anglesey. Dolyn Mon and Mencap Cymru were also very helpful.
>
> I was prepared to picket the council offices. I wrote to the local papers complaining of what they were doing. I had articles in the *Anglesey and Holyhead Mail*, the *Liverpool Daily Post* and the *Western Mail*. I said that if they sacked me from my job for not paying I would go to court and tell the judge what they were doing and how much they were paying me for my work.
>
> Social services said to me that I was not working because I needed support to do my job. I asked the social services person if he had a secretary. He said yes, so I said, 'Then you have someone who helps you do your job!'

As a result of Gary's stance the Council deferred their final decision to charge for these services.

Relationships

Nigel and Gloria were interviewed in their home in January 2006; they are proud to use their own names – 'to let everyone know'.

Nigel and Gloria have been happily married for nearly seven years; they have a daughter, Sarah, who is four years old. Sarah now goes to school full time, which she enjoys and recently started attending an after-school club, as Gloria says, 'so she can be with her friends'. Gloria thinks it is important for Sarah to have friends and doesn't mind that at the moment all Sarah's friends are boys and she plays 'bang, bang you're dead'!

Nigel and Gloria have purchased their own home and last year bought a conservatory which is now Sarah's playroom, 'so all her toys are together and gives us some space,' said Nigel. Gloria enjoys gardening; the house has a garden at the front, down the side of the house and at the back. She doesn't let Nigel do any because he pulls flowers up as well as weeds.

Nigel has worked part time at Tesco for thirteen years and as Sarah is now going to school Gloria recently went back to work for a few hours each week. Sarah's grandmother helps with childcare in the school holidays and enjoys having Sarah to stay some weekends. Someone from the Family Support Team calls once a week to help Gloria with sorting bills and checks that everything is all right with Sarah. Sarah has a bath at 8 pm and Gloria reads her a bedtime story, then she goes to sleep at 9 pm. Nigel wants to learn to read so he can share in telling bedtime stories and playing on the computer.

Nigel said: 'Tell me this: some parents on this estate go out at night and leave little children alone in the house why doesn't social services; come after them? Are they better than me?'

Nigel is concerned that if anything happened to him or Gloria Sarah would be taken into care – he is determined that will not happen.

Nigel and Gloria think everyone with learning disabilities should be able to have the same opportunities as them, to have relationships, get married and have children if they want to. Nigel and Gloria remember their families, friends and social workers: 'Everybody said we wouldn't be able to cope but we showed them we could', said a very proud Nigel.

Independent living

Marion is an older carer in her seventies.

> We've been trying to find somewhere for David to live for fifteen years. Although I don't want him to move out, I'm getting older, like many people I know, and I have seen what happens when people aren't given a chance to settle. Too often if a parent dies people are sent all over the place, emergency placements are upsetting for everyone and people end up living away from home and all the people they know. When they've just been bereaved this is the last thing they need.

It is right to acknowledge that whereas in 1970 nearly 50 per cent of people with a learning disability lived in large institutions, either hospitals or hostels, we have made tremendous progress and about 50 per cent of the population now live independently in their own communities. At the time of writing, however, a small number of people still live in hospitals, although by the end of 2006 no one with a learning disability should live in a hospital in Wales unless they have serious health needs as well as a learning disability. Fifty per cent of adults still live at home with their families and about 1,500 people live with carers over the age of seventy. The needs of older carers are one of Mencap Cymru's priority areas for the future. Many experience the same fight that Marion has been through. Helping older carers to have choices and opportunities is fundamental to our vision.

Mencap Cymru's aspirations

Mencap Cymru's aspirations are to help people with a learning disability and their families to gain the necessary political knowledge and skills to be able to control and change their lives. If people are given the tools to enable self-advocacy, to campaign, to support each other mutually, then no ambition is too great.

Shaun Galletley took part in the Partners in Politics Project:

> Went to Brussels. To the European Parliament. Lovely trip. We met a man . . . in an office and talked about mad cow disease. We went to meetings with people from Wales, Denmark and other countries. We learnt about money, transport, work and carers.
>
> Rhodri Morgan gave me my certificate. I presented flowers to the lady.
>
> David met Jane Hutt and Angela met Edwina Hart. I saw David on the TV – jealous of it.

We want to see people with a learning disability and their families not only aiming high, but achieving these aims. We have obtained money from the Big Lottery Fund to work with children and young people with a learning disability through their schools and other young people's groups. Our work will be focused on ensuring that the voices of children and young people are heard by decision-makers and on helping the young people themselves to develop the necessary skills to be able to take control of their lives.

We will also be focusing on ensuring that people with a profound learning disability and their families are included within all we do. The communication barriers and complex needs of people with a profound learning disability mean they are some of the most excluded people in today's society. As well as people with profound and multiple learning disabilities, people from black and minority ethnic communities are also not receiving their fair share of help and support. In all our campaigning work, skills development of children and young people, listening to older carers and direct services, we want to make sure that whoever you are, and wherever you come from, you can be part of Mencap Cymru.

In the next sixty years we hope that we can reach everyone with a learning disability in Wales and their families and to help them to take control of their lives.

Maureen Edwards, a member from Llandudno, remembers that when her daughter Paula was a young girl forty years ago there were very few support services. She attended a specialist playgroup three days a week until starting at school. The special school had untrained teachers and was in a building which had previously been a church school but was no longer thought suitable for school purposes. Maureen said: 'Respite care enables parents to cope and helps people with a learning disability to learn new abilities, away from their parents.'

Today we can undoubtedly say that services are available to more people and individuals have choices about education; it is also recognised that people with a learning disability should be supported by trained and skilled staff. Inequality, however, is still ingrained in our society and has to be repeatedly challenged. Only three years ago people with a learning disability in Cardiff found themselves attending a day centre where it was necessary to have security guards on the doors and where the surroundings were appallingly run down with many dirty needles littering the grounds. In the past this may well have continued unquestioned and unaltered. Not in the Wales of the twenty-first century; the people with a learning disability using the centre challenged this, asserted their rights to a clean and safe environment and demanded the centre move. They were victorious; and perhaps, in the echoing and ghostly corridors of former long-stay hospitals throughout the Principality, there could have been heard a faint ripple of applause and the murmur of hope.

Mencap in Northern Ireland

Maureen Piggot
Director, Mencap in Northern Ireland

Northern Ireland is the smallest and most recent of the countries in which Mencap works. We are on the other large island on the western edge of Europe and the only part of Mencap to share a land border with another European member-state. Our unique geopolitical position means that we are different in some ways, including our experience of working against the backdrop of the Troubles, the Peace Process and the comings and goings of the Northern Ireland Assembly. This is a brief history of what that has been like, the role Mencap has played and some of the people who are part of our story.

First, some facts about us and where we live. The total population of Northern Ireland is 1.7 million. This is a largely rural country with a concentration of people and services in the east, especially around Belfast. All roads lead to Belfast and the transport links beyond the commuter belt are poor. The beautiful scenery, with mountains, glens, loughs and rugged coasts, makes it a wonderful place to live. The downside for people who can't drive, don't have cars and need access to services is that those very features cut them off. Mencap local societies and Gateway clubs have been focal points in these communities. The impetus for the development of new services has often been the demand of parents in the local Mencap group or the actions of a committed group of volunteers getting together to provide what was needed themselves. That is at the centre of the Mencap story.

Mencap's story in Northern Ireland starts in 1965 at a public meeting in the Belfast City Hall. In its marbled halls and panelled chambers hundreds of people gathered at the invitation of the National Society for Mentally Handicapped Children (later known as Mencap). The response far exceeded the expectations of the organisers, and the newly appointed Regional Officer, Evelyn Greer, had to negotiate hastily with the Lord Mayor for the use of the ballroom rather than his parlour to accommodate the crowd.

Who were these people and what attracted them in such numbers? They were mostly parents of people with a learning disability but there were also many supportive professionals. They had travelled from all over Northern Ireland, united by their concern. Some were representatives of parents and friends groups, associations linked to the hospitals and other services operated by the special care system, which at that time ran all services for children and adults with a learning disability. What attracted them was the idea that by joining forces with the National Society they could give a stronger voice to their issues. Being part of the larger organisation would mean they had advice and support for their activities, an infrastructure that would increase their capacity and effectiveness. In a landmark decision they voted to join and Mencap in Northern Ireland was born.

'When the parents formed together we became a pressure group, naturally. Mencap was a very powerful voice on behalf of learning disabled people as our Department of Health and Social Services recognised that the parent's voice is a very powerful voice,' said Evelyn Greer, reflecting on her experience as Mencap's Director from its inception to 1990.

Northern Ireland was one of twelve Mencap regions. Each had a Regional Council made up of nominees of each local society. The first chairman was Roy Lewis. Two members were elected to represent the region on a National Council. The first national representatives were Roy Lewis and Jim Martin. Such is the commitment of Mencap's founding members that many of them are still active in the Society. We are not talking about faithfully attending meetings and nodding off under 'matters arising'. Instead, there is the example of Ian Millar, former Northern Ireland Chairman and national trustee who last year trekked the mountains of New Zealand, one of our toughest adventure challenges, and raised £15,000 for both the Bangor local society and Mencap in Northern Ireland, or Annabel Poots, the President of Gateway who, at a distinguished age, still runs a flower-arranging group for women with a learning disability. A tireless campaigner Greta

McIntyre MBE has advocated on behalf of the residents of Muckamore Abbey Hospital and their parents and continues to do so, although her own daughter has been resettled from the hospital. She, and others like her, can be found at the street collections, bring and buys or bed-pushes raising funds for their local society or Gateway club or at the public meetings debating the burning issues and standing up for people with a learning disability and their families.

The first regional office was above a hairdresser's shop at 230 Ormeau Road, Belfast. In a very short time it became apparent that bigger and more visible headquarters were needed to support the growing network and to provide space for demonstration projects, like the nursery, which had been established in a house on Knock Road. Fortunately, at about this time, a large semi-detached house at 4 Annadale Avenue was left to Mencap in a legacy. This made it possible to move the office and nursery to a new and, importantly, safe location in south Belfast, from which we still support all of Mencap's activities in Northern Ireland.

Although the adapted and extended Victorian semi-detached villa is not ideal for our activities, it has served the organisation well and has a special place in many hearts. The building was named Segal House in honour of Lord Segal of Wytham, the Chairman of Mencap and a supporter of the new region. It also has a ghost, as you would expect of any house of note in Ireland. Our ghost is known as Grandpa McClean. He got a name after the family who once lived in the house came to visit and told us about the death of their grandfather and how he had passed away peacefully in the general office. All of a sudden we had an explanation for the doors that banged in the far reaches of the house when anyone was working late or the sudden appearance or disappearance of objects from desks or shelves. All of us who work there know he might have some fun but he looks after us.

In the 1960s, Mencap's second network of groups began to grow. They were the Gateway clubs. Formed in response to the needs of young people for a social life outside the family, the clubs rely on volunteers to organise an interesting and entertaining programme and provide support to members to participate in the activities they choose. In 1965, the first Northern Ireland Gateway club was formed, the Ards Gateway Club in Newtownards. The network continued to grow in the 1970s as local societies and Gateway clubs were formed serving major towns and their surrounding districts. In recent years the greatest growth has been in clubs for children and adolescents. Increasingly they involve brothers and sisters or link with a youth club or other facility to share in activities and make friends with non-disabled children their age.

The Gateway clubs participate in a programme of regional events that bring groups together at different times during the year. The Gateway Forum, chaired by Stephen Lenaghan from Lisburn Gateway, plans and coordinates sporting and arts events and helps with the annual Christmas concert and conferences. The Northern Ireland football team they have created has distinguished itself in the international tournament in Geneva by their skill and their team spirit. That same team spirit motivates the volunteers who support the regional events. Without them we would not be able to run such an active programme, as there are few of us on the staff.

In the first few years Mencap only had the one Regional Officer, Evelyn Greer. As she recounts:

It was wonderful. In 1971 there were thirty-eight local societies. There were none when I started so I had to travel extensively through Northern Ireland. Much of this development took place against a background of violence, and therefore I had to make a personal decision, 'Did I not go out at night and did I stay in my headquarters?' But I decided that I couldn't do that. So many times I would be driving around the Province late at night. One instance, I went to a school about ninety miles away. I could have stayed over but I always wanted to go home, and this particular night I was flying home about 11 pm – I used to run about at all hours – and I saw lights flashing to stop. But that day police uniforms had been stolen by one of the paramilitaries in police uniform, and I drove through the block and then I jammed on the brakes and stopped. These pounding feet came running up and a policeman said, 'Why did you do that? You could have been shot dead.' And so I could because they had said, 'Stop!' 'Show me your identification,' I said. I was afraid. So he said, 'You go on ahead and we will alert every stop along the way that you're coming so that you needn't be frightened.' Wasn't that good?

In 1973, the indefatigable Evelyn also led the establishment of Special Olympics in Northern Ireland. The first Northern Ireland team went on to compete in the International Games at Brockport, USA. Twelve years later 200 athletes represented Northern Ireland and in 2003 the whole island of Ireland thrilled to the spectacle of the opening ceremony of the World Games in Dublin. Towns and villages participating in the host town scheme opened their hearts and homes to welcome the delegations from all over the world. Evelyn, who retired from Mencap in 1990, remained involved with Special Olympics and has continued to make an outstanding contribution to the lives of people with a learning disability and their families. Evelyn Greer's achievements and boundless energy were appreciated within the organisation and were also recognised with an MBE in 1979 and OBE in 2003. In September 1990 I was appointed and am the Director to the present day and, hopefully, beyond, for this excursion into writing has dissuaded me from tackling the novel I thought was one of my future tasks!

In the 1980s, as in the rest of Mencap, the new development was in residential care. There was great excitement when Brian Rix opened Mencap's first residential scheme in Princetown Road, Bangor. This was followed by a second large group home, Ashley House, in Omagh. Grant and contract conditions are often less favourable in Northern Ireland. Funding uncertainties and changes in the approach to providing housing and support made Mencap decide not to commit to large-scale development of residential services. In 1991, we campaigned for the introduction of Hostel Deficit Grant and succeeded in having it made available in Northern Ireland. Without this additional revenue funding the housing association and other jointly managed services in the voluntary sector would not have been able to operate.

Two further Mencap residential developments have taken place: one a small shared house in Keady, and the most recent, Riversley, a complex of flats for older people and people with a learning disability and an eight-person shared house in Banbridge. Each has demonstrated different ways of supporting people, thereby adding to the range of alternatives that should be available for people who need to move on from the family or from care in a hospital. In the next planned development we are designing services for older people with a learning disability. Using new technology to support and to entertain is one innovative aspect of the design brief. Combating isolation by developing a sense of community will be another of the features of the new Princetown Road facility.

Although it hard to get definitive statistics, it is clear that Northern Ireland has higher numbers of people with a learning disability and that they and their families need to speak up and be heard if they are to enjoy the same rights and services as are available in the rest of the United Kingdom or Ireland. Getting heard against the clamour of competing voices is a challenge anywhere. In Northern Ireland it has been complicated by extraordinary and constantly changing arrangements for government and by single-issue politics.

When the Northern Ireland Assembly was first formed we entered the new era with hope and the determination to ensure that learning disability would soon be on the agenda of our 108 Members of the Legislative Assembly (MLAs) and eleven ministers in the Executive. To begin that process we held a reception in the Long Gallery at Stormont, Northern Ireland's Parliament building. In the lead up to the event we got a call from an MLA to alert us to the fact that there was a move afoot in the DUP (Democratic Unionist Party) to get support for a motion to exclude Sinn Fein from the Assembly. If the required number of signatories was obtained there would be a vote on the motion on the day of our reception. Needless to say nobody would come to our party. In the days leading up to the event we paid more attention than usual to party politics while we waited to hear if we were going to have to cancel. Thankfully that did not happen and the event was well attended. Northern Ireland's elected representatives heard people with a learning disability and their parents tell them how their lives were affected by poor transport, the shortage of housing and support, lack of respite and all the other issues.

Hilary Gammon, a young woman with a learning disability whose parents, Nell and Jim, had been founder members of the Belfast Society and the Mencap Regional Council, spoke eloquently of the aspirations of the people she knew in day centres who wanted proper jobs:

> I would like people to understand and respect people with a learning disability. We have feelings too and it hurts when we are stared at or teased.

I would like people to see our abilities not disabilities. We can work as hard and do as much for our communities as everybody else.

We should be free to live where we want, with who we want and if we need help it should be there for us.

We should be paid fairly for the jobs we do, not just a token payment.

We should be able to go to college and choose whichever courses we want and have support if we need it.

Finally, there should be more money available for organisations like Mencap and Pathway to help us train and find jobs and give us the support that some of us need.

The political undercurrents were there. Volunteers helping with arrangements were briefed to ensure that Bairbre de Brun, then Minister for Health and Social Services and Public Safety, did not come face to face with Sir Ronnie Flanagan, Chief Constable of the RUC. Care went into planning who could be seen with whom in the photographs taken for the local and regional papers.

In the period that the Assembly was up and running, learning disability issues made it to the floor of the debating chamber more than once. The most extensive debates were about the shortage of day services, shortcomings in transition and the need for services for children and adults with autism. An all party group on disability was established and encouragingly a number of MLAs championed the cause of people with a learning disability. As a result, development funding was made available for additional day service places, assessment and early intervention for children with autism and an Inter-Departmental Group was set up to review transition. It began to feel like we had politicians who listened. Unfortunately it did not last. The Assembly collapsed.

The next major Mencap event at Stormont was the Learning Disabled People's Parliament in January 2005. In the disused senate chamber people with a learning disability called on politicians from all parties to debate with them the rights of people with a learning disability. The rights to vote, housing, jobs, personal safety and respect as equals were powerfully asserted by people from the Democracy in Action and Shout Out groups. Just as Northern Ireland had discovered that parents of people with a learning disability were a lobby to be taken seriously, now it is discovering that people with a learning disability can make their own case. They are no longer 'shadow people', as Trevor Rhodie, one of the self-advocates put it.

The groundwork that created this opportunity and enabled people to find their voice took place in self-advocacy groups like the Strule Buzz Group in Omagh as Joanne McDonald, a member of the group, writes:

> This group is a self-advocacy group made up of ten people with a learning disability who meet up once a month to talk about things that are important to us as people with a learning disability. We learn how important it is to speak up for ourselves and we also have training to be able to do this. We meet with other groups on a regular basis to tell them what life as people with a learning disability is like; groups such as people who work within the health service and members of the public. Our aim is to make them more aware of people with a learning disability so that they will see that we are not that different from anyone else, we just need more support.

It is hard now to remember what an achievement this is. To recall how far we have come from the days when having a learning disability meant living in the shadow, not being taken seriously, even within Mencap. *Focus on the Future*, Mencap's five-year plan published in 1995 after extensive consultation, rang the changes. The large national conferences that for the first time brought the local societies and Gateway clubs together in one event were the spectacular evidence that Mencap was doing things differently. People with a learning disability took their places on that conference platform and inspired us all. The Mencap Events Team and Communications Department worked magic to pull off complex programmes to cater for all interests and abilities and to ensure the conference presentations were accessible to all.

Northern Ireland supported the conferences well. In buses, planes and trains we travelled, looking out for each other on the journey. The members and staff who attended always came back with lots to tell and new ideas to try. At one of those conferences, in Bournemouth in 1998, a new constitution was adopted that ensured full inclusion at all levels in the organisation.

At our Northern Ireland conference the following year we provided time and space for hustings as a strong field of candidates for the National Assembly vied for members' votes. The ten candidates were: Sam Bell, Cathy Gribbon, Margaret Hazley, Alison Hutchinson, Mary Johnson, Ann McGinley, John McKee, Ian Millar, Theresa O'Connor and Trevor Rhodie. To ensure the process did not disadvantage people who had not had public speaking experience, we provided a stall for each candidate and support to get set up. Conference delegates were encouraged to meet the candidates, look at their material and find out their views. It was all new and exciting: a hard lesson in democracy for those not elected as they were extremely disappointed; useful lessons for all in making processes accessible and fair. The first duly elected National Assembly representatives for Northern Ireland were Ian Millar, John McKee and Mary Johnson.

Mencap in Northern Ireland has its own committee, accountable directly to the Board of Trustees. It is made up of representatives of each of the four district committees and includes the National Assembly members for Northern Ireland. It is fully inclusive and works well, ensuring a range of perspectives on any subject. The committee rotates its meetings around the districts, choosing a venue in one of the major towns and inviting members and staff to meet with them for an exchange of information and views before the formal meeting. This brings the business to life and gives interested members the opportunity to meet their representatives. The longest-serving Chairman of the new committee, Neill Wilson, has provided steady guidance and positive leadership to Mencap in Northern Ireland through all the changes. Annette and Anetta Crawford, a mother and daughter team, bring their enthusiasm for, and commitment to, Mencap's work in Northern Ireland to the National Assembly in which Annette serves as the Vice-Chairperson.

Northern Ireland is the most youthful region in Europe with 25 per cent of its population under twenty-five years old. It is therefore not surprising that Mencap's flagship service, established in 1969, was for pre-school-age children and that now, in 2006, we have young people meeting the Commissioner for Children and Young People, speaking up for themselves. By their example and by offering equality training in schools and youth clubs they are changing the attitudes of other young people.

In the thirty-seven years since the first pre-school playgroup was established in a house in Knock Road, Belfast, around 2,000 children have benefited from the early intervention services that Mencap has continued to offer. The nursery at Segal House is known throughout Northern Ireland for the excellence of its multi-disciplinary approach and the supportive atmosphere, welcomed by parents. Anne McBride, the Principal for twenty-nine years, set the tone: 'To me Mencap is there to provide support to families who have a child with a learning disability not just for a month or a year but for life.'

Coffee and chat sessions for parents and toddlers, information evenings and fundraising activities bring parents together and foster life-long friendships.

For the nursery's twenty-fifth birthday we brought together former pupils and their parents for celebrations at Segal House and a family day out at Castle Ward in scenic Strangford. Among the stories told was one about a mums' weekend break to Jersey. The parents' committee and Anne had arranged the expedition. Dads, grandparents and respite services, who had been called on to give the mothers a well-earned treat, were more than a little suspicious when they got calls on the Sunday evening to say that fog had delayed the women's return and they were forced to stay an extra day. Those mums had a memorable time – one of many.

The value of Segal House and its approach is encapsulated by Joanne Tunnah, whose son Patrick is a recent 'graduate' from the nursery:

> We were initially gutted as all our dreams and aspirations seemed shattered. How wrong we were! Very soon after Patrick's birth we were advised that Mencap had a specialist nursery unit that provided in-house therapies, support, information and much, much more. Our family cannot praise Segal House nursery staff and therapists enough. I needed a lifeline and they provided it.

In the early days children travelled from all over Northern Ireland to attend the nursery or the advice clinic which was added. Segal House was the forerunner of child development centres and community paediatric teams that now see children and their families closer to home.

Getting allied health professionals to work in the community and take a special interest in learning disability was a radical idea at the time Mencap established the Segal House multi-disciplinary team in 1977. With funding from the Eastern Health and Social Services Board, a therapy wing was added and a team of professional staff comprising Dr Nan Hill, the paediatrician, Alison McCullough, speech and language therapist, Isobel Thompson, physiotherapist, and Audrey Patton, occupational therapist, were dedicated to work alongside Mencap's own staff and the South Belfast social work team. In one place, children and their families could have access to health, education and social services facilitated by Mencap in one seamless service. A plaque on the wall records that Sir Richard Needham, then Minister for Health and Social Services, opened the building. Little did he know that nineteen years later that plaque would lead us to tracking him down and inviting him to head the Blue Sky Appeal in Northern Ireland.

Building specialist expertise is a continuing need. The nursery plays a part in the training of therapists, nurses and care staff through providing placements and maintaining links with the universities and colleges. The value of working together is the other lesson from Segal House nursery. The children are our common concern; their parents are the most important people in their lives. Mencap's role is to provide the right conditions for everyone to focus on doing what they do best in a way that promotes the child's development and total well-being. Segal House works in partnership with a local day nursery, the Forward Steps programme for children with autism and peripatetic teachers for children with sensory impairments. Children leave to start school or may progress to a mainstream nursery class. Leaving is a wrench for all concerned but the door is always open and many choose to stay in touch, as Marian Nicholas's story illustrates:

> I got involved with Mencap for very selfish reasons. My daughter Laura had been born with a learning disability and we needed help because I was scared and felt I owed it to her to get help and to get as much information and advice as possible. Mencap has been a constant support, probably the only thing constant in the world of disability.

Because of Mencap I have made myself do things that I probably would not have dreamed of, for example, giving speeches at functions, going on radio, having wonderful arguments with people in the Trusts, trying to get our point across.

As we speak, we are looking at building on the Segal House experience to develop the next generation of services to children and their families. We have outgrown the building and plan to replace it with a new regional centre of excellence.

Mencap has services across Northern Ireland. In the 1990s we worked to reach beyond Greater Belfast and to establish Mencap offices in major towns in the south, west, east and most recently the north of the country. The first office outside Belfast was the Southern Area office in Armagh. Established with a grant from the Southern Health and Social Services Board, we were able to employ the first area manager, Róisín Foster, who energetically set about developing services in that area.

Development is determined by funding and means that we are more visible in some areas than others. The expansion in the 1990s took us from services and activities worth £500,000 to a broad-based programme of over £3 million. The major initiatives were the development of the Mencap employment services and the information and advice services. Other smaller but no less significant services are the community summer schemes, play advisers and advocacy and self-advocacy projects. Our aim has been to reach more people, work across the age range and ability spectrum of people with a learning disability and to introduce new solutions, new ways of working. 'Innovation with care' is how our approach was characterised in the most recent independent evaluation of Mencap in Northern Ireland.

One of our achievements was producing the first-ever Government report in accessible formats. This was the executive summary of the Department of Health and Social Services' *Review of Policy for People with a Learning Disability 1995*. Bravely, they agreed to our suggestion that a policy for people with a learning disability ought to be made accessible to them and commissioned Mencap to conduct an action research project, the result of which would be an accessible version of the report. With a team of advisers from the Speech and Language Therapy Department,

Media Studies and others at University of Ulster, the Special Library Service, the Northern Ireland Centre for the Blind, a number of illustrators and proofing groups of people with a learning disability, we produced the accessible report and an audio version. The Mencap Northern Ireland Information Service continues this work and gives advice or undertakes the task for a wide range of agencies. Publications include guidance on the Disability Discrimination Act, Direct Payment and many others.

Mencap's impact is felt across many fields and beyond the boundaries of Northern Ireland. We have influenced the law on special education, hate crime and discrimination in Northern Ireland. Through participation in the European TIDE (Telematics for the Integration of the Disabled and Elderly) programme we got cognitive disabilities into the work plan for future research and contributed to thinking about how technology could be used to support people with a learning disability to learn, to find information and to be more independent. We hosted the end of programme Helios conference for the whole of Europe.

Mencap has a high profile in Northern Ireland and engages with Government across all eleven departments. Through the constant submission of thoughtful responses to policy documents and draft legislation we keep the needs and unique circumstances of people with a learning disability and their families in front of decision-makers. Through facilitating consultations every year we connect hundreds of people directly with Government, giving them the opportunity to make their own case. Our press and PR work keeps the issues and the organisation in front of the public in Northern Ireland. The *Snap!* competition has been an outstanding example for which we won awards at national and Northern Ireland levels. To launch the competition here we arranged an exhibition and reception in Belfast's showcase venue, the Waterfront Hall. Brian Ingram, an award-winning photographer from the *Belfast Telegraph*, gave a master-class to prospective participants. Media coverage of the exhibition helped us to make the case to get the intimate and moving images and stories of people's lives into 'the corridors of power'. British Telecom took it to display in BT Tower; the exhibition was also seen in Stormont, the University of Ulster and the police headquarters and training college. Joanne Tunnah, one of the winners, reflects, 'I think to date my most poignant memory of my time with Mencap is of the *Snap!* competition, and of course my son being the first child from Northern Ireland to win a category. Silly as it may seem, but being able to enter a photo of your most beloved child and hearing that he had won filled me with such overwhelming pride that I was able to show the world how beautiful and accomplished my brilliant son is!'

So much of what we do is dependent on fundraising. While project grants and contracts for services make up most of the money we work with, it is the freely given money we get through appeals that make it all work. The complex patchwork of funding we put together each year has very narrow seams and pieces missing. That's where our fundraised income is needed. Fundraising is a necessity but it has other value. It brings people together, united to help and have fun although sometimes, as with the personally challenging treks and hikes, the fun is in the storytelling afterwards.

Joanne and Marian's stories above are typical of the way families become involved. The treks and hikes have brought large numbers of people in touch while raising money for us. Many have family or other personal reasons for wanting to help. The commitment of some trekkers is extraordinary. Among them is Flo Creighton who has been on every Mencap trek since we started doing them. Flo, with all the others, has walked the remotest parts of the planet in Mencap's name.

The other amazing women who have supported us down the years are the members of the Special Events Committee and their network of family and friends. Angela Holland, the current Chairperson tells her story:

> During my time on the committee we have raised approximately £50,000 annually through a wide range of fundraising events, equating to £1 million!
>
> My most poignant memory during the past twenty-two years was the untimely death of two close friends and committee members who brought laughter and fun to everything we did for Mencap. Ten years ago I was honoured and proud to accept the chair and follow in the footsteps of one of those friends.

What, with typical modesty, she does not say is how much time she and the committee give, the numbers of tickets they have collectively sold, the prizes they have negotiated, the favours they have begged, the miracles they have worked when the caterers let us down or the main act failed to arrive because of trouble at the border. Events run by the Special Events Committee are always special. The behind-the-scenes stories are the best. Someone should collect them; there is a book in it: 'The things I've done for Mencap'. Perhaps Brian Rix will do that next.

The biggest fundraising story of all was the Blue Sky Appeal. Mencap in Northern Ireland really flew its kite (the symbol of the Blue Sky Appeal was a kite). Sir Richard Needham, Patron of the Appeal, set the pace for the high-powered committee. They knew he would be a hard act to follow when his personal Blue Sky challenge was to water ski round Strangford Lough – in a suit. From the day he agreed to take us on it has been a pleasure to hang on to his coat tails as he took off to raise the target £1 million and kept going. Not a moment is wasted nor an opportunity missed to press Mencap's advantage. With Sir Richard's help and Aine Gibbon's guidance as the first Fundraising Manager in Northern Ireland, we put together an influential Appeal Committee under the chairmanship of Dr Maurice Hayes. Each committee member led a sector of the appeal and had a personal target. Sir Ronnie Flanagan, then Chief Constable of the RUC, threw himself into that challenge and led the police force in raising a quarter of a million pounds for Mencap. Some of the events probably not in other fundraising repertoires that year included Land-Rover and helicopter pulls. The RUC also linked in with our local groups to hold joint events like the Family Fun Day in Fermanagh.

Local groups rallied to the call. Most held at least one Blue Sky event. There were parties, raffles, dances and music and drama such as the Ards Gateway Club sell-out concert. The staff did the same. A team challenge for Blue Sky day brought out hidden talent and some shenanigans as staff teams competed to produce the best kite, best outfits and best poem. The mural on the wall of the Derry office is a lasting memento. Blue was the colour theme. Neighbours were astonished at the procession of strange visitors to Segal House that day. The photos show blue 'trekkies', nuns, charladies, pilots, clowns and a host of other characters. The 'craic' was good as we struggled to identify each other and competed for the team honours. The photographic record still has fundraising potential for blackmailers.

With a combination of grants and appeals we raised our target and established the Family Advisory Service, responding to the pressing need for information and advice so that families and people with a learning disability can find their way through the increasingly complex system of services, benefits and other entitlements. The Northern Ireland Information Service was built on the Blue Sky income. The enquiry service still serves the whole of Northern Ireland and local advisers are available to offer more personalised support in the northern and southern areas and in Londonderry. Out of the fun and the fuss we have a lasting benefit and a lot of fond memories.

Looking to the future, Mencap will continue to be vital to the community of people with a learning disability and those who care for and about them in Northern Ireland. The strategy for the Province is to be a 'forward and outward looking region', so too for Mencap in Northern Ireland. Marian Nicholas echoes this viewpoint: 'My hopes for Mencap are that it continues to grow and thrive, to keep up to date with our changing world and to be around to support people like us forever.'

As an integral part of Mencap we benefit from the depth of knowledge and the breadth of talent the organisation has within it. Connected through our network to people with a learning disability, their parents and other family members, we are in touch with what is important and are strengthened by them speaking up for themselves and for Mencap. Joanne McDonald writes:

In my opinion the greatest achievement that Mencap has done is to help people with a learning disability become more involved within their work, such as have people with a learning disability sitting on their boards, become volunteers in their Gateway clubs but also supporting them to be part of their local community by supporting them to get employment, to get the right support within all parts of their life, giving them the same chances in life as anyone else, and also to be there to support the people who care for them. I just hope that Mencap will help more people become aware of people with a learning disability and see the person before the learning disability.

We will continue to improve on how we listen, how we connect people and how we get our concerns heard. We need to track changes in the big picture. That means looking beyond ourselves and watching the UK, European and even global trends. Evelyn Greer writes that she

> always felt that Mencap should have more of a world focus. That is not easy to do. Because I travelled extensively with the Special Olympics I did not often see major voluntary organisations in different countries but the reason for that is that the cultures are different, so you can't imprint what Mencap does in, say, Italy or France, but I think Mencap should have contact with departments throughout the world. There used to be a directory called the International Directory of Countries with Mental Handicap and I used it for my Churchill Fellowship, but I feel that Mencap could almost be a world leader in learning disabilities if not a European leader, because we are now in the European Union, and in my time we did not have very strong links. It seems to me the projects could be exchange visits by major officials, exchange of students, major world conferences. I think we're too inward looking.

For us in Northern Ireland there is a particular east-west and north-south dimension to that 'watch' function. We have a continuing part to play in bridging the divides that have blighted Northern Ireland. There are also people right here for whom we need to do more, children and adults with profound and multiple learning disability, new populations of immigrant and migrant families from Eastern Europe and other places, new technology to explore and harness. In those tasks we will achieve more if we work in partnership, building on the good relationships we enjoy with others in the learning disability sector, the cities, the wider voluntary sector and the business community. To conclude with a quote from Joanne Tunnah: 'My wish for the future is that through Mencap's endeavours, they can bridge the gap in equal opportunities, so that my son and others like him can enjoy a brighter, more colourful and varied future.'

Acknowledgements

I would like to thank the following for their contributions: Evelyn Greer OBE, Anne McBride, Marian Nicholas, Angela Holland, Joanne McDonald and Joanne Tunnah.

Other Enterprises

I have bracketed the Open University, Local Societies, Gateway and Golden Lane Housing together because although they seem different they are actually all intertwined. Each and every one of them offers support of one kind or another at a local level, with an umbilical cord reaching out to Golden Lane, Mencap's head office. Gateway thrives around the country and provides the greater part of Mencap's membership, as well as the volunteer force. Local societies are, as the title makes clear, *local* and are also very concerned that Golden Lane Housing can reach out to support the housing needs of people with a learning disability in their locality. The Open University disseminates its educational works to the entire nation and pays particular attention to Mencap and people with a learning disability with some targeted courses.

The Dream Team:
Mencap and the Open University

Professor Dorothy Atkinson BA Mphil PhD
Professor of Learning Disability at the OU

In a productive partnership, already spanning the best part of a quarter of a century, the Open University (OU) and Mencap have worked together to bring knowledge, skills and best practice to as wide and as diverse an audience as possible. The original idea – to create an OU course open to everyone involved in learning disability – was both innovative and timely. Nothing like this existed at the time.

At the beginning of the 1980s, many people with a learning disability were still living in long-stay institutions and community care was more of an aspiration than a reality. There were examples, here and there, of good services and 'best practice' but no effective means of sharing them. What was needed then was a means of disseminating the best of the best practices so that everyone could adopt them; but even more important

Left: Let's celebrate
Mencap's sixtieth
anniversary!

Below: Brian and
Elspet Rix

Pictures from
Understanding Us

Top: John Brown:
'This is me in my
football kit. I am going
to play for Manchester
United and England…
Then I will be famous.'

Middle: Lizzie Howes:
'I like this photo of me
on my birthday.
My friends at Safeway
bought me a watch.'

Bottom: Jordan Wright
is blind but laughed as
Meg, the dog, jumped
up and knocked the
football off his lap

Pictures from
Understanding Us Volume II

Top: this picture captures Sally Creighton's happiness and enthusiasm for life, even though she was in hospital only a few days earlier

Middle: Andrea and Paul Kinnear, whose story is told in Chapter 10, married in September 2004

Bottom: Jonathan Welsby: 'I use a hose to wash cars for our business at school. We make money.'

Some people with learning disabilities and their families have a big advantage ...it's called Mencap

Learning disabilities are caused by genetic factors or damage to the brain and cannot be cured. There are over one million people with learning disabilities in the United Kingdom. But Mencap reaches only one person in 20. We want to reach more.

mencap · Caring and campaigning... the first 50 years

When it comes to the big decisions in life, it helps to have someone to talk to

Mencap's Family Adviser Service. Helping families at all the crucial moment. Supported by the Blue Sky Appeal

mencap · Caring and campaigning... the first 50 years

You learn something every day. So does Elizabeth

Mencap runs three colleges which help young adults acquire skills for life

mencap · Education... developing skills for life

Angela's learning disability has never got in the way of a good day's work

A job means a wage, self-esteem and a chance to contribute. Mencap's Pathway scheme has helped more than 7,000 people into worthwhile jobs, by bringing employers and job-hunters together.

mencap · Employment... helping people into real jobs

Advertisements for the Blue Sky Appeal in 1996

Top: Gateway performers enjoy tea between shows at London's Royal Festival Hall during the eighties

Bottom: Mencap's Trans-active project started in Birmingham in 2001 to help teenagers with a learning disability move more easily to adulthood through activities with their non-disabled peers

Red

Red is the round juiciness of tomatoes
the sweetness of ripe strawberries.
Red is the texture of delicious cherries
the hard crunchiness of raw peppers.
Red is scented, soft rose petals
the smooth gloss of shiny lips.
Red is a cold metal postbox
And the soft warm beat of a loving heart.
Red is gentle, beautiful and romantic.

Tricia Clark, Helen Louise Fish,
Robert Capstaff, Laura Cawood
and Vicki Carruthers

I want

I want to go swimming.
I want to do sport.
I want to do cooking.
I want to do football.
I want to have a kiss.

I don't want to go on a plane.
I don't want to eat chips.
I don't want to drink beer.
I don't want to have a fit.

Eugene Grice

I wish

I wish I was kissing Anthony Dunn
outside at Dilston common room.
Tall, handsome,
I like to look at your nice blond hair
and beautiful arms.
I look at your beautiful blue eyes.
Can you make me happy?
Put your beautiful arms around me.
Look at me with your beautiful blue eyes.
Anthony, take Jane out every night.

Jane Baxter

My friend Craig

My friend has bright green eyes
behind round circle glasses,
brown dark skin
and pink round lips
like a cupid's bow.

When he smiles
he shows his white teeth
and gums.
Sometimes he talks
about love and kisses.

He likes writing
and playing computer games.
He is good on the internet
like me.

Just once he cooked
me a jacket potato.
He put tomato on it
just for me.

Donna Kearton

Trish

Trish has black, glossy hair,
brown, gentle eyes,
a lot of smiles.
She works hard,
sits with me at dinner,
listens to me,
tells me her troubles.

And she has a temper,
walks away,
scowls.
I run after her,
give her a hug.
She hugs me back,
says sorry.
I say it's OK.
We laugh about it.
Trish is my friend.
Princess Trish.

Jack Hope

Pages from *We too have a voice* – a collection of poems by students from Mencap National College, published as part of Mencap 60 celebrations

Photographs from Mencap's
corporate plan 2006–07
showing people with a
learning disability at play and
at work

was the need to change hearts and minds so that everyone could see the need for change.

This is what the first OU course in learning disability, financed and produced in partnership with Mencap, set out to do – to bring about change at all levels: changes in the attitudes, approaches and skills of the workforce but also real changes in provision and the quality of people's lives. Conceived as an idea in 1982 by Brian Rix (then Secretary-General of Mencap) and Chris Pym, from the OU, funding of the proposed course took a further two years but by the end of 1984 a course team was in place at the OU. This was when I joined the then Department of Health and Social Welfare at the OU (headed by Malcolm Johnson) as a member of the original course team.

This was a dream job for me. I joined a core team – Ann Brechin, Lydia Chant, Linda Ward and Jan Walmsley, together with Mary Holland (from Mencap) – which had ready access to key people and good practices from all around the UK. It also had a dedicated BBC producer, Alison Tucker, and resources for a series of television programmes. The course, *Patterns for Living*, was launched to great acclaim in 1986. It pioneered the use of real-life case studies, people's stories and authentic voices (on audio cassettes and on television, as well as in the course workbooks) as a way of engaging students' interest in the issues but also as a means of enabling them to learn, to understand and ultimately to think differently about people with a learning disability.

The course was taken up on an unprecedented scale in health, social care and educational settings to such an extent that a reprint of course materials was needed only six months after the launch. A later independent evaluation to the course (by the Health Education Authority) estimated that 16,000 students had successfully studied and completed it in its first two years. The equally good news was that it had reached all parts of its target audience, which included parents and volunteers as well as staff and practitioners, not forgetting local societies.

Undoubtedly, *Patterns for Living* was a great success. However, although it put people with a learning disability at the centre of its course materials, the one audience it did not reach (with some notable exceptions) were those very same people. As a result, a new OU course was developed called *Working Together*, which was launched in 1988. This was the first OU (and as far as we know the first in the world) course for people with a learning disability who had, *inter alia*, learning difficulties, the term we use in an educational context. The course pioneered the use of audio drama, illustrated workbooks and accessible assessment for people with a learning disability, many of whom later 'graduated' at local award ceremonies, where they received their signed and personalised certificates from local dignitaries, to family – as well as local press and radio – acclaim.

The successful OU–Mencap partnership has continued over the intervening years. In 1988, James Cummings from Mencap joined an OU team to produce a second-level undergraduate OU course. This was called *Changing Perspectives* and was launched in 1990. At its heart was an anthology of people's stories (in prose, poetry and art), entitled *Know Me As I Am* (Atkinson and Williams, 1990). Widely available in bookshops as well as to registered students, it proved to be a landmark book, influencing and inspiring people throughout the learning disability field not only in the UK but in many other parts of the world as well.

In a three-way collaboration in the mid-1990s, the original partnership (now including Brian Fairchild from Mencap) was joined by members of People First (Lloyd Page and Anya Souza) to develop another course. Called *Equal People*, it was launched in 1996, exactly ten years after the original OU course had come out. Uniquely, this later course aimed to engage everyone in the learning disability field in working and learning together as equal partners including the whole spectrum of students this time, ranging from people with a learning disability, their families and friends to care staff, volunteers and practitioners.

The stories of people's lives, which over the years have so informed and inspired students from all walks of life, have also provided the inspiration for a group of researchers at the OU – the Social History of Learning Disability Research Group – to embark on another ambitious project. This is to make sure these stories, and others, are heard in the wider world. Some of the stories of people with a learning disability have appeared already in the group's series of books: *Forgotten Lives* (1997), *Crossing Boundaries* (2000), *Good Times, Bad Times* (2000) and *Testimonies of Resistance* (2006); and a collection of family stories over seventy years of the twentieth century appeared in *Witnesses to Change* (2005).

This is not the end of the story. A longer-term plan is to create an archive so that the stories of people with a learning disability and their families have a proper and lasting home where they can continue to be a source of information and inspiration not only for practitioners, scholars and historians but also for the people and families most directly concerned.

Local Societies

The Open University has produced six booklets on local societies by Sheena Rolph based on two research projects, the first being *Reclaiming the Past: The Role of Mencap Societies in the Development of Community Care in East Anglia, 1946–1980*, and the second, *A Hidden Heritage: Local Mencap Societies and the Provision of Social Care in East Anglia, 1946–1990*.

Admittedly, these studies are concerned with only one part of the country but the findings therein could be replicated in practically every local society, no matter where they are located. When I was Secretary-General, Judy Fryd used to ask anxiously at every meeting if we had achieved her target figure of 500 local societies. We never did, although we were up in the 480s. Since then, of course, the number has decreased for all the present-day demographic reasons – ageing parents and youthful hubris – the belief that it is no longer necessary to band together to achieve change. How successful that banding together proved to be is illustrated in Sheena Rolph's histories, which are published by the OU, Walton Hall, Milton Keynes, and the societies are:

* Cambridge Mencap
* Norwich and District Mencap Society
* Bedford and District Society for People with Learning Disabilities
* Lowestoft and District Mencap Society
* Great Yarmouth and District Mencap Society
* South Norfolk Mencap Society

Sheena writes a foreword to each booklet which sums up the situation regarding local societies rather neatly:

Since 1946 a voluntary movement has been working and campaigning in the community to change lives. Local Mencap societies have emerged in many towns and cities since World War II . . . Although affiliated to the Royal Mencap Society, these are local societies, working at grass-roots level and with a degree of independence from the national society. These societies are remarkable in that they broke with the traditional approach of the existing voluntary societies, such as the Central Association for Mental Welfare which had endorsed the Government policy of segregation. Instead, in the 1940s and 1950s, parents challenged the Government and set up societies to confront policies and demand change. Research has only recently begun to take account of these local societies, which is surprising in view of the enormous impact they made nationally on the provision of local care for people with learning difficulties.

You will notice that Sheena chooses to use 'difficulties', which she says is the preferred term of the self-advocacy movement. However, the OU often use 'learning difficulty' instead of 'learning disability' in their literature because they are involved in education rather than health or social security. It can be very confusing at times.

Sheena Rolf goes on to write: 'There are large gaps in the story, and as older and founder members of the societies retire, there is a real danger that the history will remain hidden, and that a collection of memories, stories and archives might disappear.'

That is why I have tried to recapture as many of those memories as I possibly can in this book without, I hope, wearying the reader. There is a real and present danger that some of the stories will be repetitive in certain details; early diagnosis and prognosis as related to parents being a classic example but, as I have already mentioned, I believe a history of learning disability and of Mencap should be placed on record so that future generations will be able to recognise the battles fought and won by so many of us over the years – particularly since 1946 when Judy Fryd started this great movement – and also appreciate our hopes and ambitions for the future. Perhaps, then, they will realise just how much they owe to parents, carers, educationalists – even the odd politician – who lived in the second part of the twentieth century but, above all, see how our endeavours to change attitudes have enabled people with a learning disability to discover they *do* have a voice after all.

Mencap: Looking Forward, 2006

Val Brittin
Head of Community Development, Mencap

The Royal Mencap Society still has the advantage of being a membership organisation. We have over 700 groups affiliated to us, including local societies and Gateway clubs. This is a sound base upon which to build strong campaigns, for we still need to work to make a better world for people with a learning disability and their families. This has not changed since the Society began in 1946, even though much progress has been made, and our plans for community support insist we be responsive and accessible to all who are involved – people with a learning disability, their parents, their families, their carers. We are also looking at developing a friends' scheme which opens up Mencap to those wishing to be involved in a supportive role rather than as an active member. We need to draw them in and find out what they can do for us and what we can offer them.

In England the new structure of Mencap's Community Support Business Unit (CSBU) reflects the key aims of our Vision for Change. The new teams are finding out all we need to know and how we can influence and improve matters for the better. Collectively the teams will provide a range of support for people with a learning disability – especially those with the most profound needs, as well as those unsung heroes, family carers and, of course, carers across the board.

Other projects in advocacy, older carers, parenting and information are all part of our local network and many of these projects are breaking new ground, very much like those early ones in the 1960s. All the resources available, and knowledge garnered by the new teams, will be captured within the Mencap Helpline, there for callers who may have a simple question or a problem which our caseworkers can then take on. We also have a range of arts, leisure and sport projects with national and international influence. These have identified people with a learning disability as leaders in their field, showing real talent and commitment. Gus Garside, Mencap's National Arts Development Manager, has already written about this particular subject in Part III Chapter 11.

The new Community Development Team is working with local groups, creating strong local partnerships, sharing knowledge and experience, for many of these groups provide services and have positive links with their local politicians and partners. However, current legislative and regulatory demands can be hard for volunteers in small groups to carry out, hence the need for partners. We believe that one of these should be the Royal Mencap Society, for the new membership agreement between local groups and Mencap will ensure a coordinated approach, as it sets out clearly the role and responsibility of each partner with agreed objectives, giving us all the opportunity to make a difference and put forward the Mencap view which is both clear and unambiguous. We need to share the brand, for the Royal Mencap Society is well known and respected, and by adopting minimum standards and good practice our groups can operate to the highest standards. It must be stressed, though, that we already have some excellent groups who certainly achieve these standards and we, in turn, need to learn from them.

The constitutional change of 2000 gave us one member, one vote and enabled people with a learning disability to take a full part in the governance of the organisation. Currently over 50 per cent of representatives on our district committees and National Assembly are people with a learning disability. Representation needs to be meaningful and we need to ensure all our delegates have the support they need to fulfil their role. We need to be responsible in the development of our governance and ensure a balance of representation. Participation of members from local groups will provide a valuable link to relevant local issues and need. The balance of participation is a key issue and one which Mencap is currently addressing.

I trust Val Brittin's short paper emphasises the need for powerful partnerships.

Local societies, of course, have to raise their own funds and, rather as I did in the old days, they generally resort to all the usual fundraising activities which can take place in a particular city, town or village. Some, naturally, are more successful than others because of their location. It's easier in Chelsea or Westminster to raise larger sums of money than in, say, Foston on the Wolds in East Yorkshire. However, there was one way which was devised by Mencap in the late 1940s which provided much-needed cash for both local and national societies. That was the Christmas card scheme which stemmed from Doris Drown's first meeting with Frank Kerry and her initial sale of remaindered Raphael Tuck Christmas cards to make money for her local group, which was soon extended to take in the whole country (see 1952–55 in the Mencap diary). The local groups sold the cards, the national society provided the administrative back-up, the profits were shared out and everyone was happy.

Mencap Christmas Cards

Peter Pascoe
National Christmas Cards Coordinator, Mencap, 1967–99
As told to Justine Williams

I saw an advertisement that they wanted a Christmas Card Officer so I went along – I started on 30 October 1967. That was fun because your grandfather [Alan Phillips, then Assistant Secretary-General] met me and took me to Newman Street and showed me this showroom which we'd bought for the Society. It was a large room with a couple of fluorescent lights in it, no floorboards on the floor, and he said, 'I'm glad you've turned up because Hayley Mills is opening this as your Christmas card shop in two weeks!' It was hard work but we did it. We managed to get it looking quite decent in the end but it didn't matter too much because most of our contacts were outside with the local societies and they were doing most of the sales. We worked with Webb Ivory, a commercial firm, and they were great – a chap called Frank Kerry ran it. He was an extraordinary bloke, very generous, and he and Doris Drown had started the whole thing off; we received very generous terms of business. That meant Auntie Doris had to be around most of the time and I became her sort of lieutenant, as it were.

I thought you were in charge?

Yes, but you didn't work like that with Doris. She was a voluntary lady and on the National Council, along with her husband. When I first saw her I thought she looked a bit like the Rock of Gibraltar wearing a very smart, all-enveloping fur coat, but when you got to know her she was great and she did an awful lot for us. That was the set-up – George Lee and others liked me because I could handle Doris fairly well, on the Christmas card side of things at any rate.

To start off, Webb Ivory used to provide the catalogue for us and the cards were mostly sold through the local societies. The great thing about the job as far as I was concerned was working with the local societies because they were wonderful people and I had to go around the country talking to them all, persuading them to sell Christmas cards and gifts – if they weren't already – and looking after the ones that were already trading; if there were any problems it was my job to sort them out. We used to have card conferences, too, around the country, chaired by Neville Thompson but always attended by Auntie Doris, and there was intense rivalry between various local societies to see who could make the most sales. Funnily enough, the winner always seemed to be the Chairman of the conference, Neville Thompson, for the sales effected by his local society, Greenwich Mencap.

How much money did this generate?

£2 million a year in the end. We'd reached £1 million sales by 1973. How it worked in those days was that National Society got a cut of local society sales and local societies got 27.5 per cent of the retail value of their sales, and they used that money for their own local projects,. They could do what they liked with it.

What did you do, apart from selling cards?

One of the good things, at the beginning especially, was being able to do extra things. Although I wasn't sitting around twiddling my thumbs most of the time, in those days – when when there was a much smaller staff – you were encouraged, or begged, to do other things. For instance, the bookshop is the easiest way to start. They decided to have an exhibition on books about mental handicap, so I sat down and rang round publishers and said, 'Can you send me a catalogue and anything you've got on mental handicap because we want to have an exhibition' and got together about 200–300 titles. Books were just one of the extra things. They had a mobile exhibition unit which the Duke of Edinburgh had given to them, and they said, 'You can do this can't you, you're not selling Christmas cards that much at the moment, You can go around agricultural shows with the publicity officer and one or two other people' and so we ended up going round with the exhibition unit selling books, cards and telling people about 'mental handicap'. The mobile unit didn't last long because at an agricultural show people are wandering around looking for something to buy in the way of farm equipment or a flock of sheep or something, and only people who are desperately interested will come on board. It sounds quite exciting if the Duke of Edinburgh says, 'Look, old chap, you can have this', but you've got to keep the mobile unit somewhere and maintain it, although you start off thinking, 'If we put Mencap posters on it, people will rush in to see what the National Society is all about', but they didn't really, so we decided it wasn't any use and got rid of it.

Anything else?

Yes. The other thing I got involved in was Brian's *Let's Go!* in the 1980s. On that I did distribution; the BBC couldn't do it and we had to deal with dispatching the slides and the videos and the workbooks (which were written by Fred Heddell) and that type of thing. I had some input at the beginning. In those days you had general meetings about a product like that and anybody who was concerned had a say, which was great. Brian's good at that; actually he's good at heading a team and getting everybody involved.

We also did toys for a toy library exhibition – Lena Baum was our toy lady. We got quite a lot of publicity and I'm pretty sure that it did a lot to kick-start the Toy Libraries Association. The Association had already existed but I'm sure the exhibition did quite a bit to help raise awareness to really get it off the ground. The other exhibition we did, which was terrific, was called *All Our Own Work* and showed products made by learning disabled people and that was great fun.

I think it was that exhibition which started us including stuff made by learning disabled people in the catalogue and we got quite a few items in eventually. Some of them were such good sellers we had to keep on repeating them. Bird-boxes sold a bomb! The first year items were in the catalogue it was difficult to keep supplies going, but it was worth it.

The other thing I'm proud of is selling cards which are designed by learning disabled people. I got involved with an art exhibition by people with a learning disability and persuaded a small firm to make general greeting cards from some of the paintings and offered them to local societies. They sold rather well. Then I got Webb Ivory interested and the first one they produced was by a Russian with a lad pulling a sledge and that sold well, too. From then on we've done at least one card by a learning disabled person every year, and they are almost without exception in the top half dozen of all cards sold by the Royal Mencap Society and by local groups, too. I was – and am – very pleased with that.

Where would you like to see Mencap going in the future?
I don't know where it is now, any more – it's six years since I retired. One thing I'd like to mention though are the Regional Officers (as they were in those days), the majority of whom were absolutely terrific, people such as Doreen Flint, Glenys Jones and Joyce McCarthy, who'd keep an eye on things for you on their patch and, as I've said, they'd invite you down to talk to new local societies and the cards helped to get them going. But that's all in the past. I believe that nowadays the cards and the catalogues continue with Webb Ivory as before, although the financial arrangements have probably changed. In my day, though, local societies were all trying desperately to raise money for their various projects including, of course, their Gateway club if they'd formed one. I'm grateful I had a hand in making some of those projects possible. I'd do it all again, if I had the chance.

Gateway

Now we come to Gateway. Originally conceived in 1966 by Ken Solly and Alan Phillips (then respectively Deputy Secretary-General and Assistant Secretary-General of Mencap), and stemming from a number of local societies attempting to provide leisure activities for their learning disabled sons and daughters, the subsequent achievements and exploits of Gateway members and volunteers could well fill a book on their own. However, I will try to tell their story through interviews conducted with Alan Phillips and John Oliver, while paying tribute to Mike Mackey and Tim Gadd, Vice-Chairman and Treasurer respectively of Gateway for many years. I will finish with Roger Galletley's story, as he was the second, and last, Chairman of Gateway, for when the constitution was changed at the end of 1998 it was decided to rebrand Gateway's national activities as a department, under the umbrella of the Royal Mencap Society, with the name Mencap Leisure. Local Gateway clubs continue to describe themselves as before, but there is now only one overall chairman and he is the Chairman of Mencap, Brian Baldock.

Sadly, Ken Solly is no longer with us, but as the first Chairman of Gateway and, to start the ball rolling, there now follows his introduction to Gateway's Silver Jubilee celebrations in 1991, still using the term 'mental handicap' which was extant in those days.

Reflections Along the Jubilee Road

Ken Solly OBE
Chairman, Gateway, 1966–87

Changes were on the way in the 1960s. Alternatives to living in large hospitals were being considered; possibilities emerged for employment for people with mental handicap; the Mental Health Act encouraged the development of training centres. But these provided for only a few hours on weekdays. What was to happen afterwards and at weekends?

Mencap's first nationwide professional team, led by Secretary-

General George Lee, was involved in the changes. A demonstration hostel and workshop opened at Slough, teacher training began in Birmingham, social and rural training at Pengwern Hall and Lufton Manor. A year was spent examining the leisure needs of people with a mental handicap. Some local societies already organised leisure activities. How should these develop? Should people with a mental handicap be encouraged to join local youth organisations?

In a dynamic youth club, would the slower-learning individual become a spectator rather than a real participant? The answer seemed to lie in a leisure programme aimed first at the needs of people with a mental handicap, building bridges to the rest of the community on the way so that integration became a natural process. The Society allocated resources and staff to establish a federation of clubs, to link those already existing and encourage development and experiment.

The name 'Gateway' was the inspiration of Alan Phillips, then Assistant Secretary-General, to whom Gateway was to owe much in ensuing years.

A constitution was adopted in June 1966. In six months fifty clubs had joined; in two years there were 140 and from then on the federation grew by a new club every ten days for twenty years. Organisational back-up and local leadership were provided by the Society's Regional Officers. Growing contacts between clubs assisted the pooling of ideas, especially those brought in by the growing army of volunteer helpers. Few volunteers had prior experience of mental handicap; they were caught by the infectious enthusiasm and warm welcome in every club. Their skills helped the expansion of club programmes, towards an objective: 'not to copy and do badly what goes on in other youth organisations but to explore together the frontiers of achievement for people with a mental handicap'. These frontiers continued to recede as Gateway grew.

The *Gatepost* newsletter, started in 1968, helped inter-club communication; a *Garden Gatepost* issue helped publicise a pumpkin-growing competition, with staggering results.

More resources, expanding programmes and members' increasing competence opened up new horizons. An international soccer eleven competed annually in Geneva and Genoa from 1982, bringing home all the trophies from their first visit, until their rivals caught up with their skills. On their third visit, Gateway won nothing.

The first UK participants in International Special Olympics were recruited from Gateway clubs for the Rochester, N.Y. Games in 1979. UK competitors won most of the swimming events, a tribute to the local provision at home. The founding of Special Olympics UK and of the UK Sports Association for People with Mental Handicap followed directly from the Rochester Games and Gateway has continued a close relationship with them both.

For the International Year of Disabled People 1981, clubs combined to raise over £10,000 to support the United Nation's Water Decade by helping water supplies in African villages. After three months' training, a team of members and helpers flew to Mombassa for a 2,000-mile trek through the bush to deliver Gateway Aid, providing water pipes for two schools for disabled children and a submersible pump for a well in a Kikuyu village.

In 1989 a Gateway team took part in Operation Hannibal to follow the elephant route over the Alps, mapping the journey on the way. Increasingly, local clubs have provided holiday expeditions abroad as well as camps and mountain walking at home.

But as one annual report said, adventure doesn't belong only in mountains and foreign lands; it belongs as much in the mind and in human relationships. Among the twenty-five Gateway clubs in long-stay hospitals there was much adventuring. In the late seventies profoundly handicapped members, on hospital cots, could be seen to react to a 'music and movement' programme with the faintest of movements – a tiny stirring of participation. Then, in 1985, young helpers in Belfast learnt Makaton to help communicate with their members who could not talk. Gateway has endeavoured to be for everyone.

Twenty-five years of Gateway have left memories with many who have shared them:

> 'When the so-called helpers and the so-called handicapped enjoy what unites them, the world all of a sudden seems a much more enjoyable place.' Trevor Milner, Chilterns Gateway Club, 1978

'These six years have added a new dimension to my experience and understanding, without which life would have been that much poorer. The magic of Gateway still has me in its clutches.' Francis Stuart, former Chief Education Officer, on retiring as Gateway's National Officer, 1980

'We parents should wear the Gateway badge; a way of informing people outside the world of mental handicap that loving kindness is alive and well and thriving in Gateway clubs.' Elizabeth Thompson, a mother, 1982

'The Gateway club provides more than a place to go to one or two nights a week; it provides status and friendship. I'm very impressed. Long live Gateway clubs! It would be worth copying in my own country.' Martha D. Brockwell, Director, Parent/Family Training, North Carolina, USA, 1981

And, finally, in 1991, Gateway members were undertaking a number of other exciting and imaginative projects, which included a tour with the Corinthian Casuals Football Club to Florida, USA, where they played a number of challenge matches. A group of ten members, accompanied by the same number of volunteers, travelled in the opposite direction to climb Mount Elbrus, Europe's highest mountain, as part of the Russian Adventure. They reached the peak, too, and their self-confidence had increased beyond all recognition.

Now we turn to Alan Phillips, the co-founder of Gateway with Ken Solly. He was interviewed by his own granddaughter, Justine Williams, and extracts from their question and answer interview follow.

Alan Phillips OBE

Assistant Secretary-General, 1968–80
Deputy Secretary-General, 1981–7

I had only joined the National Society for Mentally Handicapped Children as the Regional Welfare Secretary for London in 1966, the year Gateway began. Ken Solly went to a filing cabinet and showed me suggestions from about sixty groups, all connected with local societies, and all wanting to do something in the way of leisure and sport. Ken thought that what I'd learnt in the YMCA could be brought to bear. So we called a conference, which was held at the ice rink in Oxford Street (which is now the Salvation Army headquarters), and about forty of the groups who were interested had representatives there. As a result of the meeting we decided to go forward, but then a big question arose about what this new group would be called. Various names were discussed and after a year Gateway was decided upon, because if things went right it would indeed be a gateway of opportunity for people with a learning disability. We then asked the Hornsey College of Art (offering a small prize) if students would design a suitable emblem and they came up with a five-bar gate which became the badge of Gateway. Of course we couldn't stop people creating clubs! Within four years more than 600 clubs had sprung up round the country and very soon members (all with a learning disability) and volunteers were taking part in outdoor adventures – rock climbing, canoeing, football, national swimming competitions – every activity which up to then had been denied them.

We used to hold five-a-side football games in the centre part of the country. The second one we held at Birmingham in the sports grounds of a hospital which had a hall, so if wet weather intervened there was some form of shelter. We'd thought about a marquee but they were very expensive to hire so we decided to take a risk with the rather small hall instead. It bucketed down. There were a number of pitches so we could have three or four games at the same time, but the pitches were virtually under water and people came dashing in and were provided with towels to dry them off. There was a chap who was refereeing the next match, peering through the misted-up window, who said, 'We can go on playing after this stops,' and I said, 'Well, you better go out now as your teams for the next match are already out there.' He couldn't believe it. There was all this rain pouring down, he was looking like a drowned rat and there were both these teams out there waiting patiently for him to go out and get the game started. I never bothered with a marquee for any outdoor event after that because I thought even if there was a blizzard it would go on, such was the enthusiasm of the Gateway members.

Our clubs were mostly run by volunteers, although as the movement developed we received grants just like any youth organisation, with youth workers getting grants for leadership and helping to organise the volunteers. And if a local society wanted a club, one of the club leaders would talk it through with them and tell them how they could set it up and hold their hand for a bit. In the end we had something like 50,000 members who were learning disabled, with about half as many helpers. Clubs didn't run on a one-to-one basis except in very exceptional circumstances.

I felt it was extremely important that many thousands of volunteers were supporting Gateway in one way or another because that meant those volunteers didn't cross the road when a learning disabled person was on the pavement walking towards them – that used to happen, people used to dodge them. But our volunteers got to know people and realised they were human beings and had something to offer.

We started the Gateway Festival to encourage development within the programme. From previous experience with the YMCA, I realised that you always have to have targets, as young people like to know they are going somewhere – reaching out – so you have to think of activities which give them that certainty. One way, to develop the programme and encourage the clubs to think along those lines, was to develop the festival. This meant that they could produce an item which had entertainment value: soloist, musician, comedian, performer in comic sketches, anything which would please another person. We then had regional festivals, so the performer's target was to be accepted at a regional level, while the ultimate target was to be chosen out of the regional festival for the national festival, so there was always that kind of progression. We used to have the Royal Festival Hall on the South Bank for the whole day and the first time we just had one programme but we were so overwhelmed with disappointed people that I could see that we would have to have two houses. We decided that one way out of it was to take the Royal Albert Hall, which we did, and to have one house, as the Albert Hall has more than double the number of seats in the Festival Hall. But the atmosphere wasn't the same; it was too big an arena, so we switched back to the Festival Hall and had the two houses from then on. We were at the hall by 9 am, setting up by 9.30, and it was organised that clubs from the North had accommodation the night before so that they could come in early to rehearse, whereas people travelling in locally would come in later in the morning to do their stuff before a hurried walk-through rehearsal; we had no time for a proper dress rehearsal. The producers, who were part of the team going round the regional festivals to choose the acts, in a sense knew what was coming and were able to instruct the voluntary stage crew where to place microphones and props and scenery and then they marked out the stage with coloured blobs and circles so that for each act they knew exactly where everything went. It was pretty hair-raising. Then we had to arrange for all the groups to have lunch (as well as a huge tea before the second house) and get ready for the show. There was much excitement and feverish activity backstage with about 200 artists milling about and another 100 or so helpers to see that they got onstage on cue; everyone getting made-up, dressed and waiting for their turn. People with a learning disability were running between dressing rooms, acting as call-boys and certainly the full house out front hadn't a clue what was happening backstage. Despite all the apparent chaos and lack of rehearsal, the show was remarkable, demon-strating what people with a learning disability can do if given the chance. The artists, the organisers, the stage-hands, the staff of the Festival Hall, all deserve the highest praise for many a memorable show. Certainly I, for one, will never forget them.

Two volunteers, who served the Gateway movement for years were Mike Mackey MVO BEM (who appears in Chapter 2 among Mencap's Vice-Presidents), who was Vice-Chairman of the Federation and Chairman of the Festival Committee for nearly a quarter of a century. He worked first with Ken Solly as Chairman and then Roger Galletley came on board in Ken's place. Along with Tim Gadd, who was the Hon. Treasurer, they became a fantastic triumvirate known, hardly originally, as the Three Musketeers. Mike continues to vet the applications to the Renton Foundation, which Lord Renton set up in memory of his wife, Paddy, supporting projects put forward by Gateway clubs. Mike says: 'It must be a positive, constructive project and we also ask for a report about what has happened.' Tim Gadd says:

> I served on the Executive Committee for twenty-odd years and became the Treasurer of Gateway when Alan Phillips retired. I think Alan and Ken were very foresighted in coming up with the concept of the National Federation of Gateway Clubs and in seeing that people with a learning disability needed that gateway through leisure out into the wider community and – in turn – the wider community needed a gateway back into the lives of people with a learning disability.

John Oliver

National Holidays Officer, 1979–94
Director of Mencap's Holiday Service, 1994–8
Director of the National Federation of Gateway Clubs, 1980–94
As told to Justine Williams

I joined Mencap on 1 February 1965, and worked as an administrator in the North-West regional office in Manchester for about fourteen years, from 1965 to 1979, and quite early on I heard about an organisation called the National Federation of Gateway Clubs which had just been established in London. So, round about 1969–70, I just asked if I could help develop this Federation in the North West and we held an initial conference in Manchester Town Hall to formalise its establishment. One of the speakers who came along was Alan Phillips who, apart from all his other duties, was also the Secretary of the National Federation of Gateway Clubs, but the star turn was Dr Benjamin Spock, the famed child expert, who just happened to be in the Manchester area at the time. I managed to track him down and asked him if he would be willing to address this conference, which he did. This gave it some glamour and a good reason to come along. Members of local societies, those who were running a club and those who were thinking of running a club flocked to the Town Hall, as you can imagine.

Did the conference have the desired effect?
The clubs joined at a startling rate. Part of the success was that we had a Regional Executive Committee which was made up of club leaders themselves, so it was very much a region of can-do people at a local level who were interested in extending the range of activities at a regional level. My job was to support and encourage this motivation. There was lots of enthusiasm and we set up junior, senior and hospital-based Gateway clubs because back in the 1960s – before the famous White Paper *Better Services for the Mentally Handicapped* – the majority of Gateway clubs were established when young people left junior training centres, so the club was a source of respite for parents. Of course, these were teenagers and, as the model proved successful, parents were then looking for provision for their younger sons and daughters, so Junior Gateway clubs were formed. These catered for youngsters who would enjoy playgroup provision. Because in those days large numbers of people with a learning disability were living in long-stay hospitals, Mencap was encouraging the affiliation of clubs there, as well. The interesting thing about the hospitals was that they had excellent facilities, gymnasiums, swimming pools, large grounds – even theatres – which were hardly ever used and Mencap was keen to encourage affiliation to the Gateway clubs so full use could be made of them. Another reason was to try to bring the hospitals closer to the community and to bring the community closer to the hospitals.

This work continued for me until 1979 when I accepted appointment as the National Holidays Officer for Mencap. One of the most pressing needs was – and still is – for respite care, so both parents and their learning disabled sons or daughters can have a break. One opportunity for respite was when the Mental Health Officer noticed stress within the family and arranged for the child to go into hospital for a week or two, which was fine in a way, but not all parents felt happy about their child being 'shunted off' to the back ward of a hospital. So Mencap set up some holiday homes, but eventually these were either sold or transferred to provide faciltities for further education. Although they had enabled people to have short-term breaks, they had also proved to be a drain on the Society's finances and the homes were seen to be yet further isolated buildings housing people with a learning disability, not altogether dissimilar from the long-stay hospitals which had upset so many parents and carers.

The National Council recognised that another way needed to be found. As an alternative, the founders of Gateway, Ken Solly and Alan Phillips, seeing that the demand for holidays was seasonal, thought there might be some advantage in looking at a work camp-type initiative where young people were recruited as volunteers, very much like Camp America. The idea was that Mencap could follow the work camps and instead of owning premises they could borrow them, and run the camps for a period for a week or two, encouraging young people, many of whom were following courses of further and higher education, to allow themselves to be worked to death for a fortnight for free accommodation and the benefit of gaining some first-hand experience of working with people with a learning disability. As well as this sort of holiday, which was seen as a type of demonstration, we also started to run holidays for people in guest houses, adventure holidays and ones which many thought were the most important of all, special care holidays for people with profound and multiple learning disabilities who needed one-to-one care. We usually ran these in residential schools, so part of the trick was to approach the headmaster of a residential school and say, 'When you're closed over the summer can we borrow your million-pound pad and look after it while we run a week or two with volunteers?'

What was the reaction to that?
The good thing was that many people in the teaching profession had been through that experience themselves, so they recognised that here was a good opportunity for young people following further education to gain some first-hand experience. It was useful to do it with Mencap because we could assure them that we were properly insured and we'd look after the place. What we used to do was go in and remove anything that was breakable, take the pictures down, make a note of them and put everything away; we provided sheets and bedding and catering, recruiting

volunteers attending catering colleges to take care of all that. The
Holidays Office was based in Rochdale – Alan Phillips said, 'Go and find
somewhere like a shop, John, where the rent's cheap, because all you
want is somewhere to store the gear for the holidays' – and when Brian
Rix came to visit us he said, 'It's like a veritable quartermaster's store'.

We used to have scrapbooks, which were very important, because
each day we had the volunteers write up a daily diary so parents would
know what their sons and daughters had done on the holiday, especially
those who couldn't communicate.

The holidays were run all over the country. They were made special
by the skills and the interests which the volunteers themselves brought
to them. We had a day shift and a night shift. On the special care holidays
we had to administer medication, so that was another skill we had to
learn. I cannot speak too highly of all those who made the holidays such
a great success.

Had your interest in Gateway ceased when you took over the holidays?
Oh no! In 1980 I was appointed the National Officer for the National
Federation of Gateway Clubs, in addition to my duties as the National
Holidays Officer. This took me down to London, where I was managed
by Alan Phillips and survived fourteen years. My brief was to develop
more Gateway clubs.

When I went into the job in 1980 there were 500 junior, senior and
hospital clubs affiliated to Mencap. By 1994 there were over 700,
providing for about 50,000 members and an almost equal number of
volunteers. We instituted the Gateway Charter, establishing some basic
standards which we would expect every affiliated Gateway club to abide
by. We developed the Gateway Award Scheme – for most young people
challenge is an important part of their personal development and the
Duke of Edinburgh Award Scheme is a prime example of that. The
Gateway Award gave members an opportunity to choose the type of
activity they wanted to do, but the activity would then be conducted at
the member's pace, depending on their level of ability. Eventually we
applied to the Department of Education and Science for a grant which
enabled us to have the Award scheme updated and revised in tune with
modern practice.

You must have been a busy man.

Well, there was a lot of travel involved, quite apart from the fact that I commuted between Rochdale and London every two or three days. There's also much I haven't been able to mention, because I know it is somewhere else in this book. At least, I hope it is. But the pleasure of seeing people with a learning disability – quite apart from their parents, their carers and volunteers – thoroughly enjoying themselves, thanks to holidays, Gateway clubs, Gateway Awards and the Gateway Festival – made it all very much worthwhile. I retired from Gateway in 1994 and as the National Holidays Officer at the end of January 1998. Thirty-three years of service and I can honestly say I enjoyed, well, if not every minute, at least an awful lot of them! Also it was such a pleasure to work with so many of them: Ken Solly, your grandfather [Alan Phillips] and Roger Galletley [who succeeded Ken Solly as Chairman], quite apart from Gateway's Vice-Chairman, Mike Mackey, and the Treasurer, Tim Gadd. They were a great bunch and between us I believe we created a Federation of which we could be justly proud and which benefited, and continues to benefit, thousands of people, young and old, with a learning disability. What more can a man ask?

I realise I have given a great deal of space to Gateway already, but it would be a serious omission not to include Roger Galletley in these tributes. As you can see from his biographical details in Chapter 2, he is a man who has devoted much of his time to voluntary work for the Royal Mencap Society, not only with Gateway, but now with Golden Lane Housing, the Governance Committee and the Renton Foundation. Here is his story.

Life with Mencap

Roger Galletley
Vice-Chairman, National Federation of Gateway Clubs, 1984–7
Chairman, National Federation of Gateway Clubs, 1987–2000
Chairman of Golden Lane Housing, 2000–
Chairman of the Governance Committee, 2004–
Chairman of Trustees, the Renton Foundation, 1991–

Although I didn't know it at the time, my life was about to change dramatically during the early hours of Wednesday, 13 February 1968. A rather fearsome staff nurse at the now non-existent St David's Hospital in Cardiff told me that it was not the slightest use my hanging around for the imminent birth of my wife Susan's second child, as it wouldn't happen for at least twelve hours and anyway husbands in delivery rooms only got in the way, so the best thing I could do was go home. Being a little less confident at crossing swords with officialdom than I am today, I did as I was told. Two hours later our first son, whom we subsequently named Shaun David, was born.

Apart from a little difficulty with feeding, everything appeared to be normal and after the regulation ten-day stay I proudly went to collect Susan and Shaun from the hospital. Just as we were about to leave the ward sister asked us if we would go into a side ward as the consultant gynaecologist wanted to have a word with us before we left. In he came and his first words to us were in the form of a question and I quote: 'Have either of you ever heard of mongolism?' to which we replied, 'Yes, but we don't know anything about it'. He then came out with the statement that was to devastate us and again I quote: 'Well, your son is a mongol, there is nothing you can do about it and you will just have to learn to live with it. Good morning.' He then turned on his heel and walked out.

For three days we were both struck dumb. All our family lived hundreds of miles away and there was absolutely no support whatsoever from social services. So we were forced to set about 'learning to live with it' and for the next three years or so that is what we did. Then one morning we had a letter from someone whose name was Langdon Doidge, who introduced himself, if I remember correctly, as the Divisional Manager for the South Wales Region of an organisation which was then called the National Society for Mentally Handicapped Children. This was when our lives really began to change.

The letter invited us to attend a meeting to create a new branch of the Society in Monmouth, which is about fifteen miles north of where we live in the town of Usk. Sensing that this was not my cup of tea at all, I said to Susan that this was just the sort of thing she would enjoy, organising coffee mornings and raffles and other fundraising ventures.

So off she went and duly came back a few hours later to find me in bed reading a book. I asked her how things had gone and she then droned on about how they had started a new committee and set in motion the usual things I have mentioned, while I half-listened, carrying on reading my book. Then something she said stopped me dead in my tracks and I suddenly started to take notice because what she said was this: 'Oh yes, there's one thing you ought to know – we elected you as the chairman'. And that, as they say, is how it all began to happen.

Just a few weeks later after I had rather reluctantly agreed to see how things went and had chaired my first meeting, we received a letter inviting us to send a representative to a South Wales regional meeting of something called the National Federation of Gateway Clubs, which I had never heard of before. No one else seemed interested so I agreed to attend. The meeting was held in the offices of the Society in Cardiff on a Saturday afternoon and the first thing that happened was the Chairman, a consultant at Cardiff General Hospital, resigned due to pressure of work and, for reasons that I have still to understand, I found myself elected to take her place. I can vaguely remember bumbling my way through the meeting and just about picking up the fact that Gateway was the leisure arm of the National Society. At the end of the meeting I was taken to one side by Langdon Doidge's assistant, a rather delightful young lady by the name of Jane Harrison, and told that the position of chairman also involved my attending a few meetings a year in London representing South Wales on the National Executive Committee of the Gateway Federation. Things suddenly began to sound interesting.

Sure enough, a few weeks later, in September 1975, a large brown envelope arrived inviting me to attend the next meeting of the National Executive Committee of the National Federation of Gateway Clubs in Pembridge Gardens, Notting Hill, London. This sounded extremely interesting stuff to be getting involved in and I duly travelled to London, something I had never done before, and sat round a very impressive table along with new colleagues from all over England, Wales and Northern Ireland. For the next few hours I sat and listened to what became to me one of the most boring days of my life because what seemed to happen for the majority of the time was having to listen to the various representatives going on about how successful their own coffee mornings and raffles and sports days and trips to the nearest zoo had been. Nothing at all was said about the formulation of future policy or how we were going to improve things in the field of leisure for the people we had been elected to represent. Anyway, I sat through all this without saying a word and returned home quietly fuming in the train.

When I got home Susan asked me how I had got on and then had to endure my sounding off for the next half an hour about what I thought my day in London had achieved. This, I might add, is something she still does to this day. Her advice after I had shut up was to ring Langdon Doidge and Jane Harrison and tell them my thoughts. This I did and they both told me the same thing. If you don't agree with what is being said, say so and put your own point of view as strongly as you can. That advice is something I remember and still use to this day because at the following meeting of the NEC I caused something of a fuss when I erupted into action and said that the meeting was nothing more than a complete waste of time and that we should be spending our time doing far more important things. To put it mildly there were a few murmurings of discontent. Anyway, at the end of the meeting I approached the Chairman, Ken Solly, and offered my apologies for causing such a row. He immediately told me it was the most enjoyable thing he had ever witnessed round the NEC table. I'm told that was when a certain reputation was born.

The next ten years were spent hammering away at getting the Royal Society for Mentally Handicapped Children and Adults, which it had now become, to accept that as Gateway was now the largest element of the work of the Society that fact should be recognised by devoting a considerably larger proportion of its resources to leisure. That battle was particularly memorable as it involved plenty of table thumping and violent clashes of personality before it came to fruition. But come to fruition it did, and it set Gateway and the Royal Society on a path that was to lead to tens if not hundreds of thousands of people with a learning disability enjoying a position in society that a few years earlier would have been unthinkable.

This leads me to that part of my life with Mencap that saw my role begin to change rather dramatically. I had been the South Wales representative on the Gateway NEC for nine years when, in 1984, Ken Solly decided he needed a Vice-Chairman and to my surprise I was elected to that position not ever thinking that a mere three years later Ken would decide to call it a day and retire and I would be elected as Chairman in his place. At this time the number of Gateway clubs was growing at an astonishing rate and at one point a new one was being created every three days. This, of course, could not last and when it reached something over 800 clubs, it began to slow down. This meant that there were approximately twice as many Gateway clubs as local societies and thought began to be given to a complete overhaul of Mencap's constitution, which would bring Gateway under the Mencap umbrella and do away with the NEC. This was met with a lot of opposition, myself included, but gradually we began to see the sense of what was being proposed and I was finally won over during a very pleasant lunch at the House of Lords with Brian Rix and Fred Heddell.

It was at this lunch that the three of us dreamed up the idea of touring the country over the following eighteen months or so with a roadshow which would promote the benefits of accepting the new draft constitution, which would mean giving people with a learning disability the same rights as everyone else, including having a minimum representation of one-third on the new National Assembly. These roadshows provided us with many lively and sometimes hilarious evenings (which I won't go into detail about here) all over the country but at the end of it all we were successful and today I am very proud of what we have achieved and of subsequently being given the opportunity to continue to fight for the rights of people with a learning disability as a member of the new Board of Trustees.

One of the last important decisions the old National Council took was to create a new subsidiary charity called Golden Lane Housing and, having relinquished my role in Gateway, I was delighted to take on a new challenge as a trustee and subsequently Chairman of this new charity. This took off in a spectacular way and today sits at the forefront of provision of independent housing for people with a learning disability, with over 700 people now living in their own homes. With Golden Lane Housing being a wholly owned subsidiary, Mencap can feel justly proud of the success that its financial backing has given to Golden Lane and of the opportunities it has given and will continue to give to hundreds and hopefully thousands of people with a learning disability. After all, this is no more than the rest of us regard as a right.

So here I am thirty years later and never regretting for a moment the day I got involved. It has given me opportunities that I would never have dreamed of all those years ago; it has given me the opportunity to meet and become friends with people whom I would never have otherwise met. But above all it has given me the opportunity to make the lives of people with a learning disability more like the one I, and millions like me, take for granted. I hope, in some small way, I have succeeded.

Golden Lane Housing

As Roger has ended his story with reference to Golden Lane Housing, this would seem to be as good a place as any to quote a few of the remarks by residents in some of the properties. Of course, before Golden Lane Housing there was Mencap Homes Foundation, but these were houses acquired through the good offices of housing associations, including Mencap's own arm's-length housing association, New Era. We continue to run several hundred houses, with several thousands of residents, by this method, but Golden Lane Housing actually gives people with a learning disability the chance to own, part-own or rent their properties, in conjunction with Mencap. Here are a few appreciative remarks from those who have taken advantage of this new, and somewhat sophisticated, method of providing housing.

When six people with a learning disability in Wiltshire faced the prospect of being homeless, Golden Lane Housing saved the day. The six were living in a block of flats owned by a private landlord who got into financial difficulties. The building society was preparing to repossess the property. Golden Lane Housing stepped in, buying the building, extensively refurbishing it and sorting out a major damp problem.

'It was a huge relief when Golden Lane Housing took over the flats,' said tenant Matthew O'Callaghan, who shares a flat with his fiancée, Sue Ellis. 'Sue and I get on really well with all the other tenants so we would have been very upset to be separated from each other.' Golden Lane

Housing also helped them claim their full housing benefit entitlement. All six are now planning their long-term future, safe in the knowledge that they are now secure tenants.

'When I finally got a flat of my dreams, it felt like I'd won the lottery,' said Stephen McDonald, who is aged forty-five and lives in Cornwall. Stephen, who has a learning disability, moved from Scotland in 1995 to be close to his aunt after his mother died. He lived in a shared house run by a local charity but, said Stephen, 'I desperately wanted my own place'. It was Golden Lane Housing which guided Stephen through the tricky flat-hunting process. 'I had to try and try again,' said Stephen. 'Golden Lane were really helpful, and in the end I found the perfect place – a ground floor flat in a nice area close to the shops.' Apart from a few hours' support a week, Stephen lives independently, getting by on benefits and income support and doing voluntary jobs. He spends the weekends at his aunt's. 'She can't move around as much as she used to,' says Stephen, 'so it's good that I'm nearby.'

Three young women with a learning disability lived separately in rather unsuitable accommodation near Doncaster. Doncaster social services, who had been supporting the women, turned to Golden Lane Housing to find a solution, which they did, finding and buying the perfect house for the three, Samantha, Marie and Tracy. An extra bedroom enables a support worker to sleep over at the house every night. Tracy said: 'I really like it here. It was good to move in with two girls of my own age – we are like sisters.'

And finally, for quotations like this could go on for a very long time, such has been the success of Golden Lane Housing, here is the story of twins with a learning disability, Anne and Elizabeth, who live in Surrey and needed to live near their elder sister, Mary. Finding a suitable house nearby was one thing, but purchasing the perfect two-up, two-down, complete with garden – only four doors away from Mary – was nothing short of a miracle, but Golden Lane Housing achieved it.

'It's fantastic here, much better than before,' said Anne, one of the twin sisters. 'We've now got central heating and we are closer to Mary.' Elizabeth also values her independence and freedom: 'We haven't got other people checking up on us all the time.'

And if people were minded to peep over the garden wall they'd see two ladies who are now safe and secure for, 'without Golden Lane Housing,' says their sister Mary, 'they could have been living in a high-rise block miles and miles away. That was the prospect that was facing them.'

The trustees of Golden Lane Housing are researching the possibility of creating a network of interested partners willing to work operationally and financially with them. It is hoped that the establishment of such a network will enable Golden Lane Housing to make a step change in tackling the continuing problem of the 'housing timebomb' awaiting people with a learning disability and their families in the years ahead.

PART VI

Families

Families

It's pretty obvious that the story of Mencap couldn't have begun if it were not for families, the very term 'family' presupposing a couple of parents (at the outset, anyway) and at least one child. If that one child has a learning disability then it is quite natural for the parents to do all within their power to make his or her quality of life as good as is humanly possible. Some even devote all their working lives and waking hours to the support of that child, while others fight to establish as independent a lifestyle as is possible for their son or daughter. Some beget more than one child with a learning disability, while many have other non-disabled children who are drawn into a far more complex family relationship 'twixt parents and siblings than exists in most households. In this part of the book which is mainly penned by the contributors themselves, parents, siblings and carers, I will try to illustrate the various problems which all of them have encountered – their successes, their failures, their hopes and fears. Again can I say how deeply grateful I am to each and every one for all the time and effort they have spent in writing their personal histories.

I will begin with two inspiring and thought-provoking stories by that well-known and exceptional sportswriter for *The Times*, Simon Barnes, and my younger son, Jonathan, for – as a father, a brother and a lecturer at the OU closely associated with learning disability – he is in a unique position to comment. Furthermore, both are fathers of sons with Down's syndrome of a similar age (five in 2006) and as they are the youngest scions appearing in Part VI of this book, I have afforded them pride of place. Mind you, some family stories have already been recounted under different chapter headings but the sum total of their impact on the reader will, I am certain, be unforgettable, for they are both memorable and moving. It may be that some of the contributors have very little day-to-day connection with Mencap – indeed, the last two parents in this part of the book, Carol Boys and Damon Hill, are the respective Director and President of the Down's Syndrome Association – but all are there to ensure that future historians will be given as wide and as accurate a picture as possible. I am sure they will recognise that Mencap's endeavours over the past sixty years have had a dramatic effect on all our lives, whether we be parents, carers, siblings, relations, workers in the field of learning disability or members of the general public. Above all, though, those with a learning disability themselves have gained immeasurably from Mencap's work and are now an integral part of all that lies ahead. It would be an exaggeration to state that Mencap had enjoyed 'sixty glorious years', but I think the Society can claim that those six decades have been notable, exciting and productive – bringing forth changes which were unimaginable when our daughter, Shelley, was born in 1951 – as well as redounding to the credit of *all* concerned.

Judy Fryd will rest content.

CHAPTER 18

Eddie

Simons Barnes
Chief Sportswriter, The Times

The thought hit me with such extraordinary power that my legs almost gave way beneath me. I walked a few steps to one of the benches that surround the duck-pond on the edge of Barnet, and sat down. My heart was racing, my breathing shallow, I was covered in a sweat, and I thought for a moment I might pass out, or throw up. After a while, quite a decent while, I decided I would do neither. And I got up and went to the supermarket, for my wife was in hospital and was filled with a passion for fresh fruit.

What if he has Down's syndrome? That was the sudden question that had overwhelmed me. My first child was to be born any day, and there were complications, which was why my wife was in hospital. So naturally I was full of nerves, as a first-time parent must be. The duck-pond incident was an attack of the horrors: I imagined a situation so terrible that it almost robbed me of consciousness. Down's syndrome! The horror, the horror!

Well, he didn't. Joseph was born the following day by Caesarean section, and has no problems beyond his own singularity of nature. Joe is great; Cindy and I were, if you'll forgive the word, blessed, and life carried on in a new and extraordinary way. So far so ordinary.

Seven years later, we had another child. He does have Down's syndrome. We had been told after the second scan that there was a 50 per cent chance of this. I accepted this as a 100 per cent certainty. Or was there just a tiny one per cent pinhole of hope? Hope against hope? But no, I told myself, resign yourself. And I remember very clearly another of those moments of pre-birth terror. I'm sure we'll deal with it, I thought, whatever happens. And they'll say, Simon, well, bloody hell, you know, he's a saint, the way he looks after that boy. And I thought: I don't want to be a bloody saint. I want to enjoy my life, not dedicate it. I have no ambitions at all when it comes to sainthood.

And do you know what? I haven't become a saint. It's a complete triumph; I have found no need for canonisation whatsoever. Nor did I have to work hard at resisting sainthood. Unsaintliness came quite naturally. Eddie – Edmund John Francis – was born on 23 May 2001. He has Down's syndrome all right. He has me as his father, and his father is not a saint. His father also enjoys his life very much, and Eddie does not compromise that, *au contraire*. Eddie enjoys his life very much too, most of the time; he makes that quite clear. And when he doesn't, he makes that pretty clear as well, being a child.

The human imagination can do many extraordinary things. But we can't imagine love. Or perhaps I mean loving: love as a continuous state, one that carries on in much the same way from day to day, changing and growing with time just as people themselves do. The great stories of literature are about meeting and falling in love, about infidelity, about passion. They are very seldom about the routines of married life and having children.

We can imagine dramas and turmoil. People make films about them. In our own minds, we often put together the most terrific stories about thrilling or devastating events that might befall us. But what no one can imagine is the day-to-day process of living with things and getting on with the humdrum job of loving. We can only imagine the beautiful and the terrible. We are drama queens, and our imaginations are incapable of giving us any help about coping from day to day. Marriage is not the same as falling in love; nor is marriage an endless succession of terrible rows and monumental reconciliations; it is about a million small things: things beyond our imagining.

By the way, I hope you are not too squeamish. This piece is not going to pull any punches. If you find the idea of love uncomfortable or sentimental or best-not-talked-about or existing only in the midst of a passionate love affair, then you will find problems with what I am writing. I am writing of love not as a matter of grand passions, or as highfalutin idealism or as religion. I am writing about love as the stuff that makes the processes of human life happen; the love that moves the sun and other stars, which is also the love that makes the toast and other snacks. Love is the most humdrum thing in life, the only thing that matters, the thing that is forever beyond the reach of human imagination.

So no, I couldn't imagine what it was like to live with a child who had Down's syndrome. I could only imagine the dramatic bits: the difficulties, the people in public places turning away in shock and distaste; the awfulness of a child who couldn't say his own name. I could speculate on the horrors of living with a child who could not do a thousand things. I could create a dramatic picture of life with a monster.

But I could not imagine what it was like to live with Eddie. You know, from day to day. That doesn't make Eddie unique. I couldn't imagine what it would be like exchanging a childless life for life with Joe. I don't think anybody can do that sort of thing; it's not what the human imagination does. You imagine bits that make you proud and bits that make you fearful. You can imagine reading him the *Narnia* stories, reading his glowing school reports, watching him score the winning goal and getting applauded after his solo at the school concert. But you lack the machinery for imagining the routine of living with a child who grows up with you.

The fact is that nothing to do with love seems so terribly difficult when you get down to it. Nothing seems to be an impossible demand on your time, your resources, your patience, your temper, your abilities; not because you connect with your inner saintliness but because you just find yourself getting on with it, muddling through. Most non-parents imagine they could never change a nappy. Then parenthood happens and they do it. It was the same thing when it came to living with Eddie. It's just parenthood; everyone who has done it knows it.

So Eddie was born, and I have spent the subsequent five years living with him. Not living with Down's syndrome, what a ridiculous idea. Living with Eddie. Who is my boy. And that really is the beginning, the end of it, and the humdrum day-to-day routine of it.

At the hospital, when they first discovered on the scan that Down's syndrome was a possibility, they very kindly offered to kill him for us. They needn't have bothered. My wife is, unlike myself, an exceptional person in the field of loving and caring. Please do not read this as a brief genuflection, one of the ploys of married life. Nor is it a literary trick. It is the rather the literal truth. One small example: I have two goldfish in my study, both the size of salmon. When one fish was about a quarter that size, Cindy found him dead, flat on the bottom of the tank. She somehow lifted him out and revived him. It was a long and elaborate process, and it worked. That is the sort of thing Cindy does. The idea of not caring for something that is in your care is an abomination to her. The idea of not caring for her own child was a monstrosity impossible to contemplate. Amniocentesis? Not a chance, it puts the child at risk. And no matter what such a test would say about the child, she would go ahead. There was a life that had to be cared for.

This was not negotiable. It sounds, I know, a little dreadful, to put it this way. Certainly, I lack the courage to stand between Cindy and someone she loves. The devil himself lacks that sort of courage. Had life turned out differently, had I been married to another, had that woman preferred to go the way of amniocentesis and termination, I have no doubt I would have gone along with that, too, and treated parents of Down's syndrome children with a lofty pity.

But thank God, I did not marry someone else. And that left me with a straightforward choice. I could either say that Eddie wasn't part of the deal and bugger off, or I could keep on keepin' on with the humdrum routines of life, and hope that this would be enough for the arrival into our lives of this unimaginable creature we already knew as Edmund, or Eddie. Well, we needed a name right away, many weeks before he was born and Joe, to whom I had indeed read *Narnia*, was especially keen on the name.

We needed a name. It does, I know, seem rather jarring: to have an abnormal child and to give him a normal name. As if he were a normal child. I, certainly, have always found the giving of normal names to abnormal children rather disconcerting, almost pathetic, as if you were trying to pretend that the dreadful things suffered by the child were not dreadful at all. Perhaps Eddie should have been called Down, or maybe Syndrome. But that's what they say about animals, isn't it? Don't give it a name or you'll get fond of it. A name changes everything and even in the womb we were not wondering about how we would cope with A Child With Down's syndrome. We wondering about living with Eddie.

And I thought – I hoped – that somehow, we would 'make the best of it'. What an absurd notion that now seems. So Eddie was born and in a week or so it became very clear that the important issue was not how I would cope with the fact that he had Down's syndrome, but whether or not Eddie was going to die. He had two holes in his heart, and required open-heart surgery at the age of four months; this was a problem associated with the protean forms of Down's syndrome.

I remember those few months of illness with great clarity: this little blob of life, draped over my left shoulder, both arms held slack at his sides, too weak to do anything but flop. Treacherous voices had spoken to me during the late pregnancy: perhaps I'll be let off. Perhaps there'll be complications. Perhaps he'll die in childbirth. Knowing, all the time, that this let-off would be no let-off at all, but a worse horror than anything I could imagine about Eddie's future life. Such terrible voices will speak to us, and we can't always silence them. It is part of the way we dramatise our lives.

And, of course, the reality is very different from the things you imagine. When Eddie was on my shoulder, I wanted him to live with all my heart; indeed, if my heart would have been any good to him, I'd have given it and welcome. That doesn't make me a saint, by the way, just a parent.

I remember the medical phase of Eddie's life, before and after his birth, and the twenty-four hours in intensive care, with the scrap of life seemingly living. I remember, too, the amazing confidence of the doctors and nursing staff at Guy's. Their certainty quickly became Eddie's certainty and eventually ours. Truly remarkable people.

So Eddie lived, and lives: burly and merry and on the whole, pretty healthy. And once the surgery was done and the emergencies and the dramas were over, it was time to get on with the business of living. And that is really rather an easy business. You live one day, and then you live the next.

Well, maybe easy isn't the right word, but parenthood is not supposed to be easy. Nothing worthwhile is. Down's syndrome brings in a number of physical problems. After his operation, we suffered – all of us, but Eddie by far the most – with Eddie's agonies of constipation, a weekly rising barometer of hideous discomfort ending in blessed and stinking relief. Here, and in many other ways, we looked for help and found it. But in an unexpected way: Peter Walker, a cranial osteopath, had the hands and the mind to help Eddie through his difficult patches, and he continues to do so. As Eddie belatedly began to crawl, his – naturally lax – stomach muscles tightened up, and the problem eased, just as Peter predicted, incidentally. And no one else had a clue.

There are various bits of assistance provided by the state; if you have a child with special needs, you will find a cluster of them. Some of these people are great, some are less great. There are times when we feel invaded by people with negative mindset and poor understanding, dominated by an eagerness to fill in forms and keep their arses covered. There are times when we feel that Eddie is state property, a public problem that somehow has to be organised. It seems sometimes that Eddie's principal function is to provide employment for unpleasant and insensitive people. Steps have been taken, words spoken. Problems still occur and are distressing. No doubt there are forms and files that have us down as obstructive and difficult parents.

Eddie's education continues, and at Eddie's pace, which is slow, and demands repetition and then repetition. He has a few words now, and a vocabulary of Makaton signs, with a very cheering capacity for understanding. He goes to the local nursery school, which he enjoys very much, and we hope that he will be at school in the next village in a term or two.

Eddie's education is slow but continuous. Frustrating? Not at all. Progress of any kind, in any context, is enthralling. It's not about a child passing an exam, it's about a child growing into himself; and for every parent that ever drew breath, that is a great and glorious thing. It has been the same with Joe in many ways: he hates sport, has no musical gifts, and has never got on with school life. He has a thousand other strengths, and is improving them. That's education for you. The fact that Eddie counts doo, doo, dee, rather than performing differential calculus, does not affect this truth. Eddie is learning stuff and becoming more himself.

I am not in the front line of the teaching part of Eddie's life. I see myself as more in the front line of arsing about. Giggling is an aspect of life underrated by the chart-makers. Eddie has a huge relish for giggles. He also loves a ball game, and our improvised games of chucking the ball into the wastepaper basket or kicking the ball for the dog are a constant delight. The dog is one of Eddie's special joys. He will climb into her basket and curl up with her, and the dog, a Labrador of gentle disposition even by the standards of the breed, utters no more serious complaint than an occasional sigh. She has a generous nature, but perhaps she has also fallen under Eddie's spell. He has gifts that way.

Children with Down's syndrome often seem to have a charismatic side to them, at least when they are up and cheerful and everything is going well. Eddie has a gift for laughter, for a joyous, shared laughter. He loves to laugh, but from a very early age it was clear that he also loves to inspire laughter. He has, for example, a taste for preposterous hats. On most occasions, he will reject a hat very firmly, but when the mood is on him, he will take a hat and wear it, the more ludicrous the better. When he visits his grandfather, he always wears his grandfather's bowler. This clownish nature is not something to be pitied; it is something Eddie quite deliberately assumes. But not to order.

Cheerful little soul? Certainly not. He's a four-year-old boy, and more prone than most to frustrations. His need to communicate is acute and therefore frequently painful, when his vocabulary of signs and words is inadequate for his own very clear idea of what he needs. That brings on a wounded-buffalo roaring of fury and distress.

Generalisations about Down's syndrome are as hopeless as any other generalisation. Cindy and I often talk about 'they', in reference to the generalisations people make – often good-heartedly – about Down's syndrome. The most frequent is 'they're very loving'. We often quote to each other in the midst of a fit of the roars.

It's not a matter of they, it's a matter of him. It always is; everything always is. I don't have a child with Down's syndrome; I am Eddie's father. There is a huge amount of difference between the two things. The first is almost impossible to deal with; the second is the way I live from day to day. I don't even think about it much.

Eddie is lucky in many ways, not least in his choice of a brother. Joseph is seven years older than him; not a usual gap, but the one we've got. And it is a very good one, we discovered; they are not competing on the same level or for the same things. And Joe, too, has his mother's generosity.

He and Eddie have wonderful big brother/little brother games, full of piggybacks and tumbles and chasing and pouncing. And giggles; Eddie's games are always full of giggles. The only area of competition is when Eddie's charisma overwhelms a social gathering, leaving Joe a little ignored. Eddie makes everything fun when he's up; naturally he becomes the centre of attention. Joe, however, takes that in stride and enjoys Eddie's social triumphs.

I don't want to sound too matter-of-fact here, any more than I want to sound saintly. Of course it's difficult sometimes. That's true for any parent and, God knows, many parents have more difficult times than Cindy and I do. I don't, above all, want to give the impression that everything is easy because I am such a sane, balanced and admirable person. I am not any of those things. I'm just a parent, playing the hand I've been dealt as best I can.

Some bits are hard, some bits are easy, some bits are fun, some bits are a frightful bore. That's true of life with Eddie; it's also true of life with Joe. But you don't even begin to break it up into categories; it is the one long endless complex business of being a parent. You don't go into parenthood in order to make sure that the benefits outweigh the deficits: you go into parenthood out of – brace yourself, but really no other word will do – love.

Parenthood is not really about the traditional round-robin Christmas letter: Jasper is school captain and is having trials for Middlesex at both cricket and rugby and played Hamlet in the school play of the same name while Oxford and Cambridge have both offered scholarships. He has just passed grade eight on the cello. Parenthood, like anything else in life, is not about perfection. It's much more interesting than that; it's about making the best of what you've got. Define best, then? Do that for yourself, but I'll give you a clue: if you think it's all about A levels, you're on the wrong track.

So my task, then, is to bring the best out of Eddie. That is unlikely to involve A levels. I know that there will be many harder things to face as he grows older. No doubt we will take these things in the order in which they come. We can imagine a few horrors, of course, but we will live through the actual events day by day. And we will continue with other important tasks like giggling and playing ball and providing hats and dealing with the world that can't imagine the dreadful fate of being a parent to a child with Down's syndrome.

What is it like to have Down's syndrome? How terrible is it? Is it terrible at all? It depends, I suppose, on how well loved you are. Like most other conditions of life. Would I want Eddie changed? It's a silly question, but it gets to the heart of the matter.

Of course you'd want certain physical things to be changed: the narrow tubes that lead to breathing problems, for example. But that's not the same as 'changed', is it? If you are a parent, would you like the essential nature of your child changed? If you were told that pressing a button would turn him into the infant Mozart, or Einstein, or van Gogh, would you press it? Or would you refuse, because you love the person who is there and real, and not some hypothetical other?

I can't say that I'm glad that Eddie has Down's syndrome, or that I would wish him to suffer in order to charm me and fill me with giggles. But no, I don't want his essential nature changed. Good God, what a thought. It would be as much a denial of myself as a denial of my son.

What's the good of him, then? Buggered if I know. The never-disputed terribleness of Down's syndrome is used as one of the great justifications for abortion; abortion has to exist, so that we don't people the world with monsters. I am not here to talk about abortion – make your own mind up – but I am here to tell you that Down's syndrome is not an insupportable horror for either the sufferer or the parents. I'll go further: human beings are not better off without Down's syndrome.

A chance gathering in my kitchen. Three people: my wife, who has some gypsy blood; Eddie; a friend who is Jewish. And the realisation that under Hitler all three would have been bound for the ovens. Down's syndrome, no more than Jewishness or gipsyhood, is not something that needs to be wiped out for the good of humanity. Down's syndrome is not the end of the world. In fact, for me, it was the beginning of one.

I am not here to make judgements on those who have gone for termination, being unwilling to cope with something they could not imagine. I am here to tell everybody that Eddie is my son and he's great. And I am now going to behave in a thoroughly unseemly manner. I am going to boast. I have a life that a lot of people envy. Mostly, they envy my job: I am chief sportswriter of *The Times*. People say: 'You're going to the World Cup, you're going to the Olympic Games, you lucky thing, can I come? I'll carry your bags.'

I live in a nice house in the country, it stands in a few acres of ground, and I keep five horses. People tell me, 'You are lucky, I'd love to live in place like this.' I make decent money, for all that I'm not seriously rich. I can, for example, spend a week in the African bush with Joseph or take the family for a winter break in southern Spain without worrying about the costs too much.

All these things people envy me for. But I have a child with Down's syndrome and, for that, people pity me. And I am here to say: wrong. Wrong, wrong, wrong. I am not to be pitied; here, far more than elsewhere, I am to be envied.

What is a child with Down's syndrome for? What does he do to improve the lot of the human race? Is he just a parasite on the species, and drag, a deadweight? I can answer that one, too. Eddie's function is to love and to be loved. Same as any other human being. And if that does not improve the lot of the human species, then what the hell are we all doing here?

CHAPTER 19

From One Professional to Another

Jonathan Rix BEd (Hons) MA
Lecturer in Inclusion Curriculum and Learning, Open University

I do not think that my expectations on becoming a parent of a child with Down syndrome (as it is now often called) were the same as many parents, because my sister, Shelley, had prepared the ground for me. Growing up as a sibling of a person with Down Syndrome allowed me to understand that people really are people first regardless of the labels we give them. This head start meant that I knew from the word go that I would be as proud of my son, Robbie, as any other child I might have been given (for example, his fab older sister, Isabel). This did not prepare me for what a parent has to go through with professionals however. Neither did many years of working in education.

Professionals give parents a huge amount of work to do. This has a wide range of practical, emotional and psychological consequences. Explaining this impact to other people, whether they be professionals or parents of typically developing children is difficult, but it is immediately recognised by other parents of children with an impairment. We all have our own versions of the tale, of course, but I'm going to try and explain mine.

It begins with the diagnosis. No one really wants to tell you what it is they have identified. And can you blame them? They know that it is going to upset you, that it is going to turn your life upside down. But of course, every baby does that. It is the social construction about what a baby should be that makes it different. We learn our notions of normality from our earliest days. We throw away a doll that has lost an arm or a leg. We are told not to stare or to ask questions. A baby is an image of perfection. It is meant to make us smile and feel protective. So when one comes along that does not fit this model we get in a tizz. Suddenly, the midwife who knows perfectly well that a child has an impairment is not allowed to talk to the parents about this. Someone in authority has to take on this role. We knew that our lovely lad had Down Syndrome the second time we looked at him. Robbie was sticking his tongue out at us. We had to ask if people agreed. No one would say, of course. Not until Caroline and I got the midwife to ourselves and finally she told us that we were probably right, though we weren't to tell anyone that she had told us. When the consultant paediatrician visited the next day, he sat very nervously at the end of my wife's bed and told her the news. He didn't do a bad job. He didn't say anything truly insensitive . . . well, apart from saying she could take Robbie to the United States to have plastic surgery on his eyes . . . but everything about the way he did it made it clear that this was bad news. And so it was again the next day, when he ran through all the medical problems that might be stored up for Robbie, and the ways in which his development might be impaired. Of course, his discomfort and his lists just played into the fears we had about having a baby that didn't fit in with everyone's idea of perfection. It did not help us reach the obvious view that our baby was a human being who would develop in his own way. It encouraged a vision of our child as a baby who needed to be assessed and measured and treated differently from the rest. It encouraged a sense of sadness and loss.

Over the next few days, the medical staff did their best to be positive. They were always popping in to say something cheerful:

'He doesn't look very Down's.'

'Well, at least he can get a job in Sainsbury's nowadays.'

'He's not a bad one, is he?'

Hardly surprisingly, none of this really helped. Neither did the constant comparison of our son to the norms and averages that fill the medical discourse. But after a week or so we had Robbie at home. Our lives together as a family could begin. This life now required us to visit doctors and therapists on a weekly basis, of course, or to have them come into our home. We have spent hundreds of hours answering their questions, describing Robbie and our lives, coming up with strategies and plans, making decisions based on possible outcomes and norm-based goals. Over the years the frequency of these visits has decreased but the impact of them has not.

Lots of these people we have met have been very kind to us. All of them have been overworked. Most of them have been underpaid. We have had some arguments and complaints, but we have also shared many valuable moments with them. We have met paediatricians, various other types of doctor, various types of nurse, hearing specialists, speech and language therapists, portage workers, physiotherapists, Sure Start advisers, health visitors and educational psychologists. Robbie has had heart tests, thyroid tests, blood tests, hearing and sight tests, and has been constantly measured (sometimes discreetly, sometimes openly) against developmental norms. We have been encouraged by this process to focus less on what Robbie can do now and much more on what we want him to do next. Our lives with our son have been filled with exercises and games that are designed to move him forward, to overcome those delays in development that the consultant paediatrician first mapped out for us on that hospital bed. It has been made absolutely clear to us that if we carry out these interventions then Robbie will develop as fast as he possibly can, and by implication that if we don't carry them out then he will not.

So let's talk about guilt and a sense of failure. We are given a target for our son, one among many, for example to say the sound 'S'. With the professional we come up with some possible strategies to get him to say or hear this sound. Sometimes it goes brilliantly. You have a hoot. Your morning is energised because you had such a successful session. But the next time you see this person, Robbie is not yet saying 'S'. Nor is he for the next five visits. We are not achieving the targets set for us. We have failed. Robbie has failed. There must another strategy out there to make him say the sound. We have to try harder, but Robbie isn't interested in the strategies we come up with. He loathes sound cards, he won't collect objects together that begin with 'S', he doesn't like me singing 'Sing a Song of Sixpence' . . . well, he just doesn't like me singing – the list goes on. We are aware of errorless learning techniques, using small steps, mirroring, scaffolding, slow, passive modelling, and we are totally up on avoidance tactics and the need for consistency to develop appropriate behaviour. But none of this seems to . . . HELP!

And then you are told that because he can't do this it means he must have dyspraxia. A new label. A new bad bit of news. And whose fault is that? Quite possibly, it is the fault of the research community. Quite possibly it is because we have a tradition of giving a label to a child on the basis of what they cannot do. Quite possibly it is because we are fixated on the search for symptoms. That's how you can make someone better. But it takes a while to reach that realisation. In the meantime, you look into the black hole of uselessness and feel like shit.

Our measure of effectiveness as parents of Robbie is in so many ways fundamentally different from our effectiveness as parents of Isabel. Generally speaking, we avoid forcing Isabel to do things just because we believe it will be good for her in the end. We are firm believers in discipline: we make her eat a couple of sprouts, we expect her to go to bed at a particular time, we tell her she is going to go on that walk with us, but we would never make her play a game she did not want to play nor come up with cunning strategies to keep her standing up for longer. But with Robbie that is exactly what we are expected to do. We are faced with confrontations about all kinds of things that we would let come naturally with Isabel. They come out of trying to teach him the sounds he should be saying, the way that his body should be moving, how he should be doing a jigsaw, or insisting that he makes himself understood. Throughout the day, there are possible points of conflict not because of the person you would typically be with your child, but because you have become a person delivering a programme in conjunction with a professional. And to make it worse, you know that the professional would hate to think that they were the cause of even the slightest bit of conflict. They are good people. People you like. But because of the relationship you have built with them, you now judge the effectiveness of your parenting against their targets, not your child's.

This change in our way of thinking is a surreptitious process, of course. It does not come about as a result of witnessing huge changes in Robbie because of these activities. We could not put our hands on our hearts and say that any of the interventions have had a clear-cut impact on Robbie and who he is now. The change in thinking comes about through learning the language of the professionals, and through the routine nature of carrying out the process. We get used to finding moments to fit in the activities, and gradually it becomes second nature to think of new ways to carry them out, of creating situations in which the activities become play. We don't notice what has happened until we lapse in this role. And, of course, all parents lapse. There are periods of time when life is too busy to carry out properly what we and the professionals are expecting of us, or when we lack the wherewithal they require. So, for example, I remember very clearly spending a weekend with Robbie when I had carried out none of the activities, and waking up on Monday morning, lying there at 6 am, thinking to myself, 'I'm a useless father,' then realising what I was doing to myself. So, I went back over the past week and realised that I had played with him quite a lot . . . just played with him . . . and I thought, 'What's wrong with that? Aren't I allowed some time off? Isn't he?'

We have recently moved into a new phase in our relationship with professionals. Robbie has started attending the local primary school. We are no longer responsible for carrying out his learning programme. Now, like every other parent, we just have to support his school and encourage him to engage with all they offer. But, of course, it is not quite as simple as that. Legally, Robbie only has special educational needs if he is provided with additional support, but it is largely up to us, his parents, to make sure the school receives the appropriate resources from the Local Education Authority (LEA) so that they can provide that additional support. We have to make sure that Robbie has a suitable statement of special educational needs or else everyone suffers. This may sound a touch over-dramatic, but there are plenty of children with Down Syndrome in schools who have only fifteen hours of support during their thirty-five-hour school week. Now, of course, some of these children are quite capable of doing very well with just a minimum of support, but the vast majority who receive this level are being under-supported, and therefore so are their schools and their peers.

This, of course, takes us to the heart of the dilemmas that parents face when placing their children into the current education system. We are told that we have choices. We are told that schools must aspire to the highest grade-related standards. We are told that schools should be inclusive. All these aspirations pull in different directions.

- If we choose a school, we are dependent on 1. that school or LEA choosing our child over all the others who have applied and 2. the LEA being willing to fund our choice.
- If a school is pushing for high academic standards then they are less likely to have the sorts of teaching practices that work to the advantage of children with learning difficulties.
- For a school to be inclusive it must be filled with teachers and support staff who see it as their role to work with children with learning difficulties and who are fully supported and appropriately funded by the LEA.

Underpinning all this is a mass of perspectives driven by a notion of rights. We all now seem to have rights to be educated together, to make choices about where we are educated, and to receive a high-class education. Somewhere along the line this notion of rights has bamboozled us into thinking that a right should act as some sort of guarantee of excellence. Since when has education been about excellence? The vast majority of us had a very indifferent education. Some days were better than others. Many of us loathed large chunks of our schooling; there are people in special schools who hated being wrapped up in cottonwool and treated like little children and there are people in mainstream schools who felt picked upon and isolated. There is a never-ending variety of ways in which education has failed us. In many ways the best we can hope for is a school that is least likely to undermine our child's sense of self while they are there, and least likely to under-prepare them for their future.

On top of that we are caught in the crossfire between inclusive education and special education. We are told that special schools are closing down and that there has been an inexorable march towards inclusion. We are also told that the majority of teachers believe inclusion is the right way forward, but not for those with social, emotional and behavioural difficulties, and only if they receive the right levels of support and training. Many of us feel we are trapped between schools that will definitely undermine our child's sense of self, or fail to prepare them for their future.

And, of course, the picture changes from LEA to LEA, from school to school and class to class. In some LEAs you will find your child is being pushed into a special school; in others you will find your child is being pushed into a mainstream school. Figures from the Department for Education and Skills (DfES 2004) show that 1.2 per cent of pupils are in special schools today, compared to 1.6 per cent in 1984, but that in some LEAs this is below 0.5 per cent while in others it is above 2.5 per cent. Proportionally almost as many secondary schools have closed as special schools, but today 5.14 per cent of schools are special schools compared to 5.95 per cent in 1984. However, with the opening of Pupil Referral Units (where lots of teenagers with SEBD – social, emotional and behavioural difficulties – are now placed) there were more segregated settings in 2005 than there were in 1984 (DfES 2004). This confusion of policies in relation to special schools across the UK is echoed in the mixed training of our mainstream staff. A recent *Times Educational Supplement Survey* (Bloom, 2005) of 511 primary and secondary school teachers revealed that 37 per cent had had no initial teacher training in working with pupils with SEN (special educational needs), 23 per cent had had a day or less, 14 per cent had had between two and five days, and 18 per cent had received more than five days. It was clear, however, that the vast majority of those who had received the most training had been most recently trained, and that it was these teachers who felt most capable and committed to work with all children. These are the teachers who will have learned that they have most of the skills they need already, that a belief in their own ability is paramount.

When you look at this flurry of statistics and policy issues, it becomes clear that, once again, as parents of a child with a learning difficulty, our choices and understanding of the needs of our children are being fundamentally framed by the professionals who run the services which support us.

Robbie had his first statement when he was two and a half. We were told by all the professionals that we spoke to that Robbie was too young to have anything in his statement except for the most general outline of his educational needs and how these should be met. It was explained that at this age things change so fast it is hardly worth getting things in writing. What really mattered was having the hours of support guaranteed by the LEA. Maybe they were right. But in hindsight I doubt it. What it actually meant was that they were able to get away with woolly targets and woolly descriptions of practice, which gave us no insight into how our son should be supported in his early years' settings and no leverage when they patently failed to carry out strategies recommended by other professionals – strategies which were not included on the statement, of course.

When it came to reviewing Robbie's statement for the start of primary school, we were slightly more wary. We received the reports from various professionals and wondered if we had enough to work with. The special school that Robbie had attended for eighteen months had written a reasonable description of Robbie, but made only the most superficial of recommendations about possible strategies to use with him. The educational psychologist reissued a report based on an assessment she had carried out when Robbie was three. Only the speech and language therapist had presented a full, specific, up-to-date report. Nonetheless, contained across all these reports were enough details for a suitable description and set of strategies to be mapped out. What is surprising is that we were surprised when the proposed statement arrived from the LEA. As with the majority of parents, our statementing process had fallen far outside the timelines required in the code of practice. We should have been prepared. Why were we expecting anything but the vague and woolly document that we were presented with, and one which offered that meagre fifteen hours of support? Maybe it was our naivety. Maybe it is that faith in authority and the professionals who represent authority that has been drummed into all of us in our early years. Whatever the cause, that does not excuse the flagrant attempt of the LEA to fob us off with something that was patently failing Robbie and the school he would be attending. There is no question that the LEA officers must have known what they were doing. They must have produced statements for many children with profiles similar to Robbie in the past. Robbie is certainly not the first child with Down Syndrome in West Sussex.

Of course, the reason that they do it is because they can. For example, in a recent piece of research (O'Connor *et al*, 2005) only 18 per cent of parents had requested a rewrite of their statement. Like us, people feel they can trust the professionals, or they don't have the energy or wherewithal to challenge them. The LEA has got away with it with all those other parents, so why not try to get away with it with us? And what makes it worse is that because we will fight we will get what our child and his school deserves, but this will change nothing for all those who follow. The LEA ignore as much of the law as they can get away with, and if they are ever punished it is only ever for the individual case on which they have been caught out. Of course, much of the problem lies with the Government's tendency to pass enabling legislation in relation to education, legislation that acts as guidelines rather than as absolutes. A cynic might say that it gets this name because it is merely enabling the authorities to do as little as possible.

So, on receiving the statement, we immediately started to kick up a stink. We got in touch the Head Teacher of Robbie's former special school, and she phoned the LEA to say the hours were wholly inappropriate. 'Oh,' said the LEA and then announced that these hours were only for when he was part time. They wanted to reassess his needs after he had been at the school for a few weeks. This was not a practice anyone we have spoken to has heard of before in West Sussex in relation to a child like Robbie. So, we got this in writing, and then sat down to rewrite the statement. We went through the literature on Down Syndrome, we had discussions with people at the Down Syndrome Educational Trust who knew Robbie well, and we sent back a document to the LEA that clearly defined what Robbie would need to make his schooling effective. And they ignored the lot. They told us it should go in an individual education plan, not a statement. Again they wanted us to place our trust in the professionals, to trust our son's teachers to know what to do and to carry it out. Now, as it happens, we did trust our son's teachers. We had spent a year preparing them, with the help of a heroic speech and language therapist, for the arrival of Robbie. The class teacher concerned had started to learn sign language. They had gone ahead and appointed new staff even though there was no new money guaranteed from the LEA. Until now they had, by and large, done us proud, but things can change. Teachers move on, pupils change classes, new problems and opportunities emerge. Without a clear statement we have no control, and the school has no guarantees or guidelines. So today, as I write, we are preparing for our tribunal. We have had our meeting with the LEA officer. And a very friendly bloke he was, too. He has made it clear that they don't want to go to the tribunal. But who knows? And what is it all about? Just three pages of clear description of how Robbie learns best; a request that they specify how many times a year the different professionals will visit; and our need for the statement to state that the short activities recommended by the professionals are carried out daily, activities of the sort that we spent so many hours carrying out in our home.

The ironies of it all are not lost on us, of course. We have become the professionals now. We are the ones driving them to list our son's needs, to create their checklists, to make sure that they get on with it. In the early days, it felt as if we were just passing through the lives of these professionals. We were in transit. Now, after so many of them have passed through our lives, we realise that they are the transient ones. We are the long-term providers and Robbie is the only constant. We are Robbie's mum and dad. That's all.

It has been a long journey to here from the day when that first professional sat on our bed and began to make us doubt our ability to cope as parents. Along the way we have met many good people, many lazy ones, and many who really need to be a bit more reflective. Some of them have had an essential humanity, others have not. They have challenged us and changed our ways of thinking. They have damaged us at times and supported us at others. They have made this a very public experience and yet one that has turned us inward and become intensely private. Of course, many parents of typically developing children will see echoes of their own struggles with their offspring in this tale. They will feel that they have been as much concerned with the schooling of their children as we have, that they too struggle to get them to the next stage of learning. Many will feel they have given as many hours to swimming lessons, reading and writing and the learning of a musical instrument, and so on, as we have to Robbie's development. They too will see themselves as just as much revealed to the world by bringing up kids. Once I might have argued with them about this. Now I am not so sure. After all, we are all just parents. Robbie is just another child. But, when I look at my peers and at my early relationship with Isabel, I do feel there is a small difference that is worth noting. And as with all things this difference is both a blessing and a curse. The difference is that with Robbie everything is just a bit more. Life with Robbie involves just a bit more planning, more patience, more determination, more frustration, more reward, more extremes, more learning – more professionals.

So what, after four years of being in the company of these trained individuals, would I wish them to do differently? Well, I think I wish that they were better at encouraging us all to value our children for who they are rather than worrying quite so much about who they could be. I wish they would look less for the barriers to be overcome and more for the opportunities that are presented. After all, when all is said and done, Robbie is just a red-headed kid with a life of his own.

CHAPTER 20

Four Decades of Change:
A family perspective on learning disability

Dr Philippa Russell CBE
Disability Rights Commissioner
Disability Policy Adviser to the National Children's Bureau

Since the birth of my son in 1963, we have seen huge changes in attitudes, expectations and provision for people with a learning disability. In the early 1960s, the birth of any disabled child was seen as a disaster. Institutional care was often offered as a solution for the well-being of families. Hotels, cinemas, even shops or cafés regularly rejected customers who 'looked different'. But life was changing. The energetic Peggy Jay and Maureen Oswin laid bare the sterile, lonely lives led by many children with a learning disability living on hospital wards. Jack Tizard demonstrated the lifelong negative outcomes of bringing children up in environments which did not see child-centred policies and individualised care as relevant to learning disability. Professor Stanley Segal campaigned for the right to education and the 'parents' movement' was born. And of course Lord Rix was and is a tireless champion for people with a learning disabilitiy and their families; we have been fortunate in our supporters.

It is also interesting to reflect that although we all endorse a social rather than a medical model of disability in the twenty-first century, much of the energising and advocacy for children with a learning disability in the sixties and seventies came from paediatricians such as Simon Yudkin, Hugh Jolly, Ruth Griffiths, Ronnie McKeith and of course the inimitable David Morris. I knew many of them personally and valued their strong advocacy and passionate belief that 'every child matters'. Then, as now, personal belief systems mattered and we parents were profoundly influenced by their support and their conviction that our children did have a future.

The start of a 'pilgrim's progress'

My first child, Simon, was born in November 1963. The night before his birth, my parents, some New Zealand relatives and I went to the Whitehall Theatre to see Brian Rix (as he was then) in one of his famous Whitehall farces. My aunt commented that she had heard that he had a disabled daughter and she was very pleased that he was still performing. People hide away too often, she said emphatically, but life goes on. I did not imagine that night that I would over the years see Brian Rix on many occasions and that Simon, like Shelley, would not follow the life-path anticipated by his family.

All parents vividly remember their children's births, but we had more reason than most to remember Simon's. President Kennedy had been assassinated and every midwife, new parent, doctor – probably even the babies themselves – felt that this was an ominous reminder of human vulnerability and changes in the old order. Like many other emotional parents at the time, we named our son after the President. We did not anticipate that Simon John Fitzgerald Russell and we would eventually meet the Kennedy clan, go to Hyannisport (for the matriarch Rose Kennedy's 100th birthday celebrations) and have a kindly correspondence over some years between Simon and John Kennedy Junior. Simon received his last card from the former President's son a week before he died in the tragic flying accident. Our contact with Rose Kennedy was another example of parent power. The formidable Rose Kennedy had always insisted that her daughter Rosemary should be treated like any other daughter of one of America's 'first families'. She was also a passionate believer in parents as change agents. Never one to suffer fools (or cowards) gladly, she ensured that Rosemary was presented at court, complete with family diamonds and ostrich plumes in her hair. She was also and, unusually for the time, very open and public in discussing learning disability in the family.

Rose Kennedy was also a wonderful correspondent, spending hours writing regularly to those parents from all over the world who got in touch with her and exhorting optimism and courage. In 1964, she visited the UK and an interview with a *Guardian* journalist on learning disability prompted many letters from parents. We were one of those families and we were left in no doubt about her belief that families could change society and move mountains (as indeed the Kennedy family did in the USA). Families need sensitive support but sometimes we need the crucial push in order to make a difference. Judy Fryd, the Founder Member of Mencap (and another parent who also met Rose Kennedy), once described her as the only person who had ever told her to 'straighten her spine and get on with it and do something'.

When Simon was born, we of course had no idea that we might 'need to do something'. He was a beautiful baby. There was no indication of the troubles ahead. He was rosy cheeked, blue eyed and had a head of blond curls. Even more importantly, he slept all night and I was the envy of friends for having such a trouble-free child. But by the time he was ten months old, the good times were ending. He got infections, serious enough to mean hospital admissions. He was slow to sit up, to crawl and to stand. Finally, he was admitted to Coppets Wood (the London regional hospital for infectious and tropical diseases) with suspected encephalitis. He recovered but at our discharge home, the consultant sat me down and somewhat brusquely said that while she was not a paediatrician, she felt sure that Simon was not developing normally. She gave me the names of three paediatricians (all, I subsequently discovered, with international reputations). She had no 'bedside manner', but I appreciated her directness.

Unfortunately, her concern was well founded. Within two weeks Simon was referred, in hospital and having the painful and frightening surgical investigations which preceded the MRI scans. On one occasion he was given a private room because of the terrible headaches which accompanied the examinations of the time. After a day we were told to move him because a private patient was being admitted. I refused and prepared to face up to an elegant (and clearly very affluent) woman and her small girl who was a reluctant candidate for a tonsillectomy. I was about to deliver a passionate speech about Simon's obvious pain, his need to be kept apart from the noisy ward and my absolute refusal to go anywhere, when my contestant grasped her daughter's hand, looked at Simon and me and said that she was going – Simon clearly needed the bed more than Amy. Delighted as I was to have stood my ground, my heart sank. I saw her lingering sad and pitying look and I realised just how ill my son really was. Amy and her mother walked away and I wished I could follow them.

Changing lives

But we did walk away eventually. It was agreed that Simon had an arrested hydrocephalus, that he had probably experienced a subdural haemorrhage at birth and that he should now make progress. We had expected to be a typical Foreign Office family, spending large parts of our adult lives overseas. Most of our contemporaries hankered after high-profile urban postings in the major European cities, the USA, Canada. But hoping that the climate and rural lifestyle would improve Simon's health, we accepted a posting with the High Commission in Malawi.

We were exhausted when we left England and our new house – high on the slopes of Mount Zomba and looking across the bottom of the Great Rift Valley to Mount Mlanje and Mozambique – seemed like paradise. But alas paradise is easily lost. Simon did not make progress. He eventually learnt to walk, largely due to the efforts of Caesar, the huge German shepherd dog belonging to a neighbour whose wife had gone back to England with a tropical illness. Caesar arrived on our veranda at 6.20 every morning and stayed until dusk. He was Simon's self-appointed nanny, portage teacher and general protector. He suffered in the process from endless hugs, pokes and kicks but he would regularly haul Simon to his feet and endlessly nudge him forward. But notwithstanding Caesar's best efforts to turn Simon into a thoroughly sociable and well-mannered puppy, the difference between Simon and his brother Christopher, born one year later, became daily more apparent.

And notwithstanding a sunny and moderate climate, Simon was increasingly ill. Severe illness and pneumonia were major risks to a young child in a country where our medical advice came from the Medical Officer with the King's African Rifles (if he was not out on distant manoeuvres). I brought the children home and Simon went into the then Evelina Children's Hospital for more tests. We returned to Africa and waited for the results. The letter when it came was almost a relief. Simon had brain damage, probably from a haematoma relating to the earlier bleed. He had a learning disability and would have long-term difficulties. The Foreign Office was horrified. The children and I would have to go home – at once – but we had no home to go to. Our house was rented, and I had no intention of being exiled because I had a disabled child. To its credit the Foreign Office changed its mind; there is now a very active organisation of officials and partners with disabled children and a lot of peer support for life in various overseas postings with a child with special needs. Careers are not put on hold because you have a disabled child. But disability (in particular learning disability) was not discussed openly at the time and long-stay residential care was a serious option and offered, given our circumstances.

Much has been written about the impact of diagnosis of a disability. All parents are shocked – this is not the life they expected. I sat and read the final letter and reports on Simon (I had retrieved them from the diplomatic bag and driven up to the plateau on Mont Zomba to read them on my own). The weather was cold and grey, remarkably similar to the gloomy weather of an early English winter. The only difference was the sudden appearance of a family of baboons, hungry and scraggy in the cold snap, who pattered around me hoping for bananas, sandwiches, any of the picnic-box food, which they had learnt to expect from visitors to the mountain. I felt some empathy with them – we were all scrabbling for survival. In some ways the news was a relief to me. I knew something was wrong, it was not my fault and I hoped (unrealistically) that we could 'do something' about it. My husband had not expected the diagnosis and we learnt the hard lesson that even in a single family there can be very different expectations.

We came home to England for, like many other families, our own careers had to change overnight. Simon's health meant that remaining in

Malawi or indeed any other Foreign Office posting was unrealistic. We also came back to the terrible realisation that while healthcare might have improved dramatically in the UK, other provision left much to be desired. In 2006, with a Disability Rights Commission and equality legislation, some of the attitudes of the 1970s and early 1980s now seem unbelievable.

Partnership in change

The ILEA (Inner London Education Authority) was progressive and interested in disabled children. But at the end of the 1960s, they were obliged to inform us that Simon was 'ineducable' under the 1944 Act. In effect, he had no right to go to school. The educational psychologist apologised profusely and gave us by hand the crucial letter excluding Simon from education. In the days of typewriters, most had a ribbon which provided type in red or black. To ensure that we had no illusions about the future, the dreaded red ribbon recorded Simon's ineducability. But we, like many other parents, did not accept that any child was ineducable. We were lucky. Our charismatic paediatrician, Dr Ronnie McKeith, had sent me off to Mencap as part of Simon's assessment plans and we were rapidly involved in a big Mencap campaign which led finally to the 1970 Education (Handicapped Children) Act and amendment to the 1944 Act. Alice Bacon, then Minister of State for Education, led the celebration and Simon and Anya Souza presented the inevitable flowers. We were now in the 'swinging sixties' and Simon and his brother's emerald green velvet 'loons' and ruffled shirts were greatly admired, albeit now greeted with shrieks of horror that anyone could wear clothes like that.

Simon had in fact been to school before the 1970 Act was implemented. Dr Trevor Evans, a community paediatrician, had ensured that Camden's health services paid for the education of children with a learning disability. The flexibility with health budgets seems unbelievable now, as does the level of services, such as speech and language therapy, which we received. We had a specialist social worker and access to respite, short breaks and other provision, which is now so tightly rationed. But of course provision was very variable and public attitudes were often extremely negative.

Simon (like most children at that time) went to a special school. After Malawi (where there were a number of disabled children, all of whom were of necessity included in everything because of the absence of any special provision), it was a shock to be regularly excluded on our return to the UK. But he had a better start in life than many of his peers. We were one of the first pilot families to receive portage (virtually unknown at the time, but a lifeline for parents who had very little guidance about helping their children). With the help of the health authority and social services, we and other parents set up our own nursery. Housed in the large living room of some generous Hampstead grandparents, the nursery ran until it was (as intended) taken over by the local authority and merged with a new day nursery. I had learned early the value of working with other families and the importance of peer support.

Like many parents, we were closely involved with a range of parent support groups. My husband chaired the Camden Mencap and we joined Kith and Kids. Simon attended a local special school and subsequently became a boarder at a residential special school in Surrey. The debate about residential education is often heated, but Simon was happy. An intensive speech and language therapy programme improved his communication skills. The school was unusually open and inclusive of the local community. Volunteers from the local police overcame his fear of water and he acquired the status of silver and gold medals and various awards at local swimming galas. My other son and his friends longed to go to school with Simon – everybody was always welcome (many ex-pupils came back to visit and stay), their approval was the marker of a real sense of community and an assumption that all children can learn and achieve.

Looking to the future – achieving an 'ordinary life'

Simon was in many ways fortunate – we have no criticism of his education and he was able to go on to further education college and Mencap's rural training unit at Lufton Manor. That in turn led to United Response in West Sussex, where he lives today. He owns his own house (of course, with a mortgage like everyone else), he works in 'organics' (albeit unwaged) at the Aldingbourne Centre, which was also created by parents. But we, like other families, worry desperately about the future.

Life can seem like a sequence of assessments, eligibility criteria and concerns about 'what if' we are unable to provide personal and financial support to secure a good future.

Thinking positively, Simon's 'pilgrim's progress' has been very different from what we might have expected. He has his own home, he has good support, he has travelled and he is more independent than we expected in the early sixties. But on the downside, he is now middle-aged and needs much more support as he gets older. We live in a community care system where there is a 'postcode lottery'. We have the vision of an ordinary life, but its delivery will be challenging.

As a family carer, I see myself as an ally as well as a parent to my son. In the USA, disability discrimination legislation formally recognises the concept of 'allies' between disabled people and family members. But I fear that we are sometimes not always fully valued in the UK. There is nothing informal about the care and support which we offer throughout our children's lives. I would often prefer – like so many parents – just to be Simon's mother. But I also know that we too often have to be warrior parents in order to get good enough services.

If my own personal 'pilgrim's progress' has taught me anything, it is that partnership matters. I have learnt that you have to respect people in order to change them. In the 1970s, I was 'sent to Coventry' by the children's nurses in one long-stay hospital because (as a member of the visiting local Community Health Council) I had dared to criticise the children's toys hanging tantalisingly immaculate from the ceiling rather than sitting grubby but loved on their beds or tables. The staff argued that parents visiting 'didn't like their gifts to be spoiled' and 'it was more hygienic that way'. MRSA didn't exist in the seventies and eighties, but people trained to be good nurses valued hygiene over childcare. I realised that we needed to give them permission to run more child-friendly services and to persuade the families that a little chaos and confusion could mean more personalised care rather than poor standards. Most importantly, we needed to move children into appropriate settings and we needed to help parents to care for children at home.

As David Towell notes in Chapter 21, we have had a major cultural shift away from institutions towards an ordinary life. Children with a learning disability then – as now – are the citizens of the future. When I saw my son go off to vote in the last election, I realised that life was changing for people with a learning disability.

As *Valuing People* (2001) concludes:

> We must not underestimate the difficulties involved in delivering our ambitious new vision for people with learning disabilities. The principles of rights, independence, choice and inclusion . . . are challenging and have far-reaching implications for everybody . . . But getting it right for people with learning disabilities will show what can be achieved with and for one of the most vulnerable and socially excluded groups in our society.

I did not expect to work in my current field. I envisaged a very different life in 1963 when Simon was born. But I feel privileged by the people I have met, by the solidarity and mutual support in the learning disability sector and I feel proud to have known the many people with a learning disability who have taught me much and made me see the world in a different way. I am proud of Christopher and his sister Emma, and particularly proud of Simon. He has had many challenges but he is generous in spirit, loving, creative (in his garden, his pride and joy) and like many people with a learning disability, he has the wonderful gift of always finding the best in everybody.

CHAPTER 21

Brothers and Sisters as Change Agents: From the personal to the political

Dr David Towell MA (Cantab) PhD (Cantab)

Director of the Centre for Inclusive Futures and Visiting Senior Lecturer in Social Policy at St George's, University of London

Introduction

It is a privilege to be asked to contribute to this sixtieth anniversary compilation. This book is both a collection of vivid stories about people's lives as these have changed over the period since World War II and the history of the social movement, most concretely reflected in the work of Mencap, which has struggled to produce the conditions in which everyone with a learning disability can live full lives as valued members of our society.

Brian Rix's invitation to me was to contribute to both aspects of this collection from the perspective of a sibling. It is only right therefore that I should start by introducing my sister Pat.

Pat is now sixty-nine years old. If you met her, you would find her a dignified senior citizen, living an ordinary life in south-west London, sharing her modern home with four other people, two of whom have been friends for more than a quarter of a century and two of whom are younger and bring additional spice to everyday activity in their household. You would find that Pat has a wide range of interests, from swimming to theatre to Indian food, and a full range of home entertainment in her room, among which perhaps she likes best a projector which creates patterns of coloured light on her walls and ceiling, especially at bedtime. You would also notice that Pat uses a wheelchair, needs significant assistance in everything she does, from eating to moving, and doesn't speak – rather her eyes tell us whether she is interested or otherwise in what is going on around her.

It's my impression now that Pat has a good life, in many ways like other, non-disabled people of her age, although it is also essential to remain eternally vigilant about how she feels and whether there are ways in which she could do better. But this wasn't always so. Our story goes back the full sixty years covered by this book and both Pat's experiences and my responses to them have been a modest factor in the movement for social change which it celebrates. Indeed, if some of Pat's – and therefore my – negative experiences are now untypical, this is itself welcome evidence of our progress.

As my title suggests, it is the interplay between family experience and social change, between 'the personal and the political', which provides the focus for this contribution. It is a common observation, when we come across someone in professional or public life who seems especially interested in people with a learning disability (a good teacher, a sympathetic journalist, a committed MP) that it turns out they have a close relative with a learning disability. Our movement, not least of course in Mencap itself, has largely relied on the volunteer contributions of families – indeed, perhaps too much. Often our allies – well represented by the other contributors to this book – also turn out to have a personal reason for their professional interest.

My thesis is that this linking of the personal to the political (meaning what we do outside the family in the professional or public sphere) partly depends on the greater knowledge and awareness of learning disability which family experience brings. But, especially for brothers and sisters, our motivation to get involved also springs in part from our feelings about the huge inequalities typically evident in the differences between our own and our disabled sibling's lives, and the desire to make reparation for these inequalities.

To be more concrete in our case, both Pat and I received considerable financial support from the state in our first twenty-six years. Pat never went to school but by twenty-six had lived in institutional care with twenty-four-hour staff support for eighteen years. Meanwhile, her brother was still at school (just completing a PhD after eight years at Cambridge University, about the most expensive schooling the state can provide). At the equivalent period in our lives, one of us was living with hundreds of other disabled people in poor conditions and with no apparent way out. The other was just starting his first well-paid job in the UK's leading applied social research institute, with a promising career ahead.

How siblings act on both their personal knowledge and motivation of course varies. Beyond the immediate family relationship there are many ways in which these can be linked: for example, becoming a key advocate with and for one's disabled sibling; playing one's part (volunteering) in civil society associations (such as Mencap) which try to promote broader change; or joining a profession which offers opportunities to make a specialist contribution in this field.

In my own case, I have had very good opportunities to do all these things while at the same time always struggling to make sense of my unusual relationship with Pat – about which, more below.

Brian offered me up to 3,000 words for this contribution, which is not enough to tell our sixty-year story comprehensively; perhaps even 300,000 wouldn't suffice! In what follows therefore I have drawn out three 'slices' of history from across this period which perhaps best illuminate what it has meant to me to be a sibling.

The lost decades: finding my sister

Pat was born in 1936, the first child. Not long afterwards she contracted a severe case of whooping cough through which she suffered major brain damage. Very attractive as a small girl (I still have a lovely photo of her supporting herself with a spade on the beach at Yarmouth), she nevertheless became very hard work to look after and didn't develop as other children did, the extent of her disabilities becoming increasingly clear. Of course the bulk of this work was done by our mother in the rather unfavourable conditions of life in London during World War II (indeed the family was bombed out in 1941).

They managed after a fashion – people helped each other a lot during WWII – but shortly after the war ended, Pat suffered her next disaster. Our parents gave birth to their second child and, as was not uncommon in this period, doctors advised that they should concentrate now on me and place Pat in institutional care. Indeed, more painfully, I believe the advice was to 'forget her'. Thus, at eight years old, Pat began what was to become nearly fifty-two years in institutional care, never again having her own bedroom until Normansfield closed and she moved to her current home in 1997.

Of course, they never did forget her. She started her institutional career at Leavesdon, a few miles from what was then our home in Feltham, where I suspect they went often. Then, for administrative reasons, Pat moved further away, to Royal Earlswood, and I think they gradually saw her less. Indeed, I think they had stopped visiting altogether when I was a teenager and it was not until more than thirty years later, after my father's death, that I was able to reintroduce Pat to Mum.

I don't know when I first realised I had a sister. Or when I first formulated the intention to find her. On the former point, I recall that every Christmas Mum would knit Pat a bedjacket (which must have shaped my ideas on how she spent her time). I also remember going with our parents when I was about twelve to Royal Earlswood but being left in the car while they did the visiting. Clearly they found this painful and didn't want me to share their experience. And then there were the early childhood photos . . .

On the latter point, I think that as a teenager I decided that I needed to know my sister. Even so, it was not until after I left university that I first got to meet her. I can't explain why this took me so long, beyond the point that if one has already missed someone for twenty years, it is a bit difficult to work out when to start. I think I sensed that Pat had become something of a closed chapter in our parents' life and they might find it hard for me to reopen this book. I also wonder now whether, at least unconsciously, I was reluctant to let reality challenge the fantasy I had built up about my sister in the absence of information about her.

My main evidence for this last idea came at our first meeting. I finally turned up at Normansfield, where she now lived, having signalled my intentions to staff there. I was shown into an elegant lounge in the old building (where the Langdon Downs had once lived) and, after a while, house staff brought Pat from her ward, the South Wing (which I later discovered was very much less elegant, housing fifty women with varying capacities, all sharing a single dormitory at night and all milling around in a single large room during the day).

I was very happy to be meeting Pat, then in her late thirties, but also completely surprised. On the one hand, she was clearly one of us, with our mother's rich wavy hair and our father's eyes and nose. On the other hand, she looked completely different from how I had imagined: the fantasy I had carried with me for a long time, based in part on those early photos, was of an attractive young woman (illogically, younger than me) with long blond hair.

So this was the beginning. We looked at each other for perhaps an hour or more. We didn't touch. I think I did some talking. And we were visited by the Medical Director, Dr Lawler, and his secretary, who were keen to learn more about this 'new relative on the block'.

Scandal and opportunity: rising to the challenges

My early plan was to get to know Pat and her situation better, as indeed I have. I think it is perhaps fair to say now that I have known her for more than thirty years while she has known me for an hour or two many times over the same period. What I mean by this is that we can be confident Pat has no conception of family or brother and it is certainly my impression that, while sometimes when I am with her she takes an interest in me (other times less so), she doesn't recognise me as someone who has been spending time with her regularly over this whole period.

At the personal level, I have understood my role as loving Pat as my sister, looking out for her in any way I can, both to encourage more positive things in her life and be alert to problems, and speaking up for her both informally and at times when she is the centre of decision-making, as in the annual reviews of which services attend to her needs. I also think I have extended her identity with the people she meets day to day. She is of course Pat, but she is also David's sister, and the David in question is a small part of her life, seems to know quite a lot about the lives of people with a learning disability more generally and even sometimes seems quite influential with managers and policy-makers in this field.

Things might just have continued at this personal level but not too long after I first met Pat, fate took a hand and shifted my concern for her into the public sphere. First, there was the scandal at Normansfield, coming to public attention when care staff walked out in the middle of the night, leaving their dependent residents (including Pat) unsupported as a dramatic protest at the controlling and stifling leadership of Dr Lawler. Thus began the last major inquiry into hospital scandals in a series dating back to Ely and Farleigh in the mid sixties.★

Second, at roughly the same time, I was recruited to a senior post at the King's Fund (a long-established London-based charity) with responsibility for leading its work on long-term, or as I soon relabelled this, community care. With the support of my new colleagues★★ my first major initiative in this job was to get together some of the most able and committed people across the country both to spell out a new philosophy to underpin services for people with a learning disability – *An Ordinary Life* – and to provide detailed design guidance on how to implement this philosophy, including for people (like Pat) with the highest support needs.

This initiative was timely because the early 1980s was a period in which, partly because of the institutional scandals, the NHS was finding significant amounts of money, especially capital, to invest in new learning disability services but wasting much of it on building new smaller institutions, often misdescribed as 'community units'. The King's Fund publications argued authoritatively that everyone is able, with the right support, to live in 'an ordinary house in an ordinary street'.

★ As other siblings (and of course parents) who have read my contribution point out, while the role of advocate and supporter has many rewards, it also brings big responsibilities which *in extremis* can be concerned with taking a stand in life and death situations.

★★ My life's work in this field has both relied on and learnt from a huge network of people in different walks of life, many of whom became good friends. In this story, I have only named those who are either well known or to make links with other parts of this book. I am however indebted to them all.

At Normansfield, a task force led by Professor Joan Bicknell was established to 'turn the institution around,' following Dr Lawler's dismissal, and Government offered large sums of revenue and capital for modernisation. I was myself professionally expert in this kind of cultural change and offered my volunteer support to Joan in her team's programme of improvements. Even so, we were not able to persuade the authorities to invest this money in genuine community services; rather all the capital was used to build a new day centre and a set of twenty-four-place bungalows in the hospital grounds, only to be knocked down again less than fifteen years later when Normansfield closed. My first effort at public influence on behalf of Pat and her fellow residents can be judged a disappointing failure.

Goodbye to institutions: partners in social change

Families learn to stick at it however long it takes. And as the look in Pat's eyes often said to me, 'nothing much ever happens fast round here'. Indeed, this next part of our story is another ten years on from the new building at Normansfield. In that time, Pat had moved to one of the bungalows, now sharing a bedroom with only two other people and a day room with twelve, both men and women. It was here she got to know the people who moved out with her to her current home. The physical conditions in the bungalow were of course immeasurably better, the smaller numbers of residents making for a more domestic life but actually with other aspects of the institutional routines not much different.

Over the same period, the King's Fund had sustained its efforts to spread innovations based on the *Ordinary Life* philosophy, attracting influential allies like the Joseph Rowntree Foundation. Earlier – in 1975 – the Government had established the National Development Group and National Development Team to push forward improvements in learning disability services, the former focusing on policy and guidance, the latter on inspecting and helping local services. However, in Mrs Thatcher's 'quango hunt' of 1981, the NDG was abolished. Fortunately, I was able to use the good offices of the King's Fund to bring together the main national voluntary organisations in our field, to create an independent alternative, the IDC (Independent Development Council) in which Brian Rix (by then, Mencap Secretary-General) was the first Chair (followed by Philippa Russell) and I was the first Secretary.

Through this kind of multi-track approach, we were having increasing success in winning both central and local support for positive change, perhaps best represented initially in the pioneering All Wales Strategy for community-based services which drew heavily on the *An Ordinary Life* work. Elsewhere, for example in south-east Thames – where Audrey Emerton's leadership (now Baroness Emerton) was the pivotal influence – the shift away from institutions was gaining pace. Indeed, there was enough concrete progress that by 1987 we were able to publish *An Ordinary Life in Practice*.

In my own professional work, I had also taken on the post of Associate Director of the National Development Team (supporting Derek Thomas) and in my voluntary activities, graduated to become Chair of the Normansfield Parents, Relatives and Advocates Association.

Normansfield, working with the Mencap Homes Foundation (in which Elspet Rix was playing a key local role) had made some start on moving more able residents into community settings, but by 1990 was clearly lagging behind this wider movement for reform. However, the NDT was able to use its inspection function to demand new managerial leadership and a programme for closure, and the new managers found ready allies in our Association. Indeed, while not far away rather conservative parents' associations linked to institutions were trying to preserve the past, we pushed hard to speed up the process of change and became active partners in achieving an exemplary transition to community. Thus Normansfield closed in 1997. Pat was in one of the last groups to move out to her new home (last, partly because she had benefited from the earlier period of new building).

In turn, families had to find fresh ways of advancing the interests of their disabled relatives in this new pattern of community living. We merged our Association with Richmond Mencap so as to be campaigning alongside the established community-based advocacy organisation in our locality and I accepted the invitation to become a Board member in the independent housing association ('Owl') responsible for Pat's everyday support.

Into the twenty-first century: Valuing People *and beyond*

Of course, this is not the end of our story. Pat is ageing slowly (our dad and mum made it to eighty-seven and ninety-five respectively) and I hope she still has much life to come. Two of her friends have however died and in Owl we are working on both providing better support to people in their later years and ways of reshaping housing options to fit our commitment to individual solutions better.

At the policy level, I now think that closing all the institutions was no more than a first step in advancing the agenda for a more inclusive society, one that values all its members. Indeed, I was able to use the networks established through the experience described above (this time round including Sheila Hollins, Rob Greig and Oliver Russell) to help ensure that the New Labour Government in 1997 put learning disability firmly on their agenda and produced a radical policy framework for twenty-first century progress, *Valuing People*. Making a reality of this positive agenda is the new frontier. Meanwhile, I have been lucky enough to add international advocacy to my own voluntary portfolio, working as an adviser to both Inclusion Europe and Inclusion International (similar organisations to Mencap at the European and global levels) as they seek to protect human rights and promote *An Ordinary Life* for everyone.

Looking back on this sixty-year story, we can see now that as Pat's brother but also as part of our movement, I was able to play some part in shaping the second half of Pat's life for the better. Equally, and without ever knowing that she has a brother, Pat has profoundly shaped mine. Together, we still have much to do to advance the shared values we have gained through this experience.

CHAPTER 22

On Families

Russell Burton

Russell Burton is the father of Catherine, who has just started at Mencap's Lufton College. He has raised, to date, over £20,000 for Mencap by taking part in Sinai desert and China bike rides and a trek in Tibet. He is currently training to run the New York Marathon on 5 November 2006 to raise more funds for Mencap.

Russell was interviewed by Tim Segaller.

Catherine's going to Lufton College has been the biggest step in her life, the biggest decision for us all in terms of her future. Before this, everything that has happened to her has been pretty much predestined and structured, i.e. nursery school, then primary school and secondary school (though she left the latter halfway through to go to a moderate learning difficulties special school). So no big decisions had to be taken.

After special school, she went to the local sixth-form college and did a three-year ASDAN (Awards Scheme Development and Accreditation Network) Towards Independence course. Halfway through this it dawned on us that the next stage was mind-blowing, when decisions had to be taken, and that she really wasn't ready for the real world; she was still very dependent on her parents and three younger sisters, and would be until her late twenties or early thirties.

So in the last twelve months I have been pushing, cajoling social services, Connexions, psychologists, occupational therapists and her then college to get them to agree that somewhere like Lufton would be the best next place for her. In the end they didn't need much persuading to fund this because they didn't have anything else to offer and because it tends to make life easier for them if they agree with the parents.

So Catherine did a three-day assessment, and this made her realise for the first time that she wouldn't have her comfort zone at home forever. The hardest thing was getting her to realise that going to Lufton was not the same as leaving home, her room would always be hers and would always be the same as when she left it and came back in the holidays. But she needed a huge amount of reassurance about this. In fact, this whole issue of her room has been an ongoing thing with her – i.e. difficulties when going on holiday and packing a suitcase and her not liking this and wanting the room to be left untouched (to do with feeling secure), so rather than her taking the things she needed for Lufton out of her room at home, we deliberately bought new things specifically for Lufton. So we were dreading taking her there in this context. In the end it went incredibly well, though she needed constant reassurance and kept asking why we wanted her to leave home.

When she arrived there she had totally normal reactions about not knowing anyone and being new. But soon she started to meet people and she was fine when we left her. She phoned us the first three nights and was still fine, and she has written lots of letters all saying the right things, but going over the same ground repeatedly (which perhaps shows she's not ready yet for full independence). The picture I'm painting is that Catherine has been brought up as part of a loving family with three sisters (aged seventeen, fifteen and eleven in 2006), with loving parents who have been married for twenty-seven years, and that she has been treated much the same as her sisters, but has needed more attention, particularly in these latter years, for when she was younger her differences were less marked.

In 2000 I decided to leave work after twenty-three years with Lloyds TSB. My decision may have had something to do with worrying about Catherine and her future. At this point Catherine was fourteen and a half and had just moved to a special school from a mainstream secondary school because it had become apparent there that her learning disability was a problem and that the gap between her and the other pupils was widening. It was particularly relevant then that she was the eldest child because we didn't have the comparison of what normal children would be doing at that stage.

She'd gone to the mainstream secondary school in the first place because we had wanted her to stay with her peer group, plus the non-teaching assistant (NTA) who'd been with her at primary school was going to go with her to secondary school. But we misjudged how much the gap between Catherine and her peers would widen. And by giving her the crutch of the NTA, she was even more isolated – a fish out of water. The special needs coordinator at school admitted they just couldn't provide the level of support needed. The special school was much better equipped to cope with her.

In the last five years I've applied more of a business approach to dealing with Catherine's affairs – probably annoying people at the college in the process – challenging their targets; for example, that Catherine should get to her lessons on time. My view is that one target should be to help her to understand the concept and process of planning her time, not just about being on time. Being off work and being a house husband, I constantly worried about securing Catherine's future, and the fundraising I have done for Mencap (and will continue to do) was all about reassuring myself that if I ever wanted to call on Mencap's help I would have done something for them already.

I've raised a little over £20k. People say that this is a lot, but in the banking context it's peanuts.

In five to ten years' time Catherine can be more independent, but if you talk in those time terms to social services, they just can't handle it. It's really hard trying to get them and Connexions to see the options. Another difficult thing is that – as any parent will tell you – other people's (for example, teachers') opinions of their kids are very different from how they are at home, where they can let off steam. This is magnified several times for Catherine as she has a learning disability. And as she gets older her emotions bubble over. By the end of her three years at sixth-form college she became more confused and upset and uncertain and she wasn't handling the idea that she couldn't do a job. She kept coming up with new ideas for her career, such as, 'I'm going to be a solicitor,' and was worrying about leaving home. She was also asking about other awkward things, such as 'when can I learn to drive?' or 'when will I able to get married?'

Regarding jobs, Julie, my wife, investigated voluntary work at an old people's home. Catherine's been helping out there for the last year and has been trusted like a member of staff, doing valuable jobs, including chatting to the old people. This is a real niche activity for her, but it could never turn into a job because she didn't have experience of living away from home and didn't really understand the commitment required to do a job (she would go in to the home as and when she felt like it) but this was all good experience about the world of work.

All the above problems show why Lufton is just right for her, for she is experiencing:

- living away from home,
- work experience,
- a secure environment – a halfway house.

The key learning point will be about handling money – numeracy – which, hopefully, Lufton will teach her. Her funding is at present for only one year given, reluctantly, by the local Learning and Skills Council but we trust this can be increased.

What has been the effect on family life?
We've already noticed a big difference. My wife and I have been able to spend time doing things together and this isn't because she needed round-the-clock care, rather it was because we always felt that we had to try to get her to be more active (which is very difficult once someone is an adult) and do things, and so couldn't really settle into doing what we wanted to do. Knowing that she was at Lufton being well looked after meant we could relax and get on with life.

What about her sisters?

The absence of Catherine hasn't really changed them. Of late, they'd being giving her a much wider berth because she'd been so difficult, but they chose to go to Lufton to see her off, and the youngest one even wanted to go there herself! However, Catherine's letters home include questions about her sisters, which shows she is thinking about them and has affection for them even though she can find it hard to show, especially seeing sisters overtaking her in everything they do. Despite this, there is genuine sisterly affection. The way Catherine has reacted at times would have made most siblings run away, but it just hasn't happened like that.

And, after Lufton?

Well, some fear that she might regress, though she'll be in a much better position to move on to the next stage of her life.

And what are your conclusions?

Well, I'll list them. First – a constant theme – Catherine is lucky as she's got us to fight for her; we're reasonably affluent and well educated, but this isn't always the case for other families and carers. Second, she is lucky to be part of a family, but it can be hard for her to cope with not being able to do the same things as her sisters. Third, from her sisters' point of view, they don't need to think about what learning disability is – they don't see it as a label. They see her as she is on a day-to-day basis. They see her 'condition' purely in terms of how she behaves. They will grow up with a greater insight of what learning disability really means and will be more tolerant and understanding. We've seen this in the way that they treat Catherine's friends – as equals. Plus they also understand why their parents aren't always on top form.

Postscript

A year ago Catherine was really struggling to cope with the idea of leaving home to go to Lufton. We were struggling to get funding. A year on, Catherine has won her struggle in the sense that she accepts that she can go away and when she comes home it is all still there for her, including us. Our struggle to secure funding beyond year one of the three-year course has finally succeeded; just two weeks before the end of the third term we had an agreement to fund the remaining two years. Our goal is for Catherine to gain enough confidence and skills in those two years to move from Lufton to some sort of community living and have some sort of meaningful job. We shall see.

CHAPTER 23

Another Parent's Story

The Rt Hon. The Viscount Tenby
Secretary to the All Party Parliamentary Group on Learning Disability

When Brian Rix, my cross-bench colleague and friend in the Lords, asked me to contribute to this publication I hesitated. Not only is it inevitably an intensely personal area, but I was doubtful whether I could bring any fresh or original insights into what, over recent years, has become a well-covered area of interest and concern. What finally persuaded me otherwise was that, first, a sharing of personal experience with others must in some degree be beneficial, and secondly, my involvement as trustee and Chairman of a residential home for women with a learning disability in north Hampshire enables me to set down some of the problems from, as it were, the other side of the picture.

Our daughter, Sara, who is now forty-eight, was born with benign congenital hypertonia. By school age it was apparent that she had special needs due to learning disability. In addition, because of her medical condition, at the age of eleven she had to have an operation to straighten her ankles and this had to be repeated at seventeen. So much for the medical background.

It was clear that Sara would have to go to a special school and one was found in Surrey, which involved boarding during the week. The school, which no longer exists in its old form, was not dedicated solely to girls with a learning disability, but also embraced those from difficult home backgrounds and the like. Looking back, it must have been daunting for Sara to adapt to these conditions, but with characteristic courage and good humour adapt she did, supported, it must be added, by caring and committed staff. It was not a perfect solution, but it was the only one available to us at the time.

After leaving at sixteen, Sara lived at home and was enrolled at Alton Bay Centre. In the seventies, county social services often tended to 'think big' and the custom-built centre, on the outskirts of the county town of Alton and facing the famous Lord Mayor Treloar Hospital, was a focal point, drawing in clients from across east and north Hampshire. The centre was run by a dedicated staff under a highly motivated and charismatic Head, whose views did not always coincide with those of the more cautious social services in Winchester. Although, in current thinking, it was not an entirely satisfactory way of meeting needs, the fact remains that for most clients it was an enriching and fulfilling experience due entirely to the excellence and commitment of the staff.

Times were, however, changing. Starting in the eighties, the emphasis began to shift towards smaller groupings, not only in residential living (more of which later) but also to smaller centres nearer to clients' homes and therefore involving less daily travelling. At the same time it also became apparent that, with old age rapidly approaching, we would be irresponsible not to make arrangements for Sara. We accordingly embarked on a programme of visits to various homes with a view to seeing whether there would be one suitable for her, bearing in mind that sheltered accommodation which involved any large measure of independence would be unsuitable because of her disability. For example, although she could more than hold her own socially, certain basic skills – telling the time, being aware of the value of money, tying her own shoelaces – were more or less beyond her.

The solution came from an unexpected, but very welcome because of its proximity, quarter. There was a residential home for women with physical and learning disabilities only five miles away and most of the residents also attended the day centre to which Sara had been going. Accordingly, she had been well known to them for many years. It also happened that I had been invited to become a trustee some years earlier, so I had knowledge of its situation, ethos and attitude to life generally. Vacancies were a rarity and there was accordingly no waiting list on which to put Sara's name. However, sadly and unexpectedly, one of the residents died and I asked my fellow trustees if they would accept my daughter, to which they readily agreed. She has now been a resident for more than ten years and it is thankfully very much a second home for her, spending the week there and the weekends with us. In addition, she attends a day centre in the neighbouring town of Fleet and here her self-confidence has been steadily built up to a remarkable degree, thanks to the skill of the staff there.

At the start of this piece I mentioned wearing my second hat as Chairman of the Trustees of a home and this has been what I can only describe as a full and demanding experience. The home was opened in the early 1950s by a single lady who had an adopted daughter with a learning disability. With the introduction of new regulations in 1987 relating to the amount of space and light per resident, the trustees were left with a major decision: either to build a new wing or to reluctantly ask some residents, who had been promised a home for life, to leave. To the trustees the latter was never an option. Despite the daunting implications of financing a large addition to the original building, the task was completed and, thanks to the support of the local community and the generosity of others, paid for after a relatively short time.

Owing to changes in social service policy by successive Governments in recent years, homes with twenty residents are now frowned upon and I think it is true to say that ten, or even fewer, would be regarded as the optimum size. So, after all the expenditure incurred, we are back to square one. And this factor alone, I would suggest, leads to a perfectly legitimate question: after expenditure on a substantial scale what guarantee is there that some twenty years down the line there will not be another change of fashion by Government or social services? Waste, alas, is not often a word to be found in the vocabulary of either.

Perhaps I can illustrate the dilemma by reference to the home of which I am Chairman. We are now the 'wrong' size. Accordingly, we do not get referrals from Social Services either within, or outside, the county. If a client dies, or has to leave because she has to be in, say, a full-time nursing home, our gaps are accordingly not filled. Revenue goes down in consequence, but we find it difficult to attract staff so we have to use agencies, which are more expensive. We are caught between a rock and a hard place and it is a difficult situation to turn round. All organisations working in this field will confirm that there are acute staff shortages throughout the United Kingdom and this at a time when many of the new strategies, if anything, require greater staffing levels. In future, units being built may have to take account of this factor by including staff accommodation in their plans in order, say, to attract staff from places like Eastern Europe, whose countries have a tradition of working in this field.

I do not think that there can be many who mourn the passing of the old, Victorian piles of fifty or more years ago with their grim facades and soullessness. But meaningful relationships were forged there and there was in many of them a feeling of community. Accordingly, whenever authority recommends a breaking up of the old order and values, it is important to ensure that something very much better and more life-enhancing is put in its place. Living in the community is an important and noble aspiration, but before it is embarked upon too thoughtlessly in a surge of euphoria certain factors must be taken into account. First, and I suppose most obviously, the clients must be able to live in the community without danger to themselves or others. Secondly, the community must be able to accept and welcome these unsure venturers into a new world. Sadly, there have been reports of antagonism to such settlements in the past on the grounds of irrational fear, the possibility of a drop in the value of local housing as a consequence of their arrival, and so on. Such misgivings are almost always the result of ignorance and inability to cope with something of which they have no experience, but these are nettles which have to be grasped and there is no substitute for gentle education and good public relations in dealing with them.

What effect has Sara had on the lives of myself and my family? It has inevitably affected all of us in different ways; I would say very much for the better. From a very early age my other daughter and son have been fiercely protective of her interests and would resent anything they perceived as a slight to her, however innocent that might have been. That love today is as strong as ever it was in the early days. Obviously the greatest burden falls on the mother in such circumstances and in this context both Sara and I have been very fortunate. The amount of extra work and worry will be familiar to all facing the same circumstances, but it is a critical factor surely that there should be at all times a totally committed or caring parent, a demand which precludes much social activity which others take as a matter of course. It is useless to pretend that being in such a situation does not affect one's social life. Unless one is dealing with someone similarly placed, who has knowledge of what is involved, it is sometimes difficult to get across the reason for the refusal of an invitation, or the need to get home by a certain time. Travelling, too, can present difficulties, particularly on long-distance flights.

Sara has a happy and loving disposition and can on occasion astound those around her with knowledge that no one knew she possessed. All the more reason therefore to stretch her and others like her. Parents can often be over-protective, due to their proximity to the person over many years, but we have seen Sara respond to challenges which we ourselves would not have thought possible. What effect has Sara had on our lives? Quiet simply, she has enriched the lives of all of us and in doing so, opened the doors of another world. It has truly been an enriching and humbling experience.

CHAPTER 24

The Down's Syndrome Association

People with Down's syndrome make up a significant number of those with a learning disability. And as Mencap has many members with this condition, I felt this all-encompassing book would not be complete unless mention was made of the Down's Syndrome Association which was formed in 1970.

The Down's Syndrome Association (DSA) which was formed in 1970, began as a local support group for families who had a child with Down's syndrome. Since those days it has grown to become a national organisation with over 19,000 members, giving advice, support, information and training to a wide variety of people. The DSA has also become a recognised voice in the world of learning disability, often working with other learning disability charities, such as Mencap, to influence Government policy and champion the rights of people with Down's syndrome.

Much has changed in the thirty-five years since the DSA was founded. In that time the average life expectancy of someone with the condition has more than doubled. These days all children can expect a long school career, whereas before the 1970 Education Act they were deemed ineducable. Not everything has changed, however, and people with Down's syndrome are not given the same chances as everyone else, and the DSA continues to work to achieve those ends.

The Chief Executive of the Down's Syndrome Association, Carol Boys, first became interested in the issues facing people with a learning disability when she had a son, Alex, who has Down's syndrome, in 1983. Her struggle to obtain a suitable education for Alex led her to become a more active member of her local parent support group, and eventually led to her appointment as Chief Executive, a position she has held since 1996. Previously she had been the Association's Chairman. While she was working in that capacity, the DSA acquired its most hard-working patron, Damon Hill. Damon and his wife Georgie had a son, Oliver, in 1989, who also has Down's syndrome. When Oliver was born they contacted the DSA, as many new parents do, for advice and support. When Damon subsequently became a Formula One racing driver he offered his services to the charity and, along with Georgie, who became a trustee at the same time, has worked hard to raise awareness of Down's syndrome and the DSA ever since.

Alex

Carol Boys
Director, the Down's Syndrome Association

If I could have known, twenty-two years ago, in those awful dark days immediately after the birth of Alex, my son with Down's syndrome, just how dramatically my life was going to change, I think it would have helped me a lot. I don't think that I would have believed it, but change it certainly did. He was born by emergency Caesarean after I developed nerve-rackingly high blood pressure. At that point, I was the sole focus of medical attention. Alex just lay quietly in his cot, maybe not feeding too well, but making no fuss. He was the welcome completion of our family, joining me, his older brother Andrew and my husband Paul. My only concern was to get better and get home.

The first inkling I had of something being wrong with our perfect baby was when a nurse, fussing around my bed two days after Alex was born, said chirpily, 'Oh, I don't know what was happening last night. The Senior House Officer was having a very close look at your son, I can't think what she was doing with him.' Two hours later, the doctor who had shown such unnatural nocturnal interest in my baby perched herself on the edge of the bed. Full of foreboding, I was desperate to have my husband Paul with me, but he was due to visit that afternoon and no one, it appeared, was prepared to wait until we could be together. One of my most vivid memories of those agonising first few weeks was of her quizzing me. 'Do you think Alex looks different at all? How does he compare to your older son at birth? Do you think there is anything unusual about the shape of his eyes?' Completely perplexed, I blurted out: 'What on earth are you talking about? Does he have Down's syndrome or something?' She demurred, but recommended a meeting with the consultant.

Later that day, Paul and I were summoned to see the consultant, who was already in a little room examining Alex. He reassured us by saying that he was '99.9 per cent sure' that Alex didn't have Down's syndrome, but recommended a blood test to rule it out entirely. After all the initial confusion, we were too shell-shocked to be relieved. I was at home with Alex some days later when the telephone call came. The message from the consultant was that he was 'very sorry'. As far as I could tell, he was extremely sorry that he had been wrong and apparently even more sorry that Alex did have Down's syndrome, after all. Despite the warnings and the emotional tension of the previous few days, the news was devastating.

You would never believe it now, with stories about new and better antenatal tests being reported in the newspapers almost weekly, but in the early eighties the possibility of having a child with Down's syndrome just wasn't the issue it is today. It simply never occurred to me, as a thirty-three-year-old relatively young mum, that Alex might be born with the condition. Like all the other mothers, I was vaguely aware of the amniocentesis test, which was something mysterious and rather gruesome involving a needle in the womb. That was only offered to the really 'old' mothers because, surely, they were the only ones affected, we reasoned complacently. Anyway, it must be an incredibly rare condition (we would all have concluded if we had even bothered to discuss it), because you hardly ever saw anyone with Down's syndrome just walking down the street.

Wrong, wrong, wrong. Of course, the statistics just trip off the tongue now – how, in fact, 80 per cent of babies with Down's syndrome are born to women under thirty-five – women like me. As for it being an incredibly rare condition, that depends on your point of view. The fact is that now most of us know someone with Down's syndrome, perhaps serving in the local shop or living in the next street.

People with Down's syndrome are no longer expected to live their lives in institutions, tucked away out of sight and living half a life. As a teenager, I had worked as a volunteer in a psychiatric hospital and remembered seeing many patients with Down's syndrome, blank-eyed after decades in institutional care. Other vague memories were of rare sightings of adults in childish clothes walking around the shops behind elderly parents. Although many of our friends were robust and supportive, a colleague at my husband's office mentioned a friend of his who had a daughter with Down's syndrome. 'They managed to keep her until she was five,' he said, 'but then they had to give in and send her away.' 'What on earth happened when she was five?' I remember saying frantically to Paul, looking down at our tiny, vulnerable son. Here I was, looking after a baby whose needs were, to all intents and purposes like any other, but apparently, in a few short years, a monster was going to replace him, testing our family to its limits.

To make matters worse, the first visit from our GP was a devastating blow. She breezed in, took one look at Alex and turned round to me saying, 'Well, he's certainly not a poor grade mongol, Mrs Boys'. Sadly, I think that she was genuinely trying to be positive.

We frantically searched around looking for information (of course there was no Internet access in those days). Just by sheer fluke, I came across a book by Professor Cliff Cunningham and the whole family read it from cover to cover. Looking back now, we couldn't have read anything better. Cliff was a staunch advocate of early intervention for babies with Down's syndrome and we very quickly realised our baby would reach his milestones, but much later than his brother, and maybe some he might never reach at all. We decided then and there that we would try to give Alex all the opportunities that we could to develop his full potential. We joined the Down's Syndrome Association, as instructed by Cliff in his book. This was very much against my better judgement; under normal circumstances I would have run a mile from a membership organisation.

My first encounter with another family and their child with Down's syndrome was a real turning point for me. I remember going along to a house not far from my home on a sunny afternoon. I was invited into the garden where there were five children bouncing on a very large trampoline, four boys and a little girl. The children were oblivious to me and my tiny baby and it was only when their mum came out of the kitchen with drinks and biscuits for them all that I realised that the little girl had Down's syndrome. Her name was Jacqueline and she was nine, her language was great and she could read books far more advanced than my five year old. This was such an uplifting experience; I rushed home to tell everyone I could think of about this young girl that I had met. I now know that Jaqueline was and still is a very able young woman with Down's syndrome and not everyone with the condition will develop such skills, but that didn't matter to us then, it just gave us the boost that we needed to be really positive about our new son.

Alex continued to progress, managing to escape all of the various medical problems he could have had. He was in fact a picture of health and we considered ourselves to be very lucky. He spoke very early and by the time he was three years old he had a good vocabulary and could make himself understood. However, nothing could have prepared us for the battles that were to come over his education.

Alex went to playgroup with sons and daughters of friends. We were fortunate enough to live in the university area of Reading, which had a fantastic mix of families from all walks of life and all parts of the world. It had never occurred to us that Alex joining his new friends at school would be a problem. We couldn't have been more wrong. An educational psychologist friend of mine told us that there had never been a successful placement of a child with Down's syndrome in mainstream school in Berkshire. I was devastated.

I think my first encounter with the professionals that were called in to assess Alex's educational needs was the start of the passion for campaigning which is now such a huge part of my life. They all seemed so negative. I was told by the educational psychologist that children with Down's syndrome very rarely learnt to read or write and those that did were very much the exception. I knew from what I had read that this was rubbish. I found myself battling with the LEA because the headteacher of our local primary school was quite happy to take Alex into her nursery and all my friends and their children wanted Alex to be there, but he had this label 'Down's syndrome' and that made everything much more complicated. Eventually he did go into the primary school nursery with his friends and then into the infants class, but with no support for the first two years because that's how long it took the local authority to realise that we were not going to back down and send him to the local special school several miles down the road. To us as a family, it seemed ridiculous to take Alex out of his circle of friends and away from his brother, who was already established in the primary school.

Alex did manage quite well in mainstream school, eventually receiving the extra support he needed up to the age of eleven. He continued to make friends and develop the tremendous social skills and sense of humour that he is so well known for today. Increasing difficulties with the academic side of life, and the fact that most of his friends went off to grammar school, brought about the end of his career at mainstream school. Depressed about being separated from his primary school friends (although many are still in touch), he repeated a year and lost confidence and self-esteem. On the advice of Berkshire Education Authority, we visited Boveridge House Special School. We were told that there we would find a peer group that Alex could relate to and an ethos that we would approve of. We arrived on a visit to the school to find all the children playing a game of rounders against the local middle school. They were having a great time and Alex was asked to join the group; he loved it. The school had its own stables and there were cows and sheep everywhere. Chickens wandered in and out of the classrooms and the students all seemed to have a great sense of purpose. The only problem as far as we could see with this school was the location. It was in Dorset and this meant that Alex would have to board. The prospect of weekly boarding did not seem to deter him; in fact, the following term, after two weeks of coming home, he announced that he would like to stay for the weekends because it was more fun with his friends.

Alex continued to enjoy his time at Boveridge for the next two years. I, on the other hand, found it very difficult to come to terms with the fact that he was so far away. The school was, to say the least, quirky. The students were a mixture of privately funded and LEA pupils, some who came from very wealthy backgrounds and others whose family circumstances were very different. The school was run by a lady called Miss Harper in a beautiful Grade II-listed Georgian house rented from the Gascoine Cecil Estate in Cranborne, Dorset. In its heyday, the school catered for up to seventy pupils living in the school itself and in cottages around the village. Pupils were referred to the school from all over the country and indeed all over the world. Alex was extremely happy there and we were happy with his progress. Although Miss Harper was obviously coming to the end of her career, we assumed that she would see Alex through the next few years. However, this was not to be the case and in fact towards the end of his second year we began to get the feeling that there were problems. We had been told at Alex's annual review that Ofsted were unhappy with the way that the school did not conform to the National Curriculum, and it was soon after the beginning of the new school year that we heard the devastating news: Miss Harper announced her retirement and the fact that the school would have to close at Easter following a report from Ofsted. She told everyone that she would be giving up the lease on the school and all the pupils would have to leave. This was a devastating blow to everyone; there were twenty-two children in the school and the vast majority were funded by LEAs. Where would all the children go, and what would happen to the friendships they had made? More importantly for us, once again Alex would be wrenched away from his peers; where to next?

I contacted the DfES and asked them if anything could be done to save the school. I had been given a copy of the Ofsted report, so I knew that the school had fallen into 'Special Measures' for a number of reasons, including the need to improve the facilities and the accommodation in the school. I was told by the DfES that Boveridge had been an important school in the circle of provision over the years and that the Department would be very keen to see it turned around. I decided then and there that the school had to be saved. I enlisted the help of a group of parents, including my husband Paul. We registered the school as a charity, put together a business plan and I set about trying to find a sponsor to put up the £500,000 needed to make the necessary changes to the accommodation. I remember going to Hatfield House to see the agent for Lord Cranborne. Would they give us a thirty-year lease on the property? Who were we? They didn't know us from Adam. Miraculously, the Estate agreed to give us a lease with three years rent free and I managed somehow to secure funds from the Philip Green Memorial Trust to upgrade the accommodation. More importantly, we found a new headteacher who would be able to put the all-important action plan in place for education in the school. Five years later, I'm very proud to say that Boveridge came out of Special Measures and the Philip Green Memorial School is now a thriving and well-respected residential special school for children with a variety of special needs. The most important thing is that we have managed to retain the wonderful ethos that first drew us to the school as a place for Alex.

Alex left school three years ago and he is now living with seven other people with learning disabilities in a house run by Robert Owen Communities in Newton Abbot, Devon. He is a well-adjusted, confident twenty-two year old, who has the same hopes and dreams as everyone else. He has a job and a hectic social life, he is fiercely independent and his approach to life is very much 'if you want it, go out and get it'. Although I would have preferred to have had him at home with us when he was younger, I think the fact that he made the break from home at thirteen has helped him to enjoy his independence now. As he keeps reminding me – 'I'm an adult now!'

My own career developed when, having joined the Down's Syndrome Association when Alex was young and having worked with parents at a local level, I found myself being asked to stand for election as a trustee. Eventually I was elected as National Chair of the organisation. Some years later, I was asked to by my fellow trustees to take on a caretaker Director role as a volunteer, following the sudden departure of the Director because of health problems in pregnancy. This was meant to be a temporary situation to cover an emergency, and yet here I am ten years later. I just don't seem to be able to resist a challenge.

Fate seems to have intervened in our lives a lot over the last twenty-two years. The most recent example of this occurred four years ago when Paul, then working as a property developer, came home and announced that his team had bought the old Victorian Normansfield hospital site in Teddington. Their intention was to build a prestigious housing development around the old listed hospital building, which very few people knew contained a beautiful Victorian hand-painted theatre. The listed building would be handed over to a charity as part of a section 106 planning agreement. I very quickly realised the building he was referring to was the family home and hospital of Dr John Langdon Down. It had been a place where people with a learning disability were looked after and educated by that great Victorian pioneer. He was the first to realise that some of his patients shared similar characteristics; in fact, he was carrying out early research into what we now call Down's syndrome. What Paul and I didn't know at that time was that there were other people with a keen interest in the fate of this building, not least of all Lord Rix, whose daughter Shelley had been a patient there when Normansfield was an NHS long-stay hospital. I first began to take a real interest in Normansfield when Professor Conor Ward, author of *John Langdon Down, a Caring Pioneer*, and medical adviser to Down's Syndrome Ireland, contacted me. Professor Ward knew nothing about my personal connection with the developers. He was worried that the building was going to be turned into a theatre museum by the Theatres Trust and he felt that Dr Langdon Down's work would be lost and forgotten. He also told me about the wonderful archive of Dr Langdon Down's photographs and papers that he had managed to rescue from the derelict building. Yet another challenge presented itself: to form a trust and find the funds to bring Normansfield back to life, and to tell the story of Dr Langdon Down and his pioneering work. Thanks to Lord Rix, Professor Ward, Richmond Borough Council and of course my husband and Laing Homes Ltd, the Langdon Down Centre is now a great building. It is a busy conference venue, the headquarters of the Down's Syndrome Association and is regularly used by other local community groups. Dr Langdon Down's papers are being archived and they will soon be available on the web for all to see (www.langdondown

centre.org.uk). People come from all over the world to see the theatre and to learn about the work of Dr Langdon Down and his family.

Having children can be a challenge. Having a child with Down's syndrome brings its own special challenges. I am so grateful to my son Alex for giving me the opportunity to make a contribution to the world of learning disability. I hope that I have been able to help to make a difference for other families like mine, and I hope that I will carry on for a little while yet.

Oliver

Damon Hill
President, Down's Syndrome Association

I first met Oliver in the hospital at Hammersmith; lots of long faces – except for his. He just wiggled there while they (the staff and doctors) stuck pins in his foot and things like that, so they could be sure that he was in fact a 'Down's' baby. Obviously, they did all the right things as best they could, but inevitably it came across as though the worst thing in the world had just happened. Georgie, my wife, was in shock but quickly took Oliver under her wing and off we went to start our new lives together. The DSA was crucial to us in providing the colouring-in of what was a very blank picture at the hospital. The odd thing is that this story is repeated over and over with parents of Down's syndrome babies. It's as if the hospital feels responsible for what has happened. What has happened? A baby unlike most has been born; a human baby, with emotions and needs and a personality that will probably be forceful enough to make the world compromise to suit it, rather than the other way round. You can't argue with a person with Down's syndrome if they believe something is not right. Gandhi has nothing on Oliver.

Slowly the relationship grows away from suspicion and fear of the unknown to acceptance and love of the infant. I must say that I fell in love with Oliver the first day I saw him clean. All babies are a bit slimy at first, but he scrubbed up lovely. I knew the first time I looked into his eyes, and he looked at me, that we were going to have a lot of fun together. And we have! I've been skiing with him, cooking with him, dancing, we've been to the Bootleg Beatles together, we know every Disney video, song and DVD that has ever been made, all the Warner Brothers cartoons, the *Wizard of Oz* inside out. Shall I go on? He swims like a seal. He will stay under for an alarming amount of time, only to surface with an expression of complete calm and contentment. I can't get him in a boat because he had one bad experience, so now he will force himself into a state of self-inflicted panic until he gets an ice-cream or drink of Coke. Then he will nervously board the vessel, only to choose the best moment to create the maximum havoc with the semi-digested treats. He did this routine once on board a multimillion-pound motor boat we had generously been invited to purchase. The white upholstery was not what we were looking for, especially after Olly had given it 'the treatment'. See what I mean about him getting his own way?

If there is one thing that you can count on with Oliver, it is that you have to go one step at a time. The first year I took him skiing, I managed to get the boots on. The next year, we tried the skis. The next year he moved enough to gain sufficient momentum to cause a minor catastrophe, involving a deckchair, table and someone's hot chocolate. He was beginning to enjoy it! After a few more sorties, he was hooked. Literally, since the only way to prevent him from becoming Britain's next Konrad Bartelski was to keep him attached to two lengths of dog leash and a mountaineering harness. This enabled me to steer him quite effectively down the slopes without too much strain. However, just as he was starting to get really good, he decided he didn't like skiing, after all. I will have to content myself with the sheer joy of moments like this one, when he first tried the chairlift: a few feet into the trip and as the chair was rising Poppins-like into the air, he yelled out at the top of his voice, 'I'm flying!' I cling dearly to the belief that he truly thought he was flying as he said it, but if I know Oliver at all, he was probably pulling my leg. Another time, he escaped at the top of the drag-lift just before I had reached him to clip on the safety harness. The lift monitor, thinking he was helping, stopped the lift so I had no way to reach Oliver before he set off on another one of his hair-raising adventures. I tried running across the deep snow between the lift and the piste that Oliver was now on and picking up a good speed. This is difficult wearing skis. So, waddling like a electrocuted penguin, I hurled myself onto the slope and tucked into my 'plummet like a comet' position in a desperate attempt to catch up with someone already travelling close to their 'V-Max'. God came to my rescue as Oliver stayed upright (despite my screeching, 'F-A-L-L D-O-W-N, O-L-I-V-E-R! F-A-L-L D-O-W-N!'), as I vainly chased him down the slope, which must be the only slope in the world with 500 yards of flat run-off.

Eventually, I caught him. He was shaking and laughing with excitement and fear. I wonder if that's what put him off?

We have just looked at the moon together. It's a thin slice of white brilliance low in the evening sky and looks a bit like a nail clipping. I get excited and command everyone to come and join me outside, where it is –2°C. Not many takers. Then out comes Oliver with the telescope. He will not be marginalised. I never knew astronomy was one of his interests, but right now he makes Patrick Moore look like a dilettante. 'Beautiful,' he says. Oliver is seventeen now. He has three siblings: a brother eighteen months younger, and two sisters of ten and seven. Everyone just treats him as Oliver. There is a small degree of autistic-type behaviour. He likes to be alone quite a lot. He repeats songs and film scripts to himself. He has a virtual world in his head which occasionally escapes. This can be slightly annoying when you are trying to think. It also underlines the importance of human interaction and activities which bring him into reality. Isn't he a bit like you and me? ('Nowhere Man': the Beatles)

What will the future hold for Oliver? Georgie and I hope there will be a world fit for all kinds of people with varied levels of ability. To get there we need people like Brian Rix of Mencap and Carol Boys of the DSA and all their teams of helpers. But it will not work without a general and all-pervading attitude of help and cooperation for one another within society. This invariably means people need time. Life in the West can be very hectic. Trying to get Oliver to understand 'hurry up' is like trying to make the grass grow by pulling it out of the ground. Life needs to slow down, which perhaps is why we often find isolated communities of people with extra special needs. But, practically, we can't and most don't want to live in remote places. Within towns and cities there are precious few places of refuge, but this could be improved. I would like to imagine Oliver going to the shops on his own one day, and maybe looking forward to social activities. The thought that he will atrophy in some God awful institution just watching television is a nightmare that Brian knows all about, and changed for thousands of people like Oliver into a more rewarding reality. Perhaps global warming will reduce the number of cars on the road? There is an old person with Down's syndrome who lives near us and goes about on a trike. It has a number plate with his name on it: Nige. He wears a helmet and a brightly coloured jacket. Oliver can ride a trike. I'd like to think he could be independent like Nige.

Afterword

The Rt Hon. David Cameron MP
Leader of HM Opposition
Vice-Chairman, All Party Parliamentary Group
on Learning Disability

It is a privilege to be able to add a few closing thoughts to what has been a most impressive tribute to the work of Mencap.

I have worked closely with Mencap and other organisations in my capacity as Vice-Chair of the All Party Parliamentary Group on Learning Disability. For me there are two main lessons from this book.

The first is that, for Mencap's founders, the world of 2006 would have been unrecognisable. To read of the challenges faced by parents of children with a learning disability in the 1950s and 1960s is to appreciate just how far services – and, even more fundamentally, attitudes – have been transformed. It does great credit to that generation of parents that so many of them did so much to bring that transformation about. Personal recollections, such as those of Paul Annear, and the extraordinary life story of pioneer Joey Deacon, further remind us of how far things have come.

But the second lesson is that, down the ages, people with a learning disability, and those who are close to them, have also shared many experiences and emotions. That is true not least for parents. As Sheila Hollins puts it so clearly: parents should trust their judgements as the most powerful advocates of their children's needs.

As the father of Ivan, who has epilepsy and cerebral palsy, I found the accounts by Simon Barnes, Jonathan Rix and Carmel Kinnear three of the most inspiring articles I have ever read. They show that some needs will always remain the same, especially the need to understand and support families, from simply finding the right words at the right time to providing the services and respite care on which they depend.

It has clearly been a mammoth task commissioning and arranging such a wide array of articles. That task fell to Brian Rix. He completed it as successfully as ever. The result is a lasting tribute to all those who have made Mencap what it is – from the earliest pioneers to all its workers, fundraisers and supporters today. And not least to Brian himself. Clearly there is much still left to do in the years ahead. But the many thousands of lives which have already been transformed stand as a more lasting tribute still.

Learning Disability Time Line
Spinal column for a history of leglislation
on learning disability

Researched by Brian McGinnis OBE
Member of the Royal Society of Medicine's Intellectual Disability Forum

Introductory note: The first principle of the 1904–08 Royal Commission on the Care and Control of the Feeble-minded neatly sums up the overarching purpose of most laws on people with a learning disability: 'Our first principle is that persons who cannot take a part in the struggle of life owing to mental defect . . . should be afforded by the state such special protection as may be suited to their needs.' (Protection includes protection of rights.)

At different periods in history this has meant different things, depending on the social and economic circumstances of the time, and of course on how long people with a learning disability lived. (When most of those more severely disabled died in childhood, provision for severely disabled adults was a less pressing concern.) What is most striking is that precisely the same issues of capacity for decision making, substitute decision making, financial affairs, protection from abuse, civil rights and obligations, and health and social care, were being addressed over a thousand years ago.

Greek and Roman times and other early civilisations: We have terminology to describe learning disability from Classical times (Greek *idios*, Latin *idiota*) and evidence of a range of attitudes from putting to death through amused tolerance to respect. (Seneca's wife kept a blind imbecile [*fatua*] as a companion.)

The Bible: It is by no means clear that the Bible refers specifically to learning disability. In the Authorised Version (1611) St Paul refers to comforting the feeble-minded (First Letter to the Thessalonians Chapter 5 verse 14), but later versions translate this as spiritual not mental weakness.

The reference by St Paul, in his First Letter to the Corinthians Chapter 1, to God choosing the weak to shame the strong has also been claimed by later Christians as referring to the role of people with a learning disability in the Church. Again, this is unlikely to be a specific reference.

In the Old Testament, Leviticus Chapter 19 verse 31 enjoins respect for old people, and Leviticus Chapter 19 verse 14 and Deuteronomy Chapter 27 verse 18 urge patience with deaf people and avoiding making things difficult for blind people. On the other hand, Leviticus 21 forbids the involvement of anyone blind, lame, disfigured or deformed in officiating as a priest.

The most convincing exposition of the Old and New Testaments is that in portraying a God who cares about people, including marginalised people, they encourage followers of that God to care about people, including those with physical or mental disabilities. That has been the majority view in both Jewish and Christian history, with the extremes ranging from the view that people with intellectual impairment are holy innocents and due special reverence to the view that they have no consciences and are the devil's progeny.

In the fourth century St Nicholas, Bishop of Myra, cared for idiots and imbeciles.

The Koran: The Koran dates from about AD 610. In the Chapter on Women – the chapter traditionally numbered 4 – there is a reference which seems to cover men as well as women: 'Do not give to the feeble-minded the property with which Allah has entrusted you for their support, but maintain and clothe them with its proceeds, and give them good advice.'

AD 939: (Athelstan) Writ to King's reeves to provide food and clothing for those who are destitute on the King's estates.

1247: Bethlehem Royal Hospital established in Bishopsgate. (Saxon monasteries cared for sick. The Normans had almshouses, bede houses, *maisons de dieu* and lazar houses. On the whole, medieval hospitals did not knowingly care for people with mental disabilities. We know of only two sixteenth-century hospitals catering specifically for idiots. The role of the monasteries in providing for people with a learning disability or mental health problems is unclear. The inspection reports long before Henry VIII's phased dissolution suggest that their role was not substantial. Religious orders probably played a more significant role in residential provision in comparatively modern times.)

1275: (Edward I) Protection of freehold for those of good memory (*de bone memoire*). We have a later reference to, but no extant copy of, a law of Edward I giving the King the right to take custody of the lands of idiots (*idiotarum et stultorum*). This must have derived from older feudal tradition.

1322: (Edward II) Justices to determine management of property of idiots (*etas fatuitas seu quicunque actus defectus*).

1324: (Edward II) The King to have custody of lands of natural fools (*fatuorum naturalium*). Separate provision was made for those who had had capacity but had lost it (*aliquis qui prius habuit memoriam et intellectum*) and might have lucid intervals (*lucida intervalla*).

1349: (Edward III) Alms restricted to impotent beggars.

1483: (Richard III) Protection of those not of whole memory.

1488–9: (Henry VII) Protection for those not of whole mind.

1491: Thirteenth-century Holy Cross Hospital (Bath) for lepers reconstituted as Morotrophium, i.e. place for caring for morons.

1531: (Henry VIII) Beggars Act, again distinguishing the impotent from those physically and mentally able.

1536: (Henry VIII) Parishes to care for aged, poor and impotent by voluntary and charitable alms to discourage begging. There were different definitions of who is vulnerable in this way in the same Act: 'poor, impotent, lame, feeble, sick and diseased'; 'poor, maimed, decrepit, indigent and needy'; 'poor, needy, sick, sore and indigent.'

1542–3: (Henry VIII) Wills or testaments of idiots ineffectual (non-sane memory).

1548: (Edward VI) Penalties for those 'untruly' finding someone to be 'lunatic, idiot or dead' as a means of dispossessing them.

1563: (Elizabeth I) Act for Relief of the Poor.

1572: (Elizabeth I) Impotent poor outdoor relief and almshouses, but the impotent poor are still whipped if they insist on begging.

1576: (Elizabeth I) Act for Relief of the Poor. Stocks of material to be kept for poor to work on. Houses of correction for those unwilling to work.

1581: (Elizabeth I) Protection for those of unsound mind (*non compos mentis*).

1598: (Elizabeth I) Act for Relief of the Poor. Houses of dwelling for the impotent poor. Emphasised family responsibilities. Hospitals and almshouses supported by local tax.

1601: (Elizabeth I) Consolidation of Poor Laws. (Made 'permanent' 1640.) Impotent persons who begged found themselves classified with the rich variety of mendicants who wandered the roads of Tudor England: real or pretend scholars, shipwrecked mariners, fortune-tellers, charity collectors, fencers, bear-keepers, wandering players, minstrels, discharged prisoners, jugglers, tinkers, pedlars, victims of fires, Egyptians.

1623: (James I) Time limits for recovery of debts do not run while someone is of unsound mind (*non compos mentis*).

1690: John Locke in *Two Treatises of Government*: 'Any one who comes not to such a degree of reason wherein he might be supposed capable of knowing the law . . . he is never capable of being a free man. So lunatics and idiots are never set free from the government of their parents.'

1731: (George II) Act to Enable Idiots and Lunatics Possessed of Estates to Make Conveyances, etc.

1742: (George II) Act to Prevent the Marriage of Lunatics.

1744: (George II) Act to Make More Effective Laws on Rogues, Vagabonds and Other Disorderly Persons. Included locking up those 'who by lunacy or otherwise are furiously mad'. Flogging for stepping out of line.

1744: (George II) Churchwardens and Overseers of Poor to fix Poor Rate. Unexpected fluctuations in the rate had caused discontent.

1753: (George II) Prevented clandestine marriages with those *non compos mentis*.

1763: *Report of the Committee to Enquire into the Situation of Private Madhouses.* The first of a long line of parliamentary and Government scandal reports.

1774: (George III) Act for Regulating Mad Houses.

1789: Visits to lazarettos in Europe by John Howard FRS. Included idiot provision, and illustrated the mixing of groups at that time, for both children and adults.

1796: (George III) Dealt with lunatics holding Bank of England stock. The *Writ de Lunatico Inquirendo* is paralleled by *Writ de Idiota Inquirendo*, and we have examples of both sorts of enquiry into mental competence. In many cases, appearance and inability to talk were evidence enough. In other cases, the old sixteenth-century test of a very basic understanding of money and being able to say who your parents were seems to have lasted well into the nineteenth century.

1800: (George III) Act for the Safe Custody of Insane Persons Charged with Offences.

1802: *An Account of the Discovery and Education of a Savage Man* by Itard. One of a number of optimistic eighteenth-century exercises in socialising 'savages', that is, children or young people who had missed out on education and were living wild.

1805–7: Select Committee on Lunacy.

1808: (George III) Act for Better Care and Maintenance of Lunatics, Beggars, Paupers and Criminals, included 'dangerous idiots', who were commonly excluded from the harmless category and classified and accommodated with dangerous lunatics.

1812: *The Law Concerning Idiots, Lunatics and Other Persons Non Compotes Mentis* by George Dale Collinson. One of the earliest British surveys of the history of legislation on learning disability and mental illness.

1815: *Report on Madhouses.* One of many scandal reports.

1815: (George III) Scottish Act on Asylums.

1817: (George III) The Irish Counterpart Act.

1818: (George III) Regulation of Native Insane Hospitals in India.

1828: Sir Andrew Halliday in *General View of the Present State of Lunatics and Lunatic Asylums in Great Britain and Ireland and in Some Other Kingdoms* argued for better institutional provision. 'Thousands of our fellow men are hurried to an untimely grave in all the horrors of raging madness or helpless fatuity.'

1832: (William IV) Act on Care and Treatment of Insane Persons. Covered idiots and persons of unsound mind. Allowed for without-notice visits and night visits.

1832: (William IV) Act to Amend Representation of the People Act in England and Wales. Excluded potential voters with legal incapacity. Neither this nor subsequent Acts directly denied the franchise to men with a learning disability or mental illness, but the property qualification could be expected to exclude them because they lacked capacity to manage their affairs.

1834: (William IV) Poor Law Amendment Act. Expanded role of workhouses, but also outdoor relief. Outdoor relief orders included mental infirmity and mental imbecility. Poor Law Commission and Unions with Board of Guardians.

1837: Seguin Bicetre Hospital for Idiots and Imbeciles in Paris.

1837: (William IV) Will Act. Testamentary capacity does not impose a very onerous test.

1839: Guggenbuhl Cretin Colony in Abendberg.

1841: *Construction and Management of Hospitals for the Insane* by Dr Jacobi. Introduction commented on number of patients in large asylums with congenital idiotism or hopeless fatuity.

1840: *Sketches in London* by James Grant. Brilliant Boz illustrations and telling descriptions of workhouses and asylums.

1842: Poor Law Commissioners' *Report to the Home Department on the Sanitary Condition of the Labouring Population*. Showed why institutions might be better for pauper patients, and the dreadful domestic conditions experienced by some boarders and by some of those living with their families.

Reports of the Commissioners in Lunacy 1844–1915; Reports of the Board of Control 1915–38. Fascinating evidence about both the community care of the time and the institutions.

1844: [American] *Jurisprudence* by Ray. 'In reasoning power, idiots are below the brute.' Largely a matter of state law rather than federal law in America, and a number of states remove most rights from mentally impaired people, but not voting rights.

1846: *Idiocy and Its Treatment* by E. Seguin.

1847: Royal Earlswood founded.

1848: (Victoria) Poor Law Amendment Act. Provided for medical relief.

1848: Park House, Highgate, first charitable asylum for idiots.

1859: Essex Hall.

1862: Starcross (Western Counties Asylum).

1862: (Victoria) Lunatics Amendment Act. Promoted return from asylums to workhouses of chronic and harmless patients to facilitate the curative and/or custodial role of the asylums.

1863: Broadmoor. Supposed to be for convicted people only and not mental defectives.

1866: *A Manual for the Classification, Training and Education of the Feeble-minded, Imbecile and Idiot* by P. Martin Duncan. Four categories: idiots, imbeciles, simpletons and feeble-minded. Envisaged the possibility of moving from first to fourth category.

1867: (Victoria) Metropolitan Poor Act. Asylums to replace workhouses. Led to St Lawrence's and Leavesden. London Metropolitan Asylums Board led the way for nearly fifty years in public authority provision for mental defectives.

1867: (Victoria) Criminal Lunatics Act. Dangerous idiots and imbeciles to county asylums.

1867: St Lawrence's. *Observations on an Ethnic Classification of Idiots* by John Langdon Down, the famous treatise associating various conditions with ethnic characteristics.

1868: Northern Counties Asylum for Idiots and Imbeciles (Royal Albert Hospital).

1868: White House, Hampton Wick. Metropolitan Licensed House, later Normansfield Training Institution for Imbeciles.

1871: (Victoria) Anatomy Act. Medical schools could have unclaimed bodies of patients.

1876: (Victoria) Elementary Education Act. Experience of universal elementary education highlighted the challenge of defective children.

1883: Sir Francis Galton propounded his eugenics theory.

1886: (Victoria) Idiots Act. Gave facilities for the care, education and training of idiots and imbeciles. Separate systems for idiots and lunatics. Registered placements. Inspections. Repatriation to place of origin.

Idiots and imbeciles did not include lunatics. (But see 1890 Act below.)

1888: (Victoria) Local Government Act. Daily grant from guardians to maintain indoor paupers, including those in institutions for idiots and imbeciles. Defined feeble-minded by vulnerability.

1888: *Lunacy in Many Lands* by G.A. Tucker. A multi-volume survey. Admired Illinois Asylum for Feeble-minded Children. Noted that in many areas number of idiots exceeded numbers with mental illness.

1890: (Victoria) Act to Consolidate Certain of the Enactments Respecting Lunatics. Defined lunatic as 'idiot or person of unsound mind'. Commissioners in Lunacy. Medical and Legal Visitors. Local Asylum Visiting Committees. Separate accommodation for lunatics in workhouses.

1893: (Victoria) Sale of Goods Act. Necessaries sold to incompetent person had to be paid for. (Re-enacted 1979.) Dealt with the situation of people who would lack capacity to enter into a contract.

1894: *Lunatic Asylums: Their Organisation and Management* by Charles Mercer, Senior Assistant Medical Officer, Leavesden, encouraged person-centred planning. 'No restriction is justified that is not required by the circumstances of the individual case . . . All arrangements will be made with special reference to the individuality of the patient.'

1896–8: Departmental Committee on Defective and Epileptic Children. Followed up an earlier study of the needs of other disabled children. Mental defectiveness and epilepsy were closely aligned in the thinking of the time.

1896: National Association for Promoting the Welfare of the Feeble-minded.

1899: (Victoria) Elementary Education (Defective and Epileptic Children) Act. Authorised but did not require special schools. (First official schools for defective children, 1893.) For children not imbecile and not merely dull or backward and not capable of benefiting from instruction in ordinary public elementary school, but capable of benefiting from a special class.

1901: Inclusion of feeble-minded category in the census raised the mentally defective population to 133,000, against 1891 estimate of 97,000.

1904–8: Royal Commission on the Care and Control of the Feeble-minded. Considered existing methods of dealing with idiots, epileptics, imbeciles, feeble-minded and defective persons not certified under lunacy laws. Major landmark in collection of evidence, debate and recommendations. Favoured colonies, but left open wide range of provision. Rejected case for sterilisation, but accepted inherited degeneracy arguments. Recommended separate education system.

1905: *Mental Defects* by Martin W. Baker. Noted range of terminology and attitudes: 'Les enfants du Bon Dieu', 'Children of the Great Spirit'.

1907: Indiana law allowing sterilisation of defectives. By 1936 twenty-five states had such laws. California had the only large-scale sterilisation programme.

1908: *Mental Deficiency (Amentia)* by A.F. Tredgold. The standard textbook through successive editions.

1909: Stoke Park Colony.

1911: *Feeble-mindedness in Children of School Age* by Dr C.L. Lapage and M. Dendy. About 700 children in boarding schools for the mentally defective.

1913: (George V) Mental Deficiency Act. Favoured colonies, but allowed for wide range of alternatives. Set pattern for more than forty years, but the Great War delayed effective implementation, although, like World War II, it gave mentally impaired people jobs, including jobs in institutions. Repeal of 1886 Idiots Act. Institution or guardianship. Relatives apply; doctors certify. Care and control.

1914: (George V) Elementary Education (Defective and Epileptic Children) Act. Local authorities to provide education for backward and defective children, and report those incapable of benefiting to Mental Deficiency Committee. Essentially the children's counterpart to the 1913 Act.

1914: Prudhoe Hall Colony.

1914: Royal Eastern Counties Institution.

1918: (George V) Electoral Reform Act. Tripled franchise, removing property qualification, and seen by critics as bringing in rootless and irresponsible people. No specific exclusion of people simply because of impaired intellect.

1921: (George V) Education Act. Strengthened 1898 Act requiring schooling for children not imbeciles but requiring special class or school.

1926: Rampton Hospital.

1927: (George V) Mental Deficiency (Amendment) Act. Amended definitions: idiots, imbeciles, feeble-minded, moral defectives. Allowed into mental deficiency those with damage acquired before age eighteen. (*Encephalitis lethargica* outbreak peaked 1924.) Board of Control and Board of Education could jointly certify combined institution for mental defectives and school for defective children. Training and occupation requirement included, the forerunners of day centres.

1928: Middlesex Colony (Harperbury).

1929: (George V) Local Government Act. Poor Law Authorities replaced by counties and boroughs. The end of more than four centuries of the Poor Law.

1929: Wood Committee recommended compulsory sterilisation.

1930: (George V) Mental Treatment Act. Amended Lunacy Acts 1890–1922 and Mental Deficiency Acts 1913–27. Reorganised Board of Control. Asylums became mental hospitals. Ended pauper category, now rate-aided. Ended lunatic category, now persons of unsound mind.

1931: Dovenby Hall Mental Defective Colony.

1931: Sterilisation Bill introduced but defeated.

1933: Moss Side (after delayed start).

1938: St Andrew's Colony (Northgate).

1942: *Social Insurance and Allied Services* (Beveridge Report). Silence on learning disability.

1944: (George VI) Education Act. LEA to report to local authority children 'suffering from a disability of mind of such a nature or to such an extent as to make him incapable of receiving education at school,' including those not considered to be accceptable if educated in association with other children.

1944: (George VI) Disabled Persons (Employment) Act. Quota scheme.

1946: (George VI) National Health Service Act. Colonies, etc. brought into NHS; local authority role defined; Junior Training Centres for children with severe learning disabilities. Block transfer to NHS of residential provision differed from the course adopted with elderly people's services.

1946: Association of Parents of Backward Children. Parents often not much involved in some of the earlier voluntary sector initiatives because regarded as part of the problem.

1948: (George VI) National Assistance Act. Consolidated welfare provisions and local authority role, including residential care and day and domiciliary services.

1949: (George VI) Representation of the People Act. Votes for detained patients while still on local electoral register.

1950: European Convention on Human Rights.

1954–7: Royal Commission on the *Law Relating to Mental Illness and Mental Deficiency*. Noted widespread ignorance of mental deficiency, and widespread confusion with mental illness.

1956: (Elizabeth II) Sexual Offences Act. Included offences against defectives.

1958: (Elizabeth II) Disabled Persons (Employment) Act. Revised employment services for disabled people.

1959: (Elizabeth II) Mental Health Act. As later amended, the Act was mainly concerned with detention and safeguards around this. Originally, it went much wider in separating out health and social services responsibilities. (These broader provisions were subsequently incorporated in other legislation.) Removed centralised controls. Emphasis on voluntary treatment. New terminology. Moral defectiveness became psychopathy. Entwining of mental defects and moral defects had been a problem for centuries, and overshadowed the 1913 Act, despite distinctions made in Classical times. Guardianship partly replaced old community supervision arrangements.

1959: Danish Act Concerning the Care of the Mentally Retarded and Other Exceptionally Retarded Persons. Encouraged community care.

1967: Swedish Act on Provisions for Certain Mentally Retarded Persons.

1967: (Elizabeth II) Sexual Offences Act. Defined severe mental handicap.

1967: (Elizabeth II) Abortion Act (amended by Human Fertilisation and Embryology Act 1990). Allowed late terminations where child might be seriously handicapped by physical or mental abnormalities.

1967: Stanley Segal – 'No child is ineducable.'

1968: (Elizabeth II) Health Services and Public Health Act. Grants to voluntary bodies such as Mencap.

1969: *Report of the Committee of Inquiry into Allegations of Ill-Treatment of Patients and Other Irregularities at the Ely Hospital, Cardiff.*

1969: *Put Away* by Pauline Morris.

1970: (Elizabeth II) Local Authority Social Services Act. Unified social services.

1970: (Elizabeth II) Chronically Sick and Disabled Persons Act. Rights to information and services.

1970: (Elizabeth II) Education (Handicapped Children) Act. Children with severe learning disabilities no longer excluded from school.

1970: (Elizabeth II) National Insurance Act. Attendance Allowance introduced. (Additional lower rate added under 1972 National Insurance Act.)

1971: UN *Declaration on the Rights of Mentally Retarded Persons.* Enjoyment of the same rights as others to the maximum extent of feasibility.

1971: *Better Services for the Mentally Handicapped.* The White Paper that marked out a course for a continuing shift towards community care.

1972: Willowbrook, New York. De-institutionalisation precedent.

1972: *The Principle of Normalisation in Human Services* by W. Wolfensberger.

1973: (Elizabeth II) NHS Re-organisation Act. End of Medical Superintendents. Community Health Councils.

1973: Belgian law on prolonged minority for people with intellectual disability. This still continues for people with severe intellectual disability.

1974: *South Ockenden Report.*

1974: (Elizabeth II) Juries Act. Mental handicap and severe mental handicap disqualify for jury service.

1974: *Social Security Provision for Chronically Sick and Disabled People.* Report to Parliament in accordance with Section 36 of the 1973 Social Security Act.

1975: *Report of the Committee on Mentally Abnormal Offenders.* Wanted mental disorder rather than mental abnormality as a generic term.

1975: National Development Group and National Development Team created respectively to advise on mental handicap policy and inspect mental handicap facilities and encourage good practice.

1975: UN *Declaration on the Rights of Disabled Persons.*

1975: Swedish Act prohibiting involuntary sterilisations.

1975: (Elizabeth II) Social Security Benefits Act. Non-contributory

Invalidity Pension (later Severe Disablement Allowance) and Invalid Care Allowance (later Carer's Allowance).

1975: (Elizabeth II) Social Security Pensions Act. Mobility Allowance.

1976: California Developmental Disabilities Services Act.

1976: Alberta Dependent Adults Act (amended 1985). Allowed guardians to be appointed.

1977: (Elizabeth II) Housing (Homeless Persons Act). Mentally handicapped person living with family can be homeless.

1977: (Elizabeth II) NHS Act. Included new legislative basis for day centres.

1978: *Report of the Committee of Enquiry into Normansfield Hospital.*

1979: *Committee of Enquiry into Mental Handicap Nursing and Care* (Jay Report).

1979: Review of the Mental Health Act 1959. Justified inclusion of mental handicap; turned down idea of parallel legislation; but wanted clarification that mental handicap on its own did not justify detention.

1980: *Report of the Review of Rampton Hospital.*

1980: *An Ordinary Life* by the King's Fund. Start of a series of booklets encouraging new-style community care.

1980: *Mental Handicap: Progress, Problems and Priorities.* A review of progress on the 1971 White Paper.

1981: (Elizabeth II) Education Act. Reclassification of education-related disability, and preference for mainstream education.

1982: Spanish Law for the Social Integration of the Handicapped. Paved way for four-level classification of learning disability. (There was a threefold classification of capacity in a 1984 decree.)

1983: (Elizabeth II) Mental Health Act. New system for detained patients. Included patients with mental impairments. Receiverships. Reduced scope for guardianship.

1983: (Elizabeth II) NHS Re-organisation Act. General management.

1983: *All Wales Strategy for the Development of Services for Mentally Handicapped People.* Offered hopes of an integrated approach to community care supported by dedicated funding.

1983: (Elizabeth II) Health and Social Services and Social Security Adjudications Act. Authorised discretionary charges for services.

1983: (Elizabeth II) Representation of the People Act.

1984: (Elizabeth II) Registered Homes Act. Included definition of mental handicap. (Small homes included by 1991 Act.)

1984: (Elizabeth II) Police and Criminal Evidence Act. Defined mental handicap. Right to an 'appropriate adult' when being interviewed by the police.

1984: (Elizabeth II) Health and Social Security Act. Severe Disablement Allowance.

1985: Social Services Committee *Report on Community Care*. Special reference to adult mentally ill and mentally handicapped people. Government response to Committee. The Government said: 'Community care is a matter of marshalling resources, sharing responsibilities and combining skills to achieve good-quality modern services to meet the actual needs of real people, in ways those people find acceptable and in places which encourage rather than prevent normal living. It is firmly opposed to revamped institutions and to artificial ghettos, which have nothing to commend them except someone else's convenience and which have nothing to do with community care.'

1985: (Elizabeth II) Transport Act. Concessionary fares.

1985: Swedish Act confirms citizenship of people with severe intellectual disability. (Institutional provision officially ended in Sweden in 1999.)

1986: (Elizabeth II) Disabled Persons (Services, Consultation and Representation) Act. Improved assessment rights. Section 11 required an annual report to Parliament on mental handicap and mental illness services.

1986: (Elizabeth II) Social Security Act. Income Support and ICA (Invalid Care Allowance) extended to married women.

1986: Audit Commission Report: *Making a Reality of Community Care.*

1988: *Griffiths Report.* New approach to Community care.

1988: (Elizabeth II) Local Government Finance Act. 'Poll Tax' exemption for people with severe mental impairment.

1988: (Elizabeth II) Road Traffic Act. Severe mental handicap disqualifies for a driving licence.

1988: Wagner Report *Residential Care: A Positive Choice.*

1989: *Caring for People.* Government policy on community care.

1989: (Elizabeth II) Children Act. Bringing disabled children into the mainstream.

1989: (Elizabeth II) Local Government Act. Disabled Facilities Grant.

1990: (Elizabeth II) NHS and Community Care Act. NHS Trusts. New procedures for community care.

1990: Americans with Disabilities Act (USA).

1991: (Elizabeth II) Criminal Procedure (Insanity and Unfitness to Plead) Act 1991. Allowed trial of facts, separate from guilt issue.

1991: (Elizabeth II) Disability Living Allowance and Disability Working Allowance Act. DLA replaced Attendance Allowance for those claiming under pension age, and Mobility Allowance. People with a learning disability were significant beneficiaries from the lowest rates of DLA. DWA was created as a new benefit for disabled people with low earnings. Workers with learning disabilities were significant beneficiaries.

1992: (Elizabeth II) Further and Higher Education Act. Included an educability condition for funding further education.

1992: (Elizabeth II) Local Government Finance Act. Council Tax exemption (from the personal element of the tax) for those who had been exempted from the Poll Tax.

1992: German 'Caretaking' Act replaced rigid guardianship law with flexible guardianship provisions; strengthened civil and personal rights of people with a learning disability.

1993: (Elizabeth II) Education Act (now consolidated in 1996 Education Act). Further changes in special education.

1993: Health Committee Report on Community Care.

1995: (Elizabeth II) Disability Discrimination Act. People with a learning disability covered.

1995: (Elizabeth II) Carers Recognition and Services Act. Recognition of family carers in their own right.

1996: (Elizabeth II) Housing Grants, Construction and Regeneration Act. Disabled Facilities Grant.

1996: (Elizabeth II) Community Care (Direct Payments) Act.

1997: (Elizabeth II) Police Act. Better vetting for vulnerable people.

1998: (Elizabeth II) Human Rights Act.

1998: Health Committee Report on the *Relationship Between Health and Social Services*.

1999: (Elizabeth II) Disability Rights Commission Act.

1999: (Elizabeth II) Protection of Children Act.

2000: (Elizabeth II) Representation of the People Act. Eased voting restrictions on those in hospital.

2000: (Elizabeth II) Carers and Disabled Children Act. Extended direct payments.

2000: (Elizabeth II) Learning and Skills Act. Learning and Skills Councils.

2000: (Elizabeth II) Care Standards Act. New regulatory framework for quality standards.

2000: (Elizabeth II) Welfare Reform Act. Abolition of Severe Disablement Allowance for new claimants.

2001: (Elizabeth II) Health and Social Care Act. Care Trusts, definition of nursing care, and new consumer interest structure. Tougher requirements on Direct Payments. Section 62 replaced Section 11 of the Disabled Persons Act, requiring an annual report to Parliament on 'development of health and social services for persons with learning disability'. Defined learning disability for the first time.

2001: (Elizabeth II) Special Educational Needs and Disability Act. Further encouragement of mainstream schools for children with special needs, and extension of disability rights to the education system.

2001: *Valuing People* White Paper.

2002: (Elizabeth II) Tax Credits Act. A range of provisions recognised disabled workers and disabled children.

2003: (Elizabeth II) Telecommunications Act. Some recognition of the needs of disabled people in the new integrated IT environment.

2003: (Elizabeth II) Sexual Offences Act. Included provisions to protect persons with a mental disorder.

2005: (Elizabeth II) Mental Capacity Act. Governed decision-making on behalf of adults who lack mental capacity.

2005: (Elizabeth II) Disability Discrimination Act. Strengthened and broadened the DDA 1995 and gave public bodies a duty to promote equality of disabled people.

2005: (Elizabeth II) Equality Act. Provided for the establishment of the new Commission for Equality and Human Rights (CEHR), a single integrated body to underpin legislation on race, gender, disability, religion or belief, sexual orientation, and proposed legislation on age and human rights.

2005: Disabled Facilities Grant helping to pay for changes in the home to accommodate disabled people no longer to be means tested.

2006: (Elizabeth II) Electoral Administration Act 2006. Changed various aspects of electoral law. It removed the offensive terms 'idiots and luntics' and made it clear that people with a learning disability have the same right to vote as anyone else.

2006: (Elizabeth II) Childcare Act 2006. Placed a duty on local authorities to improve outcomes and reduce inequalities for all children under five, to secure sufficient childcare to meet the needs of working parents and parents who wish to work.

Other Bills which will almost certainly become Acts before the end of 2006 are the Safeguarding Vulnerable Groups Bill, the Education and Inspections Bill and the Welfare Reform Bill.

Note: Scottish legislation runs broadly in parallel from the time of the Act of Union to the re-creation of the Scottish Parliament, but there are significant differences, particularly because of the different legal system in Scotland.

Scotland already has its Adults with Incapacity Act 2000 and its Mental Health (Care and Treatment) (Scotland) Act 2003. These are the Scottish equivalents of the Mental Capacity Act and the abandoned Draft Mental Health Bill. This latter Bill has now been withdrawn and an Amending Bill will take its place, which has not yet been laid before the UK Parliament.

BIBLIOGRAPHY

(Government reports, White Papers and publications
mentioned in the Appendix are not included here)

A Day in the Life. London. Mencap. 2002

Advocacy Strategy. London. Mencap. 2004

Anon. Editorial. *BMJ*. 1864; 1:42

Arts for All. London. Mencap. 2002

Atkinson, D. *et al. Good Times, Bad Times*. Kidderminster. Bild Publications. 2000

Atkinson, D., Jackson, M. and Walmsley, J. *Forgotten Lives*. Kidderminster. Bild Publications. 1997

Atkinson, D. and Williams, F. *Know Me As I Am*. London. Hodder and Stoughton. 1990

Behind Closed Doors. London. Mencap. 2001

Bloom, A. 'Staff starved of training to help disabled pupils'. *Times Educational Supplement*, 14 October 2005.

Breaking Point. London. Mencap. 2003

Breathnach, C. 'Henry Hutchinson Stewart (1798–1879)'. *Hist. Psychiatry*. 1998; 9:27–33

Brigham, L. *et al. Crossing Boundaries*. Kidderminster. Bild Publications. 2000

Changing Places. London. Mencap. 2006

Clark, J. *A Memoir of John Connolly*. London. John Murray. 1868.

Connolly, J. 'The physiognomy of insanity.' *Medical Times Gazette*. 1858–9; 16:2–4

Cunningham, C. *Down's syndrome: An introduction for parents*. London. Souvenir Press. Reissued 2006

Deacon, J. *Tongue Tied*. Deacon. 1974

Department for Education and Skills. *Statistics of Education: School in England*. Norwich. HMSO. 2004

Doing, Showing and Going. London. Mencap. 2002

Don't Count Me Out. London. Mencap. 2001

Duncan, P. M. *A Manual for the Classification, Training and Education of the Feebleminded, Imbecile and Idiotic*. London. Longman Green. 1866

Equal Chances. London. Mencap. 2004

Hogg, J. and Sebba, J. *Profound Retardation and Multiple Impairments*. Vol. 1 *Development and Learning*. Vol. 2 *Education and Therapy*. London. Croom Helm. 1986

Hollins, S. and Hollins, M. *You and Your Child: Making Sense of Learning Disabilities*. London. Karnac. 2005

Housing Timebomb. London. Mencap. 2002

Impact Review 2001/2002 and *2002/2003*. London. Mencap. 2002, 2003

Langdon Down, J. *Mental Affections of Childhood and Youth*. London. Churchill. 1964

Little, W. J. 'The influence of abnormal parturition, difficult labours, premature birth and asphyxia neonatorum on the mental and physical condition of the child especially in relation to deformities'. *Trans. Obstet. Soc. of London*. 1862; pp293–347

Mencap Welcome Pack. London. Mencap. 2005

Millard, W. *The Idiot and his Helpers*. London. Longman. 1864

Mitchell, D. *Testimonies of Resistance*. London. Jessica Kingsley. 2006

No Ordinary Life. London. Mencap. 2001

O'Connor, U., McConkey, R. and Hartop, B. 'Parental views on the statutory assessment and educational planning for children with special educational needs'. *European Journal of Special Educational Needs*. 2005; 19: 2, 251–69

Oswin, M. *The Empty Hours: Weekend life of handicapped children in Institutions*. London. Penguin. 1973

Pim, J. *On the Necessity of a State Provision for the Education of the Dumb, the Blind and the Imbecile*. Dublin. Webb. 1864

Reed, A. and Reed, C. *Memoirs of the Life and Philanthropic Labours of the Late Andrew Reed*. London. Strahan. 1863

Report. *Medical Times*. 28 June 1879

Report. *Quart. J. Geograph. Soc.* 1892; 48:47–48

Review. *BMJ*. 1866; 1: 387–8

Rolph, S. *Witnesses to Change*. Kidderminster. Bild Publications. 2005

SR 392/2/1/5. *Board Minutes*. f8

SRO 392/2/116. f281

SRO 39211/2/1

To Know is to Understand. London. Mencap. 2002

Towell, D. (ed.) *An Ordinary Life*. London. King's Fund. 1982

Towell, D. (ed.) *An Ordinary Working Life*. London. King's Fund. 1984

Treat me right! London. Mencap. 2004

Understanding Us. London. Mencap. 2004

Understanding Us, Volume II. London. Mencap. 2005

We too have a voice: Poems by students from Mencap National College. London. Mencap. 2006

Ward, O.C. *John Langdon Down, a Caring Pioneer*. London. RSM Press. 1998

Ward, O.C. 'Down's syndrome' in Ed. P.J. Koehier, G.W. Bruyn and J.M.S. Pearce, *Neurological Syndromes*. Oxford University Press. 2000

Ward, O.C. 'Langdon Down's 1864 case of Prader Willi syndrome'. *RSM*. 1997; 90:694–6

Westminster Watch. London. Mencap. 2002, 2003, 2004, 2005, 2006

Index